OCCUPATION

NEW PERSPECTIVES ON EASTERN EUROPE AND EURASIA

The states of Eastern Europe and Eurasia are once again at the centre of global attention, particularly following Russia's 2022 full-scale invasion of Ukraine. But media coverage can only do so much in providing the necessary context to make sense of fast-moving developments. The books in this series provide original, engaging and timely perspectives on Eastern Europe and Eurasia for a general readership. Written by experts on—and from—these states, the books in the series cover an eclectic range of cutting-edge topics relating to politics, history, culture, economics and society. The series is originated by Hurst, with titles co-published or distributed in North America by Oxford University Press, New York.

Series editor: Dr Ben Noble—Associate Professor of Russian Politics at University College London and Associate Fellow at Chatham House

DAVID LEWIS

Occupation

Russian Rule in South-Eastern Ukraine

Oxford University Press is a department of the
University of Oxford. It furthers the University's objective
of excellence in research, scholarship, and education
by publishing worldwide.

Oxford New York

Auckland Cape Town Dar es Salaam Hong Kong Karachi
Kuala Lumpur Madrid Melbourne Mexico City Nairobi
New Delhi Shanghai Taipei Toronto

With offices in

Argentina Austria Brazil Chile Czech Republic France Greece
Guatemala Hungary Italy Japan Poland Portugal Singapore
South Korea Switzerland Thailand Turkey Ukraine Vietnam

Oxford is a registered trade mark of Oxford University Press
in the UK and certain other countries.

Published in the United States of America by
Oxford University Press
198 Madison Avenue, New York, NY 10016

Copyright © David Lewis, 2025

All rights reserved. No part of this publication may be reproduced,
stored in a retrieval system, or transmitted, in any form or by any
means, without the prior permission in writing of Oxford University
Press, or as expressly permitted by law, by license, or under terms
agreed with the appropriate reproduction rights organization.
Inquiries concerning reproduction outside the scope of the above
should be sent to the Rights Department, Oxford University Press, at
the address above.

You must not circulate this work in any other form
and you must impose this same condition on any acquirer.
Library of Congress Cataloging-in-Publication Data is available

ISBN: 9780197811092

Printed in the United Kingdom by Bell and Bain Ltd, Glasgow

CONTENTS

Maps vii
Acknowledgements ix
Note on Transliteration and Naming xi
Glossary and Acronyms xiii

Introduction: Occupation 1
1. Ideas 19
2. Attack 51
3. Government 85
4. Violence 123
5. Propaganda 175
6. Money 219
7. Liberation 261
Conclusion: Futures 283

Notes 293
Index 365

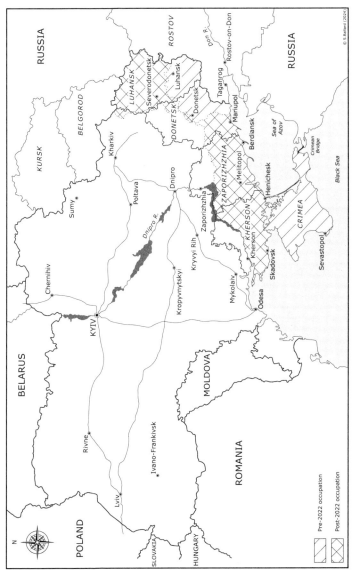

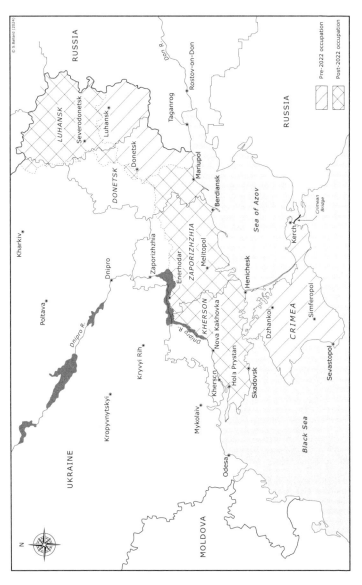

Russian-Occupied Territories in Ukraine

ACKNOWLEDGEMENTS

I am indebted to many people for help in the preparation of this book, not all of whom can be named in the present circumstances. I am particularly grateful to colleagues and friends in and from Ukraine who helped me with numerous interviews, sources and contacts and provided intellectual discussion and challenge. I was privileged to work in a research project at the Serious Organised Crime and Anti-Corruption Evidence (SOC ACE) Programme while writing this book, which enabled me to research economic aspects of the occupation. I am indebted to the UK Foreign, Commonwealth and Development Office (FCDO) for funding that project and to SOC ACE Director Professor Heather Marquette of the University of Birmingham, my research colleagues in the UK and in Ukraine and the team at SOC ACE for their support. I am also grateful for the many insights I gained from colleagues during a period spent on secondment in 2019–22 as an ESRC Knowledge Exchange Fellow and subsequently Research Fellow in the FCDO. All opinions, conclusions and errors in the book are of course my own.

I was invited to present aspects of this research at the Institute for European, Russian, and Eurasian Studies (IERES) at George Washington University in October 2023; at the Columbia-NYU Russia Public Policy roundtable in February 2024; and at the International Studies Association Convention in San Francisco in April 2024. My thanks to those institutions for hosting, and to fellow-panellists and audience members for stimulating questions and comments on the work.

ACKNOWLEDGEMENTS

As always, I am grateful to colleagues at the University of Exeter, who provided me with such a stimulating intellectual environment for research over the last decade. I would also like to thank two anonymous peer reviewers for their invaluable comments and suggestions on the manuscript. I am very grateful to Dr Sebastian Ballard for the maps that accompany the text. Last, but not least, I am indebted to Michael Dwyer and the editorial and production team at Hurst & Co. and to Series Editor Dr Ben Noble for all their support, input and encouragement.

My main debt is as always to my wife, Olivia, who was a constant source of support, inspiration and insight during the writing of this book.

NOTE ON TRANSLITERATION AND NAMING

The transliteration of geographical and personal names in Ukraine has become highly politicised. Transliteration from Ukrainian and from Russian produce slightly different English forms (most obviously, Kyiv or Kiev) and using one or the other form hints at different political positions. Where the term is a geographical place in Ukraine, I have used the official Ukrainian name and the standardised English-language version transliterated from the Ukrainian—Kryvyi Rih, for example, not Krivoi Rog (Rus.), or Odesa, not Odessa. I make occasional exceptions for well-established English names, such as Crimea. Russia and Ukraine often use different names for the same place, with Russian sources continuing to refer to names that were in use prior to the 'decommunisation' process initiated in Ukraine in 2015–16. Ukrainian forces in Bakhmut and Russian soldiers in Artemovsk were fighting over the same ruined town. In each case I use the Ukrainian version, except in quotes from Russian media or officials. At times, the difference is primarily in transliteration, so Luhansk (Ukr.) and Lugansk (Rus.). In such cases I also use the Ukrainian version, except in direct quotes from Russian sources.

For people's names I have tried to follow their own preferred spelling in English on personal or official websites (so *Vladimir* not *Volodymyr* Saldo). Where their preferred usage is not obvious, I have used a standard transliteration system from Ukrainian to English to transliterate Ukrainian names. I have compromised for any well-known names, such as 'Zelensky', for the ease of read-

NOTE ON TRANSLITERATION AND NAMING

ability and in most cases have preferred a familiar version of a name as used in the media rather than a purist application of the transliteration rules. I use the terms Luhansk region and Donetsk region to refer to the administrative oblasts in Ukraine, but I refer to the Donetsk People's Republic (DNR) and Lugansk People's Republic (LNR) to reference the political regimes that occupy part of those regions and the unrecognised territorial entities that Russia claims to have incorporated into the Russian Federation. Use of these terms does not imply any recognition of their legitimacy, but simply conveys the political reality of control of territory at the time of writing.

GLOSSARY AND ACRONYMS

ATO	Anti-Terrorist Operation. Ukraine's anti-separatist military campaign in the Donbas after 2014.
CEC	Central Election Commission (Russia)
CMR	*Tsentr mezhdunarodnykh raschetov*. Centre for International Settlements. Russian bank.
DNR	*Donetskaya narodnaya respublika*. Donetsk People's Republic.
DOI	Department for Operational Information. FSB Department (Russia).
DVKR	Department of Military Counter-Intelligence. FSB Department (Russia).
EGRYUL	Unified State Register of Legal Entities. Russian corporate register of companies and organisations.
ER	*Edinaya Rossiya*. United Russia. Russia's biggest political party.
EZSS	*Edinnyi zakazchik v sfere stroitelstva*. Single Contractor in the Construction Sphere. Russian state holding company.
FBK	Anti-Corruption Foundation. Campaigning organisation founded by Alexei Navalny.
FSB	*Federalnaya sluzhba bezopasnosti*. Federal Security Service (Russia).
FTsRPSP	*Federalnyi tsentr razvitiya programm sotsializatsii pod-*

GLOSSARY AND ACRONYMS

	trostkov. Federal Centre for the Development of Programmes for the Socialisation of Teenagers (also known as the Federal Teenager Centre). Russia.
GSB	*Gosudarstvennaya sluzhba bezopasnosti*. State Security Service. Unofficial (Russian) security service in Kherson in 2022.
GU (GRU)	Main Directorate of the General Staff. Russian Military Intelligence.
HUR	Ukrainian military intelligence
ICC	International Criminal Court
ICRC	International Committee of the Red Cross
KGB	Committee of State Security. Soviet-era intelligence agency.
KPRF	Communist Party of the Russian Federation. Russian political party.
KRO	*Kongress russkikh obschin* (Congress of Russian Communities). Russian political party.
LNR	*Luganskaya narodnaya respublika*. Lugansk People's Republic.
MChS	*Ministerstvo chrezvychainykh situatsii*. Ministry of Emergency Situations (Russia)
MFC	Multifunctional Centres. Russian registration and documentation agencies.
MRB	*Mezhdunarodnyi raschetnyi bank*. International Settlement Bank (Russia).
NKVD	Soviet People's Commissariat for Internal Affairs
NRC	National Resistance Center (Ukraine)
Oblast	A region in both Ukraine and Russia. Except in quotes, I use the term 'region' to refer to oblasts.
OCU	Orthodox Church of Ukraine
OHCHR	Office of the United Nations High Commissioner for Human Rights
OSCE	Organisation for Security and Cooperation in Europe

GLOSSARY AND ACRONYMS

OUN	*Orhanizatsiia ukrainskykh natsionalistiv.* Organisation of Ukrainian Nationalists.
OUN-B	Faction of the OUN founded by Stepan Bandera.
PFP	*Proverochno-filtratsionnyi punkt* (Screening and Filtration Point).
POR	Party of Regions. Ukrainian political party.
PSB	Promsvyazbank. Russian bank.
RSFSR	Russian Soviet Federative Socialist Republic
RVIO	*Rossiiskoe voenno-istoricheskoe obshchestvo.* Russian Military-Historical Society
SBU	*Sluzhba bezpeky Ukrainy.* Security Service of Ukraine.
SIZO	*Sledstvennyi izolator.* Detention centre.
SK	*Sledstvennyi komitet.* Investigative Committee (Russia).
SRZP	*Spravedlivaya Rossiya—Za pravdu* (A Just Russia—For Truth). Russian political party.
SSR	Soviet Socialist Republic
TOT	*Tymchasovo okupovani terytorii.* Temporarily Occupied Territories.
TRNC	Turkish Republic of Northern Cyprus
TsISM	*Tsentr izucheniya i setovogo monitoringa molodezhnoi sredy.* Centre for the Study and Network Monitoring of the Youth Environment (Russia)
UNESCO	United Nations Educational, Scientific and Cultural Organization
UOCMP	Ukrainian Orthodox Church (Moscow Patriarchate)
UPA	*Ukrayinska povstanska armiia.* Ukrainian Insurgent Army.
VGA	*Voenno-grazhdanskaya administratsiya.* Military-Civilian Administration (Russian occupation authorities).
VSK	*Voenno-stroitelnaya kompaniya.* Military-Construction Company of the Russian Ministry of Defence.
VSU	Ukrainian armed forces (Russian acronym)

GLOSSARY AND ACRONYMS

ZNPP	Zaporizhzhia Nuclear Power Plant
ZSU	*Zbroini syly Ukrainy.* Armed forces of Ukraine.
ZZRK	Zaporizhzhia Iron Ore Plant

INTRODUCTION

OCCUPATION

In September 2022, at a grandiose ceremony in the Moscow Kremlin, President Vladimir Putin announced the incorporation of four provinces of southern and eastern Ukraine into the Russian Federation. It was the biggest land grab in Europe since World War II, leaving Russia occupying more than 100,000 square kilometres of Ukrainian territory. On these occupied lands, Russian forces and their proxies kidnapped, tortured and killed civilians and officials, seized businesses and properties from their Ukrainian owners, erased any evidence of Ukrainian culture, rewrote Ukrainian history and subjected the population to a barrage of constant propaganda. The story of how Russia occupied and annexed these territories is the subject of this book.

It is a story that unfolds on different levels. It is about grand geopolitics and abstract ideas of world order. Russian officials talked of 'ending US hegemony', while Western diplomats worried that a successful Russian offensive would upend the 'rules-based international order'. Russia's invasion and occupation of Ukraine were viewed as potential precedents, perhaps encouraging China to conquer Taiwan or leading to further Russian offensives against the Baltic States or Poland. The tropes of 1938, of appeasement, the Sudetenland, reminders of Nazi occupation, were all widely invoked. There was a 'whiff of Munich in the air', according to British defence secretary Ben Wallace.

OCCUPATION

It is also a story about two countries, Russia and Ukraine, whose concepts of nation-building in the aftermath of the Soviet collapse had come into violent collision. This was identity politics at its most brutal. The war meant many different things to different people, but at heart it was a bitter dispute over what it meant to be Ukrainian or Russian. This was a fight over history, over culture and language. And a struggle over the future—between a European, pluralistic future in Ukraine or an increasingly isolated and authoritarian Russia. The occupation was also intensely local. The fighting took place street by street, along the banks of canals, through abandoned factories, from treeline to treeline. The occupation entered people's homes, as Russian forces trampled through apartments, gardens and houses. It even entered people's minds, in what Ukrainians started calling a 'cognitive occupation', as Russia's propaganda and education sought to change how people thought, about history, about the present, even about their own personal experiences of the war.

The word occupation implies something static and fixed, but its direct consequence for millions of people was forced mobility. It sparked a huge exodus from Russian-occupied territory; only a small minority welcomed the prospect of Russian rule. Some joined the six million Ukrainian refugees in Russia and Europe. But many displaced people settled as close as possible to their homes, in cities such as Zaporizhzhia, Mykolaiv and Odesa, which were only a few hours' drive away from Russian-occupied territory. But they might have been a continent away. All direct routes across the front line were closed, and travelling to Mariupol or Melitopol now required a long and arduous multi-day trip through Russia. For many it was too dangerous. Europe was divided once more. The boundaries of the occupation ran like a scar through the steppeland of south-eastern Ukraine.

Most of those who left thought it would be for a few weeks, or months, at most. They left behind family, friends, homes and businesses. Most could only watch from afar as they saw the occupation authorities and some locals on the make seize their shops or factories or occupy their houses and apartments. A Mariupol resident told me bitterly that squatters in her home had thrown her per-

INTRODUCTION

sonal possessions out onto the street. Others talked with barely concealed anger about former friends who were now working for the Russians. The resentment against collaborators ran deep.

Between those who left and those who remained there was a growing divide. Living under occupation forced you to make a series of existential choices almost every day. There was little room for moral purity for anybody who wanted to survive. Russian rule forced everybody to make a choice: to take a Russian passport, to open a Russian bank account, to send your children to a Russian school. Resistance continued, but as time went on it was harder to maintain the hope that things would change. After the failed Ukrainian counteroffensive in 2023, more people left the occupied territories, preferring to leave their homes rather than face a future under Russian rule. Among those who stayed, there was also an armed resistance: Ukrainian underground networks targeted Russian soldiers and collaborators with poisonings, car bombs and shootings. But for most people, the aim was to adapt and survive.

This was a 'belligerent occupation' under international law—an occupation that occurred as the result of a wider military campaign. The geography of the occupation was shaped by the relentless fighting on the front line, which shifted back and forth over the first two years of the war. If not for a determined Ukrainian defence, this book might have been discussing the occupation of Kyiv and much of north-eastern Ukraine. But Russian forces withdrew from northern Ukraine in April 2022 and were then forced out of Kharkiv region in September. In November 2022 Russian forces abandoned Kherson city, despite claiming to have annexed it a few weeks before. Those retreats still left Russia occupying a swathe of land across south-eastern Ukraine, from the eastern banks of the Dnipro River across to Mariupol and the Donbas. Despite offensives and counteroffensives by both sides, and huge losses in military personnel, this front line remained largely static during 2023 and 2024, with Russia controlling about 18% of Ukrainian territory.

The offensives and counteroffensives of the first years of the war have been explored in detail in several excellent books.[1] Other works provide accounts of the 'entangled histories' of Russia and

Ukraine.² This book attempts something different. It focuses on what happened behind the front lines, in the territories that Russia continued to occupy two years into the war. I set out to explain how Russia maintained control of these territories, despite hostility from the population, international condemnation and Ukrainian military pressure. While much of the media attention was on victories and losses on the battlefield, what happened behind the front line in the occupied regions was also critical to the outcome of the war. If Russia's occupation faced deep-rooted resistance and high costs, Ukraine would have a much greater chance of winning back these territories over the long run. On the other hand, if Russia were successful in maintaining control, questions would rise about whether it could reproduce its occupation regime in other places—either in other Ukrainian territories or even in other countries in Europe or Eurasia.

My argument in the book is that Russia built a highly effective occupation regime, but it was aided by the political and social dynamics of south-eastern Ukraine. It achieved a high level of control through its occupation regime, but it was not clear that it could be reproduced elsewhere. It is true that with sufficient violence, any military force can assert control in the short term, but authoritarian regimes struggle to survive in the longer term against widespread political opposition if they rely solely on repression. A contemporary military occupation requires a more sophisticated policy toolbox than simply a thuggish occupation force. Russia also introduced its political institutions, laws and regulations—an administrative occupation that was highly effective at forcing compliance from the population through legal and bureaucratic controls. Contemporary authoritarian regimes also need to control political discourse: a recent book talks about the 'spin dictators', referring to those authoritarian regimes that manipulate society through mass propaganda and information control.³ Russia's media managers were masters of manipulation, and they rushed to saturate the information space in the occupied territories. Any occupation regime also requires control of physical space—of highways, roads and urban areas. This is achieved not only through military patrolling and surveillance, but through urban design, symbolism, the built environment and infrastructure. Finally, an effective occupation regime also needs control of financial flows and economic resources to co-opt local elites and placate local society. I explore these different elements through the four pillars of occupation—governance, violence, propaganda and money—to try to understand the mechanics of Russian rule.[4]

One way of thinking about Russian policy in the occupied territories is to use the distinction made by the sociologist Michael Mann between 'infrastructural power'—the power that stems from the state's penetration of every aspect of society through bureaucracy and institutions, laws and regulations—and 'despotic power', its direct power over the life and death of its citizens.[5] In Chapter 3, I examine one aspect of this 'infrastructural power'—Russia's expansion of political, legal and governance institutions into the occupied territories. In September 2022 Russia held rigged referendums in these regions on joining Russia, and then began to introduce Russian political, legal and economic systems. It held elections for regional councils in Kherson, Zaporizhzhia, Donetsk and Luhansk regions in September 2023 and for the Russian presidency in 2024. These elections were entirely fraudulent, but the crucial point was not their outcome. They demonstrated that Russia had the ability to impose its political infrastructure across the occupied territories, setting up local governments, ministries and civilian agencies to extend Russian governance across the territories. At the same time, Russia embarked on a 'bureaucratic occupation', forcing people to adopt Russian passports, observe Russian laws and regulations, and adapt to Russia's legal system, its regulatory regime and its bureaucracy.

In Chapter 4, I turn to what Mann calls 'despotic power', the use of coercion against citizens to enforce the power of the state. Russian governance in the occupation was heavily reliant on shocking levels of violence and repression. Without the Russian security forces, Russia's political institutions in the occupation would have collapsed overnight. Russia's military campaign was accompanied from the very first days by violence against civilians. The Federal Security Service (FSB) led a campaign to target potential opponents of the occupation, including local officials, journalists, activists and religious leaders. The rest of the population were forced to undergo a process known as 'filtration', in which every individual was checked for ties to the Ukrainian military and their potential disloyalty to Russia. Those who were detained by Russian forces faced torture, sexual violence and, in some cases, extra-judicial execution. Millions of people also faced forced migration, and there were shocking accounts of many Ukrainian children being deported and separated from their families.

The third pillar was a mass campaign of propaganda and indoctrination. Russia took over all communications and internet links and ended Ukrainian television and radio broadcasts. The new authorities set up television stations, newspapers and social media channels for the occupied territories. They also embarked on a rapid process of Russification in culture and education, trying to erase any evidence that these territories were part of Ukraine. The main Russian emphasis was on changing the minds of young people, through exchange programmes, study tours and a myriad of new youth groups and youth programmes. Russia was betting that within a few years it could produce a new generation of pro-Russian youth in the occupied territories.

The fourth pillar of the Russian occupation regime was the economy. Russian spending in the occupied territories amounted to around US$12 billion a year, less than 0.5% of Russian GDP, but these were substantial funds in these relatively poor regions. Russian development programmes were not primarily aimed at the well-being of local people, but at buying off local elites and ensuring compliance in the local population, through the provision of pensions and welfare payments. A mass programme of expropriation of Ukrainian assets and business provided huge opportunities for self-enrichment—both for locals and for Russians. A well-funded reconstruction programme was marked by extensive allegations of corruption and profiteering. Occupation was also a way to make money.

Taken together, these four areas of Russian activity comprised a highly repressive and integrated occupation regime. It effectively combined infrastructural power, which penetrated and saturated

INTRODUCTION

the occupied territories through Russia's rules, institutions, media and money, with egregious use of despotic power, enabling Russia to rule through fear and violence. Russia's ultimate aim was to produce a compliant population in the occupied territories to reduce the need to rely on extensive repression. Over the longer term, Russia would almost certainly encourage Russian citizens to move into the occupied territories, as tens of thousands had done in Crimea since 2014. Demographic change would help Russia achieve a sense of permanence and inevitability to the occupied territories and challenge the label of 'occupier' and 'occupied'; instead, in the future, Russia would assert that these lands were once again part of Russia and should be recognised as such by the international community. But any such recognition was very unlikely, because it would be a radical departure from the post-1945 international order, in which the world had decisively rejected the legitimacy of military occupation and military conquest.

Defining occupation

The areas of Ukrainian territory occupied by Russia are best understood as three distinct geographical zones, which have taken different historical routes to their annexation by Russia. First, Russia annexed Crimea and the city of Sevastopol in March 2014, after a one-sided referendum that no international body has recognised as legitimate. Russia spent the next decade introducing Russian laws and regulations into the Crimean Peninsula to make it an indistinguishable part of the Russian Federation. In a second territorial zone, Russia did not initially annex territories controlled by the separatist regimes in the Donetsk People's Republic (DNR) and the Lugansk People's Republic (LNR), but everybody understood that Russia ultimately controlled them. Russia first recognised the DNR and LNR as independent states in February 2022 and then annexed both territories on 30 September 2022. They are still referred to as 'People's Republics' in the Russian Constitution. In some cases, the LNR and the DNR have expanded the territory under their control since February 2022, most notably in Mariupol, which is now controlled by the DNR. Finally, in a third geographical zone, after February 2022 Russia occupied about half of the territory of Zaporizhzhia and Kherson regions and claimed the full territory of both regions as part of the Russian Federation.

Russia denied that it was an occupying power in these territories under international law. When Putin launched what he termed a 'Special Military Operation' on 24 February 2022, he assured the world that 'our plans do not include the occupation of Ukraine'.[6] In reality, as discussed in Chapter 1, Russian military and security services had probably planned the occupation and annexation of at least some Ukrainian territories in advance. But for Putin, the word 'occupation' did not apply. In his warped view of history, deepened by long evenings isolated in his Covid bunker, these were historically Russian lands. Putin told diplomats that south-eastern Ukraine 'had been part of historical Greater Russia for centuries'.[7] How could Russia be occupying its own historical territories?

Far from being an occupier, Russia claimed to be a 'liberator', freeing people in south-eastern Ukraine from what Russian officials labelled a Russophobic, 'neo-Nazi' regime in Kyiv. Parallels with the Soviet Union's struggle against Nazi Germany in World War II were played out endlessly in Russian propaganda. The President of the Russian Academy of Sciences, Gennady Krasnikov, compared the 'liberation [of Mariupol] in September 1943 by the units of the 44th Army' with the 'liberation of Mariupol during the special military operation'.[8] In 2024, foreign ministry spokesperson Maria Zakharova claimed that 'the people of Kherson still hope for the liberation of their hometown from the clutches of Nazism, just as they did 80 years ago'.[9]

This idea of Russia as 'liberator' could not have been more hollow. On 21 May 2023 Putin congratulated Russian soldiers on the 'liberation of Artemovsk', a ruined city that Ukrainians knew as Bakhmut.[10] Drone footage showed what Russia's 'liberation' entailed: every building was destroyed as far as the eye could see, the black abyss between jagged smoking walls of Soviet-era apartment blocks symbolising the hollowness of Russian victory. From the pre-war population of 70,000, only a few dozen people remained. Hundreds of civilians had died; tens of thousands had fled from the advance of Russian forces.[11]

INTRODUCTION

Russia's denial that it was an occupying power is given short shrift by international lawyers. Eliav Lieblich and Eyal Benvenisti, joint authors of a definitive study of international law and occupation, conclude that 'Occupation … occurs when armed forces—usually of a state—gain effective control over foreign territory, without the consent of the territorial state.'[12] They list the formation of the quasi-statelets of the DNR and the LNR and the annexation of Crimea in 2014, together with the seizure of further territory by Russia in 2022, as different forms of occupation, despite the varied legal status of these territories at different times in Russia's eyes. The key defining feature of occupation is de facto control by a hostile military force, regardless of what claims the occupying power might make. Lieblich and Benvenisti conclude that 'Occupation […] occurs when armed forces—usually of a state—gain effective control over foreign territory, without the consent of the territorial state.'[13] Marco Longobardo agrees: 'occupation, in a nutshell, is the establishment of a foreign, hostile authority over a portion of territory'.[14]

The authoritative Geneva Academy of International Humanitarian Law and Human Rights argues that Russia has been occupying Crimea since March 2014 and 'large territories in the south and the east of Ukraine since February 2022'.[15] Almost all international scholars concur with this assessment. Kenneth Watkin argues that '[i]n respect of Ukraine the seizure of its territory by Russia directly falls within the concept of belligerent occupation, which encompasses a belligerent State seizing enemy territory during an armed conflict'.[16] As a result, Russia is legally an occupying power and it therefore carries the responsibility of an occupying power under international humanitarian law.[17] The extent of Russia's occupation is also clear. Article 42 of the Hague Regulations of 1907 asserts that 'Territory is considered occupied when it is actually placed under the authority of the hostile army. The occupation extends only to the territory where such authority has been established and can be exercised.'[18] Although Russia claimed to have annexed four regions of Ukraine in 2022, in reality it did not control all of this territory and as a result its occupation only extended to the areas that its soldiers physically controlled.

On 2 October 2022, in a rushed decision on the legality of Russia's claimed annexation, the Russian Constitutional Court dismissed these arguments. It rejected 'reproaches from a number of countries for violating the existing international borders of another state', by pointing to 'the competition of this principle […] with the principle of equality and self-determination of peoples'. The court argued that the incorporation of Ukrainian territory was legal by referring to political talking-points, rather than any reference to domestic or international law.[19] The court asserted that 'the Ukrainian SSR was formed to a large degree on lands with a predominantly Russian population', a claim that was both historically false and also irrelevant to the legality of Russia's annexation.[20] After 2014, according to the court, the Ukrainian government, under 'the external management of the collective West', conducted a policy against the 'national, linguistic, religious and cultural identity' of 'citizens who identified themselves as belonging to the Russian people'. In this context, the court argued that people used their right to self-determination, as affirmed by the UN Charter, to break away from Ukraine. They cited the referendums held in the four regions as justifying the Russian action.[21]

This was a specious argument. There is no way to legalise an annexation through historical or political claims. As Russia's judges knew very well, under international law, 'the occupying power does not gain sovereignty in the territory and thus holding referendums to annex the occupied territories is unlawful'.[22] In international law, there was no way for Russia to legitimise its annexation of Ukrainian territory unless Ukraine agreed to cede territory in a treaty. Moreover, as the distinguished Israeli legal scholar Yoram Dinstein argued, it does not matter what claims or justifications the occupying power might make: 'The fact that the Occupying Power pretends to "liberate" the inhabitants of an occupied territory does not alter the legal taxonomy, as long as the occupation does not take place consensually.'[23]

In other words, under international law, the only legitimate end-state for Russia's occupation is through withdrawal of military forces or by agreeing territorial changes in a peace agreement with a legitimate Ukrainian government. The Ukrainian government

INTRODUCTION

emphasises this temporary nature of occupation by referring to Russian-occupied territories officially as 'temporarily occupied territories' (TOT). Classic definitions under international law also assume that occupation is a temporary state, pending the completion of hostilities. But temporary occupations of this nature are rare. The US did declare itself to be a temporary 'occupying power' in Iraq in 2003: as soon as a new sovereign government was installed, the occupation ended, at least in legal terms. But in most other cases, states have either proceeded with formal annexation (Morocco in Western Sahara, Russia in Crimea, Israel in East Jerusalem and the Golan Heights) or have achieved de facto permanent control through some form of puppet regime or unrecognised state (Abkhazia, the Turkish Republic of Northern Cyprus [TRNC], South Ossetia). In the Palestinian West Bank, Israel has not formally annexed the territory, but it exercises de facto military and security control, and it has encouraged its citizens to settle in occupied territory, in violation of international law.[24]

These occupations leave the population in a legal limbo, but they can continue for decades. Occupations are more likely to become semi-permanent when the territory is geographically contiguous with the occupying power.[25] But there is still a strong international consensus against recognising any change in international borders.[26] President Donald Trump began to erode this strict international norm of non-recognition in 2019, when the US recognised Israeli sovereignty over the Golan Heights and then recognised Moroccan sovereignty over the disputed Western Sahara region in 2020. Both decisions set potentially dangerous precedents for Ukraine, which remained vehemently opposed to any suggestion of international recognition of Russia's territorial gains.

The distinction between the legal concept of temporary occupation and the reality of semi-permanent occupation reflects a paradox in international law. While the use of force to conquer territory is outlawed, military occupation itself is not strictly illegal under international law. However, it is governed by numerous laws and conventions, including the Hague Convention (1907), the Fourth Geneva Convention (1949) and the Rome Statute (2022) of the International Criminal Court (ICC). Under international law, the occupying power has extensive legal obligations and constraints, which can be summarised as an overall obligation not to interfere in local laws, customs and governance, unless there are pressing security needs.[27] The Fourth Geneva Convention, signed in 1949, affords special protection to civilians living under an occupation regime, following the horrors of Nazi occupation during World War II. The occupying power must ensure humane governance for the population and the provision of food and medical supplies. International law outlaws the forcible transfer of the population to another state, the encouragement of immigration by nationals of the occupying state, and the confiscation of private property or pillaging, i.e. 'the forcible taking of private property by an invading or conquering army from the enemy's subjects'.[28] Russia's actions in occupied Ukraine violated all these long-standing principles of international law.[29]

Scholarly debates about the definition of occupation under international law at times appear as abstractions from the violent everyday reality of alien rule. As the scholars Christine de Matos and Rowena Ward have argued, the lines between colonialism, military intervention and military occupation 'are more blurred than clear-cut'.[30] Occupation is best understood not in legal terms, but as a denial of autonomy: 'each territorial encounter assumes a loss of autonomy at the level of the individual, and/or the group, and/or the occupied state'.[31] As I explore in later chapters, this denial of autonomy is a defining feature of Russia's occupation regime. The loss of autonomy occurred at every scale—the violation of the borders of Ukraine's sovereign state, but also the spatial occupation of towns, streets, villages, farms, factories, hospitals, kindergartens and schools. Russian security agencies captured personal data on the entire population. There was no privacy under occupation. Instead, it was a constant process of violation of personal autonomy, right down to the level of the body and the mind.

Researching occupation

Researching the occupation is difficult. Not only is there an ongoing high-intensity war along the front line of the occupied territo-

INTRODUCTION

ries, but the Russian-controlled territories are very difficult for outside researchers to access. I was unable to travel either to the occupied territories or to Russia while writing this book. The security risks of visiting the territories via Russia were too high. A few international journalists visited the regions under Russian control, but such visits were controversial and posed significant risks. As a result, traditional research methods, such as in-person interviews and political ethnography, were not possible.[32] However, I did speak regularly to researchers and colleagues who were in touch with contacts in the occupied territories, and I used such information as background for the current book. Many Ukrainians still speak to their relatives and friends living under occupation, and although conversations are guarded, plenty of information does get out.

I also travelled twice to Ukraine during 2024 to interview people who had left the occupied territories. I also spoke with many Ukrainian and international journalists and officials who were following closely the situation in the occupied territories. In most cases, I have maintained anonymity for these people because of security concerns, unless they gave explicit permission for their names to be used. I have often relied on interviews that are already in the public domain, but have always tried to corroborate claims with my own investigations and sources. At times, with competing claims—or more often single-sourced claims—there is a judgment call as to whether the information is credible or not.

Fortunately, during the war, there has been some remarkable journalism. This book owes a debt to reporters writing in international and Ukrainian media, but also to detailed investigative reporting in Russian-language media outlets. Many reporters risked their lives to report from the occupied regions, including during the siege of Mariupol. Ukrainian journalists, operating under extreme wartime conditions, produced brilliant investigative reporting on many aspects of the occupation, including critical reporting on their own government's policies. Independent Russian-language journalism, operating mostly outside Russia, also contributed extensively to our understanding of what was happening on the ground. Russian-language media inside the Russian Federation operated under severe pressure and strict de facto cen-

13

sorship, but some journalists continued to provide useful reporting on aspects of the situation in the occupied territories within the constraints of Russia's highly repressive system.

Social media has also transformed our ability to research the occupation. The most widely used platform for both Russian and Ukrainian authorities and commentators has been Telegram, and it has become an invaluable resource for researchers. I have largely relied on Telegram channels that report either official positions or offer direct evidence of a particular event (photos, videos, etc.). Many Russian Telegram channels were deliberately misleading or published inaccurate or highly distorted information or interpretations of events. Nevertheless, their official channels offered important insights into Russia's plans and operations. Several Ukrainian channels provided constant updates on the situation in the occupied territories. They were invaluable sources, but some also had to be treated with caution. Ukraine, like Russia, was engaged in an information war. Other important sources included video clips on YouTube and other platforms—researchers used these to follow the reconstruction campaign in Mariupol and to track which companies were involved. Satellite photographs helped to trace shipping routes or new buildings and transport routes.

Although detailed data in Russia were often classified during the war, Russian officials often made public announcements and statements about major developments in the political and administrative occupation of Ukrainian territory. Russian laws and appointments are usually public, and some aspects of Russian expenditure can also be tracked in the state budget. Russian corporate databases provided evidence of how Russia seized control of Ukrainian companies and assets; recruitment sites and tender sites offered partial evidence of which Russian companies were working in the occupied territories. Even the occasional arrests of highly placed Russian officials shed light on mechanisms of corruption and malpractice. However, I was unable to visit Russia to talk to Russians who served in the occupation administrations or in the military, or to Ukrainians who had fled occupied Ukraine and resettled in the Russian Federation. Their voices are largely absent from these accounts, as are the voices of thousands of Ukrainians still held in prison in Russia or in the Crimea.

INTRODUCTION

Ukrainian media were much freer than in Russia, but journalists faced serious physical danger from Russian attacks. Others risked detention and violence in the occupied territories. At least eleven reporters were killed in the first two years of the war and more than a hundred journalists were victims of violence.[33] There were also military restrictions on reporting in Ukraine, and many journalists—local and international—self-censored, unwilling to criticise the government in a time of war or to contribute to the Russian war narrative. The Ukrainian authorities closed some outlets and detained or threatened bloggers and publicists considered to be pro-Russian.[34] In other cases, international journalists claimed to have had sensitive stories discouraged by editors nervous about critical reporting.[35] Some of these constraints were inevitable in wartime, but as the war progressed, pressure on the media increased and some Ukrainian journalists also reported that they were under surveillance by the intelligence agencies.[36]

This book was written during 2023 and the first half of 2024. As such, it is a snapshot of a rapidly evolving environment. The battlefield remained dynamic and the situation in the occupied territories was also evolving rapidly. Inevitably, some conclusions might be overtaken by events, but my aim was to provide an in-depth account of the first two years of the occupation, to explain the critical junctures and dynamics in Russia's establishment of an occupation regime and its annexation of Ukrainian territory. Whatever happens in the future, this process should be understood much more widely—not only for the clear policy implications, but also as part of a wider record of the Russian invasion and the violence and abuses that accompanied it.

This work aims to provide a comprehensive analysis of the Russian occupation for an English-language audience. Ukrainian scholars and writers have been providing their own accounts, based both on first-hand experience and on detailed scholarship.[37] Historically, there were often too few Ukrainian voices in academic debates, not only about Ukraine and Russia but about European and international affairs more generally. There are still very few centres of Ukrainian studies outside Ukraine, and Ukrainian authors have traditionally been under-represented in academic pub-

15

lishing.[38] Julia Buyskykh has a point when she argues that there is 'a certain epistemic violence influencing the reception of scholarly Ukrainian narratives, a violence that refuses to see them as anything other than "local" and "emotional", even illegitimate'.[39]

This situation is beginning to change, with important new work by Ukrainian scholars being published, despite the difficult conditions many academics in Ukraine faced during the war—either forced into exile or working under attack, and often without electricity or internet access.[40] On a more theoretical level, there have been important developments in the debate. Scholars have called for a paradigm shift in Western intellectual framings of Russia and Ukraine that reasserts Ukrainian subjectivity and Ukrainian voices. Some even argue for a period of silence from mainstream Western scholars to allow room for other voices to emerge in the debate.[41] Olesya Khromeychuk, a historian, has called for a 'a permanent alteration—decolonization, de-imperialization—of our knowledge'.[42]

This shift to 'decolonise' Russian studies has produced innovative scholarship, but also created new challenges and problems, which become evident when we research something as complex as the occupation. First, critiques of Western scholarship as overlooking the imperial history of Russia are often too sweeping.[43] In history and in area studies, there is a long tradition of research on both the Russian and Soviet empires and a growing application of comparative approaches and post-colonial theory. After the Soviet collapse in 1991, there was a new wave of English-language scholarship about non-Russian peoples in the Soviet empire and in its aftermath. I was fortunate to have an education in British universities in which the understanding of Russia as an empire was ever-present. My first teacher of Russian, James Forsyth, Reader in Russian at the University of Aberdeen, was one of the first Western scholars to write about Russia's expansion into Siberia and suppression of its indigenous peoples.[44] My doctoral supervisor at the London School of Economics, the historian Professor Dominic Lieven, researched the history of the Russian empire in a comparative framework with the Ottoman, Habsburg and British empires, and other cases such as China.[45] This approach also informed my doctoral dissertation on 'Stalinism and Empire', which studied the history of the remote Republic of Tyva, a 'People's Republic' which was annexed in 1944 in a similar way to the 'People's Republics' of eastern Ukraine nearly eighty years later.[46]

Second, in the current context of the war in Ukraine, the decolonial framework often risks reasserting a methodological nationalism that overlooks complex and often hybrid identities, such as those frequently encountered in the Russian-Ukrainian borderlands now under occupation. Imperialist thought played a significant role in Russia's attitudes towards Ukraine, as I explore in Chapter 1, but Moscow's visions and understandings of empire were also entwined with geopolitical thinking and with identity politics. Russia's imperialism had deep historical roots, but it was not a fixed essence of the Russian state or Russian society. Rather, it is best understood as a contingent outcome of a particular set of ideological and historical circumstances. The decolonial portrayal of the war as a former colonial territory fighting a war of liberation against an imperial power, while certainly true on one level, tended to obscure other dynamics of the conflict, including tensions and differences within Russian and Ukrainian societies. The decolonial gaze also risked overlooking economic cleavages and class differences.[47] Russian forces in Ukraine included many non-Russians—Chechens, Tyvans, Dagestanis and Ukrainians from the east—but they were almost all from the very poorest parts of society.

Finally, everybody agreed that Ukrainian voices should be central to the political debate, but which voices should be included from a diverse society like Ukraine? In the occupied territories, as discussed in Chapter 1, there was always a spectrum of attitudes towards Russia, Kyiv and the West. A wide range of views can still be heard across the Ukrainian political and scholarly spectrum. A recent special issue of a journal edited by Julia Buyskykh rightly aims at a 'rich and careful documentation of the heterogeneity of Ukraine and its citizens', not only for the purpose of scholarship, but because it 'represents one symbolic form of resistance to ongoing efforts of colonial erasure'.[48] But how far should such heterogeneity go? Volodymr Ishchenko, a leftist Ukrainian author now based in Berlin, argues that 'Ukrainian "decolonization" ... amplifies the voices articulating Ukrainian distinctiveness' but is antagonistic towards 'the voices of those who oppose this process or are simply labelled, usually misleadingly, as "pro-Russian"'.[49] He worries that 'the formalistic representation of tokenized "Ukrainian voices" helps silence other "voices" from Ukraine that are not so easy to instrumentalize'.[50] I explore some of these politics of identity throughout the book, but the polarised range of opinions in and around the occupied territories poses challenges to any researcher to represent faithfully the range of social and political attitudes towards Russia's occupation.

Although sources are complex and sometimes sparse, there is much more information available than when, as a British exchange student, I made my first visit to Ukraine in June 1988, in the last years of the Soviet Union, when it was still the Ukrainian Soviet Socialist Republic. At that time, the USSR did not appear to be in terminal decline. The idea that Ukraine might emerge as a sovereign state seemed fanciful. But by the time I went back to Ukraine, in the grim, icy winter of 1991–92, it was already a recognised, independent state. When I conducted research in Crimea in the early 1990s, many observers predicted an early conflict over the peninsula with Russia. Yet this conflict only broke out more than two decades later, in 2014. In other words, while political change can happen suddenly after decades of stasis, in other cases, deep-seated differences can be managed or remain dormant for extended periods of time. There was nothing inevitable about Russia's war against Ukraine and there is nothing inevitable about how it ends. As I write this book in the summer of 2024, Russia appears to have consolidated its military occupation of south-eastern Ukraine. Moscow's propaganda claimed that 'Russia is here forever'. But the modern histories of Russia and Ukraine suggest that the situation may yet change in unexpected ways.

1

IDEAS

In his 1992 book on occupation—a rare comparative work on the concept—Eric Carlton explains that any occupation is always reliant on ideology. Occupation begins not with the first soldiers walking down an unfamiliar, foreign street, looking warily at hostile passers-by through their balaclavas, but with the ideological debates that provide the political, strategic and even moral case for invasion and occupation. Ideology is both the framework that shapes a decision to invade, and also, as Carlton reminds us, 'certainly the most effective and least expensive means of mass control'.[1] For many years scholars had described Putin's Russia as a post-ideological regime, built on kleptocracy and cynicism, but not on ideas.[2] In reality, behind the villas and the yachts and the oligarchic bling, ideas had always played a central role in Putin's Russia, and the ideological nature of the regime became increasingly evident in the years running up to the 2022 invasion.[3] These ideas did not emerge from nowhere, but from long-standing debates in Russia that dated back to the Soviet period. Long before the first Russian soldiers appeared on Ukrainian soil, Russian thinkers, philosophers, polemicists and academics had laid the ideational groundwork for the occupation.

In this chapter, I explore the importance of ideas in four major areas. The first was grand geopolitics, a set of ideas about the world that placed the struggle over Ukraine within the global context of Russia's relations with the West. Ukraine was merely one battlefield in a much wider conflict over the future of international order. A second strand of ideas reinvented the long history of imperialist and colonial thinking in Russia. In its crudest form, it challenged the very existence of Ukraine as a nation and legitimised Russia's imperial history. This mode of thinking often presented Russia as a distinct civilisation, a 'Russian World', of which Ukraine was merely a part. A third set of ideas focused on territory, notably the territories of south-east Ukraine, transformed in Russian thinking into a historically Russian territory, a land in which Russia had rights and duties that superseded national sovereignty. Finally, there were ideational debates about Ukrainian identity—the question of how individuals living in Ukraine should define themselves in relation to a Ukrainian state-building project on the one hand, and a revanchist form of Russian neo-imperialism on the other. These ideas all overlapped and interconnected, and together formed the ideological framework that served to legitimise the invasion and occupation of Ukraine in Russian thinking.

Geopolitics

On 30 September 2022, in the vast St George's Hall in the Kremlin, President Putin signed treaties on the accession of the 'Donetsk People's Republic', the 'Lugansk People's Republic', the 'Zaporozhye' Region and the Kherson Region to the Russian Federation. Putin's speech began with a nod to the canon of historical Russian heroes who had first conquered these regions, Catherine II and Grigory Potemkin, but his speech was not primarily about these newly annexed territories or even about Ukraine. It was instead a litany of grievances about the international order and 'the West', which was 'ready to cross every line to preserve the neo-colonial system which allows it to live off the world'. To do this, '[i]t is critically important for them to force all countries to surrender their sovereignty to the United States'. If any state does not agree, 'they destroy entire states, leaving behind humanitarian disasters, devastation, ruins, millions of wrecked and mangled human lives, terrorist enclaves, social disaster zones, protectorates, colonies and semi-colonies. They don't care. All they care about is their own benefit.' That is why, in Putin's view, Russia was facing a 'hybrid war' being fought against Russia:

> They do not want us to be free; they want us to be a colony. They do not want equal cooperation; they want to loot. They do not want to see us a free society, but a mass of soulless slaves. They see our thought and our philosophy as a direct threat. That is why they target our philosophers for assassination. Our culture and art present a danger to them, so they are trying to ban them.[4]

Putin goes on amid applause from the hall, mocking the West's claim to be defending a 'rules-based international order' and accusing them of 'totalitarianism, despotism and apartheid'. They have no moral right to criticise 'the choice of the people in Crimea, Sevastopol, Donetsk, Lugansk, Zaporozhye and Kherson' since 'it was the so-called West that trampled on the principle of the inviolability of borders, and now it is deciding, at its own discretion, who has the right to self-determination and who does not, who is unworthy of it'. While announcing the biggest neo-imperial land grab in Europe since World War II, Putin also railed against Western colonialism and reminded his audience that 'we are proud that in the 20th century our country led the anti-colonial movement, which opened up opportunities for many peoples around the world to make progress, reduce poverty and inequality, and defeat hunger and disease'.[5]

It is easy to dismiss all this as Orwellian double-speak: imperialism is emancipation, occupation is liberation, war is peace. Putin repeatedly claimed that Russia was pursuing the invasion only to achieve peace: 'It's they [the West] who have started the war. And we are using force to end it.'[6] The Russian Constitutional Court echoed this view, arguing that the goal of the treaties signed to incorporate the four regions into Russia was 'to ultimately achieve peace in the relevant territory'.[7] These contradictions only make sense in the context of a long tradition of anti-Western geopolitical thought in Russia. Putin was asserting a radical ideological claim: that Russia's occupation of Ukrainian territory was a way to ensure peace, through the creation of a new international order that would overthrow centuries of Western domination. In this view, Ukraine was only one battleground in a much bigger conflict over the future of international order.

From the Russian point of view, the post-Cold War international order had radically diminished Russia's role in the world. The bipolar world, in which Moscow was one of two superpowers, had turned into a unipolar system, with Russia reduced to the status of a weak, regional power. All the big decisions in international relations were now made in Washington, not in Moscow; Russia was often not even consulted. Russia had lost its empire in Eastern Europe and now faced a challenge in its own neighbourhood, including in Ukraine, which was seeking to join NATO and the European Union.

For Putin and his advisors, this world order threatened their vision of Russia as a sovereign state and as a great power. They believed that the US was pursuing a foreign policy that promoted 'managed chaos' all around Russia's borders, including a toolbox of 'colour revolutions' that provided support for political oppositions and anti-government rebels.[8] Russian analysts saw the hand of the West everywhere: in the upheavals of the Arab Spring, in a series of major political protests in Russia in the winter of 2011–12, and in a wave of anti-regime protests from Hong Kong to Belarus, from Myanmar to Venezuela. Russia's role was to hold back this geopolitical upheaval. Moscow's global mission was to be a conservative bulwark against the collapse and chaos engendered by the US and global liberalism.[9]

Instead of this threatening unipolar system, Russian thinkers advocated a multipolar world. In such a world order, major powers—Russia, China, India—would form large geopolitical spaces in which they could promote their own ideas and their own values, not the liberal values of the West. These spaces would be based on civilisations—Russia was one of several 'state-civilisations' that could challenge the power of the US and block the flow of liberal ideas around the world.[10] The multipolar world would be a more stable world, they believed, because the dangerous, destabilising liberal ideas promoted by the US would be contained. Each civilisation could develop in its own way rather than being forced to follow the blueprint of the West.[11] Implicit in this civilisational worldview was the idea that great powers would once again enjoy spheres of influence and be able to dominate their neighbourhood, if necessary by military force. Smaller states with unlucky geography—such as Ukraine—would have to align with their more powerful neighbours or face intervention, occupation or worse.

This was not a new debate. In the 1930s—a period when occupation and annexation had once again become commonplace features of international relations—Carl Schmitt, the Nazi jurist and political thinker, argued that military occupation, far from being a negative phenomenon, could be a necessary mechanism to create a multipolar world and prevent a global war.[12] In April 1939, after a year in which Germany had annexed Austria and Sudetenland, and just weeks after German troops marched into Bohemia and Moravia, Schmitt delivered a lecture that expounded his theory of the *Großraum*—or 'Great Space'. Great powers should be permitted to expand into neighbouring territories to form a *Großraum*, from which other powers would be excluded.[13] These spheres of influence around great powers would hold back the destructive, universalist ideas of Western liberalism and would form the basis of a more stable and sustainable multipolar world. Schmitt argued that his *Großraum* concept was fully reflected in the Molotov-Ribbentrop Pact, which led to the Nazi occupation of western Poland and the Soviet occupation of eastern Poland and the Baltic States.[14] For Schmitt, this double occupation produced a sustainable balance of power and a line of division between two great powers that would preserve the peace. The occupation and obliteration of the lands in between did not concern Schmitt. The collapse of the Nazi-Soviet pact into total war and Schmitt's status as a Nazi did not prevent a remarkable renaissance in his ideas after the end of the Cold War.[15]

A nationalist thinker, Alexander Dugin, began propagating Schmitt's ideas in Russia in the early 1990s. He devoted a chapter to Schmitt in a 1997 book, *The Foundations of Geopolitics*, which resonated in military and security circles. Dugin echoed Schmitt's ideas when he wrote about 'the great Russian dream', which would be impossible to fulfil within the frontiers of the new Russian state. Instead, 'the boundaries of this dream, the nation sees, at a minimum, in an Empire'.[16] Ukraine was critical to this thinking, because—for Dugin—'the existence of Ukraine in the current borders and with its current status as a "sovereign state" is no less than a monstrous blow to Russia's geopolitical security and is equivalent to the invasion of its territory'.[17] In a review of Dugin's book, the scholar John Dunlop wrote that 'the book's implications for the future of Ukraine can be simply stated: if its ideas were to be implemented, then Ukraine would cease to exist as an independent state and would likely be dismembered'.[18]

The broad principles of Schmittian geopolitics—antagonism towards the West, opposition to liberal ideas and the right of major powers to a sphere of influence—gradually became mainstream in Russian foreign policy thinking. This trend was not inevitable, but was encouraged by a series of confrontations between Russia and the West, including the war in Georgia in 2008, when Russia had intervened in South Ossetia and Abkhazia; the declaration earlier in the same year by NATO that Georgia and Ukraine would become members of the alliance; and by events in the Middle East, first the US-led invasion of Iraq, and in 2011 the NATO intervention in Libya. Each of these events fuelled a downwards spiral in relations between Russia and the West that encouraged the growth of more radical foreign policy thinking, including the ideas of long-forgotten figures such as Schmitt and marginal polemicists such as Dugin. Russian officials became convinced that the US-led international order posed an existential threat to their vision of a future Russian state. The US and its allies viewed Russia as a growing revisionist threat to the post-Cold War European security order. Both sides saw the Russian intervention in Ukraine in 2014 as confirmation of their views, further deepening the ideological divide.

After Russia's 2022 invasion, these radical ideas became part of the mainstream of official Russian foreign policy. In October 2023, speaking at the annual Valdai conference, President Putin explained his vision of a multipolar world: rather than 'a new confrontation of blocs' or the 'soulless universalism of a new globalisation', Putin argued that, 'on the contrary, the world is on its way to a synergy of civilisation-states, large spaces, communities identifying as such'.[19] Dugin himself, who had been out of favour with the Kremlin, was back in the limelight. When a 'Multipolarity Forum' was held in Moscow in February 2024, he was the keynote speaker. He told the audience that Russia proposed an alternative, multipolar world order, based on the response of 'great ancient and unique civilisations, sovereign states, and peoples to the challenge of globalism', led by a 'Russia, awakening from its slumber' and 'China, making a rapid leap forward'.[20] The unipolar moment was over, argued Dugin, ended by

> the position of Russia and personally our President Vladimir Vladimirovich Putin, when we refused to sacrifice our sovereignty and entered into a mortal battle with the West in Ukraine. We are fighting in Ukraine not with Ukrainians, but with a unipolar world.[21]

In this mode of thinking, the occupation of Ukraine becomes the first step towards dismantling the last vestiges of 'Western imperialism'. The obvious intellectual contradictions of these arguments had already been rehearsed once before. In the 1940s, Schmitt's intellectual opponents, such as the pacifist Hans Wehberg and the liberal lawyer Hans Kelsen, had been quick to challenge his ideas. Wehberg wrote in 1941 that 'All of this has nothing to do with international law and international legal policy, but is an attempt to give a policy of imperialism a semblance of law.' Kelsen, writing after the war in 1957, dismissed it as 'a justification for imperialism with a false guise of legality'.[22] Schmitt's arguments advocating spheres of influence and military occupation as mechanisms to avoid total war ended in the grim reality of the Nazi occupation of Europe, including Ukraine. During the German occupation of Ukraine in 1941–44, at least one million Jews were killed, alongside millions of Ukrainians, Russians and other nationalities.

This revival of 1930s geopolitics in the twenty-first century was a shock to a world that believed that the idea of territorial conquest belonged in the past. The UN Charter in 1945 had outlawed military conquest ('All Members shall refrain … from the threat or use of force against the territorial integrity or political independence of any state'). Scholars argued that we had seen a shift in norms of historic importance, summed up as an 'End of Conquest'.[23] Steven Pinker made a similarly optimistic argument in 2011, noting that no country had 'conquered even parts of some other country since 1975'.[24] Iraq's attempt to seize Kuwait or the Argentinian invasion of the Falklands Islands stood out as rare exceptions to an otherwise powerful international norm. The days of military conquest and annexation seemed to be over.

This shift in norms was what made Russia's occupation and annexation of parts of Ukraine such a radical event. It seemed so anachronistic, reminiscent of the 1930s when Schmitt had been writing. But its novelty was part of the point. Russia was declaring that it was no longer bound by the rules of the old security order. Russian leaders never failed to point out that the US had intervened militarily in many parts of the world, often in violation of international law. In two major campaigns, in Afghanistan and Iraq, the US and its allies had led a form of military occupation. This fuelled a constant narrative in Russian discourse of 'dual standards', of one rule for the US, while other states—including Russia—were held accountable to different standards. In 2014, after Russia had annexed Crimea, in a flight of picturesque imagery, Putin made clear that Russia would no longer acquiesce in this world order:

> Remember that wonderful phrase: 'what is permitted to Jupiter, is not permitted to the bull': We cannot agree with this formulation. Perhaps the bull is not permitted, but I want to tell you that the bear will not ask anybody for permission. He is considered the master of the *taiga* and I know definitely that he is not planning to move anywhere else, to different climatic zones—that would not suit him. But he will not give up the *taiga* to anybody.[25]

The annexation of Crimea and its subsequent occupation was a declaration that the Russian bear would no longer 'ask for permission' in its own backyard, whether in the *taiga* or the *steppe*. It represented a growing boldness in Moscow to promulgate its own worldview, based on ideas of great powers, spheres of influence and civilisational spaces, all of which implied a potential willingness to implement forms of military occupation in Russia's neighbourhood.

Russia was now a revisionist state, even a revolutionary state, willing to challenge the norms of twenty-first-century international relations. For Dmitry Trenin, one of Russia's best-known foreign policy analysts, this was 'a revolution in Moscow's foreign policy'. Russia is now, he claimed, 'for the first time since the Bolshevik Revolution' a 'revolutionary power', that is 'pushing back more and more against the hegemonic US-centered system'.[26]

Empire

Geopolitical thinkers in Russia proposed a sphere of influence to challenge the West and to build a new international order. This worldview also overlapped neatly with neo-imperialist ideas promoted in Russia by those who wished to overcome the collapse of empire experienced in 1991. There was nothing inevitable about the Russian invasion of Ukraine in 2022. But Russia's failure to engage critically with its own imperial and colonial past always left open the possibility of a revival of elements of imperialist thought. An important strand of White Russian émigré thought was also an inspiration for a contemporary Russian nationalism that denied the existence of Ukraine as a nation.[27] From the very birth of the new Ukrainian state in 1991, powerful voices in Russia voiced alarm at the 'loss' of Ukraine and advocated its dismemberment and annexation of part of its territory by Russia. For a long time, these ideas were held in abeyance, but in 2013–14 they shifted to the mainstream, and in 2022 these arguments effectively became official Russian policy.

Russia's post-imperial crisis was more acute than that experienced by Britain or France, despite the long conflicts in Ireland and Algeria. Unlike West European colonial powers, it was difficult to distinguish where Russia as a nation-state ended and where its empire began. This was still true in the Soviet Union, although for the first time Russia—as the Russian Soviet Federative Socialist Republic—was distinguished from the Ukrainian Soviet Socialist Republic and thirteen other national republics, a process that contributed to the emergence of fifteen independent post-Soviet republics. Despite the formation of these national boundaries, the

Soviet Union also preserved the main territories of the Tsarist empire under rule from Moscow. As a result, when the Soviet Union collapsed in 1991, it also meant the end of a centuries-old Russian imperial polity. In December 2021 Putin lamented that the collapse of the Soviet Union meant the loss of 'historical Russia', by which he meant the geographical space occupied both by the Russian empire and the Soviet Union.[28]

The end of the Soviet Union remains mired in controversy. Its fate was sealed in the Belovezha Accords, signed by the leaders of Russia, Ukraine and Belarus in a Belarusian country lodge on 8 December 1991. Ukraine had declared independence on 24 August 1991, and on 1 December 1991 voters across Ukraine overwhelmingly supported Ukrainian independence in a referendum.[29] By then the collapse of the USSR was inevitable. But many Russian nationalists were appalled and claimed that the decision to disband the Soviet Union was illegitimate. The Russian State Duma—the national parliament—even adopted a resolution in March 1996 denouncing the Belovezha Accords. This idea would be revived after the 2022 invasion. Guests on the Russian talk-show *The Great Game*, in March 2024, raised doubts about the legality of the 1991 Ukrainian referendum on independence and the Belovezha agreements. As a result, the presenter Dmitrii Simes argued, Russia's presence in Ukraine could not be considered aggression against a sovereign state, because 'Russia has the right to consider this its own [territory], not only historically but from the point of view of law.'[30]

But in the 1990s, official Russia under President Boris Yeltsin rejected such views—after all, it was Yeltsin who had signed the Belovezha Accords on Russia's behalf. Instead, Russia recognised Ukraine as an independent state and affirmed its territorial integrity in the 1994 Budapest memorandum and in a 1997 bilateral agreement, despite continuing disputes over the status of Crimea and Sevastopol, home to Russia's Black Sea Fleet. Whatever the private concerns of Russian officials, there was little appetite for any boundary disputes with Ukraine at a time when Russia's own territorial integrity was threatened by a separatist war in Chechnya.

In public, at least, Vladimir Putin also adopted this pragmatic position. He appeared ready to move on from Russia's imperial past. He gave no indication that he shared the irredentist views of Russian nationalists when he came to power as president in 2000. In January 2003, when Putin visited Ukraine for talks with President Leonid Kuchma, he was welcomed by many Ukrainians, who saw him as a positive contrast to their own often ineffectual leaders. Putin seemed ready to move on from the squabbles between Russia and Ukraine in the 1990s over Crimea. He signed a far-reaching agreement, the *Treaty Between the Russian Federation and Ukraine on the Russian-Ukrainian State Border*, the result of four years of painstaking talks to delimit all 2,063 kilometres of the international frontier.

This recognition of Ukrainian independence was often grudging. Russia forced a confrontation with Ukraine in 2003 over the contested Tuzla Island in the Kerch Strait. But in April 2004, back in Moscow, Putin quietly signed the new border agreement into law. He showed no interest in what was happening in southeastern Ukraine, did not make any claims on Donbas, and did not mention any of the places that would be headline news when Russia occupied them in 2022: Mariupol, Donetsk, Berdiansk or Kherson, let alone the fictive imaginary of 'Novorossiya' that would be deployed so often in his wartime speeches. In private Putin was almost certainly sceptical about Ukrainian independence and believed that Crimea should be part of Russia, but in public, at least, Putin's team of securocrats appeared willing to accept the reality of an independent Ukrainian state within its internationally recognised boundaries.

Putin's apparent pragmatism about Ukrainian independence contained a fatal caveat. In his view, Ukrainian sovereignty was conditional on Ukrainian behaviour. While Russia was able to influence Ukrainian politics through pro-Russian parties and pro-Russian media, negotiate gas deals with its leaders and ensure that it did not get too close to the West—in particular to NATO—it would tolerate an independent Ukrainian state. But many Ukrainians had no intention of living with this form of conditional sovereignty. The so-called Orange Revolution of 2004—which prevented a pro-Russian president, Viktor Yanukovych, from coming to power through rigged elections—had huge repercussions. It emboldened a Ukrainian nationalist movement, which led a long and largely successful campaign to challenge Russian cultural, linguistic and political dominance in the country. And it prompted a rethink in Moscow of how it viewed Ukraine.

When Putin returned as president for a third term in 2012, nationalist ideologues found themselves in demand. They came together to form a loose network of around thirty right-wing thinkers called the Izborsky Club. Now they had some state support—the first meeting was attended by figures such as presidential advisor Sergei Glazyev, Minister of Culture Vladimir Medinsky (who would later negotiate with the Ukrainians after the February 2022 invasion) and Andrei Turchak—then a governor of Pskov region but in 2022–23 a regular visitor to the occupied territories as secretary of the United Russia (ER) party.[31] The Izborsky Club contained different views and schools of thought, but its disparate membership largely agreed on one thing—the centrality of empire to Russian history and political thought. They viewed Russian history as a series of imperial polities—from Rus' to the Romanov empire, through the Soviet Union and then to a proposed Eurasian Union.[32] One of the founders of the Izborsky Club, Alexander Prokhanov, argued that empire was not about domination but synthesis: 'under empire I mean not the domination of one aggressive nation against the others, but a symphony of spaces, cultures, languages, peoples, potentialities'.[33]

Different versions of this 'symphonic' empire were articulated by Russian thinkers. One version was Eurasia, a concept that was originally described by Petr Savitsky in 1927 as 'the region of the desertic steppes that extend in an uninterrupted stretch from the Chinese Wall to Galicia'.[34] In other words, the steppe of central and eastern Ukraine formed the western reaches of this Eurasian entity. In modern Russia, there were multiple versions of Eurasia. Technocrats promoted 'pragmatic Eurasianism', which owed more to the traditions of EU-style regional integration than Russian imperialist traditions.[35] In its most extreme form, however, Eurasianism was a radical, anti-Western, neo-imperialist project. It had a dual character. On the one hand Eurasia was another version of a geopolitical space dominated by Russia, a polite word for empire. But it also presented itself as a space constructed in opposition to Western 'imperialism'. The founders of Eurasianism characterised Eurasia as 'a colonized country, a potential leader of the uprising of the colonized against the colonizers'.[36] In this thinking, Russia would lead an anti-imperial empire, an oxymoron that made sense in the minds of many Eurasianists but looked very much like old-fashioned imperialism to Russia's neighbours.

Another way of talking about a revived Russian empire was the concept of the 'Russian World'. At an early stage in the mid-2000s, this was a rather benign idea that aimed to unite disparate communities of Russians and Russian speakers across the world. However, the Russian Orthodox Church promoted a version of the Russian World which provided the basis for a harder geopolitical concept. In this version, the territory of Ukraine was part of a unified spiritual space that transcended national boundaries and political entities, and where Western ideas—and concepts such as Ukrainian nationalism—were seen as alien intruders.[37] This 'Russian World' incorporated Russia, Ukraine and Belarus—and sometimes parts of Moldova and Kazakhstan. Even this notion might have been reserved primarily for spiritual and cultural ideas if it had not mapped so easily onto geopolitical divides. In 2013–14 the concept of the Russian World took on the form of a 'nationalist discourse about the necessity for Russia's revival as a great power and its revanche in the post-Soviet space'.[38] A geopolitical version of the Russian World would now be used to lay claim to large parts of eastern Ukraine, with the (almost entirely mistaken) belief that the population there would be open to being part of such a project.

In 2014 figures from the Izborsky Club cheered on the annexation of Crimea and were actively involved in promoting pro-Russian unrest across southern and eastern Ukraine—a movement they dubbed the 'Russian Spring'. But the unrest failed to turn into a mass movement and Russian nationalists were sidelined when Putin signed the Minsk agreements in 2014–15, which ended any chance of a wider Russian military campaign against Ukraine and were widely seen as a betrayal by the neo-imperialist camp in Moscow. When Putin returned for a fourth term in power in 2018, however, the ideas circulating at the Izborsky Club had already moved into the mainstream. When an amended Russian Constitution was adopted in 2020, it included a new emphasis on traditional values and was seen as evidence of a permanent shift in official thinking towards anti-Western conservatism. After the invasion of Ukraine in February 2022, the marginal philosophers of the extreme right finally took centre stage. Their ideological support for a revived form of Russian empire, their virulent anti-Westernism and their radical anti-liberalism in domestic politics all became mainstream ideas in Russian official policy. Even the Presidential Administration reportedly began consulting figures such as Dugin, once seen as an outcast, thus completing a remarkable ideological arc. As one report concluded: 'marginalised people, who Putin's administration had once wanted to keep away from, ended up infiltrating all spheres of Russian life—the government, the media, and schools'.[39]

Territory

Geopolitical thinkers wanted a sphere of influence to challenge the West. Neo-imperialists wanted to reunite the fragments of empire. But what territories should be included in any new Russian imperial polity and what should their status be? Most viewed Belarus and Russia as core territories in any new Russia-centred bloc. Some wanted northern Kazakhstan. And almost everybody agreed that a revived Russian state with expanded frontiers should include southern and eastern Ukraine, including Crimea. For a long time, official Moscow preferred to leave these territories inside Ukraine as a way to maintain political influence inside the Ukrainian state. But there had always been a school of thought that they should rightly be part of the Russian Federation.

This view goes back to the Soviet period. According to the filmmaker Karen Shakhnazarov, his father Georgy Shakhnazarov, who was a close advisor to Mikhail Gorbachev, wrote a report in early 1991 advising the Soviet leader to incorporate all of southern and eastern Ukraine into the Russian Soviet Federative Socialist Republic (RSFSR).[40] This idea had already been aired in public by Soviet dissident Alexander Solzhenitsyn in *Rebuilding Russia*, a short polemic published in 1990, in which he welcomed the end of the Soviet empire in Central Asia and the Caucasus, but called for Russia, Ukraine and Belarus to stay together if possible. At the very least, argued Solzhenitsyn, Ukraine should not claim 'those parts that weren't part of old Ukraine' such as 'Novorossiya or Crimea or Donbas'. These areas should be allowed 'self-determination'.[41] Political parties such as the Congress of Russian Communities (KRO) argued for 'an ideology of unification of Russian people (*russkie*)' to reunite what it called 'a nation split into fragments'. Its head, Dmitry Rogozin, called in 1994 for the 'integration of parts of former Soviet republics', including Crimea and eastern Ukraine.[42]

These were commonly held views among nationalists, but most Russians seemed indifferent: the KRO never gained more than 5% of the vote at elections in the 1990s. Nevertheless, at points of tension between Russia and Ukraine, Russian nationalists would return repeatedly to the status of south-east Ukraine. According to the foreign policy analyst Dmitry Trenin, after the 2004 Orange Revolution an idea began circulating in 'not entirely academic quarters' in Moscow for 'a major political redesign of the northern Black Sea area, under which southern Ukraine, from the Crimea to Odessa, would secede from Kiev and form a Moscow-friendly buffer state, to be called "Novorossiya"'—New Russia'.[43] This was the old Tsarist term for the long stretch of land on the northern shores of the Black Sea that had been conquered by Catherine the Great in the eighteenth century and dubbed 'New Russia', in conscious imitation of Europe's 'New World' in North America.

During the Maidan revolution in 2014, when a mix of Ukrainian nationalist groups and pro-Western liberals ousted President Yanukovych from power, the idea of the secession of these regions from Ukraine suddenly gained supporters in the Kremlin. Nationalist groups began lobbying the Russian leadership with separatist projects. A leaked memo, reported to have been sent to the Russian Presidential Administration in February 2014, argued that Russia should 'play on the centrifugal aspirations of various regions of the country with the purpose, in one form or another, of initiating the annexation of its eastern regions to Russia'. The memo highlighted Crimea and Kharkiv region as the most likely candidates where there was strong support for 'maximum integration' with Russia.[44]

This memo was drafted ahead of the annexation of Crimea by Russia in March 2014, but it precisely prefigured a deliberate programme organised by shadowy Russian advisors, activists and intelligence agencies to provoke an upsurge of pro-Russian unrest across southern and eastern Ukraine. Many of these protests had their roots in genuine local political concerns, but they were at a minimum amplified and financed by Moscow.[45] In April 2014 Putin argued that the 'essential issue is how to ensure the legitimate rights and interests of ethnic Russians and Russian speakers in the southeast of Ukraine'. His political pragmatism long-forgotten, Putin demonstrated a new-found interest in Russian imperial territories. He told an audience on live television:

> I would like to remind you that what was called Novorossiya [New Russia] back in the tsarist days—Kharkov, Lugansk, Donetsk, Kherson, Nikolayev and Odessa—were not part of Ukraine back then. These territories were given to Ukraine in the 1920s by the Soviet government. Why? Who knows. They were won by Potemkin and Catherine the Great in a series of well-known wars. The centre of that territory was Novorossiysk, so the region is called Novorossiya. Russia lost these territories for various reasons, but the people remained.[46]

In fact, Kharkiv had never been part of Novorossiya. The term referred to the southern lands on the northern shores of the Black Sea that Russia seized from the Ottomans in a series of wars in the eighteenth century. The region was for many centuries known as the 'Wild Fields', a desolate landscape where nomadic raiders and slave-traders held sway. On a map of Ukraine from 1648 it is labelled in Latin as *loca deserta*, deserted places. By implication, it could be thought of as a kind of uninhabited zone, voyaged through by different civilisations and tribes over millennia. The Dictionary of the Russian Academy, written in the late eighteenth century, defined the steppe as 'an empty, unpopulated, and treeless place of great expanse'.[47] However, as in other imperialisms, this claim to be occupying 'empty space' was not quite true. Previously the region was known as 'Khan Ukraine' (Khanska Ukraina) or 'Tombasar Mukataasi',[48] a region with a sparse population, mainly comprising Tatars and Cossacks.

The name 'Novorossiya' was designed to erase any previous history, but also to emphasise Russia's modernity. According to the historian Olivia Durand, 'The act of renaming the northern Black Sea "New Russia" was an ideological transformation that emphasized the modern character of Russia's southward imperial expansion.'[49] This was Russia's 'New World', representing a modern, outward-looking imperialism to match that of other European powers. The nineteenth-century historian A. N. Samoilov admitted that the new name was designed 'to eliminate any memory of the barbarians' and 'to further dazzle everyone with the brilliant achievements of the Great Catherine'.[50] The 'barbarians', of course, were not the Orthodox Ukrainian peasants who came to populate much of the region, but the Turks of the Ottoman empire, the power that Russia saw as its chief adversary.

Like the New World, New Russia became a magnet for settlers.[51] Christian refugees from the Ottoman empire flocked to these new lands. Serbs settled around the town of Bakhmut, which would later be almost completely destroyed in a Russian assault in 2023. They were followed by Mennonites, who fled Prussia for the island of Khortytsia, now in the middle of Zaporizhzhia city. In 1780, after the capture of Crimea, Russia relocated Greek and Armenian communities to the northern shores of the Sea of Azov. Greeks forced to leave Crimea founded the city of Mariupol in 1778. A significant Greek community still lived in and around Mariupol when it was attacked by Russia in February 2022, and many Ukrainian Greeks were killed, injured or displaced during the fighting.[52]

Thousands of Jews flocked to the Novorossiya region in the early nineteenth century, with Odesa becoming one of the great centres of Jewish culture. The colonisation of New Russia was not an exercise in narrow Russian nationalism, but a multinational imperial enterprise on behalf of the Russian state. But whatever the exotic mix of peoples in the region, the bulk of the incomers were Ortho-

OCCUPATION

dox Ukrainians fleeing oppressive Polish Catholic rule in right-bank Ukraine, the lands on the western side of the Dnipro River. New Russia seemed a safe haven for many Ukrainians who practised the Orthodox faith. The historian Serhii Plokhy concludes that '[d]espite its imperial origins and multiethnic bent, the province of New Russia was largely Ukrainian in ethnic composition'.[53]

Much of this southern steppe was rural agricultural land, but in the east, entrepreneurs began mining coal in the late nineteenth century, beginning an industrial boom in the Donbas—the basin of the Don River—that shaped the subsequent history of the region. Russian workers flocked to the Donbas, and it was this working class that supported the Bolshevik revolution in 1917. Local Bolsheviks even proclaimed a short-lived Krivoy-Rog Soviet Republic, which claimed a swathe of eastern Ukraine from Kharkiv down to Kherson. It did not last long, but its existence was later used as another historical precedent for Donbas separatism. The unrecognised 'parliament of the Donetsk People's Republic' that was set up in 2014 claimed a 'historical connection' between the 'Donetsk-Krivoy-Rog Republic and the Donetsk Peoples' Republic'.[54] Putin also mentioned the Krivoy-Rog Soviet Republic in a long history article he published in July 2021, 'On the Historical Unity of Russians and Ukrainians', where he noted that the leaders of the republic had asked to join Soviet Russia but had been refused and were forced to join Soviet Ukraine by Lenin.[55] In Putin's view of history, this indicated that these 'Russian lands' in the Donbas had been forced to join Ukraine by the Bolsheviks against their will and therefore were properly part of Russia.

Russian nationalist discourse found numerous ways to imagine these lands as distinct from Ukraine, as part of a Russian state and space. This approach was familiar in modern European history. It followed a pattern identified in a study of ethnic cleansing in Bosnia-Herzegovina in the 1990s:

> Places are first imaginatively constituted as ethnic spaces, as territories that 'belong' to certain groups as parts of national homelands. They are then militarily assaulted to remake them in the light of this image, initially through the violent expulsion of ethnic

others and subsequently through the erasure of their historic presence. The landscape is wiped clean and available for reinscription as an ethnically homogeneous homeland.[56]

Russia reimagined the lands of south-eastern Ukraine as a reinvented Novorossiya, a new Russia, despite its long history as part of Ukraine. The names of the Donbas and the long-forgotten term Novorossiya emerged as polemical weapons in 2014, discursive tools to prise apart the independent Ukrainian state. Russian nationalists loved to circulate maps of a dismembered Ukraine, with parts of western Ukraine swallowed by Hungary and Poland, and large parts of eastern and southern Ukraine either independent or part of Russia. In 2014 these geopolitical fantasies ceased being simply imaginary and began to be realised in a violent Russian-backed rebellion in eastern Ukraine.

In the spring of 2014, activists opposed to the overthrow of President Yanukovych in Kyiv seized government buildings in many towns in the Donbas, and on 11 May 2014 pro-Russian separatists proclaimed two new political entities: the Donetsk People's Republic (DNR) and the Lugansk People's Republic (LNR). On 22 May 2014 the DNR and LNR proclaimed a Federation of Novorossiya, with the implication that other regions of south-east Ukraine could also join the new proto-state. But the backers of Novorossiya soon had to admit that they had overestimated the 'unity of the Russian World', as an expected pro-Moscow 'popular uprising from Lugansk to Odessa' failed to materialise.[57] The obvious lesson for Moscow—that few people in the south and east of Ukraine welcomed any kind of Russian military or hybrid intervention—appears to have been lost on Russian planners during 2021–22, as they considered a new military plan, this time to take over the entire Ukrainian state.

During the 2014 crisis, Russia annexed Crimea and achieved de facto control over territories controlled by the DNR and the LNR in Donetsk and Luhansk regions. In total, Russia came to control around 7% of Ukrainian territory. Russia was reluctant to annex the two separatist states, preferring to use them as a way to influence national Ukrainian politics. In 2019 an influential academic in

OCCUPATION

Moscow admitted to me that this was Moscow's 'Trojan Horse' policy, an attempt to reinsert a Russified political entity back into the Ukrainian state. Two agreements—Minsk I and Minsk II—signed in 2014 and 2015 were ambiguous and poorly formulated, but mandated a ceasefire, monitored by the Organisation for Security and Co-operation in Europe (OSCE), prisoner exchanges and resumption of commercial trade. Officially, Russia, Ukraine and the West all supported the implementation of the Minsk agreements. In practice, Russia was only interested in implementing them in ways that would promote their influence in Donbas, and in Ukraine more widely, while Ukraine was unwilling to implement any elements that involved concessions to Russian-backed separatists. The result was Russia's first occupation of Ukrainian territory, and an impasse that ultimately led to war.

Identity

The final set of ideas that underpinned Russia's occupation related to identity. Who were the people who populated the south and east of Ukraine? Denis Pushilin, the head of the DNR, had a simple answer. A map on the wall of his office divided Ukraine into two. On the eastern half of the country was simply scrawled the word 'Russia'.[58] Journalistic cliches often reproduced this simplistic view, splitting Ukrainian society into a pro-Russian east and a pro-European west. Certainly, regional, ethnic and cultural divides had always challenged any attempt to promote a centralised, monoethnic Ukrainian state-building project, but the extent of these cleavages was a hotly contested political question.[59] Language use was one indicator of division. In the east and south many people spoke Russian as their everyday language. But this was also not a stark divide. Most Ukrainians were comfortable speaking in both languages, or at least speaking in one and passively understanding the other. Many in southern Ukraine spoke a mix of Russian and Ukrainian known as 'Surzhyk'. A version of this mixed code known as 'Neo-Surzhyk' emerged among Russian speakers who increasingly used some Ukrainian phrases and words in everyday life.[60] Moreover, other identity cleavages—generational, urban-rural, educational, class and geopolitical orientation (Soviet, European)—were often as or more important than cultural and linguistic divides. As the scholars Olga Onuch and Henry Hale concluded before the 2022 war, Ukraine was 'a divided society', but this was a 'highly blurry divide'.[61]

Russian officials were not interested in sociological nuance. They believed that the essential identity of most people in the south and east of Ukraine was Russian. Putin told officials in December 2023 that 'these are Russian historical regions. Russian people actually live there, whatever stamp they have in their passport. Their only native language is Russian, their entire culture, traditions are Russian, everything ... These are our people.'[62] Certainly, many of the towns across the south and east were predominantly Russian-speaking, although numbers were uncertain—Ukraine had failed to hold a census since 2001. Nevertheless, Putin's views were wildly anachronistic. In the south and east, the number of people identifying as 'only Russian' dropped markedly between 2012 and 2017 from 16.8% to 4.8%.[63] The proportion of people who only or mostly used Russian at home fell from 31.9% to 25.7%.[64] After 2014 there was a shift towards a deeper Ukrainian national identity across all regions. Volodymyr Kulyk identifies 'a kind of bottom-up de-Russification, a popular drift away from Russianness', as demonstrated through ethnic identification, language use and attitudes towards language policy.[65]

The vast majority of people living in the south and east considered themselves Ukrainians, and only a small minority wanted to secede from Ukraine and join Russia. Some 18% of respondents to a poll in eastern Ukraine in 2014 supported the right for regions to secede from Ukraine.[66] A poll across eight southern and eastern regions produced similar figures, with 15% supporting unification with Russia but almost 70% opposed. There was some regional variation, with support for joining Russia running at 30% in Luhansk and 28% in Donetsk. While over 70% of respondents in Kherson responded with a 'Definite No' to joining Russia, in Luhansk that figure was under 30%.[67]

A slightly different question produced similar results. In a poll across six southern and eastern regions, about 27% of respondents agreed that their region was part of the so-called 'Russian World'. Some 90% of respondents in Crimea agreed that it was part of the Russian World, but in Kherson region only just over 10% agreed, fewer than in Odesa (25%) and in Kharkiv (29%).[68] The results of these and other polls showed that an overwhelming majority of people in these regions rejected unification with Russia. On the other hand, there was a minority that was sympathetic to Moscow—and larger numbers who were suspicious of the government in Kyiv. This might have given hope to any political technologists in Moscow wondering whether there would be support for a Russian intervention.

Identity cleavages had often been politically salient in the past, splitting votes between more pro-Russian parties, which advocated closer ties with Moscow and official status for the Russian language, and more pro-Western parties, which tended to promote strong Ukrainian nation-building themes, more nationalist historical narratives and more support for Ukrainian language and culture.[69] Volodymyr Zelensky, the actor who ran for president in 2019, appeared to be the ideal candidate to overcome these continuing divides. A Russian speaker from the south-eastern city of Kryvyi Rih, Zelensky understood the southern and eastern regions.[70] His victory in the presidential election on 21 April 2019 gained votes across Ukraine, breaking with the traditional east-west split in Ukrainian politics.

Zelensky promised that his administration would do more to reach out to Russian-speaking Ukrainians. During his inauguration speech on 20 May 2019, he shifted to speaking in Russian for one section, addressing Ukrainian citizens living in the occupied territories of Donbas and Crimea. He said that 'Over these years, the government has done nothing to make them feel like Ukrainians. To know that they are not strangers, that they are ours, they are Ukrainians.'[71] Above all, he promised to end the conflict in the Donbas, the number one concern for many Ukrainian voters.

Despite Zelensky's promises, once in office he struggled either to end the conflict or to address the perceived 'alienation' of Russian speakers in the south and east. Attempts by Zelensky to revive the Minsk process in October 2019 through the so-called

Steinmeier formula—a plan to implement elections under the Minsk agreements and to grant the regions special constitutional status—broke down after protests by a Ukrainian nationalist coalition, *Rukh Opory Kapituliatsii* (Movement against Capitulation).[72] Any hint of a concession sparked political opposition. In March 2020 Ukrainian civil society activists opposed attempts to initiate talks with the breakaway DNR and LNR.[73] Zelensky was trapped. Russia showed no signs of engaging constructively to make Minsk work, while at home opposition from radical nationalists, opposition parties and civil society limited his own room for diplomatic manoeuvre. He soon shifted towards a more uncompromising stance on Minsk and in relations with Russia more widely. Far from reaching out to those living under occupation, Zelensky came to believe that they were unreachable. 'The people of Donbas have been brainwashed', he told a reporter in 2022, complaining that 'I can't reach them. There is no hope of making those people understand that Russia is really an occupying power.'[74]

According to Olga Onuch and Henry Hale's account of Zelensky's political rise, Zelensky had a vision of the Ukrainian nation that was 'defined by citizenship rather than any ethnic litmus test'.[75] Yet, paradoxically, his first term was marked by a continuation—even a deepening—of a strategy of Ukrainianisation initiated by his more nationalist predecessors. In domestic politics, Zelensky had earlier criticised a new language law that made use of Ukrainian mandatory in all official discourse and public services, but it came into effect in July 2019.[76] The Council of Europe's Venice Commission had also criticised parts of the bill as being potentially discriminatory towards Russian speakers. The law limited the use of Russian for teaching in secondary schools, although primary schools could continue to use Russian. Another provision made it compulsory for all services in shops and restaurants to be offered in Ukrainian. A further restriction in January 2022 forced all non-Ukrainian media to publish a translation in Ukrainian.[77] Concerts, films, books and other cultural outputs would now mostly be in Ukrainian.

These cultural and language policies were understandable. Ukraine had faced centuries of cultural oppression, and the Russian language had become dominant in many urban areas, including in Kyiv. A majority of Ukrainians supported the new regulations—61% were in favour of the requirement to use Ukrainian in shops and restaurants, for example.[78] Most parents wanted their children to study in Ukrainian-language schools. But there was also opposition. A large minority—34%—opposed the compulsory use of Ukrainian for serving the public, and that figure rose to 56% in the east.[79] In reality, it was hard to find any Russian speakers who experienced any serious problems using Russian in everyday life even after the law was introduced. But it fuelled a false Russian narrative about discrimination against Russian speakers that became a hackneyed trope in Russian propaganda about the war. Rapid Ukrainianisation in eastern Ukraine risked opening up vulnerabilities that Russia could exploit.

History was also highly contested in ways that would come to be a defining feature of the Russian occupation. Georgiy Kasianov argues that two mutually antagonistic versions of history competed in Ukraine: a Soviet nostalgic narrative and a 'national/nationalist' narrative. Since 2014, according to Kasianov, 'there has been an intense displacement of the Soviet nostalgic and mixed narratives in favor of the national/nationalist one'.[80] While Soviet nostalgic views glorified the post-Stalinist Soviet Union as a period of relative stability and social harmony, nationalist versions of history viewed the entire period of Soviet rule as a form of occupation, marked by political and cultural repression of Ukrainians and the deaths of millions of people in a man-made famine in the early 1930s, which Ukrainians call the Holodomor.[81] In this view, the latest Russian occupation merely continued a long historical trend of Russian and Soviet imperialism and occupation. But the story was fraught with complications. On 28 October every year, Ukraine celebrates the 'Day of Liberation of Ukraine from Fascist Invaders', commemorating the end of Nazi occupation. Millions of Ukrainians fought for the Soviet Red Army against Nazi Germany and viewed the triumph of the Soviet Union as a liberation. But other Ukrainians in the Organisation of Ukrainian Nationalists (OUN-B), led by Stepan Bandera, initially collaborated with the Nazi occupation regime in 1941 in an attempt to create an independent Ukrainian state. Thousands fought in the OUN's military wing, the Ukrainian Insurgent Army (UPA), which targeted Soviet forces as they regained control of Ukraine in 1944, and continued an anti-Soviet insurgency in western Ukraine until 1949.[82]

Many Ukrainians rejected the legacy of Bandera. A poll in 2015 suggested that Bandera was less popular in Ukraine than Soviet-era leader Leonid Brezhnev.[83] In the east, he was often viewed as a Nazi collaborator, but in western Ukraine many people considered him a nationalist hero. In 2010 President Yushchenko declared him a Hero of Ukraine. In 2015 a set of new 'memory laws' was adopted, under the aegis of the Institute of National Memory, including a new law that not only honoured the OUN and the UPA but outlawed any 'contempt' shown towards their leaders.[84] The problem was that different regions had radically different collective memories of the twentieth century, handed down by parents and grandparents. While 76% of respondents in western Ukraine supported the recognition of the OUN and the UPA, support dropped to only 27% in the east and 20% in the south, where the Soviet nostalgic history narrative was strongest.[85]

Attitudes towards the Soviet Union and to Russia remained ambivalent even after 2014, when Russia first intervened militarily in Ukraine. There was still a residual sense of strong cultural and historical links with Russia in many regions. While most people (55%) rejected the claim made in July 2021 by President Putin that 'Russians and Ukrainians are one people belonging to the same historical and spiritual space', one poll showed 41% of Ukrainian respondents agreeing with Putin's controversial claim, with the figure rising to around 60% in the east of Ukraine.[86] This surprising outcome should be treated with caution: other polls show overwhelming support for the belief that Ukraine is a separate nation. But almost 20% of respondents in one poll in south-eastern Ukraine held the apparently contradictory view that Ukraine was both a separate nation and part of the Russian nation.[87]

For many people these were not logical contradictions but rather reflected a traditional fluidity of identity in the Russian-Ukrainian borderlands. Consider a poll in Mariupol in 2020. This was a Russian-speaking city: when pollsters held interviews with

1,251 residents, only eight people chose to be interviewed in Ukrainian. According to the poll, 88% wanted Russian to have the status of a second official language. But language use did not necessarily translate into pro-Russian political positions. Journalist Ivan Synepalov noted that Mariupul had received its dose of the '"Russian World" in 2014 [...] so [not] everybody is waiting here to meet them with flowers'.[88] But while over 80% identified as Ukrainian, at the same time almost half thought of themselves as maybe or definitely Russian. More than half claimed a 'Soviet' identity, while fewer than 20% of those polled saw themselves as European—this despite Ukraine's wider moves towards the European Union. A significant majority—66%—rejected any moves to join the EU and NATO.[89]

Research led by Tetiana Bevz concluded that 18% of people living in Donbas identified with the USSR and defined their identity as 'Soviet', even twenty-five years after the Soviet Union collapsed.[90] This Soviet identity may seem anachronistic, but many older residents of the Donbas 'viewed the Soviet past as a reminder of the glorious images of Donbas workers and the industrial power of Luhansk that circulated during the USSR's existence'.[91] While Ukraine pursued a widespread decommunisation process after 2015, the DNR, the LNR and Crimea underwent a 'recommunisation' programme, in which old Soviet tropes and narratives about the Great Patriotic War, layered with contemporary Russian propaganda, formed a central part of the pro-Russian narrative. Even the memorial landscape differed sharply. As Ukraine began to dismantle many Soviet war memorials, in Luhansk an estimated 88% of all memorials were still dedicated to the Unknown Soldier who died in the Great Patriotic War.[92]

The narrative of the Great Patriotic War became a powerful legitimising device that emphasised modern Russia's continuity with the greatest achievement of the Soviet Union. But it also served as a basis for Russian claims for a political sphere of influence among the former Soviet republics. In this sense, remembrance of the war became 'a marker of post-Soviet imperialist identity', according to Olga Malinova.[93] Political scientist Tatiana Zhurzhenko writes that 'A politics of memory focusing on Russia's fight against Nazism during World War II served to counteract efforts towards a "decolonization of memory" in the former Soviet countries and to keep them in Moscow's geopolitical orbit.'[94] Now Russia also used the Great Patriotic War narrative to help promote its argument about the links between Ukrainian nationalism and inter-war fascism and to make the absurd claim that the 'Special Military Operation' was somehow a rerun of the struggle against Nazi Germany.

A key divide in eastern towns like Mariupol was between different generations. While nearly 90% of over-60s embraced a 'Soviet' identity, almost 90% of young people aged 18–29 rejected it.[95] Many young people were transforming eastern cities like Kharkiv and Mariupol into exciting, creative places with closer ties to Europe. Younger people often had quite different views from their parents or grandparents, as a result of a Ukrainian-language education and growing up in an independent Ukraine. A Russian-speaking Ukrainian refugee in Russia told journalists how irritating she found it when her daughter insisted on speaking Ukrainian.[96] A smart young Ukrainian analyst in Kyiv told me that his grandparents living in a southern region believed that neo-Nazis were running the Ukrainian government and welcomed the Russian takeover. But not all young people fitted this trend. Even among young people in Mariupol, fewer than 5% identified strongly as 'European' and more than 60% did not share a sense of being part of Europe.[97] For many locals, pro-European views were 'associated with Ukrainian nationalism, often caricatured as "fascist"'.[98] In cities with access to Russian media, many believed conspiracy theories and disinformation promoted by pro-Russian outlets.[99]

Without Russian interference, these complex processes of identity formation would probably have worked themselves out through a compromise between sometimes heavy-handed history and language policies and the widespread tolerance and pragmatism that characterised Ukrainian society. But facing opposition at home, Zelensky took a more uncompromising stance towards Russia, in ways that responded to domestic political demands but further deepened tensions with Russia. In February 2021 the Ukrainian authorities closed three television channels controlled by pro-Russian oligarch Viktor Medvedchuk, who had close ties with Putin.¹⁰⁰ In July 2021 a new law recognising indigenous people in Ukraine, but not mentioning Russians, was passed, causing more controversy.¹⁰¹

Russian officials exaggerated and instrumentalised these cultural and political cleavages and turned them into a spurious casus belli. The law on indigenous peoples appears to have infuriated Putin, who in June 2021 compared the law to 'the theory and practice of Nazi Germany'.¹⁰² In a historical essay published in July 2021, Putin set out his views at length. He argued that 'the situation in Ukraine today [...] involves a forced change of identity':

> the Russians in Ukraine are being forced not only to deny their roots, [and] generations of their ancestors but also to believe that Russia is their enemy. It would not be an exaggeration to say that the path of forced assimilation, the formation of an ethnically pure Ukrainian state, aggressive towards Russia, is comparable in its consequences to the use of weapons of mass destruction against us.¹⁰³

Putin's essay was a long, pseudo-historical excursion to explain why Ukrainians were part of the Russian nation and not a separate people. He claimed that the Ukrainian authorities 'began to mythologize and rewrite history, edit out everything that united us, and refer to the period when Ukraine was part of the Russian Empire and the Soviet Union as an occupation'. Rather than a separate nation that had been occupied by Russia, Putin argued the opposite: that Ukraine was part of Russia, but various forces—Austria-Hungary, the Germans, the Bolsheviks—had promoted Ukrainian nationalism for their own political purposes.¹⁰⁴ This referenced a long-standing set of reactionary ideas about Ukraine in Russian nationalist thinking, articulated by figures such as the White émigré Vasily Shulgin, who published a polemical book in Belgrade in 1939 that portrayed Ukrainian nationalism both as a geopolitical plot and as the result of machinations by the Bolsheviks.¹⁰⁵

These virulent attacks on Ukrainian nation-building have only deepened in Russia during the war. A meeting of the International Affairs Committee of the Federation Council (the upper chamber of Russia's parliament) in February 2024 was devoted to what was called 'the ideology of "*Ukrainstvo*" [Ukrainianism]', a term that refers to Ukrainian nationalism, often with a derogatory tone, but often served as an attack on Ukrainian identity more generally. At the meeting Vladimir Rogov, a polemicist from occupied Zaporizhzhia, called for 'political Ukrainianism' to be declared an extremist movement, just like the 'LGBT movement' (outlawed by Russia in 2023), 'behind which stood the same people'. An expert from the Institute for Strategic Studies told the meeting that they faced a conflict between 'the bearers of different identities and the national projects connected to them in one ethnocultural milieu'. Our task, he continued, is to return Russians from Ukrainianism (*Ukrainstvo*) to Russian-ness (*Russkost*). Another academic, head of the philosophy department at the Moscow State Technical University, Vitaly Darenskii, warned that 'Ukrainianism' had become a mass phenomenon, which had seized the minds of millions of people. That was why Ukrainians had put up colossal opposition, and 'fought for their cities like for Stalingrad'. As a result, in the occupied territories, he claimed that about one third of the population were '*zhduny*', literally the 'waiting ones', expecting liberation by the Ukrainian armed forces. 'Some people thought that you could work with them. But it's useless. They will die out naturally with time, and that's all', he told the meeting.[106]

Such a denial of Ukrainian identity drove a Russification policy in the occupied territories that some scholars viewed as evidence of genocidal intent on the part of Russia.[107] Russian commentators tried to finesse this position. Oleg Roi, a Russian writer, argued that the 'special operation' was being conducted, 'not against the Ukrainian people or the Ukrainian state [...] but against an ideology of "Ukrainianism"'. But what is Ukrainianism? For Roi, 'Ukrainianism' is 'a monstrous mix of Nazism with its idea of a superior nation and BLM [Black Lives Matter] with its manipulation of a sense of guilt'.[108] It was hard to imagine a more bizarre conspiracy theory than this connection between a Black civil rights movement and Nazi Germany, but it reflected a Russian belief that Ukrainian nationalism and Western progressive forces were in alignment, both aiming ultimately at the destruction of Russia. In any case, the already wafer-thin distinction between 'political Ukrainianism' and Ukrainian national identity was hard to maintain. 'Acceptable' forms of Ukrainian self-expression in Russia were reduced—at best—to apolitical folk songs or cultural expression, although in many cases even such mild expressions of Ukrainian cultural identity were seen as provocative and dangerous. It was only a short step from opposition to an ideology of 'Ukrainianism'—whatever that entailed—to a position that denied any form of Ukrainian identity, culture or language. Nikita Mikhalkov, the hardline nationalist filmmaker, ended up arguing that the Ukrainian language itself was a form of Russophobia and 'a formulation of hatred towards Russia', and that it should not be taught in schools in the occupied territories.[109]

Conclusion: Roots of occupation

The occupation had a long pre-history. Its origins can be traced at least to 1991, to the break-up of the Soviet Union, which left Russia as a middle-ranking power, shorn of its imperial lands and reduced in status in a world dominated by the US and by liberal politics and liberal values. Moscow viewed the loss of Ukraine from its self-declared sphere of influence as the most significant challenge to its claim to remain a major power, and therefore interpreted Kyiv's decision to seek NATO membership as an existential threat. This position was much more complex than simply an opposition to NATO enlargement—although the promise of Ukrainian membership certainly contributed to the long, slow spiral of Russian geopolitical thought that culminated in full-scale war in 2022. But it was not the only driver. The geopolitics of Russia and the West evolved over more than two decades: different decisions at key moments might have produced different results, but the challenge for Russia of overcoming a long imperial past was always going to cause tensions with its neighbours and a potential clash with the West.

Post-imperial Russia faced a spatial crisis—a mismatch between Russia's historical sense of itself as a sprawling, boundless imperial state and the fixed post-1991 frontiers of the Russian Federation.

Russian intellectual elites could have managed this challenge in different ways. Ideas of a revived empire—or at least territorial pretensions towards Ukraine and its neighbours—had been held in abeyance by Russian officials since 1991, but there had always been a revanchist element in Russian politics. In a new era of declining relations with the West, once-marginal ideas and thinkers came to the fore again, advocating a more aggressive policy towards Russia's neighbours and reviving old tropes about the essentially 'artificial' nature of the Ukrainian state. This latter point resonated strongly with Vladimir Putin, whose early patronising pragmatism towards Kyiv had disappeared by 2014 to be replaced by an obsession with Russian imperial history and the revival of Russian imperial power.

The occupation emerged on very specific territories which had particularly meaning for Russian nationalists. The lands that Russians referred to as Novorossiya, stretching across southern and eastern Ukraine, were especially vulnerable to a Russian narrative about reclaiming 'historically Russian lands'. Coupled with a representation of the Donbas as a quintessentially Russian region, with a strong Soviet identity, this discursive construction of these lands as 'not Ukraine' laid the groundwork for the eventual occupation. The attempt to construct a pro-Russian political project ('Novorossiya') in 2014 failed, but it left a trail that Russian propagandists picked up again in 2022. If Russia was likely to end up occupying any part of Ukraine through a military campaign, it was south-eastern Ukraine that would be the primary target.

The occupation is difficult to understand, however, without also addressing the politics of identity inside Ukraine. Although Ukrainian national identity was strengthening after 2014, there were still important differences in identity between different regions, social groups and generations in Ukraine. Many people in parts of the south and east expressed unease at the decommunisation drive after 2015, and were wary of aspects of the language and education reforms and attempts to impose an exclusive, nationalist view of Ukrainian history. Strong political leadership in Ukraine might have managed these competing forces that threatened to pull Ukraine apart, but for complex domestic political reasons, neither President Poroshenko nor President Zelensky were able to promote a state-building project that could effectively incorporate Ukraine's multiple regional identities.

There was no single factor to explain Russia's full-scale invasion and occupation of south-eastern Ukraine. But a set of ideas about the world—about geopolitics, empire, territory and identity—all contributed to Russia's actions. The geopolitics mattered, but a different trajectory for Russian relations with the West—a different ideological framing by both sides about European security—could have found a path that did not end in invasion and occupation. A lingering Russian imperial mindset played a role in the decision not just to occupy, but also to annex these territories, yet these neo-imperialist ideas only became relevant to Russian decision-making in a specific geopolitical context. The same applied to the meaning given to the territories of south-eastern Ukraine in the Russian nationalist imagination. Finally, the contested identity politics of the south and east of Ukraine were often badly handled by successive governments in Kyiv, and were manipulated by Russia to justify its occupation. Yet these were all just abstract ideas until 24 February 2022. It was Vladimir Putin's decision to turn ideas into action that transformed these intellectual battles into the sudden invasion of Ukraine by the world's fifth largest military force, the Armed Forces of the Russian Federation.

2

ATTACK

On 12 February 2022 President Zelensky travelled with his key security advisors to observe a military exercise in southern Ukraine, only a few kilometres from the front line with Crimea. Zelensky had been warned by top US officials that a full-scale Russian invasion of Ukraine was imminent. The Russian plans included a rapid incursion into southern Ukraine from the Crimean Peninsula and a simultaneous attack from DNR-controlled territory in the east. But at the exercises, Zelensky watched interior ministry and National Guard forces countering a small-scale illegal border crossing, and an exercise in which militants seized government buildings, a completely different scenario from what was about to unfold. With the exercise declared a success, Zelensky returned to Kyiv, apparently unconcerned about a largely undefended front line with Crimea.[1]

While US envoys tried to convince the Ukrainian leadership in Kyiv of the impending attack and diplomats began to evacuate their embassies, complacency reigned across the south. The mayor of Mariupol, Vadym Boychenko, told the *Financial Times* that he doubted there was a risk of war, claiming that there was no sign of increased activity by Russia and blaming Western politicians for 'pumping up the situation'.[2] On 16 February, a week before the invasion, Mariupol had hosted some important guests. Rinat

OCCUPATION

Akhmetov was Ukraine's richest man and owned two huge metals plants in the city. He arrived with his business partner Vadym Novinskyi, who would later be sanctioned by Ukraine because of his ties with Russia. In the evening on the same day, President Zelensky also arrived and met with the mayor. But nobody seems to have talked about the war. Boychenko says he discussed a new swimming pool for Mariupol, even a new airport. The mayor later admitted that he never asked Zelensky how he should prepare for a possible invasion.[3]

Even on the eve of the war, many officials still denied that an attack was imminent. On 23 February 2022 a top-secret meeting took place in the southern Ukrainian city of Kherson. Local political leaders had come to hear a report on the tense military situation from Serhii Kryvoruchko, head of the Kherson regional branch of the Ukrainian security service, the SBU. According to Dmytro Ishchenko, commander of the 124th Kherson Brigade, who was present at the meeting, there were two presentations, one from the head of the anti-terrorist centre of the SBU and one from Kryvoruchko. Both gave the gathered officials the news they all hoped for: there would be no invasion.[4] In Mariupol, officials heard the same message, according to council staffer Vaagn Mnatsakanian, who later said: 'Nobody believed that such a war could happen. At a city council meeting on February 23, everyone said we were safe and that everything would be okay.'[5]

These reports came despite visual evidence of the Russian build-up just across the border in Crimea. On 23 February, the same day as the Kherson meeting, photos on social media clearly showed columns of Russian military in the north of Crimea. Eyewitnesses saw the Russians preparing pontoon bridges along the north-eastern coast, in the desolate area known as Syvash, or the Putrid Sea. In this direction one small road wound its way along the coast, with a natural chokepoint at a bridge across a narrow channel, the Chonhar Strait. Another bigger road led through the 7-kilometre-wide Isthmus of Perekop, via the Kalanchak checkpoint. These were all crossing points that should have been possible to defend even against a larger force. Bridges were supposed to have been mined to prevent any Russian incursion.

ATTACK

Despite the scepticism of some political leaders, the Ukrainian military was on high alert on the night of 23 February. They had seen the preparations in Crimea. 'Everyone was waiting, nervous. No one slept', recalls Ivan Sestryvatovsky, a soldier stationed on the border with Crimea at the Chonhar Bridge.[6] Minutes after 04:00 on the morning of the 24 February, CCTV cameras showed Russian troops from Crimea smashing through Ukrainian checkpoints as Russian artillery and the Russian air force began to bombard Ukrainian positions across the country. Even then, wakened by the sound of bombs raining down, the mayor of Melitopol went back to sleep, dismissing the noise as a thunderstorm.[7] For unclear reasons, the mined bridges in the north of Crimea were not destroyed and the Russians rolled across the front line with almost no opposition.[8] Within the hour, the first Russian forces arrived in Henichesk, a faded Ukrainian port on the Sea of Azov, some 40 kilometres north of Chonhar. Other columns raced north-west towards the Dnipro River. Videos posted on social media from mid-morning show endless columns of Russian military trucks, tanks and armoured personnel carriers approaching the strategic town of Nova Kakhovka, site of a bridge and a dam across the Dnipro. In the videos civilian traffic continues to weave in and out of the column; many are driving in the opposite direction, towards the Russian army. There is no sign of any resistance. It is all completely shocking and unexpected.

Russian forces poured across the southern steppe at high speed. By the evening of 24 February, Russian troops had taken control of the key crossing across the Dnipro at Nova Kakhovka and seized the Antonov Bridge that led to the city of Kherson further west. From a military point of view, the bridge should have been destroyed to stop the Russian advance. Presidential advisor Mikhailo Podolyak later claimed that Ukrainians were not 'psychologically ready' to blow up their own infrastructure; they still 'could not believe that this is happening to us in the 21st century'.[9]

The Ukrainian military and scattered groups of volunteers tried to put up some resistance. Ukrainian forces even briefly took back the Antonov Bridge the next day but were quickly defeated by Russian forces who began to advance into the city. By 28 February

Kherson was doomed. 'There is no Ukrainian army here', Ihor Kolykhaev, the mayor, told reporters, 'the city is surrounded'.[10] After a few local firefights, on 3 March Russian forces entered the city. From this moment, as Kolykhaev later told journalists, 'life was divided into before and after [that date]'.[11]

As Russian forces moved north through Kherson region, they reached Enerhodar, a town dominated by the huge Zaporizhzhia nuclear power station. Russian troops began massing around the plant, which a small Ukrainian military unit was guarding. At around 11.30 pm on 3 March Russian forces launched an assault. Ukrainian troops hit a Russian tank, briefly halting the column, but Russian troops fired repeatedly at the plant's main administrative building and a training block. A live stream from the plant showed the battle in real time: at various points, the Russians appeared to shoot heavy weapons in the direction of the buildings that housed the reactors, beginning many months of dangerous tension around the plant.[12] But Russian forces had a clear advantage. By 3 a.m. the fighting was over and on 4 March Russian forces were in full control of the site of a nuclear power plant on Ukrainian territory.

Russian forces also encountered little resistance as they headed east. About 90 kilometres east of Henichesk was the town of Melitopol. After that, the M14 highway branched east along the northern coast of the Sea of Azov to the small port of Berdiansk, and then on towards Mariupol. As dawn broke in Melitopol on 24 February, volunteers went to a local branch of the Territorial Defence Forces to sign up, only to be told that there were no weapons. The only Ukrainian military presence, 500 logistics specialists of the 25th Transport Brigade at Melitopol airbase, were ordered to retreat as they lacked any heavy weaponry. When Russian troops turned up at the city, it was completely undefended. The mayor, Ivan Fedorov, remained behind: 'Imagine the situation', he told the *New Yorker*,

> I'm a mayor of a city with a hundred and fifty thousand people ... It's four in the afternoon and already getting dark. Russian tanks are at the entrance to town and all I have are five garbage trucks, three tractor trailers, and, I don't know, a metal shovel. That's it. There's not a single armed person left.[13]

ATTACK

Clashes and firefights broke out around the city with scattered groups of volunteers and veterans, but Russian forces were firmly in control by 26 February and began to move further east.

There were some 8,000 well-prepared Ukrainian troops stationed in Mariupol, because it was close to the front line after the previous round of fighting in 2014. They included some of Ukraine's best fighters in the Azov Brigade, a controversial unit because its founders espoused far-right views. But all the city's defences were on the eastern edge of the city, anticipating an attack by Russian forces from the Russian-controlled DNR to the east. Long trenches had been dug beyond the eastern suburbs along the coast of the Sea of Azov at Shyrokyne. As the war broke out, DNR troops and a Russian military force advanced on Mariupol from the east, only to be rebuffed with significant losses. But to the west, the city was wide open. When Russian troops advanced towards Mariupol from the Crimean Peninsula, they faced little resistance until they reached the city limits: 'All our defences were concentrated in the eastern part of the city, where their army was expected to arrive. You never anticipate that, when you go to confront the enemy, it will arrive from behind', Mariupol mayor Vadym Boychenko said later.[14]

By 1 March Russian forces had arrived in the western suburbs of the city and the situation became clear: Mariupol was almost surrounded. The last, slim chance to withdraw Ukrainian forces from Mariupol came and went, but Ukrainian forces—with the Azov Brigade playing a key role—regrouped and slowed the Russian advance into the city. Russian forces began a brutal siege and bombardment of the city from both sides that would last for more than two months. Despite the rapid Russian advance in the first week in the south, the failure to take Mariupol quickly was a sign that not everything was going to plan for the Russians.

In late February Russian forces had quickly advanced on Mykolaiv, home to the strategic Varvarivskyi Bridge across the Southern Buh River. If Russia could take the city, they would have an open road along the M14 highway to the vital southern port of

Odesa, just 130 kilometres away to the west. Russian tank convoys repeatedly attempted to enter the city but were repulsed by a determined defence led by Major-General Dmytro Marchenko. Later he told reporters that the defence of Mykolaiv was a kind of miracle, and that when he analysed the events with hindsight, he did not quite know how his soldiers had been able to resist the advancing Russian forces.[15] By mid-March, Mykolaiv governor Vitalii Kim was able to announce that Ukrainian forces had pushed Russian troops between 15 and 20 kilometres away from the city.[16] This was one of the most critical battles of the entire war, because it blocked Russia's advance westwards and made Russia's positions on the right bank of the Dnipro almost impossible to defend.

The other small advances for Russia came in the east, as forces pushed out from the boundaries of the territory previously controlled by the DNR and LNR. On 8 March DNR forces had taken control of Volnovakha, a key road and rail hub, but further advances in Donetsk region were limited. Russian troops had more success in Luhansk region, where they took the town of Kreminna on 19 April 2022, and expanded their control over other parts of the region over the next few weeks. In June Russia finally took control of Severodonetsk, which had been the administrative centre of Ukrainian-controlled Luhansk, although much of the city was destroyed in the fighting. Russia claimed full control of Luhansk region in July 2022 when they seized the town of Lysychansk. Further to the north, Russian forces also took control of part of Kharkiv region, although they failed to take the city of Kharkiv as Ukrainian forces mounted a fierce defence.

Occupation

When Russian soldiers first arrived in towns across the south and east, there was confusion and chaos. The FSB had almost certainly been planning the occupation for months, but their plans were often challenged by the confusing reality of the military situation on the ground and were stymied by the lack of cooperation they faced from local officials and residents. Many soldiers had assumed they would be welcomed with open arms and were surprised to find the locals telling them in forthright language to go home. Oleh Baturin, a journalist from Nova Kakhovka who was detained by the Russians for eight days in March 2022, told reporters that the Russians who held him had 'expected to be met with bread and salt', the traditional greeting in Russia and Ukraine.[17] Instead, they were met with protests, intransigence and flight. Hundreds of thousands of Ukrainians fled from southern and eastern towns and villages as the Russians approached. They grabbed what they could and joined the exodus. Most travelled west, to safer parts of Ukraine or on to Europe. From the eastern regions, Donetsk and Luhansk, many headed east to Russia, either because they sought shelter with friends and relatives there, or because other routes had been cut off and they had little choice.

In Kherson, as Russian forces took over the city, the Russian Ministry of Defence spokesperson pretended that everything was calm and running normally: 'negotiations are continuing between the Russian command and the city and regional administration to resolve issues regarding the functioning of social infrastructure, law and order and the security of the population'.[18] In reality, the situation in Kherson was dangerous and chaotic. Local doctor Elizaveta Petrovna was working in the hospital when the Russians arrived. Later she told journalists: 'People were scared to go out of the house. Men with machine guns patrolled the streets. And they were drinking like pigs.'[19] When Russian forces entered the city, 'everybody went numb', wrote the mayor's adviser, Halyna Liashevska, in a later Facebook post:

> Kherson went silent. Details flew around instantly: there's a fire here, there are soldiers on the street there, over there is firing from tanks, here there's a military convoy. I walked to work that morning—and there was nobody anywhere. You walk along empty, grey streets and feel how you are accompanied only by wary glances from behind the curtains.[20]

In the first few days, many Ukrainian officials and most of the security forces had retreated in haste. The police had left Kherson by 26 February, fearing Russian reprisals.[21] Looting broke out everywhere in the city as people took advantage of the security vacuum and began panicking about being cut off from supplies. Thieves were reported wheeling entire supermarket freezer compartments out of shops. People began to worry that the city would run out of food.[22] 'It was insane', local politician Oleksandr Samoylenko later told journalists: 'Kherson was under Russian occupation but the Russians weren't interested in taking over the administration [...]. They didn't want the headache.'[23] The Russians just imposed a curfew and waited for orders. Meanwhile, the city was descending into chaos, according to the mayor, Ihor Kolykhaev: 'in the city there [was] no protection, no police or prosecutors, no judges'.[24] For most residents, the overwhelming problem was that there was no food or medicine in the shops. Finding basic necessities became the overwhelming priority.[25]

In this chaotic situation, locals took matters into their own hands. Nightclub owner and town council member Illia Karamalikov was the kind of local businessman who could get things done. He recruited around 1,200 local volunteers to his 'Citizen Patrol' to tackle the looters and to patrol the streets at night.[26] Later, these patrols seem to have been agreed more formally with Mayor Kolykhaev.[27] Karamalikov would later end up in a Ukrainian prison on disputed collaboration charges, as I explain in Chapter 7, but at the time the volunteer patrols appeared to fill a security vacuum. Meanwhile, exhausted council workers stayed in the town hall with Kolykhaev, desperately trying to keep the city running.

Across the region, there were similar scenes of confusion and panic. The first steps the Russians took were usually the same. First, soldiers would take control of government buildings and the offices of the Ukrainian internal security service, the SBU, and the military commissariat, the local recruiting office for the military. At the SBU, FSB officers would rifle through paperwork that might help them fill out their grim target list of potential opponents, including government officials, military veterans, local activists and journalists. Personnel files at the military commissariat could help them identify veterans and reservists who might pose a threat.

Russian troops would seize the television stations and broadcasting towers wherever they arrived, and retune them to receive Russian channels. Initially, communication from the occupiers was

ATTACK

sparse and primitive. In the first weeks, there was often only a limited presence on the streets: military vehicles drove through towns announcing curfews and a ban on meetings but did not linger. Russian forces posted flyers calling for cooperation. One offered an awkwardly phrased message from Putin:

> Today's events relate not to the desire to curtail the interests of Ukraine and the Ukrainian people but to the defence of Russia itself from those who have taken Ukraine hostage and are using it against our country and its people. I call for your cooperation so that we can quickly turn this tragic page and move forward together.[28]

All communications appear to have been run through the military at this time—the planning had been so secretive that probably nobody else was briefed ahead of the invasion. Not surprisingly, they were often ineffective. The social media Telegram platform was a key source of news. The Russian military were almost certainly behind a 51-channel Telegram network that appeared on 5–7 March 2022, which covered multiple localities and reproduced almost identical messages about Russian humanitarian aid on different channels.[29] Other websites and Telegram channels also appeared, such as 'Yuzhnyi Platsdarm' (Southern Bridgehead), already operating on 25 February.[30] Later on, as I discuss in Chapter 4, the Russian propaganda machine became more sophisticated, but in the early days it was woefully ill-equipped to communicate effectively with people in the territories it was now occupying.

At this early stage, there were no clear orders about the status of the newly occupied territories. Where the LNR or DNR expanded within Luhansk or Donetsk regions, they were quick to claim control of these new lands as part of their 'Republics'. Russia had recognised the DNR and LNR as independent states on 21 February 2022, just prior to the invasion. From Russia's point of view, the lands seized in Donetsk and Luhansk regions were now part of these two 'independent' states, although they were unrecognised by the rest of the world.[31] But in much of the south—in Kherson and Zaporizhzhia regions—there was no official claim that the territories were part of Russia. During March 2022, Ukrainian flags still flew over many administration buildings and some

OCCUPATION

Ukraine-appointed officials remained in post. Russian forces often raced past villages and small settlements, leaving local government in some places almost untouched.

Russian commanders usually tried to negotiate with local officials initially, but if they did not cooperate, they quickly resorted to threats and violence. In many villages and towns, officials refused to cooperate or fled to government-controlled areas ahead of the advancing Russians. Whether to stay or to go was an existential decision for each local official, often operating without much idea of what was happening in the rest of the country, and usually without clear orders from Kyiv. Most intelligence and security officials were ordered to withdraw to Kyiv—the focus was on defending the capital, which at the time was in mortal danger.[32] But some civilian officials stayed in post. A minority actively cooperated with the Russians. In Kupiansk, in Kharkiv region, the local mayor Hennadiy Matsehora broadcast a video on Facebook on 27 February to tell residents that the Russian battalion commander had issued an ultimatum. Either there would be negotiations or Russian troops would storm the city 'with all the inevitable consequences'. Russian forces entered Kupiansk without a shot being fired, but the Ukrainian prosecutor's office the next day declared that Matsehora was being investigated for treason. Matsehora was later accused of taking part in the pro-Russian administration of Kupiansk.[33] In June 2024 Ukrainian military intelligence claimed he had been shot in an assassination attempt in Russia; he was later reported to have died.[34]

Mayor of Kherson Ihor Kolykhaev refused to collaborate, but also refused to leave. At first he stayed in his city council office, working round the clock to keep the city running, largely left alone by the Russians. But one day Russian soldiers turned up at his office and detained him for several hours. 'He returned from them grey and—somehow it seemed—even thinner', his colleague recalled later.[35] He did not cave in to Russian pressure. But his public stance was cautious: he insisted that citizens 'avoid conflict' with Russian soldiers and observe the curfew. On Facebook he wrote that 'The flag that flies over us is Ukrainian. To ensure it stays that way, we need to observe these conditions.'[36] This stance was controversial.

ATTACK

Some townsfolk wanted more active opposition to Russian rule, not caution and conflict avoidance. Activists began organising protests against the occupation on a daily basis in the city's central square, right opposite Kolykhaev's offices.

When Russian forces entered Melitopol, a sleepy town in Zaporizhzhia region, on 26 February 2022, troops headed straight for the town hall, and military vehicles drove around town announcing a curfew and a ban on demonstrations. Ukrainian police had been ordered to retreat to Zaporizhzhia. They left a vacuum, soon filled by looters and criminals who stripped the shops bare. Despite the lack of significant armed opposition when they first arrived, the Russians soon faced street protests against the occupation. Local officials were not cooperative. Things got nasty quickly, as Russian forces began detaining officials and activists on 10 March. On 11 March video footage appeared of the mayor of Melitopol, Ivan Fedorov, being frogmarched from his office by a group of Russian soldiers, his head bent forward, shrouded in a bag. He later told reporters that soldiers who claimed to be from the LNR had come into his office and told him he faced criminal charges for financing the far-right group 'Pravyi Sektor' (Right Sector), a long-standing Russian bogeyman.[37]

Fedorov, a boyish 33 years old when the war broke out, was one of a new generation of Ukrainian mayors who were intent on modernising life in these southern towns and challenging an older generation of politicians, who tended to have more pro-Russian views. While in detention, Fedorov was forced to signed an order transferring power to a representative of this older generation of fading Yanukovych-era politicians, a 57-year-old local councillor, Galina Danilchenko (Halyna Danylchenko), who later claimed that she was now the legitimate mayor ('There's an order, there's a signature, everything is legitimate and legal', she told the press).[38] Danilchenko had been a member of the Party of Regions (POR) under President Yanukovych and later a deputy in the local council from the Opposition Bloc. More importantly, she was a close associate of Yevgeny Balitsky, a former parliamentary deputy in the Verkhovna Rada from the Party of Regions and a local small-town business player, whose ambitions were increasingly thwarted after

2014. Balitsky saw the Russian occupation as a once-in-a-lifetime chance for a political comeback. In March 2022 he was appointed 'head of the Military-Civilian Administration' (VGA) in Zaporizhzhia region—the name for the temporary occupation authority, which combined military and civilian representatives.

On 12 March Danilchenko released a video. She stands in front of a blurred map of the city and stares into a slightly swaying mobile phone camera. The new 'mayor' tells the people of Melitopol that 'Our main task now is to adapt all mechanisms to the new reality', and warns local residents against 'people in the town who try to destabilise the situation'.[39] She said there would be a new 'Committee of People's Representatives', which would handle all administrative questions. The elected council of Melitopol had other ideas. They issued a decree the next day calling Danilchenko a traitor and demanding that President Zelensky investigate her. Protests continued on the streets, with hundreds marching through the centre of town with Ukrainian flags. Danilchenko dismissed them as 'a small group of marginals, who ran around with flags and insulted people',[40] but they better represented the popular mood than the group of collaborators around Danilchenko and Balitsky.

During March and early April 2022, protests against the Russian occupation continued in Berdiansk, Kherson, Melitopol and Kakhovka. Kherson—where pro-Ukrainian sentiment was strongest—became the centre of these anti-Russian demonstrations. From 5 March there were big demonstrations in the centre of the city, with protestors waving Ukrainian flags and calling on Russian soldiers to leave. Russian attempts to gather a different crowd by handing out humanitarian aid were mocked. One man who attended the protests compared the two events: '[At the protests] there were 5–10,000 people. But only the homeless, alcoholics and their puppet clowns who they [Russian forces] brought in by bus went to their humanitarian aid distribution.'[41] At first, there was public anger on the streets. Sometimes local people confronted soldiers. A group of young women began shouting at Russian soldiers in Kherson, calling them occupiers and saying, 'This is our city.' At the time it did not occur to them that this might be dangerous, one of them later recalled. 'It is not your city', replied the soldiers, 'It is a Russian city. You are Russians, you simply forgot', added the soldiers, 'You speak Russian. Study history.'[42]

Soon the situation began to worsen. The mood changed quickly on 21 March in Kherson, when Russian forces dispersed the crowds violently, shooting and wounding six protestors. Now it took extreme bravery to protest against the military occupation. With each day, the numbers at the anti-occupation protests dwindled, and the queues for humanitarian aid increased. In April 2022, the screws began to tighten across the occupied territories. In night-time raids, soldiers detained protest organisers and participants, sending them 'to the basement', the local slang for being detained in the makeshift prisons that were being set up by the Russians. People began to disappear. Reports slipped out of people being tortured or even killed. The demonstrations wound down in Kherson; now they were held only on Sundays.[43]

A woman in Berdiansk told the BBC that she had been at all the protests, but in early April 'it became really frightening'. Not only had they heard news of the shootings in Kherson, but the attitudes of Russian soldiers changed: 'If previously the military did not behave so noticeably, now they can stop you on the street and check your phone.'[44] By the end of April, the demonstrations had stopped completely. Residents realised how dangerous the situation had become. 'You suddenly realised that anything could happen to you', recalled one resident: 'You could just disappear.'[45] The occupied territories had become a space of exception, a lawless zone where there was almost complete impunity for Russian soldiers to act as they saw fit.

The resentment towards the Russians remained as vivid as ever. But the demonstrations stopped, and ordinary people and the soldiers began to live in parallel realities. 'They live in their reality', said one Kherson resident: 'They probably think there will be a Kherson People's Republic. And we live in our reality, waiting for the Ukrainian army. We don't look into their rules, we live according to Ukrainian laws.'[46] But as the occupation continued, more people sought ways to leave. At this time, in April, you could still travel out of Kherson, trying your luck to get through numerous Russian roadblocks to reach government-controlled territory.

A bus to Odesa was still running, but the price had risen from 150 hryvnia (US$4) to 3,000 hryvnia (US$80).[47]

Soon the options to leave narrowed. Most people could only escape via a single checkpoint at Vasylivka. Kateryna Protasova, a teacher who left the coastal resort of Kyrylivka near Melitopol in June 2022, passed through seventeen Russian checkpoints before reaching Vasylivka. She was forced to wait for more than twenty-four hours to get through this final Russian checkpoint—but others reported waiting for up to seven days. For Protasova, getting through the checkpoint led to a feeling of profound relief:

> We drove through roadblocks, inspections, gray areas, explosions, dirt roads, empty villages, and damaged houses to reach Kamiansk. This is the place where our people are. This is the place where the Ukrainian flag flies. And more importantly, this is the place where I can breathe again.[48]

Sometimes travellers had to pay bribes at roadblocks. At Vasylivka there was reportedly a line that charged up to US$500 for a quicker crossing.[49] At other checkpoints Russian soldiers sometimes forced Ukrainian men to undress as they looked for patriotic tattoos, a precursor of the full 'filtration' system that was being set up. One tattooist in Kherson told journalists that many people were having their patriotic tattoos covered up or redrawn to avoid suspicion.[50]

On 25 April 2022 the situation of 'dual power' in Kherson ended. Russian soldiers arrived at Mayor Kolykhaev's office, took the keys and replaced the guard with their own security. 'I left at 19.45', Kolykhaev wrote later that night on Facebook, 'and the flag of Ukraine was still flying over the mayor's office.'[51] Not for long. Now Russian military banners and Russian flags began to replace Ukrainian symbols across the occupied territories. In village after village, Russian social media showed video clips of Russian soldiers pulling down Ukrainian flags and raising Russian flags in their place.[52]

Occupation authorities

The next step for the Russians was to install their own occupation authorities. There was no legal basis or template for what they were doing, but in the territories that they occupied, they set up

ATTACK

Military-Civilian Administrations (*Voenno-grazhdanskaya administratsiya*—VGA). These were very much military first, and civilian second. Russian military doctrine dictated that it was the military that had responsibility under occupation to keep the cities and towns running and to ensure a supply of foods and other goods. The centre of power was the 'Commandant's Office', or *Kommandatura*. The formal title remained unclear for some time. And there were no clear instructions for the local population on who to talk to or how to contact them. One resident recalled: 'It is not that anybody told us that here is your mayor and here is the Russian commandant, if you need to talk to them book an appointment. It's just that everybody knows that there are Russian military there and they are the ones who run the city.'[53]

Russian military commandants were normally careful to hide their identities. The commandant of Melitopol did talk to the press, but his face was always blurred in Russian television reports. The commandant in the town of Rubizhne in Luhansk region was only known by his call-sign, 'Kambrod'. In many cases, commandants issued orders without any signature on their documents. They had good reason to remain anonymous. In Berdiansk, the commandant was reported to be a Colonel A. Bardin, who had the title 'military commandant of the city of Berdiansk and Berdiansk district' on his letterhead. On 6 September 2022 he was badly wounded when his car exploded in an assassination attempt.[54]

A leaked document appeared to show that the commandant in Kherson was a Colonel Viktor Bedrik, an officer who had served most of his career commanding Nuclear, Biological and Chemical (NBC) defence troops thousands of miles away in the Russian Far East.[55] Now he found himself in the unexpected role of occupying a city and running its administration. On 26 April, for example, according to Ukrainian reports, he was busy convening a council meeting to appoint a replacement for Mayor Kolykhaev, who had been forced to resign. This political work was the responsibility of the FSB, and the new mayor Oleksandr Kobets was evidently installed by them. Nobody had ever heard of him in Kherson. He turned out to be an ex-SBU officer who had been living in Kyiv, with almost no public profile. Journalists could not even find a photograph of him.[56]

OCCUPATION

These military commandants and their FSB minders ran the VGAs in each locality, but they also needed local Ukrainian faces. The Russians scoured around for likely frontmen for the new regime. Some had probably been on the FSB payroll before the war. Others saw a cynical career opportunity. There were pro-Russian political figures from existing political parties, such as Andrii Shevchik, an engineer at the local nuclear power plant and a town council member, who was appointed town mayor in Enerhodar.[57] Others were local activists looking for status and publicity. In Kherson, Kirill Stremousov, a local blogger and activist, was appointed as a deputy head of the VGA. Stremousov was always in the local news for some scandal or other. During the Covid pandemic he had been recording anti-vaccine conspiracy theories on his YouTube channel, and had disrupted a press conference by letting off an air pistol. He gained less than 2% of the vote when he ran for parliament.[58] Now his wish for maximum publicity was granted, at least until he died in a car crash in November 2022.

Many other appointees were also marginal, often apparently ridiculous figures in local society. In Kakhovka, Pavel Filipchuk, a former deputy in the Kherson regional parliament, was appointed deputy head of the VGA. Filipchuk had only a few hundred followers on his Telegram channel, but thousands watched his bizarre dances in the sand and strange online singing sessions on YouTube.[59] In Berdiansk the Russians appointed as acting mayor Alexander Saulenko, head of the Berdiansk branch of the Union of Left Forces, a marginal political party. The deputy mayor was Mykyta Samoilenko, who—according to Ukrainian media—worked as a janitor and 'identifies himself as a creative person who has visions in his sleep and converses with stones'.[60]

A few of these oddball figures were driven by a pro-Russian ideology. But a toxic mix of ambition and resentment was the driving force for many collaborators. Danilchenko told a local editor that 'the old city administration didn't give me a chance'. She tried to persuade a local editor to switch sides: 'If you join us, you'll have a brilliant career. You can rise all the way to Moscow.'[61] These were the drivers of collaboration: thwarted aspirations, career prospects, ambition, and resentment at a new, post-2014, Ukrainian political class that had ousted the old guard.

ATTACK

Nobody was more of an opportunist than Vladimir (Volodymyr) Saldo, a well-known local politician who had run against Kolykhaev in the mayoral elections in 2020. Saldo had been mayor of the city in 2002–12 and then a deputy in the Verkhovna Rada from the Party of Regions. He was a small-town businessman whose career was marked by constant scandals and dubious business deals, from being spanked on television by a local pop star,[62] to being arrested in the Dominican Republic on kidnapping charges in a murky feud with another businessman.[63] Kherson journalist Konstantin Ryzhenko told a newspaper that Saldo was 'a symbol of decline, economic ruin, corruption, forcible takeovers and gang violence'.[64]

Initially, Saldo did not seem to be a pro-Russian ideologue. On 14 March, he claimed in a Facebook post that he had tried to disrupt plans to form a (pro-Russian) People's Republic of Kherson, claiming: 'I did not betray my soul, my soul is Kherson, and Kherson is Ukraine.'[65] But he had already joined a pro-Russian administrative committee, the so-called 'Salvation Committee for Peace and Order', on 10 March, together with half a dozen other locals from Kherson.[66] At the end of April, Russian news sources announced that Saldo had been appointed head of Russia's VGA in the Kherson region. The lure of political advancement evidently proved too much for him.

Meanwhile, back in Kherson, although Mayor Kolykhaev had been dismissed, he refused to leave and continued running many of the city's services unofficially from another building.[67] But on 28 June he was detained. Armed men handcuffed him while soldiers took hard disks from the computers, opened all the safes and looked for documents.[67] That was the last his family saw of him for a long time. They did not know whether he was dead or alive until September 2023, when his son Svyatoslav heard from the International Committee of the Red Cross (ICRC) that his father was in captivity somewhere in the Russian Federation, but there were no more details.[69]

Two years on, in the summer of 2024, Kolykhaev was still in prison in Russia, but at times his case appeared to have been forgotten by the authorities in Kyiv. A shadow of fear hung over his story. 'Traitor or hero?' ran the strapline on a *New York Times* article about the mayor, which detailed suspicions from some opponents about his cooperation with the Russians.[70] In reality, he seems to have been careful to follow the rules, while trying to keep the city running under Russian occupation. His adviser later claimed that he ordered the Geneva Convention and Ukraine's collaboration law to be printed out, so that everybody knew the legal position.[71]

There was controversy about other Kherson politicians too. Kolykhaev's friend and political ally, the ex-head of Kherson region, Hennadiy Lahuta, had been dismissed by President Zelensky in July 2022. Lahuta had been dogged by accusations that he had 'surrendered' Kherson to the occupation forces. The SBU had opened a case against him—a relatively trivial case regarding ownership of a car—that appeared designed to target him for political reasons. On 17 September he reportedly committed suicide in hospital in Kyiv. His colleague Sergei Khlan, an outspoken former parliamentary deputy from the south, defended him and complained that the accusations were unfair and had driven him to suicide.[72] These convoluted tales were forerunners of the complex politics of occupation, marked by constant allegations of betrayal or collaboration and a growing divide between those who left the occupied areas and those who stayed.

By early May 2022, the screws had tightened further and the dividing line between occupied and government-controlled territory began to solidify. Now it became more difficult to leave Kherson to travel to government-controlled areas. The watchdog organisation Netblocks reported that the Skynet internet provider in Kherson had been disconnected from Ukrainian networks. It became harder to contact relatives who were still in the occupied territories. When the internet and telecoms were reconnected, they had been rerouted through the Russian network run by Rostelecom, the beginning of a deep communications and information divide between occupied and government-controlled territory.[73] Across the region, people tried to avoid soldiers and stay at home as much as possible. In Enerhodar the shutters were also coming down on normal civilian life. In June, life in the city was 'as quiet as a cemetery' and residents described the atmosphere as 'nervous and bleak'. Many had fled. One resident told the Institute for War and Peace Reporting (IWPR) that 'Russians largely leave the residents alone' and that 'there is no widespread repression'.[74] But selective violence continued against businessmen, local activists and anybody suspected of aiding the Ukrainian military. There was no doubt that by May 2022 the Russians were in full control across the south-eastern territories of Ukraine, even—after the most brutal siege and urban warfare—in the city of Mariupol.

The siege of Mariupol

The war had never been far away from Mariupol. After 2014 the nervous, volatile front line was only 15 kilometres away from the port city's eastern suburbs. Mariupol had already experienced occupation by pro-Russian separatist forces from the DNR for two months in 2014. They were soon pushed out by Ukrainian military and volunteer battalions and it had become a garrison town for Ukrainian troops, including the Azov Brigade—a highly controversial unit, because of its links to the far right, although far from all its fighters showed any interest in its ideological stance.[75] It later became integrated into the Ukrainian military and denied any allegations of political extremism—although it was still viewed with suspicion by some Mariupol residents. In the years before the full-scale invasion, Mariupol was a city in flux. The city was divided in diverse ways—between residents and incomers, Russian speakers and Ukrainian speakers, and those with political views closer to Moscow or to Kyiv. Mostly this did not matter—people got along and these divisions were managed, most often by trying to ignore them: 'sources of disagreement were downplayed, avoided, or ignored altogether', writes Michael Gentile, a scholar who conducted research in the city.[76]

Mariupol had traditionally been a Russian-speaking city, but a new generation was emerging with a stronger Ukrainian identity, including numerous refugees from Russian-occupied Donetsk. These incomers were often young people, who began to invigorate cultural and social life in the city. The city attracted government spending and investment because of its front-line status, and the big Azovstal metals plant and the MMK Ilyich Iron and Steel Works

OCCUPATION

employed tens of thousands of people on relatively high wages. From being a sleepy backwater, it had become one of the most vibrant cities in Ukraine. A new, younger generation held festivals and cultural events, began start-ups and opened cafes. This new sense of Mariupol as a lively, future-oriented city made its sudden descent into catastrophe even more striking.

Mariupol was strategically vulnerable and a key Russian target in the invasion. It had a working port, but three small boats in Mariupol harbour comprised the entire Ukrainian naval fleet in the Sea of Azov.[77] Although the sea was legally shared by Russia and Ukraine, in practice Russia had slowly strangled Ukrainian access by building the Crimean Bridge across the Kerch Strait. In 2018, FSB coastguards seized three Ukrainian navy vessels as they attempted to transit from the Black Sea into the Sea of Azov, en route to Mariupol port. The ships were eventually released, but Russia had gained de facto control over the Sea of Azov.

This maritime dominance allowed Russia to land thousands of troops in an amphibious landing west of Mariupol in the first days of the war. These troops were bolstered by other forces coming overland from Crimea along the coastal road. Mariupol was also under attack by forces coming from the east along the coast. That left just a road to the north-west towards government-controlled territory for Russia to capture. Russian units from the 150th Motorized Rifle Division quickly seized control of this route, and by 2 March Mariupol was surrounded.

Not many people left in the first days of the war. Evacuation trains left Mariupol half-empty.[78] The local authorities provided little information and did not encourage people to evacuate, according to Liudmyla Chychera, a civil society activist from Mariupol. Liudmyla was one of the few to leave Mariupol on 25 February, when she took her mother and children to relative safety in Zaporizhzhia. She fully expected to return to the city soon afterwards, but never did, because in the week after she left, the city plunged into crisis. Her husband, Dmytro Chychera, had stayed behind to run Halabuda, a community centre which provided humanitarian aid during the blockade. But he disappeared on 16 March, possibly captured by Russian forces.[79] In those first two

ATTACK

weeks of March, Mariupol was transformed from a peaceful European city into a hellish battlescape.

There were around 8,000 Ukrainian troops stationed inside the city, the bulk of them from the Azov Brigade and the 36th Marine Brigade. But the city was badly prepared for the Russian assault: there were no fortifications around much of the city's perimeter and hardly any arms or ammunition stores. There also appears to have been confusion in the first days of the war about tactics and leadership. Denys Prokopenko, commander of the Azov Brigade, is reported to have taken command of the defence of the city because the official military command had retreated without putting in place a clear chain of command or defensive plan.[80] According to the Ukrainian journalist Yuri Butusov, proposals from Azov's leadership to leave Mariupol and halt the advancing Russians further along the coast were rejected by the military leadership in Kyiv.[81] It is difficult to corroborate these reports, but it would not be surprising if there was chaos and miscommunication in the early days of the war.

Although outnumbered and surrounded, Ukrainian troops refused to surrender and fought fiercely across Mariupol, street by street. Russian forces pounded the city using artillery and almost indiscriminate bombing, hitting residential blocks, hospitals, shops and schools. On 2 March 2022 the entire city was left without electricity after more than fifteen hours of bombardment by Russian forces. Without power, neither the water pumps nor the heating systems worked.[82] Communications networks also collapsed, leaving people unable to call for help or to contact family and friends. The lack of any information led to panic and chaos. Mstyslav Chernov, the director of the Oscar-winning documentary *20 Days in Mariupol*, later commented that it was above all the lack of communication that explained why Mariupol fell apart so quickly.[83]

Without any news or means to communicate, without power, heat or water, life in the city began to break down. Already, by 6 March, the siege was making life intolerable. 'People are drinking from puddles in the street', Petro Andryushchenko, an advisor to the mayor of Mariupol, told reporters: 'There is no electricity, heating or telephone connections. It's absolutely horrific.'[84] Shops were stripped bare by looters as they plunged into darkness, their alarms immobilised by the loss of power. People scoured apartments for furniture to burn in open courtyards in order to cook food. A lively, modern European city had been reduced to a primitive lifestyle in a matter of days. Those who escaped the city described scenes of despair: buildings gutted by Russian shelling, bodies lying on the streets, covered in drapes or rolled in carpets, or just lying unnoticed on the ground. People gathered the dead bodies as best they could in one place, but they could not keep up with the scale of the killing. Nobody knows how many people died. An investigation by Human Rights Watch provided evidence of at least 8,000 civilian deaths, but Ukrainian officials suggested it could be 25,000 or many more.[85]

During the final days of March, Russian troops slowly took control of the city centre. Russian forces claimed to be attacking the deployments of Azov fighters and Ukrainian marines inside the city, but often their attacks were against targets with no obvious military significance. There was evidence of indiscriminate attacks by Russian forces on civilian housing, food storage depots and bomb shelters.[86] Ukrainian positions were often embedded in the infrastructure of the city, close to or inside houses, schools and other buildings, leaving civilians caught in the middle of fire from both sides. According to Human Rights Watch, Ukrainian troops were deployed in schools across the city centre, many of which were hit by Russian attacks.[87] Natalia Usmanova told reporters that she fled her home in Mariupol because a Ukrainian artillery post had been set up near a school close by her house.[88] This was a common complaint from residents in Mariupol and elsewhere. A report by Amnesty International in August 2022 criticising such practices caused a furore.[89] But in Mariupol, Ukrainian forces had little choice except to fight in and around civilian infrastructure in such a dense urban environment. Russian forces also occupied buildings across the city, including hospitals, and in at least one case were alleged to have used civilians in the Regional Intensive Care Hospital as human shields.[90] Russian forces repeated the tactics used in Grozny, in Chechnya, which had been reduced to rubble, or Aleppo in Syria, another city devastated by aerial bombardment. Residents could only cower in basements, and hope.

ATTACK

On 16 March 2022 a Russian aerial attack destroyed the Mariupol Drama Theatre and killed many of the people who had taken shelter in its underground premises. An investigation by Amnesty International concluded that 'the Russian military likely deliberately targeted the theatre despite knowing hundreds of civilians were sheltering there'.[91] There was little doubt that Russia had committed a war crime, but international investigations also demonstrated the difficulty of establishing the scale of what had happened. While Amnesty International concluded that at least twelve people had been killed in the attack, 'and likely many more', other investigations concluded that up to 600 people were dead.[92] These divergent narratives demonstrated the problems of establishing the truth about the scale of these war crimes when there was little access for independent journalists or investigators. Russia actively worked to cover up war crimes and almost certainly pressured refugees inside Russia to amplify Russian talking points. Russian media promoted their own incredible story that the Azov Brigade had deliberately blown up the theatre, and they prosecuted anybody who expressed an alternative viewpoint. In the faraway Siberian city of Barnaul, Russian journalist Maria Ponomarenko was jailed for six years for simply posting the truth: that it was Russian aircraft that had deliberately bombed the theatre.[93]

People tried to get out. During the first two weeks of March, any movement was fraught with danger. After 15 March there were attempts to organise humanitarian evacuations, but they often failed, usually because of Russian intransigence or military activity. Some residents did manage to drive out in make-shift convoys. Around 60,000 people escaped to Ukrainian-controlled territory during the second half of March, driving private cars through humanitarian corridors. A further 60,000 escaped in April, following the same route along the coast to Berdiansk and on to the Ukrainian-controlled city of Zaporizhzhia, navigating their way through at least fifteen Russian military checkpoints along the way.[94] From eastern Mariupol thousands of cars travelled east, and huge traffic jams formed at the border with Russia, with many people waiting five days or more to pass through Russia's 'registration' system, more commonly known as 'filtration', which was highly intrusive and often abusive (and discussed in more detail in Chapter 4). Other residents were loaded onto buses and trains for transport to refugee centres far inside Russia, whether they wanted to travel to Russia or not. A few residents managed to walk along the beach or swim towards the relative safety of Berdiansk. Igor Pedin walked to safety with his dog, Zhu-Zhu, covering over 200 kilometres before he arrived safely in Ukrainian-held territory.[95]

For those who stayed, conditions got progressively worse. The lack of water was a huge problem. Volunteers and staff at the local water company tried to distribute water from wells and springs, but moving around the city was dangerous. A Human Rights Watch report listed numerous cases of people who were killed while attempting to get water. One resident recalled: 'On April 2, my husband went to collect water at a well nearby, but he never returned. [...]. I looked for him for five days. I never saw him again.'[96] March was freezing cold. There was no heating or gas for cooking. People were forced to prepare meals outside on open fires, at constant risk of shelling or air attacks. For the many wounded, there was rudimentary medical care at best. With communications cut and most journalists having evacuated, there were also few people left to record what happened. The last group of international journalists left on 15 March with the footage that would make *20 Days in Mariupol*, the remarkable documentary film that shows the barbarity of the Russian attack.

By 7 April, Russian forces claimed to have 'practically cleared' Ukrainian forces from the central district, but at enormous cost.[97] A damage assessment by Human Rights Watch found that more than half of all buildings in the city centre had been hit, but of the 477 high-rise buildings in the central district, in which most Mariupol residents lived, 93% were damaged. Many were uninhabitable.[98] Despite the Russian claim to control the city, the Azov Brigade and Ukrainian marines fought on. One group of marines were based at the Ilyich Iron and Steel plant, but by mid-April they had been forced to leave. Many were captured by Russian troops, but others managed to join the remnants of the Azov Brigade in the huge Azovstal complex, which seemed almost designed to be the backdrop for a movie-set apocalypse. There were also civilians in

ATTACK

Azovstal—some were family members of the military, others were workers from the factory who had taken shelter at their workplace. But by early May, the Azovstal defenders were also at the end of their resources, with many starving or gravely wounded. After several unsuccessful negotiations, a deal was struck behind the scenes by Oleksandr Kovalov, a Ukrainian parliamentarian from the Donbas, with high-ranking intelligence officials from Russia.[99] First, civilians were evacuated to Ukrainian government-controlled areas and to the DNR. Then, on 17 May, the last members of the Azov Brigade and other Azovstal defenders left the complex and were escorted away by the Russians, after holding out against them for eighty-six days.

The battle for Mariupol was over, but the battle of narratives was only just beginning. The two sides had radically different interpretations of what had happened in Mariupol. Russia developed an entire narrative that avoided the most obvious point: that Russian forces had launched a completely unjustified assault on the city and were responsible for the deaths of tens of thousands of civilian residents, alongside thousands of Ukrainian soldiers and their own troops. Instead, they blamed the destruction of Mariupol on 'nationalists' and 'neo-Nazis' from the Azov Brigade and Ukrainian forces. Among other false claims, Russian media reported that an explosion at a maternity hospital on 9 March that killed at least three people was staged. Russian officials also claimed that the explosion at the Mariupol Drama Theatre on 16 March was the result of a bomb planted by the Azov Brigade. These claims were debunked in careful analysis by international human rights groups.[100] The Russian authorities launched court cases against several captured Azov fighters in 2023–24, on charges of killing civilians, despite their status as prisoners of war. Large parts of the Russian account were simply falsified, even without the failure to address the initial act of aggression that started the conflict. Nevertheless, propaganda that blamed Ukrainian nationalist battalions for the violence gained traction with many Russians and even with some Mariupol residents who had lived through the siege. The promotion of these narratives was aided by the lack of independent reporting from inside the city after mid-March, when all international journalists were withdrawn from the city. The lack of communications and the dangers of moving around the city made it difficult for ordinary residents to gather evidence or communicate news to their friends and families, or to the international media.

For most Ukrainians and much of the world outside Russia, the story was completely different. Azovstal defenders became the central actors in a heroic act of resistance against a murderous Russian assault. The 'Defenders of Mariupol are the heroes of our time', announced the Ukrainian General Staff. The battle cemented the myth of the Azov fighters in Ukrainian discourse: in May 2024, huge posters were hung in Kyiv celebrating Azov's ten-year anniversary with the slogan '*Vilni obyraiut borotbu*' ('The Free Choose to Fight'). Ukrainian officials argued that the Azovstal defence had held up the Russian advance and diverted its resources from the rest of Donbas. The resistance at Mariupol made it clear to Russia that the war would not be the pushover it expected. In a tweet on X, Ukrainian presidential advisor Mikhailo Podolyak wrote that:

> 83 days of Mariupol defense will go down in history as the Thermopylae of the XXI century. 'Azovstal' defenders ruined [Russia's] plan to capture the east of [Ukraine], took a hit on themselves and proved the real 'combat capability' of [Russia] … This completely changed the course of the war.[101]

There was no doubt about the horrors of the Russian assault, portrayed in powerful documentaries and numerous eyewitness accounts, nor about the bravery of its defenders. But not everybody accepted the comparison with the ancient myth of the Spartans' last stand. Two years into the war, doubts about the wisdom of Ukrainian tactics and strategy in Mariupol began to emerge in public. There were questions about the poor preparation of the city's defences against a Russian incursion from Crimea, the failure to engage Russian forces on the route to Mariupol before they reached the city, and the decision not to order an evacuation or to withdraw forces from Mariupol before they were surrounded.[102] Azov leaders themselves had reportedly requested permission to engage Russian forces before they reached Mariupol, but were refused.[103]

ATTACK

Disputes over the battle for Mariupol emerged into the open in June 2024, when Major Bohdan Krotevych, chief of staff of the Azov Brigade, made a formal complaint to the State Bureau of Investigation (SBI) about Lieutenant General Yuriy Sodol, who had been in overall command of the front around Mariupol in February and March 2022, citing failings in the defence of Mariupol as part of his accusations.[104] With hindsight, the battle of Mariupol was doomed to failure from the beginning. The outcome—the destruction of the city and the death or capture of some of Ukraine's best soldiers—was almost inevitable once the city was surrounded. But a political decision to retreat is not an easy one. Withdrawal of forces before Russia surrounded the city might have saved the lives of many Ukrainian forces and civilians in Mariupol, but it would also have handed Mariupol to Russia without a fight. The war brought everybody in Ukraine face to face with these existential decisions of historical proportions.

Retreat

Russia's victory in Mariupol appeared at first to be a Pyrrhic victory, won at a huge cost in lives and materiel, and resulting in an even further degradation of Russia's already shattered military. After facing determined Ukrainian resistance, Russian forces had been forced to withdraw from northern Ukraine—from Kyiv and Sumy regions—in early April 2022. This was a huge victory for Ukraine, but it now freed up Russian military forces to concentrate on the Donbas. On 18 April 2022 Russia launched a new offensive on the eastern front, aiming to take complete control of Luhansk and Donetsk regions. They made some progress over the next months, particularly in Luhansk region, but were dogged by low morale, poor logistics and weak leadership. Then the tide began to turn. For a few heady months in the late summer and autumn of 2022, it appeared as though Ukraine might win back large parts of the occupied territories, with Russia in abject retreat.

The first big Ukrainian counteroffensive was in Kharkiv region. Russian forces had threatened the city of Kharkiv from the beginning. It was a key target, both strategically and symbolically, viewed as a 'Russian' town in eastern Ukraine, although that reflected lazy thinking among Russian analysts rather the reality of modern Kharkiv, a city that was transforming into a contemporary, European-oriented metropolis. The Russian military and allied militias quickly occupied large parts of eastern Kharkiv region, with towns such as Kupiansk and Izyum coming under Russian rule, but they were pushed back from Kharkiv city itself by determined Ukrainian resistance. A Ukrainian counteroffensive in early May 2022 forced Russian forces to retreat beyond artillery range, giving the city some respite from Russian bombardment, but in the rest of Kharkiv region Russia began to consolidate control.

The Russians set up an occupation authority for Kharkiv region in April 2022. This Military-Civilian Administration (VGA) was based in Kupiansk and headed by a local called Vitaly Ganchev, who had previously worked as a senior official in the police force in the LNR. A regional government for Kharkiv was set up in August headed by Andrei Alekseenko, a Russian official who had previously been mayor of the Russian city of Krasnodar. A familiar litany of Russian occupation measures began to be rolled out in Kharkiv region. The authorities announced a new coat of arms for the region, based on Tsarist imagery. Schools were forced to prepare for the introduction of a new Russian school curriculum. The authorities began distributing Russian passports and introduced the Russian rouble and Russian pensions. On 6 July 2022 Ganchev told the media that the region was aiming to join Russia.[105] Ukrainian sources claimed that a referendum was planned for November.[106]

But in September 2022 Ukrainian forces counter-attacked and Russian forces began to retreat. Ganchev told the media on 7 September that the situation was under control, but two days later the entire administration, led by Ganchev, fled the region.[107] Apart from a small pocket of land on the border, the entire Russian occupation in Kharkiv region was quickly over. Ganchev, still delighting in the title of head of the Military-Civilian Administration of Kharkiv region, retreated to Belgorod, occasionally posting missives on his little-read Telegram feed.[108] Alekseenko was transferred to run the government in Kherson region, only to find that there too Russian forces were in retreat. Otherwise, the administration of the Kharkiv occupation disappeared almost without a trace, at least until May 2024 when Russian forces again crossed the frontier and took control of a strip of land in Kharkiv region. Then Ganchev reappeared in the media to report on Russian advances, only to see the Russian offensive once again end in another deadlock.[109]

The second Ukrainian counteroffensive of 2022 came in Kherson region on the right bank—the western side—of the Dnipro River. Kherson city was important for the Russians. It was the only regional centre that they had managed to seize in their early offensives, and after Mariupol it was the biggest city of any kind under Russian control. Kherson was strategically important, because its position on the right bank of the Dnipro left open the possibility that Russia could still move further west and threaten Odesa. But it was also strategically vulnerable: Russian forces were resupplied by just two bridges across the Dnipro: one in the north at Nova Kakhovka and the Antonov Bridge further south, near Kherson. The Russian position on the right bank only made sense militarily if Russia could take control of more territory—towards Mykolaiv to the west and upstream towards Kryvyi Rih along the Dnipro River. Stuck half-way to Mykolaiv, Russian forces were dangerously exposed on terrain that was difficult to defend and with highly vulnerable supply lines. Kherson's former airport at Chornobaivka was a key link in their supply chain, but the Ukrainians bombed it so many times that it became a running joke on social media.

Ukraine had begun a counteroffensive in Kherson region in August 2022. It was slow going. Village by village, field by field, Ukrainian forces slowly increased the pressure on the Russian contingent in Kherson city. By early November the pressure had become too much. On 9 November, Sergei Surovikin, at that point overall commander of Russian forces in Ukraine, announced that he had ordered Russian troops to withdraw from Kherson city and the entire right-bank area of Kherson region. He told Russian television that it was 'a very difficult decision', but had been taken 'to preserve the most important thing—the lives of our servicemen and, in general, the combat effectiveness of the group of troops, which it is futile to keep on the right bank in a limited area'.[110]

OCCUPATION

The withdrawal was met with dismay by many ideologues on the Russian side. Pro-Russian blogger Boris Rozhin said the retreat from Kherson was a 'betrayal' and the 'murder of Russian hopes'.[111] By contrast, there was unalloyed joy for Ukrainians. As the Russians pulled out from Kherson across the Dnipro and Ukrainian soldiers entered the city, residents flocked to the central square with Ukrainian flags and banners. 'Only Euphoria in Newly Liberated Kherson', was the headline on CNN. 'We feel free, we are not slaves, we are Ukrainians', a Kherson resident called Olga told the channel.[112]

That was undoubtedly true for most Khersonites. But not all. According to Russian figures, almost 70,000 people—perhaps a quarter of the pre-war population—evacuated with the Russian forces as they withdrew. The Russian military authorities had ordered an evacuation, claiming that residents were at risk from Ukrainian shelling or fighting in the city, but many people did not know whether to leave or not. Those who had cooperated with the Russians or feared the return of Ukrainian forces probably left voluntarily. Those who worked with the occupation administration understood that they faced serious reprisals if they stayed. Russian-appointed Kherson head Vladimir Saldo and his entourage all decamped to Henichesk, a small seaside town, a move that merely seemed to emphasise the failure of the Russian campaign. Doctors who had continued to work under the Russians were told that they had to leave; but some remained in hiding around the city to avoid evacuation. They could not work in any case: the Russians had removed all the equipment, furniture and patients from the hospital.[113]

Some of those who evacuated travelled to Henichesk, while others were taken directly to Russia. Two pro-Russian refugees later told the media that they started to pack their bags after hearing pro-Russian blogger Yuri Podoliak urging people to leave ahead of the advancing Ukrainian army. A text message from the occupation authority also told them to evacuate. They met other refugees early in the morning to take a ferry across the river, where they were met by a convoy of buses chartered by the Russian Ministry of Emergency Situations (MChS). When they reached the Russian border, they went through the filtration process in a huge field of tents and military personnel. Refugees were loaded into another convoy of buses and met by Russian volunteers. They were sent to camps across southern Russia, with many ending up in the Krasnodar region, in places such as Anapa.[114]

The Russians were also evacuating people from the left-bank villages on the eastern side of the Dnipro opposite Kherson, where they were building a new defensive line. Viktoria, a 43-year-old resident of Hola Pristan, a town on the left bank where Russians were setting up new defensive positions, reported that they were getting constant messages from the Russians telling people to evacuate. 'We successfully ignore them', she told a reporter, 'and so far nobody has aggressively driven us out of our homes.' But the local pro-Russian administration in Hola Pristan was closed and officials moved to Henichesk and the port town of Skadovsk, where 'Russian patriotism was concentrated' now, as Viktoria put it.[115] Pro-Russian sympathisers in Hola Pristan were worried. 'The collaborators went completely nuts', one resident, Natasha, told a newspaper: 'One of them was always talking about how she was oppressed by the Kyiv regime, and she made a great show of accepting a Russian passport.' The collapse of the Russian front led to a change in attitude: now, Natasha continued, 'she has been rushing about, asking how she can ask Zelensky for protection, like she is a political refugee. To be honest, we have been laughing at her. I don't know what will happen to her next.'[116]

There were high hopes in places like Hola Pristan that the Ukrainian advance would continue. Many people were waiting impatiently for Ukrainian troops to liberate their town. But Russian troops dug in behind the so-called Surovikin defensive lines, a network of fortifications built during the winter and spring of 2023. They were able to halt Ukraine's attempts to break through the front line in order to advance on Russian-held towns such as Tokmak and Melitopol. In truth, Ukraine had neither the manpower nor the weapons for a successful offensive against well-prepared Russian positions. Its strategy and tactics were also flawed. And it was ill-served by boosterism that raised expectations and continued to claim success even after it was clear that the counteroffensive had failed. By September 2023, after Ukraine had made only incremental gains, a commentator at the Atlantic Council was explaining that it would be 'misleading to judge Ukraine's counteroffensive purely in terms of territory liberated from Russian occupation'.[117] But the whole point of liberation was about taking back occupied territory, and during 2023 Ukraine struggled to shift the front line by more than a few kilometres.

Conclusion: Defeat in the south

Ukraine's remarkable successes against the Russian army in the north and north-east partially obscured the initial fiasco on the southern front. The Ukrainian authorities had failed to put in place substantive defensive lines to the north of Crimea that might have slowed the Russian advance. As a result, Russia's initial progress was rapid across the south. An almost unimpeded advance along the northern shores of the Sea of Azov led to an early encirclement of Mariupol and the subsequent siege and bombardment of the city. Kyiv failed to withdraw forces from an indefensible position in Mariupol before they were surrounded and had to choose between surrender and an unwinnable fight.

The most important battle in the south was not the battle for Mariupol, which was doomed from the beginning, but the remarkable defence of Mykolaiv. This was a critical success in early March, that halted the Russian advance and prevented a march on Odesa that would have cut off Ukraine from the sea. In the east, Russian forces failed to take Kharkiv and were unable to advance to the borders of Donetsk region. These dynamics on the battlefield in the first weeks of the invasion effectively shaped the front line for at least the next two years.

After Russian forces withdrew from Kharkiv and Kherson regions, the front line remained highly dynamic but did not shift significantly in terms of territory. During 2023, despite both Russian offensives and Ukrainian counteroffensives, fewer than 1,300 square kilometres changed hands between the two sides, although the cost in human lives remained horrendous.[118] Russia made small gains in early 2024, bombing the town of Avdiivka into submission, re-entering

ATTACK

Kharkiv region in May and slowly expanding its control in Donetsk region. In a surprise attack, Ukraine occupied part of the Russian region of Kursk in August 2024, but failed to halt a creeping Russian advance in the Donetsk region. Despite the continued fighting, it remained difficult for either side to make major territorial gains along the main front line, short of a major crisis or implosion among ranks on the other side of the trenches.

The failure of the Ukrainian counteroffensive during 2023 was crucial, because it gave Russia the opportunity to consolidate its control behind the front lines in the occupied territories. Moscow was able to dig in militarily and turn the front line into a resilient defensive front that was extremely difficult for Ukraine to breach. Behind this set of defensive lines, Russia turned its focus from the military to the political, to implement its administrative plans for the territories that it occupied, and to determine how it would govern them.

3

GOVERNMENT

According to a lecturer at the Military Academy of the General Staff of the Russian Armed Forces, 'military occupation is a science'. The specialist told the BBC that 'the word occupation is usually used in a negative sense, but in general occupation is simply something that you have to be able to do'.[1] Russian security and military forces had extensive experience in being able 'to do occupation'. At the sprawling FSB Academy on Michurinsky Prospekt in south-west Moscow, students could still learn lessons from the Soviet intervention in Afghanistan in 1979, or even the occupation of Czechoslovakia in 1968 or Hungary in 1956. More recently, the long war in Chechnya taught a new generation of security officials how to deal with a population that wanted you to leave—or even wanted you dead. There had been extensive preparation too. The FSB had a network of Russian agents in Ukraine—although it was probably neither as extensive nor as effective as they told their political masters. In the second half of 2021, the FSB had become increasingly active, mapping public sentiment through opinion polls to gauge the level of potential opposition to a Russian takeover. They identified local political figures likely to cooperate with a Russian occupation and lists of locals likely to lead an anti-Russian resistance.[2] And according to British intelligence shared with journalists before the war, the Russians had plans for a new puppet government in Kyiv.[3]

OCCUPATION

Despite all this planning and preparation, the reality on the ground was often confusion and chaos. This was hardly surprising. In a study of Nazi occupation regimes, Derk Venema notes that even with 'Meticulous planning, ideological determination, military superiority [and] supreme legal knowledge', occupation forces were often unprepared for the 'complexities and exigencies of organizing the administration of the occupied territory, especially when it lasts longer than a few months'.[4] In Ukraine, Russia had none of those attributes. Its planning was flawed, its ideology was vague and contradictory, and Ukraine had punctured its claims to military superiority. There was almost no evidence of planning for the legal or international ramifications of occupation. As a consequence, the period between February and September 2022 was marked by a series of ad hoc improvisations to manage the territories, as different groups in the Kremlin tried to adapt to this rapidly changing environment and to second-guess the thinking of Russia's only real decision-maker on such questions of state, Vladimir Putin.

Status

For the first few months after February 2022, there was public uncertainty around whether Russia would annex the occupied territories, proclaim some form of puppet state or impose an alternative pro-Russian Ukrainian administration. It is likely that the Russian leadership was already intent on annexing at least part of Ukraine ahead of the invasion. According to a report by Reuters, Dmitry Kozak, the veteran chain-smoking fixer who had been the Kremlin's point man on Ukraine, had almost reached a deal on the eve of war. The tentative agreement—the result of secret talks with Kyiv—would have guaranteed that Ukraine would not join NATO. But Putin allegedly rejected the deal because he was now intent not only on preventing NATO membership for Ukraine, but on annexing swathes of Ukrainian territory.[5]

The question was not whether Russia would annex territory, but how and when. On 21 February, in one of its last steps towards the full-scale invasion, Russia had recognised the DNR and the LNR as independent states. In June the Syrian government also recognised them, quickly followed by the Democratic People's Republic of Korea, but the rest of the world strongly condemned the move. Russia's recognition was accompanied by 'friendship and cooperation' treaties with the DNR and LNR that allowed for military cooperation, but also meant that Russia could now openly provide funding to the republics and dispatch official 'advisors' to run the regions. Russia had previously recognised Abkhazia and South Ossetia in the same way and stopped short of annexation. But this was a different tactic. The 'independence' of the DNR and LNR was simply the first step towards full integration with Russia.

During April and May 2022 there were rumours that a 'Kherson People's Republic' was about to be proclaimed on the basis of a fake referendum. On 16 April Liudmyla Denisova, the Ukrainian parliamentary ombudsman for human rights, told the media that referendum bulletins were already being printed in Nova Kahkovka and that the poll would be held in the first ten days of May.[6] But Russia's military failures meant that the dates of a referendum on joining Russia were repeatedly postponed.[7] Evidently, officials in Moscow hoped that the Russian military would gain more territory before any referendum was held. In March 2022 DNR head Denis Pushilin claimed that the DNR would enter Russia, but only after it had won control over all the territory of Donetsk region.[8] But strong Ukrainian resistance prevented Russian and DNR troops from winning control over major towns in Donetsk region, such as Kramatorsk and Pokrovsk.

According to Meduza's sources in the Presidential Administration, there was little enthusiasm among officials for annexing these 'depressed regions'. Bureaucrats could only see administrative problems and mounting economic costs, but it was the choice of the 'senior leadership', in other words, Putin himself.[9] Putin's vision appears to have been shared by first deputy head of the Presidential Administration, Sergei Kiriyenko. At least, according to media reports, Kiriyenko met with Putin in April 2022 and set out his proposed plans for the Russian-occupied territories in Ukraine, a vision that clearly pleased Putin.[10] By the end of April Kiriyenko had been appointed 'curator' (in the Russian parlance, an overseer) of Moscow's ties with the DNR and the LNR and by extension all the Russian-occupied territories in Ukraine.[11] He replaced the out-of-favour Dmitry Kozak, who appears to have made the mistake of questioning the efficacy of a full-scale Russian invasion and proposing further negotiations with Ukraine.[12] In his new position, Kiriyenko became a regular visitor to southern Ukraine. In April 2022 he visited Donetsk and in May he travelled with Andrei Turchak, secretary of the United Russia party, to Mariupol and Volnovakha. In Mariupol he made a speech at the opening of a new monument to Babushka Anna (Granny Anna), a semi-mythical figure who had been turned into a grotesque symbol of the Russian military campaign after she appeared to welcome Russian troops.[13]

Kiriyenko was in charge of Russian domestic politics, so his appointment to manage the newly occupied territories had the obvious implication that Ukraine was no longer viewed primarily as a foreign policy problem. A diminutive, bespectacled figure, it was hard to imagine a more unlikely political manager of a twenty-first-century occupation regime than Kiriyenko. He had been a surprise choice to manage Russia's domestic politics when Putin appointed him as first deputy head of the Presidential Administration in 2016. Kiriyenko had spent many years running Russia's nuclear energy corporation, Rosatom, and he had not been active in public politics since the 1990s. Back then, he had been widely seen as a liberal—in 1999 he founded the Union of Right Forces (SPS) party with Boris Nemtsov, the Russian liberal politician who was murdered in Moscow in 2015. Now Kiriyenko began to reinvent himself as the primary 'political technologist' of the occupied territories.

The Russian notion of 'political technology' was rooted in the work of political advisors during the dirty election campaigns of 1990s Russia, characterised by all sorts of *chernyi piar* (black PR) and *kompromat* (compromising materials) against opponents and sharp practice at the ballots. But it also had a more philosophical background in the work of Soviet philosopher Georgy Shchedrovitsky, the founder of an esoteric pseudo-scientific movement called 'Methodology'. Although Shchedrovitsky was close to Soviet dissidents, he did not share their belief in individual freedom. His ideas explored the possibility of manipulating and controlling the individual through language and education.[14] Yefim Ostrovsky, a professor influenced by Shchedrovitsky, was an advisor to Kiriyenko in the early 2000s and further developed these ideas.

The academic Ilya Kukulin described Ostrovsky's philosophy as having two basic premises: first, social movements are not spontaneous but 'the result of deliberate activity by a small group of people'; and second, 'a small and specially organised group of political technologists' can produce almost any outcomes in society.[15] Ostrovsky set out his own philosophy in the starkest terms, explaining how intellectuals—or political technologists—should transform Russian society: 'If they can't do it, we will teach them; if they don't want to—we will force them. This is our duty; it is a question of honour. It is the basis for the existence of a Country, which good and strong people, speaking in Russian, can call "Ours".'[16] This vision combined Russian nationalism with political manipulation and control—and it was underpinned by an almost unbounded belief that the techniques of 'political technology' could be used to transform almost any society. It was an ideal philosophical basis for the policies of political control and media manipulation that would be crucial for maintaining the occupation regime.

Kiriyenko began appointing his allies to key positions. In early June 2022 he visited a Centre for Humanitarian Aid set up by the United Russia party in Kherson, which was headed by one of Kiriyenko's close allies, State Duma deputy Igor Kastyukevich. Kastyukevich published an account of the visit, which ended by stating that 'the incorporation of Kherson region in Russia would be fully-fledged, analogous to the incorporation of Crimea'.[17] This was one of the first hints about Kiriyenko's plans. When Kiriyenko visited Melitopol on the same trip, the pro-Russian mayor told the media: 'We know that our future is united with Russia. The Russian Federation will be here forever. And we are beginning to prepare for a referendum.'[18] But despite these statements, there was no official word from Moscow on the government's intentions and the signals on the future of the occupied territories remained confusing.

OCCUPATION

Annexation

The problem for Russian officials was that they were always second-guessing Putin's latest thinking. Kozak had guessed wrongly and had been completely sidelined as a result. Now different factions in the Kremlin and in the occupied territories began competing to feed their own ideas into the mix. In May 2022, secretary of the United Russia party, Andrei Turchak, visited Kherson and announced that 'Russia is here forever. There should be no doubts about that. There will be no return to the past.'[19] It was an ill-fated prediction. Within four months, Russian forces would be fleeing from Kherson city ahead of advancing Ukrainian troops. But statements by Turchak and other officials confirmed that Russia's goal was not just temporary occupation, but ultimately annexation. The main obstacle to Russia's plans was the reality of the military situation on the ground.

The confusion about Moscow's intentions was also stirred up by local officials. Kirill Stremousov, the deputy head of the Kherson Military-Civilian Administration (VGA), made frequent and often contradictory claims. In early May 2022 he said that Kherson might become part of Russia without a referendum. That idea appeared to be knocked down by presidential spokesman Dmitry Peskov, who said—with a straight face—that any decision had to be 'completely legitimate, as in the case of Crimea'.[20] Peskov was at least narrowly accurate. Under Russian legislation, Russia could not simply annex Ukrainian territory. Any incorporation of part of a foreign state into Russia could only take place with the agreement of the foreign state. Since Ukraine was very unlikely to agree, Russia had a workaround. If the territory first declared independence from Ukraine and Russia then recognised its independence, this pseudo-state could then apply for incorporation into Russia, all within the letter of the law. It was just this procedure that Crimea had followed in 2014. Given that annexation was a gross violation of international law, it might seem strange for Russia to maintain this legalistic approach, but it was typical of Putin's Russia that officials tried to follow narrow legal procedures, even in their pursuit of completely illegitimate ends.

GOVERNMENT

The initial plan appears to have been to hold referendums on joining Russia in May 2022. But the decision was postponed until September, because of the lack of Russian military success. Russia controlled almost all of Luhansk region, but only around 65% of Donetsk region. Russian forces also controlled approximately 65% of Zaporizhzhia region, but not the most populated areas around Zaporizhzhia city. And Russia controlled 93% of Kherson region, although they were to lose a large part of this territory after Ukraine's counteroffensive.[21] When Ukrainian forces unexpectedly pushed Russian forces out of Kharkiv region in early September, there were reports that the poll would again be postponed.[22] Russian political technologists who had been deployed to prepare the vote were sent back to Moscow. But suddenly, on 20 September, the votes were back on again—although now without Kharkiv.[23] The Russian military defeat made that impossible. But Putin was willing to gamble that he could at least control the other territories long enough to get the vote done.

The referendums finally took place over four days on 23–27 September 2022. In the DNR and the LNR the question was a simple one: 'Do you approve of the Donetsk [or Lugansk] People's Republic being incorporated into the Russian Federation with subject rights of the Russian Federation?'. Since Russia had already recognised the two territories as independent states, the procedure was straightforward. On the other hand, in Kherson and Zaporizhzhia regions there was an awkward multiple-stage question asking voters: 'Are you in favour of the exit of Kherson oblast [region] from Ukraine and the formation of Kherson oblast as an independent state and its entry into the Russian Federation with the status of a subject of the Russian Federation?'. Another small difference: in Luhansk and Donetsk, the ballots were only in Russian, whereas in Zaporizhzhia and in Kherson, the ballot was also printed in Ukrainian.

Even by Moscow's standards of election fixing, the process was farcical. Electioneers went round houses in person to gather votes, accompanied by the Russian military. This was primarily designed for their own protection, since Ukrainian partisans were assassinating many local officials working for the Russians. But armed men accompanying the ballot box also gave everybody a strong incentive to vote the right way. Many residents tried to pretend they were not home or refused to answer the door when the vote-collectors came to visit. Others were caught at work, where they were often ordered to vote by management. Ukrainian officials claimed that people in the town of Starobilsk were banned from leaving the town and forced out to vote en masse. In Bilovodsk, a company director allegedly ordered employees to vote, claiming it was compulsory, and threatened to inform on anybody who refused.[24]

The votes in favour were clearly fabricated, but this was a scale of fraud unmatched in any Russian—or even Soviet—elections. In the LNR, an unlikely 98.4% of residents voted to join Russia, with 92.6% of the population finding time to take part. In the DNR, the electoral commission picked even less likely figures, reaching 99.9% in favour with 97.5% of the population appearing at the polls, despite the ongoing conflict. Figures were slightly moderated in Zaporizhzhia region, with only 93.1% supporting the proposal on a turnout of 85.4%. In Kherson region, the electoral commission claimed that 571,001 people had taken part, of which 497,051 had voted in favour of joining Russia, an overwhelming 87%, on a turnout of 77%. It was not even evident that there were that many people still living in the areas that Russia controlled, let alone that they all turned out to vote in favour of the proposal.[25] Voting was also permitted among refugees in the Russian Federation, and that probably served as a useful mechanism to increase the vote count.

The results of the referendum were largely fictitious, but in the DNR and LNR there probably was some genuine support for joining Russia, partly because of eight years of Russian propaganda, but also because people wanted to end the legal limbo in which they lived. Some believed that life in the Russian Federation would be at least better than under the predatory rule of the DNR and LNR elites. Others had genuine resentments against the regime in Kyiv after eight years of war. One 62-year-old lady told the BBC that she had voted in the referendum to join Russia: 'Nobody forced me to, I [did it] myself. Part of my family lives in Moscow, part in

Sevastopol. I simply want to be with my family. And for there to be peace.'[26] Elsewhere, even the television coverage seemed half-hearted. Russian journalists struggled to find any young people willing to proclaim their love for Mother Russia. Only pensioners nostalgic for the Soviet Union and a small coterie of pro-Moscow agitators seem to have voted voluntarily.

The referendum was not designed to assess popular opinion but to provide Russia with a legal fig-leaf for its illegal annexation. It also served the purpose of demonstrating the extent to which Russia was now in control of the territories. The point of the referendum was not only to produce a fraudulent result that could then be endlessly recycled as 'the will of the people', but also to demonstrate to residents, to Ukraine and to the outside world that Russia was intent on remaining in the territories, and that it had the administrative resources and security apparatus to conduct a vote across the entire territory under its military control. Despite threats from Kyiv, there was no real disruption of the vote by military attacks. A Ukrainian missile hit a hotel in central Kherson that was housing journalists shipped in to monitor the vote, and killed a former Ukrainian parliamentary deputy, Aleksei Zhuravko, who had returned to Ukraine to take part in the referendum.[27] But most of the campaign passed off without major incident.[28]

The Russian government even imported foreign observers to observe the vote. Khulekani Skosana, the head of the African National Congress (ANC) Youth League's Subcommittee on International Relations, led a delegation to Donbas. In an interview, he said: 'It's not just Donbas, we stand with people of Palestine, Western Sahara. We will always stand with those who are oppressed and those who don't have anyone to defend them.'[29] This strange logic was useful for Russian propaganda purposes and pointed to a much wider problem for Ukraine's narrative in parts of the Global South, where Ukraine's appeals to international sovereignty norms were sometimes muted by anti-Western sentiment.

At the UN, there was international condemnation of Russia's actions. On 30 September 2022 Russia used its veto to block a UN Security Council resolution condemning the referendums. On 12 October the UN General Assembly passed Resolution ES-11/4, which condemned:

> the organization by the Russian Federation of illegal so-called referendums in regions within the internationally recognized borders of Ukraine and the attempted illegal annexation of the Donetsk, Kherson, Luhansk and Zaporizhzhia regions of Ukraine

and declared:

> that the unlawful actions of the Russian Federation with regard to the illegal so-called referendums held from 23 to 27 September 2022 in parts of the Donetsk, Kherson, Luhansk and Zaporizhzhia regions of Ukraine that, in part, are or have been under the temporary military control of the Russian Federation, and the subsequent attempted illegal annexation of these regions, have no validity under international law and do not form the basis for any alteration of the status of these regions of Ukraine.

The resolution went on to call upon states 'not to recognize any alteration by the Russian Federation of the status of any or all of the Donetsk, Kherson, Luhansk or Zaporizhzhia regions of Ukraine', and demanded that Russia:

> immediately and unconditionally reverse its decisions of 21 February and 29 September 2022 related to the status of certain areas of the Donetsk, Kherson, Luhansk and Zaporizhzhia regions of Ukraine, as they are a violation of the territorial integrity and sovereignty of Ukraine and inconsistent with the principles of the Charter of the United Nations, and immediately, completely and unconditionally withdraw all of its military forces from the territory of Ukraine within its internationally recognized borders.[30]

The resolution was backed by 143 states, with only five against and thirty-five abstaining. The vote showed that the Russian decision not only to invade and occupy territory but also to annex foreign lands was a shock to the international community: few states wanted a precedent set that could threaten state sovereignty. Nevertheless, despite this overwhelming support, the abstaining states included China, India and South Africa, reflecting a belief in parts of the Global South that the war was a conflict between the West and Russia in which they did not wish to take sides. Illegal annexation was a dangerous precedent for any state, but the unwillingness of major powers outside the West to back Ukraine more fully, reflected wider concerns about the war. South Africa, for example, abstained on the resolution because although they considered 'the territorial integrity of States, including that of Ukraine, to be sacrosanct', they also wanted to see an immediate ceasefire and 'a political solution'.[31]

Legal procedures

Despite its obvious illegality, annexation followed a careful legal path. On 27 September 2022 the results of the referendum were announced. On 28 September the occupation authorities in Kherson and Zaporizhzhia regions both adopted a 'Declaration of Independence and Sovereignty', claiming that each region had seceded from Ukraine. On 29 September President Putin signed decrees recognising the 'state sovereignty and independence' of Zaporizhzhia and Kherson regions. The very next day, on 30 September, President Putin signed agreements with the leaders of the four occupied regions, Leonid Pasechnik (LNR), Denis Pushilin (DNR), Yevgeny Balitsky (Zaporizhzhia region) and Vladimir Saldo (Kherson region), for each province to become part of the Russian Federation. The Kherson agreement was titled 'the Agreement on the Accession of the Kherson Region to the Russian Federation and the Establishment of a New Constituent Entity of the Russian Federation', and similar documents were signed with the other three regions.[32]

On 30 September a ceremony was held to mark the signing of accords with the four regions on their incorporation into Russia. Putin looked a strangely reduced figure in the company of the also-rans who were put in charge of the occupied territories. Denis Pushilin of the DNR was the best known, but he had none of the charisma of his predecessor, Alexander Zakharchenko, who was killed in a bomb explosion in a cafe in Donetsk in 2018. Leonid Pasechnik, the head of the LNR, was a drab ex-intelligence officer, who came to power in 2017 but had never made his mark as a political leader. Vladimir Saldo, the Russian-installed head of Kherson, had once been an influential regional politician, but his career had been in terminal decline. Yevgeny Balitsky, declared acting governor of Zaporizhzhia region, was also a minor local businessman and politician, who saw Russia's takeover as a chance to revive his dying political career. Now Putin was reduced to sharing the stage with these provincial politicians.

There was no great upsurge in popular approval in Russia for the annexations, as there had been in 2014 when Russia annexed Crimea. The authorities did their best to create the illusion of a patriotic surge. In the evening Putin attended a concert on Red Square, where crowds of people were bussed in for the rally under the banal slogan: 'The choice of people. Always together'. Banners proclaimed 'Donetsk, Lugansk, Zaporozhe, Kherson, Russia! Together for ever!'. Pro-Kremlin singers and performers took to the stage, including Yaroslav Dronov, better known as Shaman, whose catchy tune *'Ya Russkii'* ('I am Russian') was a wartime hit. One of the performers was actor Ivan Okhlobystin, who deployed the archaic Russian word 'Goida', alleged to be the battle cry of the *oprichniki*, the notorious secret police of Ivan the Terrible in the sixteenth century. He told the crowd: '*Goida*, brothers and sisters. *Goida*! Be afraid, old world, lacking real beauty, lacking faith, real wisdom, led by madmen, perverts and satanists. Be afraid. We are moving. *Goida*'![33] This kind of apocalyptic rhetoric did not resonate with more than a minority of Russians. Many were more anxious about the impact of partial mobilisation that had just been announced ten days earlier. Almost half of Russians responded to the mobilisation news with 'Anxiety, fear and horror', according to an opinion poll.[4] But still, according to polls, 69% of Russians supported the idea of Kherson and Zaporizhzhia regions becoming part of Russia if they held referendums.[35]

In early October 2022 there were further rubber-stamp procedures in Moscow to complete the annexation. A resolution of the Constitutional Court on 2 October declared that the agreements were in compliance with the Russian Constitution. Sessions of the State Duma (3 October) and the Federation Council (4 October) convened to approve four Federal Constitutional Laws for the accession of the four regions to the Russian Federation. The laws set out far-reaching plans for integration into the Russian Federation, and detailed the timeframe and procedure for the integration of a new constituent entity of the Russian Federation into economic, financial, lending and legal systems of the Russian Federation and the system of bodies of government of the Russian Federation, as well as the relevant features of legal regulation in certain spheres of public relations.[36]

In other words, the complete absorption of the territories into the Russian political and legal system. The laws also declared that the residents of the territories would automatically become Russian citizens.

The treaties and new laws left critical questions unanswered. The new borders of Russia were now unclear. On official maps, the full territories of these four regions were indicated as part of the Russian Federation, although large parts of the annexed regions were still under Ukrainian control. Presidential spokesman Dmitry Peskov added that 'The LPR and the DPR [maintain] their 2014 borders. As for Kherson and Zaporozhye, we will continue consulting the populations of those regions.'[37] This merely confused the situation further. But having blurred borders did not seem to worry Russian officials. The military situation remained fluid, and the most important thing was to find a way to administer and govern the territories that they did control.

Governance

'Cadres', Stalin famously said, 'decide everything.' Occupying a foreign country is also a human resources challenge. The difficulty was all the greater in the newly occupied territories, where many experienced local officials, businesspeople and specialists had fled in the first weeks of occupation, or refused to work with the new administrations. The situation was easier in territories that were claimed as parts of the DNR or LNR. Here the existing DNR and LNR government structures—which had been developed since 2014—were simply expanded to the new territories. When Russian forces took control of Mariupol, which lay inside the western boundary of Donetsk region, the head of the DNR, Denis Pushilin, and his DNR government, police structures and militias, all moved in to take control, alongside the Russian military. In Kherson and Zaporizhzhia regions, on the other hand, new structures had to be set up from scratch.

One of Kiriyenko's first jobs was to find civilian officials from Russia to run the occupation authorities. The first new cadres arrived in June 2022, many of them from Kiriyenko's stable of smart young technocrats who had graduated from the Presidential Academy of National Economy and Public Administration (RANEPA), a training ground for Putinist officials. Vitaly Khotsenko was typical of this new generation of Russian officials. A graduate of RANEPA and a department head in the Ministry of Industry and Trade in Moscow, in June 2022 he was appointed as head of the regional government—or 'prime minister'—of the DNR.[38] Another RANEPA graduate, Vladislav Kuznetsov, deputy governor of Kurgan region, was appointed first deputy head of government in the LNR. In July, Anton Koltsov, another RANEPA alumnus and deputy head of the Vologda region, was appointed as head of government in Zaporizhzhia region. According to Vladimir Rogov, who described himself as a member of the Military-Civilian Administration of Zaporizhzhia, but was better known through his prolific Telegram channel, Koltsov's role would be to 'help us integrate into Russian realities and restart everything that we need to do according to Russian legislation and rules'.[39]

Officials from across Russia found a niche in the new territories. Artysh Sat, a former minister of health from the distant Republic of Tyva, 5,000 kilometres to the east, was now appointed minister of health in Zaporizhzhia region.[40] A few officials may have signed up for ideological reasons, but most saw it as a quick path to self-enrichment or career advancement. Officials could get plenty of perks and salaries two or three times higher than in Russia.[41] There were also opportunities for corruption. According to one source, officials in the annexed regions 'learn to take an excessively liberal approach' when spending budget funds. Another official told journalists that the occupied territories were a 'real school of corruption'. According to these officials, 'They have more money than they know what to do with—and no supervision. Pulling off schemes is easy, and there are locals willing to help.'[42]

GOVERNMENT

Some ambitious officials thought that a spell in the occupied territories would be an automatic ticket to promotion elsewhere. Deputy governors from Russia's regions often accepted positions in occupied Ukraine, hoping that a full governorship might be the next step. In just such a move, in April 2024 the deputy governor of Chelyabinsk region, Irina Gekht, was appointed head of Zaporizhzhia's occupation government. That calculation might also have motivated figures such as Alexander Kostomarov, who had served as a deputy governor in several of Russia's regions, and became chief of staff to Pushilin in 2022, with the job of managing all Moscow's local political initiatives, from the referendum in September 2022 to a series of fraudulent elections in 2023 and 2024.[43] But these moves did not always work out. Vitaly Khotsenko, who was head of the DNR government until March 2023, did get a plum governor's job in Omsk in return. Others were disappointed. Kostomarov left his post in the DNR in April 2024, but did not receive a governorship.[44]

Finding staff was still a challenge. Not everybody wanted to work in a war zone. In May 2022 Kiriyenko announced that Russian regions could 'adopt' towns and districts across the occupied territories (a practice called '*shefstvo*').[45] Moscow 'adopted' Donetsk and Luhansk, while St Petersburg 'adopted' Mariupol. By April 2023, at least fifty-six regions were providing assistance to the occupied regions.[46] In each case, regions were supposed to provide financial and humanitarian assistance, but also send personnel. Leningrad region was twinned with the depressed industrial town of Yenakieve in Donetsk region. In October 2023 Sergei Kharlashkin, deputy governor of Leningrad region, faced corruption charges after a complaint by the Russian Agricultural Bank, but the charges were dropped and he was dispatched to the DNR to oversee infrastructure projects.[47]

In the rush to get officials into posts, the authorities were willing to overlook past indiscretions. Donbas soon became known as a 'launderette' of reputations. Serving in the occupied territories became a potential path of redemption. Colonel Aleksei Katerinichev was a senior official in the Ministry of Emergency Situations who accompanied his boss, Yevgeny Zinichev, on a fatal trip to a remote waterfall, where Zinichev died in an accident. Katerinichev lost his position in the ministry, but resurfaced as first deputy head of the Kherson regional administration in July, only to die six weeks later in a Ukrainian artillery attack on 30 September 2022.⁴⁸ Former mayor of Krasnodar Andrei Alekseenko, whom we saw in Chapter 2 fleeing from Ukrainian forces when he was head of government in Kharkiv region, reappeared as head of the regional government in Kherson region. In December 2021, he had been questioned in a criminal case about accepting a bribe, so the transfer to the occupied territories was a useful distraction.⁴⁹ Meanwhile, the military commandant of Enerhodar in Zaporizhzhia region was reported to be a Russian official who had been sentenced to four years in prison for bribery in 2019.⁵⁰

While Kiriyenko retained oversight of the governance of what Russian officials called the 'new regions', the economic development of the occupied territories—including a mass reconstruction campaign centred on Mariupol—was largely the preserve of government agencies, overseen by the Russian deputy prime minister for construction and regional development, Marat Khusnullin. He was now in charge of a multibillion-dollar reconstruction programme across the occupied territories, including new transport infrastructure and housing. It was Khusnullin who accompanied Putin on a visit to Mariupol in March 2023, and it was Khusnullin who made a presentation to the Russian Security Council in April 2023, when officials convened to discuss the integration of the occupied regions into Russia.⁵¹

Khusnullin was a master of that aspect of the Russian political system that political scientists describe as 'patronalism'. This was 'a world of patrons and clients, patronage politics, and the dominance of informal understandings over formal rules'.⁵² Powerful officials built pyramids of patronage, incorporating political protégés, state officials, government agencies and private businesses. These hierarchical networks enabled senior officials to get things done outside the often-obstructive bureaucracy, but also provided opportunities for government bureaucrats to benefit personally from government office. Khusnullin had built a pyramid of power and influence in his native Tatarstan as a regional minister of construction, before a major promotion made him deputy mayor of Moscow, in charge of a huge construction budget, and later deputy prime minister, with a remit that covered all major state infrastructure projects in Russia.

Now he set about building a pyramid of agencies and businesses in the occupied territories. Khusnullin's ally, the minister of construction, housing and communal services, Irek Faizullin, led the team. It promoted its own people into local government: Yevgeny Solntsev, a former assistant to Faizullin, was appointed head of government in the DNR on 30 March 2023.[53] I explore this network in more detail in Chapter 6, but it elevated Khusnullin to be a key player in Russia's occupation regime. He led a working group in Moscow, in which all the security ministries were represented, meeting at least twice a week and sometimes every day in the early months. The group often travelled to the occupied regions, and the deputy minister of construction 'practically lives there', Khusnullin told his colleagues in the Security Council.[54]

Another group of civilians active on the ground came from Russia's ruling United Russia party and Russia's parliament, the State Duma. The Duma allocated certain figures to be 'curators' of each region. In Kherson region, the 'curator' from the Duma was Kiriyenko's protégé, Igor Kastyukevich. In the DNR, it was State Duma representative Dmitry Sablin, a native of Mariupol, who had close ties to the Russian military and had previously been linked to Russian 'Orthodox oligarch' Konstantin Malofeev.[55] According to Sablin, the United Russia party had ten volunteer centres in Mariupol in 2022, with volunteers from its youth wing, *Molodaya Gvardiya* (Young Guard), working alongside members of Sablin's own organisation, the *Boevoe bratstvo* (Fighting Brotherhood) veterans' association.[56] Many of these groups were interlinked: the Young Guard organisation was headed by Anton Demidov, who had previously played a role in Sablin's Fighting Brotherhood outfit.[57] Sablin also led a military contingent, a unit called 'BARS Kaskad', which offered a relatively risk-free military deployment for VIPs in a drone unit at some distance from the front line.[58] These volunteer operations disguised a much more influential role for Sablin, who was reported to have been a major player in occupied Mariupol.[59]

OCCUPATION

Understanding the role of figures such as Sablin was difficult because they operated away from the limelight in a more shadowy 'second world' of Russian politics. One way of conceptualising Russian politics was through the idea of the 'dual state', originally used by Ernst Fraenkel in a 1941 book to analyse the Nazi regime. Fraenkel identified two sides of the regime: a 'normative state', where a system of normal laws and rules applied; and a parallel 'prerogative state', where there was no rule of law and any measures—however violent or illegal—could be taken.[60] Richard Sakwa argued that in Russia a similar system was emerging, in which a constitutional state, in which there were formal processes, was contrasted with an 'administrative state', characterised by the 'shadowy and opaque structures of the administrative regime, populated by various factions and operating according to the practices of Byzantine court politics and mafia dons'.[61] As in the rest of Russia, the occupied territories were marked by this division between a formal political structure which followed constitutional norms and an informal system of power politics away from the public eye, where a very different set of rules were in place.

The formal structures of the state disguised a constantly shifting mix of figures trying to gain political kudos and financial gain. A bewildering array of businesses, criminal groups, private military companies and 'volunteer' battalions competed for influence, many of which seamlessly mixed ideology, warfare and self-enrichment. An important role was played by a network of Chechen groups, dubbed by one journalist as a 'Kherson clan'.[62] Chechen forces such as the Akhmat unit had fought in the military campaign, and Chechen head Ramzan Kadyrov sought a role in the reconstruction of Mariupol, as discussed in Chapter 6.[63]

Local politics under occupation

All these newcomers from Russia had to accommodate local political dynamics. Occupation does not completely restart local politics from scratch—it provides a second chance for all the existing disputes, grievances and political battles in each locality to be fought again—albeit in a more deadly way. From the beginning, Russia searched for local officials to work in the occupation structures. Many Ukrainians refused to cooperate with the Russians—even under threat of torture or kidnap—but a minority did collaborate. Of 112 senior officials across the four regions who were profiled in a project by Proekt media in 2022, fifty-nine were locals.[64] War and occupation offered a chance of social mobility as experienced and senior staff left the region or were forced out of their positions in favour of pliant proxies.[65] The result was the promotion of many people who had long been marginal in their communities and had little respect. A couple from Luhansk region, interviewed after they moved to government-controlled Ukraine in December 2023, told journalists that local services were in complete disarray. One complained that 'It's like anyone can get any position. Someone is a cleaner and now they're the head accountant.'[66] Similar reports were widespread. Locals who worked with the Russians could use their positions for self-enrichment or to continue long-standing feuds. The Russians also tried to find new faces. A competition called 'Leaders of the Revival' was set up to spot and promote new potential leaders from the occupied territories.[68]

In the DNR and LNR there was a struggle between the existing administrations and incoming officials from Russia. In both quasi-republics, local officials and parliamentarians had developed their own formal institutions and informal business structures since 2014, often closely entwined with Russia, above all with the FSB and GRU, and with their curators in the Presidential Administration in Moscow. There had always been some Russian citizens working in their governments and security services, but the Kremlin preferred not to advertise their presence and denied that they were there in an official capacity. After the war began, the number of Russian officials grew rapidly. In June 2022 Pushilin announced the appointment of Vitaly Khotsenko from Russia to head the government, and new ministers were brought in from Russia to take over the energy, health and education portfolios.

A similar process happened in the LNR. The head of the LNR, Leonid Pasechnik, was a wily political survivor, a former SBU officer who had a low profile but had won an internecine battle in 2017 to replace his rival, Igor Plotnitsky, as head of the republic.

Pasechnik had his own team, and local personnel still dominated the government, with only 20% of posts going to Russians in 2022, whereas in the DNR about 40% of government positions were occupied by incomers.[68] Local elites in the LNR were able to close ranks and consolidate their positions, precisely because they caused fewer worries for Moscow than in the other occupied territories. Still, even in the LNR there were signs of change. Some local officials were pushed out. Alexander Karikov, first deputy head of Krasnodar district in Luhansk, was detained in March 2023, charged with extorting bribes from businessmen.[69] In November 2023 mayor of Luhansk Manolis Pilavov was removed from office in murky circumstances.[70] Sergei Kozlov, a police officer who had headed a militia in the fighting of 2015, retained his role as head of the government but he had a new Russian deputy, Vladislav Kuznetsov, the former deputy governor of Kurgan region. Then in June 2024, Kozlov was himself replaced by another Russian deputy governor, Yegor Kovalchuk from Chelyabinsk.[71]

In Kherson and Zaporizhzhia the situation was different. Many Ukrainian specialists and officials had fled. Others refused to work with the Russians. Instead, the FSB relied on a coterie of Yanukovych-era officials transplanted back into the region and a network of local pro-Russian proxies. According to Ukrainian sources, the FSB had lined up figures from among Ukrainian exiles to staff the new administrations in the south. Volodymyr Lipandin, who had headed the Ministry of Internal Affairs in Cherkasy region before 2014, returned, tasked with running the local police. Former head of the SBU, Oleksandr Yakymenko, was drafted in to run a local security service, as discussed in the next chapter.[72] These were unannounced appointments, but they also needed a public face for the new administration. Hence the FSB cast around for likely local characters, appointing Vladimir Saldo in Kherson and Yevgeny Balitsky in Zaporizhzhia to positions as heads of the regions.

Vladimir Saldo had been mayor of Kherson in 2002–12 and a deputy in the Verkhovna Rada from the Party of Regions (POR). He ran again for mayor in 2020, but lost the election to the popular Kolykhaev. The subsequent arrest of Kolykhaev and the rise of

GOVERNMENT

Saldo to the post of regional governor under Russian rule was the ruthless outcome of this long-standing political rivalry. Saldo had a team of like-minded cronies around him, who had worked together long before the war. His ally Sergei Cherevko had helped Saldo set up the 'Salvation Committee for Peace and Order' to support the occupation in March 2022. Cherevko was later appointed deputy head of the Kherson government.

Saldo's business interests overlapped with those of Vitaly Bulyuk, who was appointed as first deputy head of the regional government with responsibility for finance and economics. Bulyuk was the ultimate survivor. In April 2022 he had written in social media that 'Kherson is Ukraine!', but a month later he was playing a key role in the occupation regime.[73] A long-time head of Kherson customs, he had his finger in every possible pie, with a strong interest in all types of trade through Skadovsk port, according to Ukrainian sources.[74] Other Saldo allies from his political party (the 'Volodymyr Saldo Bloc') also had posts in the occupation authorities. Igor Semenchev, for example, became deputy head of Kherson city administration. His son—also Igor Semenchev—was appointed as an official in the regional administration, in charge of housing and utilities. He was also reported to be in charge of the State Property Fund of Kherson region, which managed the transfer of businesses to new owners and re-registration in the Russian register.[75]

In Zaporizhzhia a small coterie of officials and businesspeople gathered around Yevgeny Balitsky, also a local businessman and politician, who ran the Melitopol brewery and a radio station in the 1990s, then took over a tractor parts factory, Avtogidroagregat, and entered politics as part of the Opposition Bloc.[76] He was elected to the national parliament, the Verkhovna Rada, in 2012 and in 2014, but failed to get re-elected in 2019. His political star was waning, and he also seems to have fallen out with Russia, having been placed under Russian sanctions in 2018 for unclear reasons. His family appeared to be as pro-Russian as possible. His elder son, Alexander, reportedly owned a French restaurant, the Bouquet Garni on October Revolution Avenue in Sevastopol, which enjoyed a 4.5 rating on Tripadvisor.[77] Balitsky also ran a local television station—which was soon pumping out Russian propaganda after the invasion. As we saw in Chapter 2, his associate, Galina Danilchenko, had been appointed as mayor of Melitopol, the administrative centre of Russian-occupied Zaporizhzhia region. Balitsky's patronage networks now attempted to consolidate their political and economic position in the new reality of occupation.

Elections

Into this toxic mix of collaboration, violence, corruption and careerism came the Kremlin's election fixers. Regional elections were held in the occupied territories on 10 September 2023, at the same time as polls were held in Russian regions. Presidential elections were held in March 2024, completing the political cycle in the occupied territories and consolidating Russia's political control. These elections were not a test of the democratic will—they were highly fraudulent and conducted under extreme pressure. But they served important political purposes. With elections to the regional and local councils, the political system would increasingly mimic that of Russia's own local governance structures. That meant a range of Russian governance mechanisms—budget transfers, government programmes—could be deployed. The polls were also a demonstration of Russian control: the ability to hold a vote, however flawed, was used by Russia to normalise its occupation, to convince residents that it was not intending to leave, and to show that it still had effective control inside the territories.

During 2023 there had been doubt about whether the regional polls could be held at all, as a Ukrainian counteroffensive gathered pace. With Ukrainian troops within 100 kilometres of Melitopol, officials at Russia's Central Election Commission (CEC) began to worry. But in a meeting with Putin on 3 July, chairperson of the CEC Ella Pamfilova announced that the elections would go ahead.[78] A vote duly took place on 8–10 September 2023 in the DNR, LNR, Zaporizhzhia and Kherson regions to regional and local councils. Even though the elections were completely managed, Moscow was not willing to risk direct elections for regional leaders—they would be elected indirectly by the regional councils.

GOVERNMENT

Indeed, voters would not get a chance to vote for any named candidates at all. Unlike most Russian regions, the elections would take place entirely through a party list system. Voters would only be able to put a cross next to a party, not an individual. The local authorities did not even publish all the names of the candidates in each party list, fearing for the 'physical security of candidates', according to the Central Electoral Commission. A Russian lawyer, Anton Rudakov, told the *Vedomosti* newspaper that publishing names risked their inclusion on a Ukrainian website that he claimed was 'actively used by people carrying out assassinations'.[79]

Despite the secrecy, journalists managed to publish an analysis of the candidates, and they provided a useful snapshot of political life in the occupied territories. Many of the candidates were local, but these were primarily people drafted in to make up the numbers for so-called opposition parties: over 80% of candidates for the Communist Party of the Russian Federation (KPRF) and the party A Just Russia—For Truth (SRZP) were local residents. Some of them were refugees from Kherson city, such as the director of Kherson port, Andrei Kharitonov, or the head of the Jubilee Concert Hall in Kherson, Yevgeny Maksimov. However, for the party that was bound to win the election, United Russia (ER), the number of local candidates was just 55%, with over 25% of those standing coming from Russia and 15% from Crimea.[80] While 54% of the SRZP's candidates were a group that Russian journalists rather patronisingly described as 'housewives, pensioners and the unemployed', only 3% of United Russia's candidates had that profile.[81] In short, anybody with a chance of actually winning a seat in a local council was handpicked by the authorities. Some 75% of United Russia's candidates were local officials or employees of state organisations.[82]

Finding local candidates was easier in Donetsk and Luhansk, where eight years of Russian control had encouraged a local elite to emerge. Here there was at least a semblance of competition: 600 people contested 100 seats in the regional Duma in the DNR and 336 in LNR. In Zaporizhzhia they could only find 220 candidates to run for office and just 191 in Kherson region. About 9,000 other candidates ran for lower-level council posts.[83] In Kherson and

Zaporizhzhia, however, many candidates came from Russia. Some of these were Russian government officials, including Oleg Nesterov who worked in the Russian Presidential Administration and whose sole claim to publicity prior to running for election was his inclusion in a US sanctions list for planning filtration mechanisms in Ukraine.[84] Another Presidential Administration official in the candidate list, Igor Deryugin, had previously served in the border guards, part of the FSB.[85]

Finding candidates was easier than getting people to vote. The same techniques from the referendum were used again: boosting the turnout through forced voting at workplaces and door-to-door visits. Instead of polling stations, the authorities introduced 'mobile voting stations', essentially a table set up in a village or on a street where everybody was persuaded to vote. To try to get even more ballots in, the authorities started voting nine days early in DNR and Zaporizhzhia region and seven days early in LNR and Kherson region.[86] The same pictures emerged of election officials being accompanied by soldiers knocking on people's doors to persuade them to vote. The authorities were desperate for at least a credible turnout, so they relaxed identity document requirements. In theory, only those with Russian passports could vote, but the authorities also permitted voting using Ukrainian passports and ID cards.[87] According to very unreliable official figures, turnout reached 76% in DNR, 73% in LNR, 68% in Zaporizhzhia region and 65% in Kherson region. The results for the different parties were predictable and evidently falsified. ER won most of the seats in each regional council, taking 75% of the votes in the LNR, with the other Kremlin-loyal parties—KPRF and SRZP and the Liberal Democratic Party (LDPR)—dividing up the remaining seats.[88] ER also took 75% of the votes cast and most of the thirty-six seats in the Kherson regional parliament, 83% in Zaporizhzhia region and 78% in the DNR.[89]

The results were not important. Elections play a quite different role under authoritarian regimes than in democratic systems. They are mechanisms to co-opt elites and wider society and to send a signal to the population that the current political status quo is both legitimate and permanent.[90] In that sense, the main point is the process, not the outcome, since it forces large numbers of officials, candidates and voters to participate in this legitimation exercise. In Russia, the electoral system was also a system of hierarchical power, reflecting the ability of the state to reach into the most remote villages and co-opt everybody, from village chiefs to school directors, to support the electoral process. The election was an opportunity for some local elites to show their loyalty to the new Russian authorities. One resident in Kherson region said that officials working for the Russians were particularly active in promoting the vote: 'that is how they try to justify their decision to work for Russia'.[91]

Organising elections requires an enormous number of personnel. Taking part was a potential crime of collaboration in Ukraine. In Kherson, after the Russians left, about twenty members of electoral commissions who had organised the referendum to join Russia were prosecuted and given the minimum prison sentence of five years.[92] Despite the potential consequences, in Luhansk region there were 5,260 people involved in organising the vote in territorial and precinct commissions, plus 336 candidates for the regional parliament and another 3,241 candidates for twenty-eight local councils. Add on election observers and other officials, and in this one occupied region Russia seems to have persuaded as many as 10,000 people to take part in the electoral process in various ways.[93]

The other important outcome of the polls was to demonstrate Russia's secure control over the territory in wartime. Ukraine had promised to disrupt the elections, and there were reports of isolated attacks against polling stations and meetings of local electoral commissions; but there was no major disruption to the voting. Yet the security situation did complicate the workings of these new bodies. In Zaporizhzhia and Kherson regions, the new regional assemblies initially had no buildings, no websites and no public meetings. In Zaporizhzhia, one local official told the Russian newspaper *Kommersant*: 'We meet wherever necessary. 40 absolutely pro-Russian people is a tasty target for the Ukrainians.'[94] The same situation reigned in Kherson, where the lack of accommodation was explained by the need 'to avoid it simply getting blown up', according to Igor Kastyukevich.⁹⁵ These threats were sharp reminders that sham elections could not wish away the ongoing fight for control of the territories.

The elections represented one more step in the process of introducing Russian political structures into the occupied territories. The regional councils now formally elected the governors of each region—Balitsky, Saldo, Pushilin and Pasechnik—who had all been 'acting' governors until the September votes. It was now possible to appoint 'Senators', representatives of the regions, to the Federation Council, the upper house of Russia's parliament. Each region sent two of these, one appointed by the head of the region and one by its regional parliament. There was hardly any pretence about making the senator role representative of local society. These positions appear to have been handed out to allies and cronies of local or federal officials.

In Kherson, the new regional council dispatched Kastyukevich as senator, while Saldo appointed Konstantin Basyuk, a businessman and former spy, who had previously been building a terminal at Khabarovsk airport before turning up in Kherson as an advisor to Saldo. In Zaporizhzhia, the two senators were Dmitry Rogozin, a well-known nationalist who had recently been running the Russian space agency, Roscosmos, and Dmitry Vorona, a rare Ukrainian in the list, who had been a deputy interior minister of Ukraine under President Yanukovych. Pushilin dispatched his own advisor, Aleksandr Voloshin, a Belarusian and Russian businessman. The other senator was Nataliya Nikonorova, a Ukrainian graduate of Kyiv University, who had been the DNR's 'foreign minister' before it was annexed. From the LNR, Olga Bas, a judge and a graduate of Kharkiv's Law Institute, was sent to Moscow. The final appointment was Darya Lantratova, who had no obvious connection to Ukraine, but was a Russian official working in the Russian Presidential Administration. Even Russia's leading business newspaper, *Kommersant*, diplomatically noted that 'the reasons for [...] Pasechnik to give the powers of a Senator to official of the Presidential Administration Darya Lantratova are still not clear'.⁹⁶

The success of the September elections in the occupied territories for Russia opened the way for presidential elections in March

2024, in which Vladimir Putin was running for his fifth term in office. The Russian authorities did not even pretend that this was a competitive poll; the vote was more akin to a public acclamation of the leader than a democratic election, but it also had important symbolic meaning in the occupied territories. Russian CEC member Andrei Shutov called it a 'historical moment', since presidential elections would be the 'absolute legitimation of the incorporation of the new subjects into the Russian Federation'.[97]

The same playbook was deployed as in the previous elections. Again, there would be additional time to vote, to allow electoral officials to visit people at home. There was more secrecy: information about electoral districts and members of electoral commissions would be classified. Photographs on social media again showed people voting under the careful gaze of a Russian soldier, hardly likely to encourage people to exercise their democratic choice. The plan, according to deputy head of the CEC, Nikolai Bulaev, was to ensure that 'the electoral campaign can be carried out successfully, that voters can vote securely, and the members of commissions can work safely at this time'.[98]

Nobody really knew how many voters were in the occupied territories, so the authorities had free rein to make things up. According to Russia's CEC there were 4.56 million voters in the occupied territories apart from Crimea, including 1.97 million in the DNR, 1.65 million in the LNR, 470,000 in Zaporizhzhia region and 468,000 in Kherson region.[99] This seemed a huge overreach—most other estimates suggested that the remaining population in the occupied territories outside Crimea was not much more than 3 million people. One expert suggested that there were no more than 2.5 million potential voters.[100] The election allowed people to vote in their nearest polling station, but the figures were also contorted by the huge military presence in the occupied territories. Soldiers could be added to the electoral lists wherever they were deployed—construction workers and other migrants could also be included, making it difficult to understand who exactly voted and where. This was the point, of course; to give the impression of a mass turnout and support for Putin but in such a way that nobody could be quite sure of where and when the electoral fraud had taken place.

Given this hugely flawed set-up, the results were not a surprise, but they were even more divorced from reality than across the rest of Russia. In Russia overall, Putin received an unlikely 88% of the vote. But in the DNR even this figure was surpassed, with a record 95% voting for Putin in a high turnout. The LNR was not far behind at 94%, and Zaporizhzhia recorded a figure of just under 93%. The lowest result was 88% in Kherson region, although even that matched the national vote.[101] The claimed turnout was extremely unlikely given the wartime conditions and population outflows, but an overwhelming vote here was politically vital for Putin. Media reports suggested that many people had not voted, although it was impossible to understand the scale of resistance because nobody wanted to discuss this topic openly. One local in Luhansk region told journalists that 'People don't talk about such topics, except perhaps with subtle hints, because they are afraid that people will turn them in to the authorities.'[102] Silence was critical to survival under occupation.

The Ukrainian authorities warned that taking part in the elections could be a crime, but it was not clear what would happen if you claimed to have voted or acted under duress. Ombudsman Dmytro Lubinets argued that anybody who helped to organise the vote would face prosecution under Article 111–1 of the Ukrainian Criminal Code on collaboration (discussed in more detail in Chapter 7), but Ukrainian citizens would not be prosecuted just for taking part. Lubinets pointed out that 'Russia's politics is cruel and totalitarian' and '"voting" is conducted at the barrel of a gun', and that 'taking part in such elections is a matter of survival in the TOT [Temporarily Occupied Territories]'.[103] The ombudsman's office often tried to maintain this pragmatic view of life in the occupied territory, but this nuanced position was not shared by everybody in Kyiv. Oleg Havrysh, chief consultant to the chief of staff of the Ukrainian presidential office, told reporters that anybody who took part in the elections—whether organising them or simply voting—was guilty of collaborationism: 'As soon as the territories are deoccupied, the facts will be established and people will be in prison.'[104] He did go on to say that where there was a threat to life the situation might be different, but this left most people without a clear understanding of what the consequences might be for having been forced to take part in the vote.

Administrative occupation

'You can't just take a standard document and replace, roughly speaking, the word "Saratov" with "Kherson"', Kastyukevich explained to the press in October 2023: 'Here everything is connected to the special features of the operational situation in the zone of the special operation.'[105] Everything was different because Russia was occupying the territory of a foreign state, but Russia's state machine was intent on introducing Russian regulations, laws and standards into the occupied territories. Since the referendums in September 2022, this bureaucratic occupation had been proceeding apace, often unnoticed by the outside world. Hundreds of laws and regulations were scrutinised to adapt them to include the newly occupied regions. By December 2023, according to Valentina Matvienko, speaker of the Federation Council, fifty-six federal laws had been adopted to enable the territories' integration into the Russian Federation. She claimed that the legal integration process at the federal level had been 'largely completed'.[106] The Russian government announced a transitional period until 1 January 2026 to complete the transition of the annexed regions to the full application of all Russian laws and regulations.[107] This was a huge bureaucratic endeavour that affected every part of the Russian government. For the most part, the Russian system was remarkably effective at imposing its bureaucracy by force on the population of the occupied territories.

As with any bureaucracy, the Russian state began with identity documents. During 2023 Russia's Federal Migration Service set up branches across the occupied territories to process applications for Russian passports. According to the agreements that incorporated the occupied territories into the Russian Federation, 'citizens of Ukraine, the LNR and DNR, and also people without citizenship, continuously living on these territories, are recognised as citizens of the Russian Federation'. As such, they were expected to apply for the identity documents of the Russian Federation, i.e. a Russian passport. Some pro-Russian residents applied voluntarily, but most residents did so because it became increasingly difficult to survive without one.

Under international law it is illegal to force people 'to swear allegiance to the hostile power', but that is exactly what Russia was demanding from its new citizens. The goal was not to win over hearts and minds of Ukrainians under Russian rule, but to erase any remnants of their legal Ukrainian identity. To this end, Ukrainian citizens were forced to accept a Russian passport, a process which in principle involved swearing an oath of loyalty:

> I (full name), voluntarily and knowingly accepting the citizenship of Russia, swear to observe the constitution and legislation of Russia, the rights and freedoms of its citizens, fulfil the duties of a citizen of Russia for the benefit of the state and society, protect the freedom and independence of Russia, be loyal to Russia, respect its culture, history and traditions.

Some accepted the passports willingly, but they were a minority. Most only did so for functional reasons. Without a passport, it became difficult to access any welfare payments, to open a bank account, or in some cases access public health services. Many people initially resisted, assuming that they would be able to continue accessing services with Ukrainian identity documents, or because they hoped the occupation would be short-lived. But as months of occupation turned into years, it became hard to survive without a Russian passport. This became literally true when the occupation authorities began limiting access to medical services. On 10 August 2023, the local head of the village of Lazurne in Kherson region, Alexander Dudka, threatened residents without Russian passports that they would not be provided with any free medicines, such as insulin, or any access to humanitarian assistance. Dudka called people who had refused to apply for Russian passports *zhduny* ('the waiting ones') and threatened them with expulsion to Ukrainian-controlled territory if they refused to send their children to Russian-controlled schools: 'If you don't like the laws of the Russian Federation, we request you to gather your things and get ready to leave.'[108]

GOVERNMENT

These measures were almost certainly illegal under international law. Article 55 of the Geneva Convention (IV) sets out the duty of the occupying power to ensure medical supplies for the population. But from 1 January 2024 medical care was only available to those with Russian health insurance, which in turn was only available to Russian citizens.[109] Some local doctors turned a blind eye, but a report by Physicians for Human Rights detailed at least ten cases where medical assistance was refused because people only had Ukrainian passports.[110] In Enerhodar, residents were reportedly warned that they would not be able to access medicines or have an ambulance call-out if they lacked a Russian passport. Similar reports came from other areas, and health workers were also forced to apply for Russian passports.[111]

The procedure to receive a Russian passport was simplified and passports were supposed to be issued in around ten days. The volume of applications meant that there were often queues at passport offices as people tried to get these otherwise unwanted identity cards.[112] More than 100 offices were opened in the occupied territories to deal with applications and distribute passports. Migration officials also travelled around the country, delivering passports to those who were not able to travel.[113] As a result, at the end of 2023, according to the Russian interior ministry, almost 90% of the remaining population in the four annexed regions—over 3 million people—had been issued with Russian passports. Figures were sometimes contradictory, but by April 2024 President Putin claimed that more than 3.2 million residents of Donetsk, Luhansk, Kherson and Zaporizhzhia regions had received Russian passports.[114] In March 2024 Ukraine's human rights ombudsman, Dmytro Lubinets, said that 'almost 100% ... of the whole population who still live on temporary occupied territories of Ukraine' had been given Russian passports.[115] But there were certainly still holdouts. In April 2024 the authorities extended the deadline to obtain Russian passports from 1 July 2024 until 1 December 2024, presumably because there were still many without Russian identity documents. Those who did not obtain Russian passports would then be considered foreign citizens and be liable to be deported.[116]

All sorts of other documents also had to be changed. The Russians required Ukrainians to apply for new driving licences and new registration documents for their cars. As a concession, drivers could change their licence until 1 January 2026 without having to retake a test.[117] Every moment of life—birth, marriage and death—would now be registered according to Russian rules and regulations. Businesses and property would also require compliance with Russian laws and corporate registries, as part of a huge campaign of expropriation and nationalisation, discussed in more detail in Chapter 6. To help with the paperwork, Russia set up a network of 'Multifunctional Centres' (MFCs)—the one-stop shop usually known simply as 'My Documents' in Russia, where Russians register births and deaths, and get any other government documents they require. By December 2023 there were sixty-eight MFC offices in Kherson region alone, including in small towns and villages.[118] The MFC network both facilitated the imposition of Russian regulatory life on Ukrainian citizens and was also another physical manifestation of the reach of the Russian state into every corner of the occupied territories.

International law on occupation demands that the occupying power change as little as possible in the legal and administrative sphere. Russia, by contrast, was intent on changing everything. Every aspect of legal and administrative life changed under occupation. Everything from Russian environmental regulations to the criminal justice system would be transformed. There was nothing temporary about Russia's intentions. They were intent on full assimilation of the territories and their residents into everything Russian. The bureaucratic occupation was less spectacular and less deadly than the Russian military campaign. But in the long term it was likely to prove as effective in consolidating Russian power in the occupied territories. The everyday interaction with the Russian state, the acceptance of Russian passports, the forced compliance with business and economic regulations—all these developments forced people to adapt to the occupation and in many cases accommodate themselves to the new reality.

Justice and the courts

The Geneva Convention could hardly be clearer about criminal justice under occupation: Article 64 states that:

/ The penal laws of the occupied territory shall remain in force, with the exception that they may be repealed or suspended by the Occupying Power in cases where they constitute a threat to its security or an obstacle to the application of the present Convention. Subject to the latter consideration and to the necessity for ensuring the effective administration of justice, the tribunals of the occupied territory shall continue to function in respect of all offences covered by the said laws.

Moreover, according to Article 54 of the Geneva Convention, the occupying power 'may not alter the status of public officials or judges in the occupied territories'.[119] In other words, Ukrainian courts should continue to function, and Ukrainian laws remain in force, even under Russian occupation. Instead, Russia rapidly introduced its own laws and its own courts, and completely transformed the legal and justice system in its own image.

The four Federal Constitutional Laws on the accession of the DNR, LNR, Kherson and Zaporizhzhia regions to the Russian Federation, passed in early October 2022, clearly set out the role of Russian laws and institutions in the new federal subjects. Article 9 of each law also set out the principles by which a new prosecutor's office would be established, and Article 10 noted that a full range of Russian courts would be introduced, and the Russian Criminal Code would be adopted.

This broad position was followed by a series of legislative acts. Four new laws adopted in April 2023 provided more details of the new court system, mandating the establishment of 100 courts across the four regions, including regional courts, arbitration courts and courts at district and city level.[120] An important legal step was the adoption of a law on 31 July 2023 which asserted that the Russian Criminal Code now applied in the new regions, but also maintained that all existing sentences and prosecutions under the previous system still had validity under Russian rule. If a sentence would have been lighter under Russian regulations, then prisoners were permitted to appeal—the principle of the legal transition was that those sentenced would not be worse off under Russian law. Article 2.2 of the new law described a major exception to this rule of continuity, declaring that any act considered criminal under either Ukrainian or Russian law would not be considered a criminal act if it were carried out 'in the defence of the interests of the Russian Federation, the Donetsk People's Republic and the Lugansk People's Republic'.[121] The legal provision created a vast state of exception in the Russian political and legal space, an even more extreme erosion of the rule of law than in the rest of Russia.

A plenum of the Russian Supreme Court confirmed that 100 courts would officially begin operating in the four regions from 21 September 2023, including 42 new courts in DNR, 35 in LNR, 8 in Zaporizhzhia and 16 in Kherson.[122] In reality, some of these courts existed on paper only—the territories over which they claimed jurisdiction remained under Ukrainian government control. Even in those courts that did exist, the authorities struggled to find sufficient judges and court employees to staff the system, although they had allowed a transition period until September 2024 to establish a fully functional court system in the occupied territories.[123] In April 2023 the Russian authorities began selecting judges for the new courts. Although potential judges were proposed by judicial qualification bodies, a presidential commission, which included representatives from the FSB and the Presidential Administration, made the final decision on who should be appointed by President Putin.[124] Political loyalty was always more important than competence.

In theory, existing judges had priority in the selection procedures, but there was a lack of local candidates in many areas. Russia had to bring in judges from Russia or from Crimea to fill the quotas, with only two of Kherson's fifty-one judges being willing to work under the Russians: the rest were incomers from Russia or Crimea.[125] A big contingent came from Crimea, including the chair of Kherson's regional court, Alexander Tsvetkov, and his deputy, Viktor Mozheliansky, well known in Crimea for his hawkish, pro-Russian views.[126] In district courts in Kherson, many judges only had limited experience, having worked as court assistants or even outside the judiciary completely. Many of the appointments were judges from the Russian provinces, who had failed to get promoted at home. Working in the occupied territories offered judges potential for early promotion and more money.[127]

GOVERNMENT

In the Zaporizhzhia region, only 10 out of 75 judges in mid-2024 were locals.[128] The region faced what the Russians call a *desant*—literally a landing of soldiers from a boat or a plane, but in everyday usage meaning a group of civilian officials brought in en masse to sort out a problematic region. In Zaporizhzhia the *desant* came from Nizhny Novgorod. Fully half of all judges in the regional court were from Nizhny Novgorod or neighbouring regions. In Melitopol city court, 6 out of 14 judges were from Nizhny Novgorod.[129] In the DNR, a team arrived from Saratov, following the appointment of Saratov judge Nikolai Podkopaev as chair of the Supreme Court. The acting chair, Yury Sirovatko, a local judge, did not take kindly to being replaced: Sirovatko reportedly refused to allow Podkopaev to take over his office for several weeks.[130] Podkopaev's appointment was followed by an influx of other judges from his region: half of the judges in the Ilich district court in Mariupol were also from Saratov.[131] Despite these new arrivals, most DNR judges were still locals: only 69 out of 194 judges in the DNR were from Russia or Crimea.[132] In the LNR, there were only 20 incomers among the 147 judges, and a local judge, Svetlana Trifanova, continued as chair of the Supreme Court.[133]

Even when the courts began operating, they were often barely functional. Judges in Mariupol were working in a half-destroyed building and there was a huge backlog of cases—it took months just to make applications to the court. There was a shortage of lawyers, and most did not want to take on any controversial cases. Anna, a resident who had lost her apartment and was appealing to the court after she was refused compensation, told journalists in 2023 that lawyers refused to take on property cases: 'They are afraid of losing their licence.'[134] In other areas, the courts were not included in the Russia-wide system of electronic courts nor did they have their own websites.[135] There was no public list of trials, hearings or judgments. However, the lack of judges and court officials did not prevent the courts from illegal show trials of prisoners of war, several of which took place in the DNR.[136]

Russia planned a new network of prisons in the occupied territories, clearly expecting a rise in the numbers incarcerated. According to a Russian government document seen by the

Associated Press, Russia planned to build twenty-five new prison colonies and open six other detention centres by 2026 in the occupied territories.[137] As discussed in the next chapter, many Ukrainian political prisoners detained by the Russians had been transported to prisons in Crimea or other parts of Russia. But Russia also took control of eleven prisons in Mykolaiv, Kherson, Zaporizhzhia and Donetsk regions, where 3,100 prisoners were held. The Ukrainian authorities had failed to evacuate these prisoners, and they came under Russian control. Prisoners reported that Russian guards severely maltreated them. They faced frequent beatings and in some cases torture—for talking back, for getting up too slowly, for not accepting a Russian passport, for refusing to vote in the referendum and so forth. 'They beat us for everything and for nothing', one inmate later told investigators.[138]

When Russian forces retreated from Kherson, they took many of these prisoners with them to Russia, in violation of international law which forbids the forced transfer of the population. Around 2,000 prisoners from Kherson ended up in the Russian prison system, although there appears to have been no official documentation detailing their transfer.[139] Many appear to have been badly treated, but the Russians did release prisoners at the end of their allotted sentences. Some took up Russian passports, nervous that returning home might lead to further punishment or mobilisation into the Ukrainian armed forces.[140] Others were transported to the Russian-Georgian border for deportation, where it often took a long time to gain permission to cross the border if they did not have valid passports.[141]

Russia also introduced a full array of prosecuting and investigatory bodies into occupied Ukraine. Russia's Investigative Committee (SK) set up special departments in each of the occupied territories—above all, according to lawyers, to maintain their institutional weight against other security and justice agencies in Moscow. The different agencies in Moscow's security bloc were in an almost constant internecine battle for influence.[142] In September 2023 four new prosecutors were appointed for the four regions, three of them from Russia. In the LNR, Gleb Mikhailov took up the post, having been deputy prosecutor in Dagestan and having also worked in Chechnya. In Zaporizhzhia, Kirill Osipchuk, previously first deputy prosecutor of Rostov region, was appointed. In Kherson, Andrei Petrov took the post. He was also a deputy prosecutor, this time from Kirov region, but also with work experience in Chechnya.[143] The experience of these officials in Chechnya was not a coincidence. The brutal Chechen counterinsurgency had been the training ground for many military and security officials who now found themselves running the occupation regime.

Conclusion: The politics of occupation

The occupation was not an unexpected outcome of Russia's invasion, but there was little evidence of effective forward planning for the administration of an occupation regime. It was one thing to take control of territory militarily, but ensuring a sustainable and viable political regime required civilian institutions and an approach to governance that extended beyond security.

Russia used fraudulent elections to produce a phoney legitimacy that was aimed as much at Russians at home and a few gullible foreigners as it was at people living in the occupied areas. Moscow used the 2022 referendums to give legal cover to its forced annexation of the regions and to provide it with the thinnest layer of legitimacy for the outside world. As we will see in Chapter 5, it developed an extensive propaganda operation to justify its annexation, both to a Russian domestic audience and to society in the occupied regions. Russia's political technologists were convinced that they could manipulate even citizens of a foreign country into believing their strategic narratives, given the right resources. Following the referendums, Moscow introduced Russian laws, regulations and institutions to integrate the territories fully into the Russian administrative and bureaucratic system, a process that was highly effective at forcing compliance on the population.

Effective co-optation was critical to the occupation regime. Although only a small minority agreed to cooperate actively with Russian governance structures, the Russian occupation regime was grafted onto pre-existing political networks. Russia was able to co-opt some local elites to front its occupation and it built a system of governance staffed at lower levels by local Ukrainians. Moscow was able to find thousands of local officials to run elections, provide basic state services and to maintain infrastructure. Without this minimal cooperation, Russia's occupation would have faced much more serious challenges. Russian officials filled more senior posts in the occupation administrations and the presence of these officials accelerated the process of assimilation and integration, just as Russia intended.

By 2024, the four occupied territories had regional parliaments, town and district heads and councils, regional administrations, governors and governments, and their own representatives in the Federation Council in Moscow. They were becoming outwardly indistinguishable from other Russian provinces. This was a remarkable demonstration of will by the Russian state, which had imposed its administration on the occupied territories and built what appeared to be a relatively stable system of authoritarian governance. But behind this political and administrative system, it was clear that the system relied heavily on coercion. The administrative system was necessary to build a sustainable system of governance in the occupied territories, but without the Russian military and security apparatus behind it, the whole occupation regime would have collapsed overnight.

4

VIOLENCE

Despite the rapid imposition of a civilian and administrative system of governance in the occupied territories, it was Russia's military and security services that designed, planned and managed the occupation regime. The most important actor was the Federal Security Service (FSB)—the successor to the Soviet-era KGB—which had extensive experience of working in insurgencies and armed conflicts, including in previous wars in Chechnya and Ukraine. It worked alongside the Russian military, which had fought counter-insurgencies at home and abroad, as had many of the parastate mercenary groups that accompanied it, such as the Wagner Group. Russian military intelligence (formally the Main Directorate of the General Staff [GU], but usually known by its old acronym, GRU) had a ruthless reputation, including a hit squad that had launched assassinations across Europe. The National Guard (Rosgvardiya) had been launched recklessly into the fight for Kyiv and retreated with huge losses. But in the occupation its skills were in demand: crushing dissent, combatting political opponents, saboteurs and rebel groups. Alongside the formal security structures there was also a string of militias, often with unclear chains of command. Chechen forces, although formalised in Rosgvardiya units such as the 141st Special Motorized Regiment, demonstrated a personal loyalty to Chechen head Ramzan Kadyrov. Military units from the

DNR and LNR were subordinate to the Russian military but often showed poor discipline.

All these forces had emerged in a Russian military-security culture that emphasised extreme violence, a disregard for legal rules and a complete lack of accountability. This security complex could trace its roots back to the Soviet state, to the terror of Stalinist rule, even to the Russian civil war, but its modern-day laboratories were the wars in Afghanistan, Chechnya and Syria, where Russian forces developed a set of brutal but effective techniques for controlling hostile populations. At times the violence appeared random and sadistic, but for the most part it was deployed as an integral part of the occupation machine, which used detention and violence to instil fear in the population, to neutralise opposition and to force people to collaborate. In response, Ukraine mounted its own resistance campaign in the occupation territories through an underground network of sympathisers and intelligence networks. They carried out assassinations of Russian military, civilian officials and Ukrainians accused of collaboration. Contrary to Russia's propaganda, the occupied territories became a zone of violence and terror.

Russia's security forces in occupied territories

The FSB was already working in Ukraine long before the invasion. Although the FSB was primarily a domestic security service, focused on counter-intelligence, internal political opposition and the threat of terrorism, its Fifth Service had retained responsibility for the former Soviet republics, the countries Russians sometimes dismissively called the 'Near Abroad'. Within the Fifth Service, the Department for Operational Information (DOI) cultivated networks in Ukraine through the usual intelligence techniques: bribery, flattery and blackmail. Ukraine was such an important target that it had its own section, the Ninth Directorate. In 2021 the DOI began ramping up its Ukrainian operations, expanding its recruitment and resources. They were tasked with developing networks of potential collaborators, including possible leaders and members of occupation administrations. They were also reported to be drawing up lists of people whom locals considered authoritative figures—either to turn them into collaborators or to 'neutralise' them, in the preferred euphemism of Russian security officials.¹

FSB officers also commissioned public opinion surveys on attitudes to Russia and to a possible war. These polls appear to have offered a relatively accurate snapshot of Ukrainian society, highlighting vulnerabilities, particularly in the south and east, that could work to Russia's advantage. For example, according to a report based on these polls, around half of respondents in the south and east indicated that in the event of war they would try to 'adapt and survive' rather than fight, indicating that Russia might be able to win over part of the population under an occupation regime.²

The FSB was later accused of misreading Ukrainian society and underestimating their willingness to fight. But it is more likely that senior officials—including Putin—interpreted polls in ways that fitted their pre-existing prejudices. It does seem probable that the FSB had claimed an extensive network of pro-Russian agents who never materialised. The apparent failure of the FSB to prepare for the invasion led to reports of purges in the agency after Russia's military disasters in the first weeks of the war. In early May 2022 two Russian spy-watchers, Andrei Soldatov and Irina Borogan, claimed that Sergei Beseda, head of the Fifth Service, was reported to be under house arrest and that the FSB was no longer the lead intelligence agency on Ukraine. Military intelligence, the GRU, was in the ascendancy. Its Ukraine operations were headed by Vladimir Alekseev, first deputy head of the GRU, a figure reportedly described by fellow officers as 'brutal and self-confident to the point of recklessness'.³ When the Ukrainians negotiated their surrender in Mariupol in early May 2022, it was Alekseev who played a key role in the talks.⁴

Talk of Sergei Beseda's demise and a degraded role for the FSB turned out to be premature. In October 2023, when head of Ukraine's military intelligence, Kyrylo Budanov, was asked to name the most dangerous generals for Ukraine, he picked out Sergei Beseda as 'a very problematic person', who 'did a lot of harm to Ukraine'; according to Budanov, he had returned to his position after a short suspension.⁵ Nevertheless, according to media reports, he finally retired as head of the Fifth Service in June 2024. The FSB remained central to the occupation regime, running a huge operation to track down potential opponents in a manner reminiscent of the post-war Stalinist operations in Eastern Europe. Those operations included a counterinsurgency campaign in western Ukraine in 1944–49 against Ukrainian nationalists. According to Soldatov, the Soviet 'pacification of Western Ukraine was an examplar' that is 'still taught at the academy of the secret service for how to pacify people when they are hostile'.⁶ Once the military was in control of Ukrainian territory, the role of the DOI was augmented by FSB officers who worked alongside the military in the Department of Military Counter-Intelligence (DVKR), one of the FSB's largest departments. The DVKR was responsible for overseeing the huge operation known as filtration, discussed below, which was designed to weed out any potential resistance and to recruit informers.⁷

While the FSB was in charge of overall security and the massive filtration exercise, they initially brought in some pro-Russian Ukrainians to run part of the security operation. Ukrainian security officials had local knowledge and could recruit more easily from among the existing Ukrainian security services. According to Ukrainian investigative journalists at the news website Babel, two key local figures returned from exile in Russia: Volodymyr Lipandin, who had headed the Ministry of Internal Affairs in Cherkasy region before 2014 and was now tasked with running the local police in Kherson, and former head of the SBU, Oleksandr Yakymenko, who was drafted in to set up and run a local security service in Kherson. Yakymenko's operation was alleged to be particularly brutal. He set up a State Security Service (known locally by the Russian acronym GSB) which set about targeting pro-Ukrainian forces, while also allegedly running a lucrative sideline in extortion and kidnap for ransom.⁸ Yakymenko had all the qualifications necessary for the job—he had run the SBU under President Yanukovych, before fleeing with him during the 2014 revolution. Yakymenko gathered old cronies and some local collaborators— including the former head of counter-intelligence for Kherson region—to build a 100-strong security apparatus.⁹

VIOLENCE

Former Ukrainian citizens also staffed the security apparatus in the DNR and LNR. Their militias and security agencies were particularly active in newly occupied regions in Donetsk and Luhansk regions. Although formally independent, two military corps in the LNR and DNR were reported to be under the de facto control of the 8th Combined Arms Army of Russia's Southern Military District. In December 2022 they were officially absorbed into the Russian military after the Russian annexation of the DNR and LNR. They were short of personnel and often poorly equipped. But analysts suggested that they were often more ideologically motivated than Russian forces, having been fighting the Ukrainian military since 2014.[10] Reports suggest that the DNR and LNR militias were sometimes more violent and more ill-disciplined than regular Russian forces. Sergei Khlan, a former parliamentarian from the south, claimed that while the FSB and the military were all involved in torture, 'the cruellest were those mobilized from the LNR and DNR'.[11] Anna Shostak-Kuchmyak, the head of the village of Vysokopole, later recounted how her village was occupied on 13 March 2022: 'DNR people arrived. These were not professional soldiers, they looked quite miserable.' Some were wearing trainers, few had helmets. They checked her Ukrainian passport. One said, 'I have exactly the same passport, I am exactly the same Ukrainian [as you]. We are all from Donbas, and we, mother, have come to have our revenge.'[12] The DNR militias were a reminder that for some at least, this war was not only a Russian invasion, but was viewed as an ongoing civil war within the Ukrainian polity. This was not a popular term in Ukraine, where the war was rightly seen as primarily the responsibility of Russia. But since 2014, Ukrainians had been fighting on both sides of the front line for very different visions of the future of these territories.[13]

These DNR and LNR militias were often involved in illegal detentions. In Lyman, in Donetsk region, Oleg Rogov, a local policeman-turned-lawyer, was detained one evening when a jeep drew up outside his house, armed men got out and rushed into his yard. They released a burst of machine-gun fire at his dog, Jesse, before grabbing Oleg, pulling a white sack over his head and pushing him into the back of the car. They were from the LNR militia and interrogated him in the local commandant's headquarters, trying to get him to confess to acting as a 'spotter' for the Ukrainian military, while beating him with a rifle butt. They claimed his neighbour had informed on him.[14] When he refused to admit any guilt, they bundled him back into the car and took him out to a Russian military position on the front line and ordered him to march forward into what they said was a minefield. At this point, Oleg had a stroke of luck. A Russian officer came by just in time. When the LNR militia admitted they had no proof that Oleg was a spotter, the officer ordered them to release him. The next day Russian forces left Lyman altogether, and Oleg—and his dog Jesse—survived.[15]

This is not to suggest that the Russian military was not involved in such detentions and abuses. The entire military-security system was built on systemic torture and violence, including numerous cases of extra-judicial killings in which regular Russian forces participated. But Ukrainians did report very different experiences of occupation by different Russian units and their proxies, and there were numerous reports that the DNR and LNR militias were among the most aggressive and abusive.

In 2023 the DNR and LNR militaries were absorbed formally into the Russian chain of command. Russian law enforcement and security services began introducing territorial divisions in each region. They also dissolved the GSB and other ad hoc security structures set up in Kherson. By 1 June 2023, the General Prosecutor's Office, the Interior Ministry and the Investigative Committee had all established their own territorial units to mimic structures in the rest of Russia.[16] Policing spread across the territories—despite reports of a serious shortfall in officers. The FSB set up departments in each of the four territories and a military unit in Donetsk city.[17]

The military, too, had begun to formalise its presence. The occupied territories became part of the Russian Southern Military District, with its headquarters in Rostov. Formal units were set up in the territories, along with training grounds in Luhansk and Donetsk regions. In each territory there was now a Russian military commissariat, responsible for recruitment into the Russian military. The main role of the military was fighting on the front line, but the Russian military police did fulfil a policing role including manning checkpoints and patrols. The Russian Ministry of Defence also took over military establishments that had previously been run by the DNR and LNR authorities, such as the Starobilsk Cossack Cadet Corps. They also set up new colleges, such as a branch of the St Petersburg Nakhimov Naval School, which opened in Mariupol.[18]

Finally, the Russian National Guard also institutionalised their presence, setting up units in each region and two military units in Donetsk region, reportedly also involved in filtration activities.[19] And there was a scattering of so-called 'volunteer battalions', usually set up by local administrations, such as a V. F. Margelov volunteer battalion in Kherson region, named after a Soviet war hero, which was actively recruiting locally and in Russia; and a Sudoplatov Battalion in Melitopol, named after a Stalinist assassin.[20] It was difficult to know how functional these groups were in military terms, but they served a propaganda purpose, to supposedly show local involvement in the war effort.

The lists

When Russian forces killed civilians as they retreated from Bucha in March 2022, they appear to have targeted people almost randomly. Bodies lay strewn along the highway. There was more method in the brutal violence of the southern occupation, where the arrests, detentions and killings were aimed primarily at potential opponents of the occupation, although in practice almost anybody could fall foul of Russian forces. It was easy to get detained—an unwise word, a dispute with a soldier, any kind of pro-Ukrainian phrase or gesture, all could get you sent '*na podval*' ('to the basement'), detained in one of hundreds of makeshift Russian detention centres hurriedly set up across the occupied territories.

The FSB had lists of potential enemies—local politicians, pro-Ukrainian activists and military veterans—that it drew up before the occupation. After the invasion, the FSB seized personnel files from the offices of Ukrainian military and intelligence agencies, augmented by active intelligence gleaned from denunciations by collaborators or beaten out of detainees through torture.[21] In some cases, pro-Russian Ukrainian officials were alleged to have passed data to the Russians from the intelligence services or from Ukrainian military commissariats, which held lists of veterans and serving personnel. According to Kherson mayor Ihor Kolykhaev, a huge amount of data was released from the Kherson branch of the Ukrainian intelligence service, the SBU. The Russians received detailed dossiers on numerous officials and activists, detailing everything 'from their wife's family tree to the name of their favourite dog', according to Kolykhaev.[22] The practice of the Ukrainian SBU of gathering extensive information on local political figures, journalists and activists proved to be a serious liability when the Russians seized their files.

The FSB assumed that the Ukrainians would mount an armed resistance behind the lines, as indeed did happen, so the most important list comprised people who had been in the armed forces, in particular those who had fought in what Ukraine termed the 'Anti-Terrorist Operation' (ATO) in Donbas since 2014.[23] Russian agents raided military recruitment offices for lists of military personnel and followed them up methodically, pressuring women to tell them where their husbands or fathers were. Not all of them were active fighters. Viktor Kushyn had been a driver in Ukraine's 53rd Brigade for a year in 2018. He was picked up by the Russians in his village in Kharkiv region in May 2022 and locked in a cellar with other veterans. Kushyn later told journalists that Russian soldiers beat them for several days and 'took a hot branding iron, pressed it on our skin and branded us with the symbol of a triangle, as is done with cattle. They did it for revenge because they hated us.'[24] Many veterans left the region as Russian forces approached or signed up with self-defence units elsewhere. But Russian soldiers continued searching for military veterans, assuming—probably correctly—that Ukraine had organised 'stay behind' cells to mount resistance and sabotage operations.[25]

A second, much broader category in Russia's hit lists targeted anybody considered to be a potential political opponent. These FSB lists included journalists, civil society activists, local officials, priests and other religious leaders—anybody with authority who was likely to challenge the occupiers.[26] These lists swelled even more when protests began in towns like Kherson—the names of the organisers were soon added to the list and led to night-time raids and detentions. One of those detained was Oleksandr Tarasov, who had been organising pro-Ukrainian protests in the first days of the Russian occupation in Kherson. The FSB arrested him and held him in the basement of the local administration building, where they tortured him. They attached electric currents to his earlobes and tried to force him to reveal the names of fellow organisers. An officer held a pistol to his forehead and cocked the trigger. 'It looks like you're fucking me around', he said. 'I had no idea if he would pull the trigger or not', Tarasov later recalled.[27]

Many journalists knew they would be targeted. Yevhenia Virlych, editor-in-chief of the Kherson publication Kavun.City, told me she was sure she was on the list. She had stayed in Kherson to document the occupation, but Russian agents were looking for her. Four men with the tell-tale accents and the pale skins of Russians from the north waited outside her house. Her husband was ready to escape through the back window with their cat in a bag. But they managed to evade arrest and eventually escaped to government-controlled territory, using forged papers under different names.[28]

Other journalists were detained by Russian forces in the occupied territories. Viktoria Roshchyna, a freelance journalist, was detained on 15 March 2022 in Berdiansk, but released a week later. She was arrested again in August 2023 and this time was not released, but was detained in a Russian prison. In October 2024 she was reported to have died while being held in prison in Moscow.[29] According to the Ukrainian Union of Journalists as many as twenty-eight Ukrainian journalists were still incarcerated in Russian prisons in 2024.[30]

The Russians also targeted many religious leaders. Attacks on religious communities largely followed political and ideological lines, with more 'pro-Ukrainian' churches being singled out for repression. Orthodox believers in Ukraine were caught in a bitter and highly politicised schism. On one side was the Orthodox Church of Ukraine (OCU), an autocephalous Orthodox community that had cuts ties with Moscow and was the closest thing Ukraine had to a national church. On the other side was the Ukrainian Orthodox Church, usually identified as the Ukrainian Orthodox Church (Moscow Patriarchate) (UOCMP), because it still recognised—at least until 2022—the spiritual authority of the Russian Orthodox Church leadership in Ukraine, and was therefore often perceived as pro-Russian. During the war, these spiritual and political divisions suddenly took on geopolitical importance. The UOCMP condemned the invasion and declared that it had split with Moscow, but its response was seen by Kyiv as too ambivalent. The Ukrainian authorities arrested some priests of the UOCMP on often disputed charges of supporting Russia.[31]

Most parishes in Russian-occupied territories belonged to the UOCMP and were largely untouched by the Russian military. UOCMP clergy in the occupied territories did not acknowledge the split with Moscow and most remained loyal to the Moscow Patriarchate. By contrast, Russian forces often detained priests of the pro-Kyiv OCU. In May 2023 Russian security forces detained OCU priest Father Kostiantyn Maksimov from Tokmak when he tried to travel to Crimea.[32] In Donetsk region, two priests of the OCU, Father Khristofor Khrimli and Father Andri Chui, were arrested in September 2023, fined for 'missionary activity' and deported.[33] The Russian security agencies also targeted parishes of the Ukrainian Greek Catholic Church, a church with strong roots in western Ukraine. Greek Catholic priests Father Ivan Levytsky and Father Bohdan Heleta were detained in Berdiansk in November 2022 and disappeared. For a long time there was no news of their fate, but they were eventually released in a prisoner exchange on 28 June 2024.[34]

Some of the most violent attacks were against Protestant and Evangelical churches. The idea that Evangelical churches were a subversive group linked to the West dated back to the Soviet period. In Lysychansk, which was occupied by Russia in July 2022, Russian forces seized a Baptist church building, and told church members that 'the military administration has banned all Baptists, Pentecostals and Adventists as extremists'. The church's leader, Pastor Nosachov, claimed that there were informers: 'when the Russians came, residents immediately reported on the church members and showed the authorities where Christians lived'.[35] On 26 December 2022 the Russian-appointed governor of Zaporizhzhia, Yevgeny Balitsky, issued a series of decrees banning four religious communities: the Grace Protestant Church, the Melitopol Christian Church, the Word of Life Protestant Church and the Ukrainian Greek Catholic Church. The churches were accused of ties to Western 'special services' and of participating in anti-Russian meetings.[36] There were numerous detentions and disappearances of church leaders. Leonid Ponomarev, leader of a Baptist congregation in Mariupol, was detained with his wife Tatiana from 21 September to 21 October 2022. On 22 November 2022 Russian soldiers abducted Anatoly Prokopchukov, a deacon in the local Christian Evangelical church, and his son Oleksandr. Their bodies were found four days later in the forest near Nova Kakhovka.[37]

Protestant churches were often openly pro-Ukrainian and very active in humanitarian activities. Pastor Britsin of Grace Protestant Church in Melitopol told Forum 18, a group campaigning for religious freedom, that the Russians 'did not like the fact that our Church openly supports the Ukrainian position, sings and prays in Ukrainian'. The church had been providing humanitarian aid, which was often a cause of repression by the occupation authorities, who preferred to monopolise any aid distribution.[38] Britsin was forcibly deported to government-controlled Ukraine in September 2022.

A third group targeted by the Russians were Ukrainian government officials. Many senior officials had fled during the first days of the war, but some local government officials remained, either out of conviction or because they were too slow to leave. Many officials were left almost untouched for weeks while Russian forces focused on the military campaign, but others were detained in the very first days of the occupation. During the first eighteen months of the war, according to a Ukrainian human rights network, Russian forces detained 132 government officials, of whom four were killed. More than half the cases (seventy-one) were in

OCCUPATION

Kherson region, perhaps because resistance to the occupation had been so high in that area. In September 2023 fourteen remained in Russian custody.[39] The most high-profile official still in custody was Kherson mayor Ihor Kolykhaev, whom we met in Chapter 2, attempting to keep the city running while resisting the Russian takeover. He was finally arrested in June 2022 and remained in Russian custody in 2024.

Another former mayor of Kherson, Volodymyr Mykolaenko, was detained on 26 April 2022. Mykolaenko was already known in Russia for his criticism of Moscow. In 2019 he had dismissed Russian historical claims to Ukraine, saying that Russia's 'ancestral territories were some swamps around Moscow' and that 'Russia is always death, humiliation, hunger, stench, ignorance and suffering. Every Ukrainian should remember that.'[40] Perhaps because he had previously featured in the Russian media, he was forced to take part in a series of disturbing interviews, made under duress by a reporter from Russia's *Izvestiya* newspaper.[41] This use of prisoners for propaganda purposes appears to have been an experiment that was later discontinued, perhaps because so few of these Ukrainian officials were willing to go along with Russian narratives. Mykolaenko also remained in Russian custody in 2024.

According to a statement by the US government in March 2023, Russian forces had detained at least thirty Ukrainian mayors, six of whom remained in Russian custody.[42] Among them were Oleksandr Babych, mayor of Hola Pristan, a small town in the river delta of the Dnipro which suffered badly from the destruction of the Kakhovka dam. Babych refused to cooperate with the Russians but had continued to work until 28 March 2022, when he was kidnapped by Russian forces at his home. Svitlana Linnyk, the deputy mayor, recalled what happened:

> I […] saw that the city council building had already been taken over [by the Russians]. A man in a military uniform without identification marks called himself Oleksii and said he was in charge. Russians had lists and already knew the names of employees. Oleksii tried to persuade me to cooperate, asked if I did not want to live amicably, as in the USSR and criticized our president. Later, the mayor was brought in a white Mercedes minibus with tinted

windows. It turned out that the occupiers had kidnapped Babych from his own yard. He was under guard in his office for some time. Then the Russian named Oleksii ordered [them] to take the mayor away. Babych took a warm jacket and gave me the keys to his house and company car. He was again put into a white minibus, in which armed men in black could be seen. The bus moved towards Skadovsk. Since then, he has never contacted me.[43]

Here—as in many other cases—local politics may have played a role. Babych's political arch-rival was Alexei Kovalev, an aspiring young agriculturalist and member of the Ukrainian parliament from Hola Pristan, who had defected to the Russians. A 33-year-old member of Zelensky's Servant of the People faction, he seemed an unlikely candidate to back the occupation. But on 8 June 2022 Kovalev posted on Facebook that he had met a Russian delegation, headed by Sergei Kiriyenko, and was convinced that 'Russia is here seriously and forever.'[44] His role would apparently have been to oversee the grain trade after he took on the role of 'deputy head' of the Russian-installed government of Kherson region. A Ukrainian member of parliament from Zelensky's party was a prize for the Russians. This also made him a prime target for the Ukrainian intelligence services. He survived one assassination attempt in June, but on 28 August 2022 he was found dead, apparently murdered, in his house.[45] On 7 October 2022, in a Russian presidential decree, he was awarded a Russian medal of bravery posthumously.

'In the basement': Detention and torture

Russian forces tried to avoid picking up people on the street, where they were likely to be filmed on smartphones or where passers-by might intervene. Typically, detentions took place at night. Russian soldiers appeared at the house of Oksana Zayarina in Berdiansk late in the evening of 25 June 2022. They searched the house and at 1.30 a.m. took her and her husband to the Russian commandant's office, which was housed in the city police headquarters at 3 Greek Street. She did not sleep all night, but at 11 a.m. she was taken to a room for questioning. Five men were in the room, three guards and two interrogators, who demanded she tell them her call-sign for the Ukrainian intelligence service and give them details about an underground resistance movement of which she was supposedly a member. One of the interviewers, wearing a balaclava and yellow glasses, called her 'a bitch', and threatened to take her to the DNR, where 'she would spend 20 years in prison'. When she caught a glimpse of her file, she was shocked to see next to her name the label 'Pro-Ukrainian activist, extremist'.[46]

Such detentions were daily events in the occupied territories: the night-time arrest, the often strange and bizarre questions intermingled with threats, frequently on the basis of dubious information or unreliable denunciations. Russian interrogators repeatedly used electric shocks to try to force detainees to confess. While in detention Oksana was forced to listen to the beatings of other prisoners: 'you could hear it clearly', she later recalled: 'We could not sleep. Anybody who had a pillow put it over their head to try to drown out the sounds.'[47] Oksana Zayarina spent eighty-three days in detention before she was finally released.

The campaign of detention, torture and violence was a deliberate mechanism to intimidate and pressure any opponents of the occupation, to spread fear in society more widely and to extract intelligence and recruit informants. Investigators from Human Rights Watch collected evidence from hundreds of interviewees who testified that Russia used kidnapping and torture against innocent civilians and mistreated prisoners held in custody.[48] All the detainees were held in grim conditions, often in makeshift prisons set up in basements, in police stations seized by the Russians, or in military camps. At least 100 police stations were taken over by Russian forces and the custody facilities and basements were used for detention, interrogation and torture.[49] After the Russians retreated from Kherson, investigators uncovered a network of torture chambers in the city. In one location in Kherson city, neighbours saw people being regularly taken into the basement with bags over their heads and in handcuffs. Some were spotted leaving with nothing, not even shoes on their feet.[50] Ukrainian officials claimed that Russia had established at least twenty major detention sites in the occupied territories in which Ukrainian officials and activists were held.[51]

Russian security and military personnel also killed Ukrainian prisoners in extra-judicial executions. The UN recorded seventy-seven summary executions of people while in detention by Russian armed forces between 24 February 2022 and 23 May 2023.[52] Some prisoners died as the result of torture, neglect or other forms of ill-treatment. Soldiers guarding the inmates often appeared to be out of control. There was little discipline or restraint. Occasionally, visits by senior officers from headquarters resulted in releases, although mainly because the prisons were overflowing.[53] House-to-house searches were often undisciplined rampages. A UN Independent Commission reported:

> Russian authorities, mostly in groups, conducted house searches, sometimes on multiple occasions. Some of the soldiers were intoxicated. They threatened and intimidated victims and their family members with weapons, including by shooting near their heads or legs. Perpetrators raped the victims in their homes, or forcibly took them to premises they had occupied in the vicinity or to locations they used as a temporary base, or raped them during confinement.[54]

Incidents of sexual violence and rape were widely reported during the Russian campaign in Kyiv region in the first months of the war, but cases occurred in every area under Russian occupation. The UN Independent Commission documented numerous cases in Kherson region, including the rape of an 83-year-old woman and of a pregnant 16-year-old girl. In May 2022, also in Kherson region, a woman who was raped by soldiers while her husband was beaten reported the case to the local Russian commander. In retaliation, Russian soldiers returned to their house and shot the couple dead.[55]

Threats of rape and sexual violence were often used in detention against prisoners as part of a wider pattern of torture.[56] Torture in Russian detention centres was systemic and practised with impunity. Yelyzaveta Sokurenko from the Human Rights Centre ZMINA, who interviewed many survivors of Russian captivity, told the OSCE that 'analysis showed that 83% of survivors reported being subjected to the most severe torture during interrogations'. According to Sokurenko's analysis, '63% of survivors reported torture by electric shocks, 81% reported "professional" beatings, and 70% reported torture by starvation'.[57] A UN report concluded that 'more than 91 per cent of civilian detainees held by the Russian Federation described subjection to torture and ill-treatment, including sexual violence'.[58] Torture was used to gain information about Ukrainian military positions or information about resistance networks. But at times it was deployed for other more mercenary ends, such as demanding a ransom or a share in a business. In many cases, Russian forces tried to coerce detainees into cooperating with the occupation forces.[59]

The most widespread form of torture was the use of electric shocks. This was a method that dated back decades. Interrogators used an old-fashioned Soviet TA-57 military field telephone, commonly known as a '*tapik*', which generated an electric current with a manual crank handle. They would attach two wires from the telephone to the prisoner's body. Then they would turn the handle to produce a current. Sasha, who was arrested in Kherson in May 2022, and spent four months in captivity, described the experience: 'It hits [you] with high-voltage impulses so that sparks fall from [your] eyes. They also hooked them on to fingers and toes. And that way they had fun all night long.'[60]

Dmytro, a brick-carrier on a construction site, was arrested in the summer of 2022 and was handcuffed to a radiator in a cell for two months. He lost so much weight that the handcuffs no longer restrained him. Dmytro was also electro-shocked: 'they tied wires to my little fingers and turned up the current'. After that, he told reporters, 'you agree to anything'. He was forced to record a video saying he was a terrorist who blew up Russian military vehicles. Perhaps because everybody realised the confession was blatantly false, they finally let him go.[61]

Viktor Maruniak, head of the village of Stara Zburivka in Kherson region, was also detained and tortured. He said that guards tied electric wires to a prisoner's toes and then poured water over the person to spread the pain over the entire body. Maruniak told reporters that he did not even notice the pain because he had already been beaten so badly. A report from a human rights group claimed that 'His torturers had beaten, kicked and used a baton against essentially all parts of his body, except his head which they avoided since that shows.'[62] Others reported ever more painful variants: what interrogators mockingly dubbed a 'call to Zelensky' involved attaching the electrodes to genitalia; a 'call to Biden' electrocuted the anus.[63]

There were several reported cases of detainees being forced to make 'confessions'. Serhii Tsyhipa, who had run a civil society organisation in Nova Kahkovka, was seized by Russian forces on 12 March 2022. He appeared in April on Russian television, apparently repeating Russian propaganda under duress.[64] In one video, an exhausted young woman standing in front of a broken window blind stumbles through a statement, apologising to Russian soldiers for calling them 'orcs' (a derogatory Ukrainian term for Russians).[65] She said that she had undergone a 'denazification' course. According to Sergei Khlan, a Ukrainian politician from Kherson region, 'courses in denazification' meant nothing more than torture.[66]

In some cases, the violence seemed chaotic, sadistic and often tactically pointless. The village head Viktor Maruniak told journalists that Russian soldiers seemed to get pleasure from the electrocutions, although even here there was a warped logic. He suggested that his abduction was part of a tactic by local soldiers to avoid being sent to the front line—by 'uncovering' a sabotage group in Maruniak's village, they could remain busy in relative safety behind the lines.[67]

Inevitably, this system of kidnap and abduction was monetised. There were reports of Russian soldiers demanding payments to release prisoners.[68] Many businessmen were detained until they agreed to pay a ransom, give up their business or pay informal taxes to whichever military unit or mafia group had abducted them. Pro-Russian Ukrainian groups were often involved in these shakedowns. The GSB security unit in Kherson was particularly notorious for extortion, according to a journalistic investigation. Their violence appeared to be primarily focused on extracting money from those being tortured rather than any political motives. Kidnapped, tortured businesspeople were forced to pay ransoms for their release, ranging from US$1,000 to US$30,000.

Others were reported to have been tortured until they agreed to hand over the title to their business.[69]

At the Zaporizhzhia nuclear power plant at Enerhodar, now under the control of Russian corporation Rosatom, torture appears to have become an everyday feature of life at the workplace. While Rosatom executives worked with the plant staff and technicians to manage the effective shutdown of the plant, the Russian military and the FSB established torture chambers in the basements to threaten and punish Ukrainian workers. They pressured workers to sign contracts with Rosatom or targeted individuals they thought were in touch with the Ukrainian military. There were occasions, according to a report by Ukrainian human rights investigators 'Truth Hounds', when Russian soldiers seized an employee straight from the office of a Rosatom executive. The two worlds of Russian international commerce and technology and the grim violence of the Russian security forces were hardly separated.[70]

Establishing the exact scale of repression is difficult. The Office of the United Nations High Commissioner for Human Rights (OHCHR) documented 864 individual cases of arbitrary detention by the Russian armed forces, including 763 men, 94 women and 7 boys, between 24 February 2022 and 23 May 2023, while acknowledging that the real figures were much higher.[71] According to the Ukrainian prosecutor's office, in Kherson region alone, Russian forces detained over 1,000 civilians in 2022, with 474 of them still in custody at the beginning of 2023.[72] In many of these cases, detainees were transferred out of the occupied territories to Russia, in violation of international humanitarian law. Often there was no information provided to relatives of the detained, who were left to search desperately for any news about their loved ones.[73]

It is true that there were abuses on both sides, but the scale and intensity of Russian human rights violations were on a much larger scale. UN reporting documented sixty-five cases in which 'Ukrainian security forces detained civilians in unofficial places of detention for periods lasting from several hours to 4.5 months, during which they were often held incommunicado.'[74] Some 57% of detainees interviewed by the OHCHR claimed they were subject to torture or ill-treatment by Ukrainian forces, often in unofficial places of detention.⁷⁵ According to the UN report, an unofficial prison reportedly operated in the basement of the central SBU building in Kyiv, where people were held without charge, sometimes for months.⁷⁶

While Ukraine showed some cooperation with international investigations into cases of illegal detention, Russia refused to engage with any international enquiries into human rights abuses. Almost all Russian human rights organisations had been banned or disbanded inside Russia, although a network of lawyers and low-profile activists continued to try to help Ukrainian prisoners. The International Committee of the Red Cross (ICRC) was not permitted access to all prisoners of war and civilian internees, despite the provisions of the Geneva Conventions.⁷⁷ Russia refused to cooperate with the Independent International Commission of Inquiry on Ukraine set up by the UN Human Rights Council on 4 March 2022 to investigate alleged violations of human rights and international humanitarian law in the context of Russia's aggression against Ukraine. In March 2024 the Commission noted that it 'has addressed to Russian officials 23 written requests for meetings, access and information, without receiving any answer'.⁷⁸

Filtration and forced migration

The violence and torture used against detained activists and officials were only the most extreme practices in a much wider system of coercive control, the system of *filtratsiya* or 'filtration'. Filtration, as defined by the UN, was 'a process used to seek to identify possible affiliation with or support for the Ukrainian armed forces or authorities, and to collect information about residents in occupied territory'.⁷⁹ FSB Military Counter-Intelligence officers took the lead role in the establishment and oversight of the filtration system, assisted by other government officials from Moscow, the local occupation authorities and units of the National Guard. According to the US government, two officials from the Russian Presidential Administration, Oleg Nesterov and Yevgeny Kim, 'oversaw the filtration of city government officials and other civilians from

Mariupol, Ukraine, including through the filtration center in Manhush, Ukraine', while Aleksei Muratov, a DNR official, and Marina Sereda, also working for the DNR, 'spearheaded the procurement of necessary equipment and technology to support filtration points in Russia-occupied Donetsk Oblast, Ukraine'.[80]

The system of filtration has a long history in the Soviet Union, dating back at least to the Soviet occupation of Eastern Europe in 1944–45. In 1944 the Soviet People's Commissariat for Internal Affairs—the NKVD—was tasked with establishing and staffing a network of 'Screening and Filtration Points' (*Proverochno-filtratsionnye punkty*, PFP) on the Soviet-Polish border and in western Ukraine to process Soviet citizens being repatriated from regions liberated from Nazi rule. Some 15,000 NKVD officers were dispatched to western Belarus and a further 20,000 to western Ukraine to run these camps.[81] By 1 March 1946, 4.2 million Soviet citizens had passed through the filtration process.[82]

Forms of filtration reappeared during the Soviet invasion of Afghanistan, but it was in Chechnya that it achieved its modern notoriety. In the first and second Chechen wars, in the 1990s and early 2000s, the filtration network in Chechnya became infamous for its brutality and violence. Filtration took place at different scales, ranging from 'on the spot' filtration—which often meant detainees being held in pits dug by the side of the road or in makeshift prisons in railway carriages—to semi-permanent filtration camps.[83] It was an extremely violent mechanism and it operated almost entirely outside the legal system, with no redress for detainees and almost complete impunity for the military running the sites. But it became a key mechanism to seek out potential and actual rebels, and also acted as an important channel of forced recruitment for the Russian military, for Chechen militias and for the FSB.

The system in Ukraine was almost certainly planned ahead of the invasion, since it was part of the standard operating procedures for the FSB's counterinsurgency operations, although it evolved significantly as the realities on the battlefield changed. It comprised different institutions and different procedures at various locations, but overall amounted to a system of registration of

VIOLENCE

the population in the occupied territories and detailed checks on any movement of people into the Russian Federation. Under international law, an occupying power has the right to register the population and—in some cases—use internment for security purposes. Yet Russia's filtration system went far beyond this. It was highly abusive, involved extensive and proven cases of torture and violence, and had no accountability mechanisms to protect the rights of the population.

The filtration system in Ukraine was initiated almost as soon as the invasion began, beginning with ad hoc checks at roadblocks and checkpoints. During such checks soldiers could inspect documents but also ask questions—about affiliations to Ukrainian groups or attitudes towards the war. But soon the FSB began to organise filtration on a mass scale in an organised way. They set up sites in schools or police stations where people could go 'voluntarily' to gain a certificate, or *'talon'*, to say that they had passed filtration. Without this certificate, people could not move around freely or leave the conflict zones.

During the first few months of the invasion, in many places Russia implemented this process of full filtration for all residents. After Russian forces took control of Lyman, in Donetsk region, in May 2022, they banned residents from going outside without a pass. To get a pass, residents had to go through the filtration process at the local police station, where the DNR security services interrogated residents. According to one resident, crowds stood in long lines to get the pass, although everybody understood that the procedure was potentially dangerous. But without filtration they would not be able to leave their homes. People were asked about whether they took part in political movements or had fought in the war in Donbas after 2014. Those who were suspected of links to the Ukrainian military or were otherwise deemed suspicious were detained and sent for further interrogation in Donetsk.[84]

Similar systems were implemented across much of the occupied territory. In Mariupol, as the brutal siege continued, Russian soldiers conducted so-called *zachistki*, literally 'cleansing' or mopping-up operations, comprising street-by-street and door-by-door checks on who was living where.[85] Men were sometimes picked up during these sweeps or detained on the street and taken away for filtration. Those who were detained were transported to a network of camps used for more detailed interrogations, such as one at Bezimenne, about 30 kilometres north-east of Mariupol. The detainees then faced a familiar pattern of ill-treatment in poor conditions with very uncertain prospects of release. A report from Yale's School of Public Health identified twenty-one of these camps or centres with different roles in the process of filtration—from registration and initial questioning to further interrogation and imprisonment.[86]

Everybody leaving the occupied territories to travel to Russia or to Crimea had to go through filtration. According to the Russian government newspaper, *Rossiiskaya gazeta*, the aim of the filtration camp was to prevent 'Ukrainian nationalists from infiltrating Russia disguised as refugees so they could avoid punishment'.[87] A statement from the Russian Embassy in Washington promoted the same idea:

> In order to avoid sabotage operations by the Ukrainian nationalists' battalions, Russian soldiers carefully inspect vehicles heading to safe regions. We will detain all bandits and fascists. The Russian military does not create any barriers for the civilian population, but helps [them] to stay alive, provides them with food and medicine.[88]

The DNR Ministry of Internal Affairs claimed filtration aimed to intercept 'persons affiliated with the security forces of Ukraine, participants in nationalist battalions, members of sabotage and reconnaissance groups, as well as their accomplices'.[89] Hardliners in Russia saw the process of filtration as a necessary security measure to respond to a series of assassinations and sabotage incidents by Ukrainian agents inside Russia. The president of a veterans' association, Sergei Goncharov, told journalists that 'so-called refugees, who received passports, are one million people. I am sure that from this one million, many Ukrainians received [Russian] passports on the instructions of the SBU or the Main Intelligence Directorate of Ukraine [military intelligence]. There are plenty of agents among us.'[90]

In March and April 2022, at the height of the fighting in Mariupol, thousands of people fled the city and were forced to go through the filtration process on the way to Russia. Many travelled in their own cars while others were transported out of Mariupol on buses by the Russian military, for example in an evacuation on 5 March. This was an organised process in which thousands of people were processed through filtration facilities and then sent on to cities and towns across Russia. The process was extremely slow, with people effectively detained in filtration camps and centres sometimes for several days or even weeks, living in completely unsanitary and unsafe conditions.

Dmytro and his neighbours drove to the filtration centre at Manhush. Getting there was fine—checkpoints were easy to pass, according to Dmytro, as long as you had cigarettes and knew how to talk to the soldiers. But when they arrived at Manhush, there were 6,500 people ahead of them and the queue was moving at a snail's pace. They were forced to camp out for days. Dmytro was finally called on the tenth day, but even then they had to pay for a better place in the queue. Local Telegram chats offered places in the line for 2,000–5,000 hryvnia (US$60–US$140).[91] The interviews were sometimes quick. It took Dmytro just fifteen minutes to get through. The main thing, according to Dmytro, was that 'if you are clean, tidy and also polite, then you do not arouse special suspicions'.[92] He received the small slip of paper which said 'Fingerprinted' on one side, and the name and date on the other, which meant he was free to travel.

There were several different camps for those leaving Mariupol. Satellite images showed about thirty-five tents set up at Bezimenne, near Novoazovsk on the border with Russia.[93] Another camp was at Nikolske (Nikolskoe), a village deeper inside Donetsk region. According to the Yale report, the facilities used there included the local school and the local police station.[94] Vitaly, a guitarist, left Mariupol on an evacuation bus with his wife and daughter, and was taken to Nikolske. The men were separated from the women and children and stood in line to enter a prefab hut, where two soldiers checked their telephones and looked for tattoos. When Vitaly entered, two men were undressed to their underpants, one with his hands on his head. They had apparently been recognised as participating in pro-Ukrainian meetings.[95]

In each case, the essential procedure was the same. Armed men—mostly local DNR forces—photographed the men, checked their passports and fingerprinted them. Then came the questions: 'They went through my phone; they asked if I knew anything about the Ukrainian army, if I had friends in the military', one woman told *The Guardian*. 'They also asked me what I thought about Ukraine, about Putin and about the conflict. It was very degrading.'[96] The process was the same everywhere. Inspecting passports and fingerprinting. Checking telephones. Asking endless questions.

Men were usually forced to undress, to see if they had any recoil marks from rifles, or any blisters or chafing on their hands from handling guns, marks on the neck from wearing a flak jacket, or patriotic tattoos on their bodies. This 'visual inspection' was humiliating and traumatic. Vitaly, the guitarist, had a tattoo of an American eagle, which provoked a long round of questions, but eventually he was released. Other tattoos also provoked bizarre discussions with FSB officers and soldiers. 'Konstantin', who left Berdiansk in March 2022, was interrogated on the border with Crimea at the Chonhar filtration point. His tattoo of an eight-pointed star, a symbol linked to the zodiac sign Scorpio, attracted attention. One of the interviewers claimed that it was the Star of David. After a long period of questioning, he finally convinced them it was not. 'I have never been so frightened', recalled Konstantin. It remained unclear why a search for 'neo-Nazis' should be concerned about a Star of David. But many of the questions made little sense.[97]

Soldiers conducted interviews 'exclusively using expletives', according to Maxim, who also passed through filtration at Chonhar. Some of the questions were strange: did he smoke? cheat on his wife? They went through every photograph on his phone. Then the threats began: 'Either give us [the names of] everybody you know who served in the VSU [Ukrainian armed forces] or the territorial defence, or you can go and fight for us. People like you they throw forward onto the front line immediately. There you'll dig some trenches, and then die.' Despite the threats, he was eventually released 'because of his son', he was told.[98]

Women, too, sometimes underwent a humiliating physical inspection. Thirty-year-old Kateryna went through filtration in Bezimenne with her two young sons. She told journalists:

VIOLENCE

> We were told to undress ... some down to their underwear, others completely naked. No explanations, no reasons. The men were taken away separately. They were held much longer. They checked all our belongings—backpacks, suitcases, plastic bags. Women who had relatives or friends in the Ukrainian army or police were threatened. They said they'd find their men and kill them, promising to send the men's heads back in boxes.[99]

In the Starobeshovo filtration camp, Alexander, who had also evacuated from Mariupol, had to wait for three days in basic conditions, sleeping on the floor and separated from his family. First, there was a form to fill in—personal data and the now ubiquitous questions about 'ties to the VSU'. Then fingerprinting, photographs and a check for tattoos and tell-tale rifle recoil marks. On to an interview with an FSB officer—straight out of central casting, according to Alexander: 'the latest iPhone, overweight, exhausted look'. He was asked whether he had ties to 'extremist organisations', presumably meaning Ukrainian far-right groups such as Right Sector, or one of the nationalist battalions such as Azov.[100] When Alexander responded with a question about what they meant by extremism and what groups they were talking about, he was met with silence and 'an evil stare'.[101]

Mostly people eventually got through the filtration process, but from time to time, travellers standing in the queue saw young men led away from the main crowds for further interrogation or detention. For these detainees, the prospects were often bleak. In many cases, their whereabouts were not properly recorded, and relatives had no idea about what had happened to them. Some detainees appear to have been effectively disappeared—in one case, official records showed that a detainee had been allowed to return to Mariupol, and yet he remained physically in a detention camp. One inmate, dubbed 'Taras' by a journalist at the *New Yorker*, managed to contact a Russian journalist and tell him about their situation:

> To put it mildly, the conditions are not for humans ... They feed us just enough so that we don't die ... We sleep on old rolled mattresses in classrooms and corridors ... We are guarded by three military police with machine guns ... Without our passports and filtration papers, we are nobody and nothing.[102]

Eventually, perhaps because of this publicity, Taras and others were released. But many more languished in these prisons, often unrecorded or in limbo between different forms of imprisonment.

It was unclear how many people were detained in this way. A DNR official involved in the filtration process told journalists that while some people were detained for more detailed checks, many of those were also released quickly after further questioning; only a few who were believed to have genuine links to the Ukrainian armed forces were detained in the DNR's prison system for further interrogation. On the other hand, a Ukrainian official claimed that between 5% and 10% of men passing through filtration were detained and taken for further questioning in Donetsk.[103] Whatever the numbers, many of these individuals remained for a long time in detention in the DNR in inhumane conditions.

The mobile phone was the source of extreme anxiety for anybody crossing a checkpoint in the Russia-Ukraine war. This was an instrument that could allow you to contact loved ones or to find help. But it could also betray your innermost thoughts and private actions. Whatever answers were given in an interrogation, a detainee could not deny an incriminating electronic trail. It was all too easy to find a serving Ukrainian military officer, a veteran or a policeman in a contacts list. And here was also a record of everything a person had read about the war—the Telegram channels, the tweets and posts reposted or liked, the YouTube videos watched—or, in the worst case, the photographs sent on messenger apps of Russian military equipment or installations.

At filtration, everybody had to surrender their phone, provide the password and allow FSB officials to link it up to a computer, presumably to download its data and analyse it. The fifteen-digit serial numbers were recorded.[104] Anybody who was facing filtration deleted anything obviously incriminating, but an empty phone was also suspicious, a sign that you had something to hide. Vitaly, the guitarist who went through filtration in Nikolske, had followed his friends' advice and deleted all his messaging apps. But having a 'clean telephone' turned out to be a problem, and he had to face long questioning about possible links to the Ukrainian military.[105] A traveller who went through filtration at Sheremetyevo airport in Moscow agreed:

Completely 'empty' phones arouse suspicion among officials and may lead to additional checks or refusal of entry. It is not recommended to delete Telegram, since FSB officers will definitely restore it in this case. If desired, they can try to restore messages, as well as browser search history and other data.[106]

Filtration allowed the Russians to develop a huge database on residents of the occupied territories. This information database could serve as a mechanism to track movement by individuals, link them to political activities or statements on social media, or as a reference for any further investigations and repressions. This digital occupation was highly invasive and all-embracing, and augmented by Russia's constant monitoring of communications and the internet in the occupied territories.

As the occupation consolidated, the filtration system became more institutionalised and less overtly abusive. Although Russia claimed that the occupied territories were part of Russia, anybody leaving the territories still had to pass through a border crossing and undergo thorough checks. There were also numerous checks inside the occupied territories: there were six checkpoints on a 200-kilometre stretch of the main E-58 highway in Zaporizhzhia region alone.[107]

The same process applied to any Ukrainian citizens travelling into Russia from third countries. Ukrainians travelled to Russia from the European Union (EU) for many reasons: to return to the occupied territories to collect elderly relatives or children, to check on property, or because families had become separated and Russia was the only place they could be reunited. Until October 2023, Ukrainians were able to travel to Russia from EU countries through land crossings (from Latvia, Estonia or Finland, for example).[108] From October 2023, Ukrainian citizens were restricted to arriving in Russia through Sheremetyevo airport in Moscow, where a filtration procedure now applied to all Ukrainian visitors, leaving hundreds of people waiting for hours to pass the filtration process.[109]

Here the system was similar. Travellers needed to fill out a form and answer a string of intrusive questions covering two sides of paper. They were asked for the names of their sites in social media. Further questions included: 'did you take part in armed conflict?' or 'have you had any contacts with the Ukrainian military?'. For some questions, it was easy to guess the right answer, such as Question 19: 'Have you been in contact with representatives of the Ukrainian security services? (Yes/No) (Name, surname of the official)'.[110]

Questions 34 and 35 on the form were more difficult. Answering 'Yes' to the question, 'Do you support the policies of the Ukrainian government?', was likely to get you deported, but the next question ('Do you support the conduct by the Russian VS [Armed Forces] of the special military operation in Ukraine?') was more complicated.[111] According to those who went through the process, you could get away with saying you were against the Russian military operation and still get through. In any case, they would probe your answers with further questions, so an honest answer to this question was best. This Kafkaesque process left travellers exhausted and humiliated.

Paradoxically, despite all Russia's protestations that the occupied territories were part of Russia, the filtration system effectively recreated the border between Russia and the occupied territories. In January 2024 the head of Crimea, Sergei Aksenov, introduced a special regime on the Crimean border with Kherson and Zaporizhzhia regions that was described as equivalent to a state border. In May 2024 a similar regime was introduced on the border with Rostov region. A 5-kilometre 'special zone' was introduced along the border by Rostov governor Vasily Golubev, in which travel would be restricted. This was to defend against 'terrorists, extremists and their accomplices'.[112]

The Crimean Gulag

On 9 May 2022, Victory Day was celebrated across Russia, the day when the Soviet Union and its allies defeated Germany after four years of brutal warfare across the Eastern Front that cost 20 million lives. It was also marked in Simferopol's Detention Centre No. 1, a crumbling 200-year-old prison which had become notorious for its ill-treatment of Crimean Tatar prisoners, even before the 2022 invasion.[113] On the morning of 9 May, prison guards banged on the door of a cell holding five Ukrainian prisoners. They grabbed Oleksandr Tarasov, the Ukrainian activist who had been detained in March for organising protests in Kherson, and forced him to stand against the wall with his head down and hands held high behind his back, in the painful pose known to prisoners as *delfinchik*—the little dolphin. 'What day is it today?', they shouted at the prisoners. 'Did your grandfathers fight? [… They] must be turning in their graves.' Whatever answer the prisoners gave, they were given an electric shock in return. Later the same day the guards were back. This time they picked on one of the prisoners and forced him to sing a well-known Soviet military song, 'Day of Victory'. Tarasov sat frozen to the floor, his eyes averted, as the prisoner stumbled through the words. If he got anything wrong, he got an electric shock.[114]

Tarasov was just one of hundreds of civilians from Ukraine held by Russia in Crimea. He was one of the first to arrive in Simferopol on 17 March 2022, but many more Ukrainian prisoners followed during the year, most of them political prisoners. There were so many that the prison authorities built a whole new block for them—SIZO (temporary holding cell) No. 2. The prisoners were reportedly held by the FSB's Department of Military Counter-Intelligence. Some were detained in other parts of Russia under the department of Military Police of the Ministry of Defence, a unit that was also under FSB control.[115] The FSB was also reported to have set up a secret Detention Centre No. 8 inside SIZO No. 2, possibly for Ukrainian political prisoners.[116]

In the new prison block the conditions were severe. The windows were blacked out and each cell had artificial light on twenty-four hours a day.[117] The prisoners were held in total isolation, with no access to news, letters or other prisoners. The prison guards were seized with a particular zeal, according to Tarasov: 'The things they say during interrogations are beyond comprehension. They are fanatics. They want a nuclear war and still believe that Russia embodies certain spiritual values. It's total nonsense.' Reports of mock executions were also common. According to the lawyer Anatoly Fursov, some detainees were forced under torture to sign confessions incriminating other activists.[118]

One prisoner in the Simferopol prison stood out. Mariano García Calatayud was a former local government official in Valencia, Spain. In 2014 he went to Ukraine to distribute humanitarian aid. He fell in love—with the country and with his partner Tetyana Marina. When he retired, he moved to Kherson. He can be seen in photographs of the early demonstrations in Kherson against the Russian occupation, waving Ukrainian and Spanish flags. On 19 March 2022 the 75-year-old was abducted by Russian troops and eventually transported to the Simferopol holding prison. He did not know Russian and was reportedly beaten and electrocuted by prison guards for not understanding instructions. At one point he suffered a heart attack: 'The prison authorities only sent him to hospital once he'd turned blue', the lawyer Fursov told journalists.[119] This ill-treatment seems to have been almost universal, whether prisoners were civilians or prisoners of war. One former detainee stated: 'No creature alive deserves to be treated like Russians treat Ukrainians in their detention facilities. Over there, you don't feel like a human being anymore.'[120]

In some cases, the FSB concocted various criminal charges against Ukrainian prisoners, many of which appeared to be fabricated. More often, they were held without any formal charges. According to Fursov, the FSB claimed that García was a citizen of 'an enemy state, meaning no laws apply in this situation'. It seemed likely that they were holding him for a future spy swap.[121] Some prisoners were interrogated by Russia's Investigative Committee (SK) about potential war crimes allegedly committed by Ukrainian forces in Mariupol, part of a campaign in which Russia put some prisoners of war on trial, potentially in violation of the Geneva Convention.[122] The FSB responded to any legal requests with a phrase about the detainees being subject to ongoing 'checks of people who resist the SVO [Special Military Operation]'.[123] This accusation—'resisting the Special Military Operation'—was used against other detainees, despite the fact that there was no such crime in Russia's Criminal Code. In the case of García, the Russian military prosecutor confirmed that he was held as part of an investigation into 'actions aimed at harming Russia'.[124]

Other high-profile detainees included the Ukrainian officials discussed above, among them current and former Kherson mayors Ihor Kolykhaev and Volodymyr Mykolaenko, together with Oleksandr Babych from Hola Pristan and three other mayors. None of them were charged with a crime, as far as is known. Despite international pressure, these prisoners had no access to lawyers and the ICRC appears to have had only extremely limited access.

In 2023 the Russian authorities began court cases against some detainees on cases of spying or terrorism.[125] In November 2023 the new branch of the SK (Investigative Committee) in Zaporizhzhia region charged a Ukrainian woman with being part of a 'terrorist group organised by the VSU'. They alleged that she had received explosives and arranged a drop-off point for them to be picked up by somebody else.[126] Dmytro Holubev, described in the Ukrainian press as a volunteer from Melitopol, was detained by Russian troops in August 2022, and sentenced to eighteen years in prison in November 2023 for an alleged bomb attack on a police building in Melitopol. Two other planned attacks were reported to have been foiled. According to the prosecution, Holubev had undergone training in Ukrainian military intelligence. A photograph of Holubev in court shows him wearing a SvaStone shirt, a clothing brand popular among far-right activists, with the slogan 'White On' on the front. The Russian newspaper *Kommersant* reported that Holubev had 'admitted the factual circumstances of the case' but denied that he engaged in terrorism, telling the court that 'I am a Ukrainian, I defended Ukraine … I did not aim for people to die'.[127]

Russia also charged some Crimean Tatars with involvement in the Noman Çelebicihan Volunteer Battalion, a volunteer group that had been founded in 2015 and had organised a blockade against Crimea. Crimean Tatars were the original inhabitants of Crimea, long before Russia annexed it in 1783, but their share of the population had been sharply reduced by Russian colonisation and forced expulsions of Tatars, most infamously in May 1944, when the entire Crimean Tatar population was deported to Siberia and Central Asia. The Soviet Union lifted the ban in 1989 and declared the deportation to have been a crime. But under Russian rule, there had been renewed repressions against Crimean

Tatars in Crimea. In 2016 Russia declared the Mejlis of the Crimean Tatar People, a representative body, to be an extremist organisation and arrested several of its leaders. Russia designated the Noman Çelebicihan Volunteer Battalion as a terrorist group in June 2022, although it was not reported to have been involved in any military activity. Human rights groups claimed that accusations of affiliation with the Noman Çelebicihan Volunteer Battalion were widely used to frame Tatar activists who campaigned against the Russian occupation.[128]

Forced migration

In May 2022 Liudmyla Denisova, Verkhovna Rada Commissioner for Human Rights, claimed that more than 1.3 million Ukrainians, including 223,000 children, had been forcibly deported to Russia. Denisova asserted that plans to deport Ukrainians to Russia were formulated prior to the invasion, implying that this was a long-term plan to depopulate the region of Ukrainians.[129] In September 2022 the US government concluded that 'Russia's forces and proxies have interrogated, detained, and forcibly deported ..., according to a broad range of sources, between 900,000 and 1.6 million Ukrainian citizens, including thousands of children.'[130] Russia denied that there had been any forced deportations, but its figures for refugee flows were even higher: they claimed that by November 2022, 4.86 million people, including 715,934 children, had crossed the border into Russia from Ukraine, with nearly 1 million cars crossing the frontier.[131] All these figures demonstrated the scale of the problem, but the actual reality of these migratory flows was hugely complex: migrants had different destinations, motivations and experiences. Some travelled through Russia back to Ukraine or found refuge in the European Union. Many remained in Russia, while others began to return to the occupied territories.

International law states that the forcible transfer of population from occupied territory is illegal.[132] The notion of 'forcible transfer' suggests people being forced onto buses at gunpoint, but the ordinary interpretation of the law makes it clear that 'forcible transfer' applies to a much wider range of scenarios, including migration in cases where there are simply no other options available to civilians. In many cases, Russia could have facilitated humanitarian evacuations to Ukrainian territory, but failed to do so, according to Human Rights Watch.[133] Many Ukrainian citizens travelled to Russia because that was the nearest territory safely away from the front line and because corridors to reach Ukrainian-held territory were either non-existent or too dangerous to use. Most travelled in their own vehicles—there were long queues at the border to get into Russia. These cases were still considered forced migration, under international law, but they differed from the coerced exile experienced, for example, in the 1940s, during the Soviet occupation of the Baltic States. Nevertheless, there were many cases in which the Russian authorities organised evacuations, usually on buses, and transported refugees to reception centres in Russia, whether they wanted to go or not.

For many people living in Mariupol and the east, Russia was still the most obvious destination to escape the immediate conflict. Travelling west meant crossing dangerous areas of fighting. Even after 2014, many people retained ties across the border—hundreds of thousands of Ukrainians still worked in Russia; many evacuees had relatives or friends who could give them shelter or help them travel to Europe via Russia. Those who had the funds could travel to Crimea or Rostov and from there travel to Moscow, and then, via a long circuitous route, reach the Baltic States. For many, that was the only way to make their way back to government-controlled Ukraine, but some went straight to Europe and stayed there. Some men did not want to travel to government-controlled Ukraine because of the restrictions on men leaving the country and their fear of being mobilised. For a long time, the only way to travel directly to Ukraine was through the Kolotilovka-Pokrovka border crossing near Krasnopillia in north-eastern Ukraine, the last open border crossing between Russia and Ukraine that thousands of people used in order to escape from the occupied territories, until it was closed in August 2024.[134] Other Ukrainian refugees left Russia through the border with Georgia.

Russia's shrinking civil society did what it could to help. The Civil Assistance Committee helped some 15,000 Ukrainian refugees with cash payments, food and legal support.[135] Other ad hoc volunteer networks assisted Ukrainians leaving Russia for Georgia, the Baltic States or going directly to Ukraine. This was potentially dangerous. Alexander Demidenko, a teacher and pacifist in Belgorod, helped hundreds of Ukrainians leave through the Kolotilovka-Pokrovka border post. The Russian security services detained and tortured him in November 2023, and he died in police custody in suspicious circumstances in April 2024.[136]

Although some Ukrainian sources claimed that the deportations had been planned in advance, it is unlikely that relevant ministries in the Russian government had prior knowledge of the invasion. A government decision from 12 March 2022 detailed how refugees would be distributed across different regions of Russia, but assumed there would be fewer than 100,000 people.[137] Although refugees reported pressure from the Russian authorities to take up Russian passports and settle in Russia, there does not seem to have been any obstacle for people to travel out of Russia—or to move to other parts of Russia—except lack of funding. Some refugees were transported to very distant parts of Russia—as far as Vladivostok and the Russian Far East. They were then permitted to travel to other parts of the country, or to depart to Europe if they had the funds and the connections. But many had no income and no possessions and so had little chance of leaving.

When Ukrainian refugees arrived in Russia, they faced enormous problems. The most fortunate ones had relatives or friends who could help. Others were provided basic accommodation in schools, hotels or holiday camps. Many arrived with almost nothing. Although they were promised a 10,000-rouble (US$111) cash payment, in practice receiving the money sometimes took time. Many needed medical assistance. Although they usually received emergency treatment, more extensive medical aid was not always available, particularly to those without Russian passports and insurance.[138] Everything became easier for those with Russian identity documents: arranging schools for children, receiving welfare payments, getting work.

Even in 2024, two years after the war broke out, there were still thousands of Ukrainian refugees living in temporary refugee centres in Russia.[139] Many found it difficult to find work—most of

VIOLENCE

these refugee centres were distant from towns with more job opportunities—some had disabilities, others had inadequate documents. Conditions in the centres were basic, usually comprising a hotel room and three meals a day, and many refugees depended on help from local volunteers.[140]

Russia used the refugee situation for its own propaganda. It exaggerated the numbers. In February 2023 TASS reported that 5.3 million refugees had arrived in Russia from Ukraine, including 738,000 children.[141] The real numbers were almost certainly much lower. The UNHCR reported 2,852,395 border crossings from Ukraine between February and December 2022, and 1,275,315 refugees as of December 2022.[142] The gap probably comprised people who had not registered as refugees in Russia or had continued their journey out of Russia and on to the EU or to Ukraine. There were just over 40,000 people still living in the temporary refugee centres in Russia in February 2023, according to TASS. The same source claimed that 12,300 million roubles (US$137 million) were spent on one-time payments of 10,000 roubles to each refugee, suggesting that 1.23 million people received the funds.[143] The Russian Red Cross claimed to have helped over 1 million Ukrainians in Russia by May 2023.[144]

The reception and treatment of refugees in Russia varied depending on the time and manner in which they had left. The worst situation was during the siege of Mariupol in March and April 2022, when people were forced to undergo a long, arduous filtration process, with the ever-present threat of violence or disappearance. The Russian authorities were not ready for such a huge influx of refugees, and many left the city with little more than a few personal possessions. When some 70,000 people left Kherson in November 2022 as Russian forces withdrew, the situation was different. Those who evacuated to Russia were still subject to filtration, but this was a more self-selecting group, less likely to face harsh interrogation or incarceration. The Russian authorities were better prepared to receive refugees, and even put in place a scheme to provide compensation to allow Kherson refugees to buy property in Russia to replace the homes they had lost in Kherson city.

One pensioner, Valya, who had been evacuated from Kherson, had strong pro-Russian sentiments. She had been born in a

Ukrainian family and lived all her life in a village in Kherson region, but she could not understand why her daughter preferred to speak Ukrainian rather than Russian, or why she had fled Russian-controlled Kherson for Odesa when the war broke out. Valya also did not understand why her neighbours back home spoke out against Putin. After she had spent a few weeks in a sanitorium with her invalid son, she received a Russian government certificate (the so-called 'Kherson certificate'), providing a 3.5-million-rouble [US$39,000] grant to buy a house. Her own house in Kherson was destroyed in the June 2023 floods when the Kakhovka dam was blown up, as discussed below.[145]

Not all the refugees from Kherson were pro-Russian. One evacuee, Nastya, sitting on the seashore, told a journalist she was pro-Ukrainian but her husband had cooperated with the FSB during the occupation and so she had decided to flee with him. She was not happy:

> this state [Russia] took everything from me. My parents' home was washed away in the flood after the collapse of the Kakhovka dam, my business was hit by a shell and everything inside was burnt, my apartment was destroyed by shrapnel, which destroyed the walls and windows.[146]

Nastya decided to get what revenge she could by getting her own 'Kherson certificate' from the Russian state. 'Thanks to the Russians', she said, 'I have nothing left, so I think that I need to take at least a tuft of wool from this mangy sheep', citing an old Russian proverb. All she needed was to show her Ukrainian passport with its Kherson stamp, and after some time she received a 2.75-million-rouble (US$30,600) grant to buy a house.[147]

For that money, refugees could buy a small house in a poorly connected town or village in one of Russia's southern districts. Since few people wanted to stay in such places, they often sold on these houses to other buyers, sometimes also using a Kherson certificate. A kind of property carousel developed, in which willing local real estate agents helped refugees effectively turn their property certificates into cash by buying and selling properties quickly, taking a commission on each sale. Many refugees then left for other parts of Russia or Europe. Igor from Kherson told a journalist he had no wish to stay in Russia, fearing that he might be mobilised. Instead, he dreamt of a small house in Germany.[148] Even people from Kherson who were already in Europe somehow managed to buy apartments in this way. One couple bought a 6-million-rouble apartment as 'Kherson refugees', but continued to live in Poland. As the journalist who wrote up their story commented: 'They [...] love Putin and comfort but are not in any rush to go to Russia, preferring to love their "strong president" from afar, while receiving Polish refugee allowances.'[149]

The case of the Kherson refugees demonstrated how complex the question of forced migration had become. According to Deputy Prime Minister Marat Khusnullin, 68,000 people left Kherson with the Russians in November 2022 and 53,000 received compensation in Russia (other officials gave lower figures).[150] Some of these migrants fled to Russia because they were afraid of possible prosecution for collaborating with the Russians. Others may have been tricked into leaving by Russian forces. Some lost everything and ended up living in temporary refugee centres in provincial Russia. Others took advantage of the situation to migrate to Europe. But these were all coping mechanisms in a world turned upside down by the Russian invasion. In the end, these different migration patterns were all the result of Russia's military campaign, even if some Ukrainians managed to adapt to new realities and achieve the best possible outcome in almost impossible circumstances.

There was little doubt about the legal status of a series of individual deportations during 2022, because the occupation authorities announced officially that these Ukrainian citizens were being deported from the occupied territories for political reasons. These deportations were official policy in Zaporizhzhia region during 2022, although there was no legal basis for such a decision.[151] The occupation authorities frequently posted videos of these deportations, in which armed men would announce an order of deportation—without any semblance of a legal process—before sending the prisoners off across no man's land towards Ukrainian-controlled territory. One video shows a man, looking lost, being ordered to leave. He stands, hesitating, before walking away from his homeland with just a bottle of water in his hand.[152]

OCCUPATION

Russian-installed governor Yevgeny Balitsky later told a journalist that he had taken advantage of a temporary measure that was in effect prior to annexation: 'We deported a very large number of families [...] those who in one way or another did not support the special operation, those who insulted the flag, the anthem of Russia, or the president of Russia.' In a strange way, Balitsky saw this as an act of great mercy:

> We understood that we could not convince them, and we would otherwise have to treat them much more harshly. Their lives could face a serious threat, so it was better for them to go to their *bandershtat* [i.e. the Ukrainian state linked to wartime nationalist leader Stepan Bandera] and build their gay-world there.[153]

This was what passed for a humanitarian gesture in the occupied territories: the expulsion of men, women and children from their homes into exile because the occupation authorities believed that otherwise they would be forced to kill them.[154]

Children

Hundreds of thousands of Ukrainian children were transported to Russia from the occupied territories. Many travelled with their families, fleeing the violence with thousands of other refugees. But there were also thousands of children taken illegally by the Russian authorities from orphanages and special residential schools. In some of the starkest cases, children were taken from their parents during filtration, or lost their parents in the war, and were subsequently taken to Russia as orphans. According to Ukrainian officials and media investigations, at least some of these children were illegally adopted by Russian families.

The International Criminal Court (ICC) made the deportation of children its first war crimes case against Russia. Allegations that Russian forces had deported children from the occupied territories constituted the basis for an ICC warrant issued on 17 March 2023, which read:

> Mr Vladimir Vladimirovich Putin, born on 7 October 1952, President of the Russian Federation, is allegedly responsible for the war crime of unlawful deportation of population (children) and

that of unlawful transfer of population (children) from occupied areas of Ukraine to the Russian Federation (under articles 8(2)(a)(vii) and 8(2)(b)(viii) of the Rome Statute). The crimes were allegedly committed in Ukrainian occupied territory at least from 24 February 2022.[155]

The ICC also issued a warrant for the arrest of Maria Lvova-Belova, Commissioner for Children's Rights in the Office of the President of the Russian Federation, on the same charges. Maria Lvova-Belova had previously announced that she had adopted a 15-year-old boy from Mariupol herself.[156]

Getting an accurate picture of the scale of the deportations is not easy. Ukrainian officials estimated that as many as 19,500 children may have been taken illegally to Russia, but it is not clear how these numbers break down. There are several potential categories. First, media reports suggested that at least some children may have been simply taken for adoption, in the most brazen manner. One baby was allegedly taken away, after a visit to a Kherson children's home by Inna Varlamova in August 2022. A BBC report alleged that Ms Varlamova adopted the baby, Marharyta Prokopenko, with her husband, Sergei Mironov, and changed the child's name to Marina Mironova. Sergei Mironov, a powerful Russian politician and head of the SRZP party, denied that the story was true.[157]

Second, and the biggest group, were children from orphanages and special schools and other institutions.[158] This included as many as 4,000 orphans, according to the Ukrainian ombudsmen's office—although here too it is difficult to find exact numbers.[159] The practice of housing children in orphanages and special residential schools was a Soviet-era leftover, and had been repeatedly criticised by Ukrainian civil society and international organisations. According to the European Commission, Ukraine has 'one of the highest rates of child institutionalisation in the world'.[160] The system included orphans, but also children who had been placed into care under temporary patronage because their parents were considered to be unable to look after them. Now, when Russians seized control of territories in which boarding schools were located, they often transferred these children—many of whom had parents or wider family—to sanitoriums and children's homes in Russia or Crimea.

Igor Kastyukevich, the State Duma deputy, was reportedly involved in the transfer of 46 children from a children's home in Kherson to Crimea in October 2022.[161] Some of these children were housed in the Yelochka children's home, an institution that had been criticised even in Russia's state media for its poor care of children.[162] In August 2023 it was announced that the children would be returned to an institution in Kherson region, although in May 2024 the intended destination, Kherson Children's School, was still reportedly being renovated.[163] While in Crimea, the children were registered as Russian citizens, with Russian birth certificates and the Russian individual insurance account number that was needed to access public health facilities.[164] A report in the *New York Times* alleged that 22 of these children had been listed as available for adoption.[165] Kastyukevich dismissed the *New York Times* story as 'rotten Western-American propaganda', claiming that Russia had saved these children, while 'they [Ukrainians] are trying to return them to Ukraine with the sole purpose of killing them or throwing them away as unnecessary'.[166]

Third, there were other unaccompanied children who also ended up in care in Russia. These included children who had been orphaned during the fighting, or—perhaps most disturbing—children whose parents were detained during filtration. These children were then placed into care—or in some cases risked being forced into adoption. Eleven-year-old Oleksandr Radchuk was taken from his mother when she was interrogated and detained during filtration on the way out of Mariupol during the siege in 2022. Two years later, he had not heard from her again. Yevhen Mezhevyi was a single father of three young children, who was also detained at filtration as he evacuated from Mariupol. He was held for seven weeks before being released, while his children were taken away to a sanitorium. He managed to collect them just days before they were due to be adopted.[167]

A fourth group comprised children who had left Russian-occupied territory in Kherson to go on holiday to Crimea or to Russia. When the front line shifted, it left their parents on the

VIOLENCE

other side in Ukrainian-held territory, leaving their children stranded. It might seem strange for parents to have allowed their children to go to Crimea during the occupation, but parents probably wanted to get their children away from a war zone to experience some form of normality with their friends. Buses full of schoolchildren went back and forth to Crimea throughout the summer of 2022 from towns like Melitopol and Kherson, and the children returned safely.

But in October 2022 the situation changed. Katya, a 15-year-old from Kherson, went with her friends to a two-week summer camp in Crimea on 7 October.[168] They were supposed to return on 21 October, but their return was first delayed until 5 November, and then indefinitely after Ukrainian forces liberated the city on 11 November.[169]

The camp authorities told Katya and her friends that they would be allowed home 'when Kherson is Russian again'. At one point they were afraid that they might be given up for adoption, but eventually their parents came and collected them in February 2023, with the help of the charity Save Ukraine.[170] Russian officials would only allow the parents of the children to collect them, but that involved an arduous roundabout trip from Ukraine to Russia and back again. Katya had few complaints about treatment at the camp: 'I missed my mother, but I can't say that they treated us badly.' They did have to listen to the Russian anthem every morning. One girl had a tee-shirt with a Ukrainian flag on it. The camp leader took it away, cut the flag out and gave it back with a huge hole in it.[171] These were traumatic separations, often for several months, with children frequently uncertain about when they would see their parents again.[172]

The fate of these children was the only issue on which there were still direct talks between Kyiv and Moscow, between the offices of the ombudsmen in both countries.[173] Other negotiations took place through the mediation of the Qatari government. The Save Ukraine charity did remarkable work helping parents travel to Russia and Crimea to locate their children and bring them home. Russian officials denied that Ukrainian children were being forcibly adopted, but media investigations suggested otherwise.[174]

When children were accommodated in Russian institutions or schools, they faced a full Russification programme, part of a much wider effort to indoctrinate Ukrainian youth that is discussed in Chapter 5. Russian officials viewed these children as essentially Russian, regardless of their Ukrainian identity documents, and saw nothing wrong with forcing them to sing the Russian national anthem or take part in the increasingly militarised school curriculum. At one institution housing Ukrainian orphans in Karaul, Tambov region, extracurricular patriotic events on their weekly schedule included '"Courage Lessons" about Russian military leaders and "Russia is My Homeland" recitation contests'.[175]

Forced deportation is illegal under international humanitarian law. Children in particular are afforded special protection, including an outright ban on any attempt to 'change their personal status', such as forcing them to adopt Russian citizenship. Under international law, the occupying power is permitted 'to undertake total or partial evacuation of a given area if the security of the population or imperative military reasons so demand', but in such cases, 'Persons thus evacuated shall be transferred back to their homes as soon as hostilities in the area in question have ceased.'[176] Many Russian officials did not believe that they were violating international law, but saw the evacuation of children as a noble deed. None acknowledged that they were at best rescuing children from the violence and destruction that they themselves had created. Yet the practice was even darker than this obvious contradiction. The deportation of children was an integral part of a wider pattern of Russification that effectively erased the personal status and national identities of many children. Some considered it a potential case of genocide.[177]

The floods

There were many ways to die in the apocalypse of Russia's invasion. During the night of Tuesday, 6 June 2023, an explosion destroyed the Kakhovka dam, resulting in a massive tidal wave of water sweeping along the Dnipro River. In the first few hours after the explosion the waters from the reservoir flooded more than 300 square kilometres of territory, sweeping away houses in low-lying villages along the river's banks and leaving thousands of people stranded. Russia claimed that Ukraine had sabotaged the dam, but most expert opinions pointed towards a deliberate Russian breach using explosives located deep inside the structure.[178] Although there were many casualties and destroyed homes on the Ukrainian-controlled right bank of the river, the worst destruction—and the most inadequate response—occurred on the Russian-controlled left bank. The water mounted very quickly in Oleshky, a settlement that jutted out into the path of the river, right opposite the Antonov Bridge that led into Kherson city. Many traditional one-storey houses in this low-lying village were submerged, forcing their residents to either risk fleeing through the water, or to take their luck with any neighbours who had an extra storey on their house.

The Russian authorities did little to help initially. Only two days later, on Thursday, after many houses had been submerged and some had collapsed, did Russian troops begin an evacuation, which volunteers described as 'too sluggish and too late'. Local Telegram channels published appeals from stranded people. One posted: 'Ozerna Street, Hola Prystan village, an elderly couple are on their roof, water is rising, please help!'; another announced: 'School no. 61, three people on the roof, the situation is critical!'[179] In Oleshky, volunteers claimed that thirty people had died on one street alone and that Russian forces had refused to evacuate people with Ukrainian passports (although local authorities denied this to reporters).[180] Another local resident said that when Russian soldiers arrived to evacuate villagers, some people refused to go with them.[181] They were probably concerned that they would be forcibly evacuated to Russia.[182]

In Hola Pristan, Valentina was one of the lucky ones. 'The current was so fast', she told reporters, and 'the waters rose quickly, it literally knocked you off your feet. We just managed to grab some drinking water, our documents and carry some food upstairs.' From their second-floor windows they watched the chickens and a dog who were sitting together on the roof of the shed, which the water almost reached. From time to time—when there was a connection—her daughter would call her from abroad. Crying, she would plead with her to evacuate. Valentina explained that for three days they had not seen any volunteers or emergency services. 'Imagine, [my daughter] thinks that there are volunteers everywhere and the MChS is saving people', she said, referring to the Russian Ministry of Emergency Situations (MChS).[183]

The MChS rescue mission was slow to start but did eventually begin to evacuate people from flooded villages. By the weekend, the local authorities claimed that about 5,000 people had been evacuated, although on Saturday morning, volunteers claimed there were still 1,751 requests for evacuation—including 117 children. According to the volunteer network, relatives had lost contact with a least 395 people in the flood zone, in Oleshky, Hola Pristan, Krynky and Kokhany.[184] In the end, Russian officials claimed that fifty-nine people died in the flood in territories they controlled, but an investigation by AP concluded that hundreds died in Oleshky alone. The occupation authorities allegedly manipulated death certificates as part of a deliberate pattern of undercounting.[185]

Their fate was all the more poignant because those in occupied territory could see signs of the Ukrainian response on the other side of the Dnipro River, where emergency services flocked to help. President Zelensky visited Kherson, but no Russian official was visible on the other side of the river. According to Zelensky, Ukrainian services tried to help residents on the left bank but were shot at by Russian forces. He claimed that 'the occupiers simply abandoned people in these terrible conditions. Without rescue, without water, just on the roofs of houses in flooded communities.'[186]

Ukrainian resistance

The smartphone was the ultimate mechanism of control—the first thing that interrogators in filtration camps inspected or soldiers at checkpoints examined. But it also provided the means to wreak revenge, to inform on the whereabouts of Russian troops or collaborators to the Ukrainian military or intelligence agencies. Alina, who had worked in a school in Kherson before the invasion, resigned from her job to avoid working with the occupiers. She had two phones. 'On one I was a good girl, but on the other I passed on the coordinates of Russian military equipment for attacks by the ZSU [Ukrainian military]', she told journalists later.[187] This so-called 'spotting' for Ukrainian firepower was relatively easy while people had access to Ukrainian cell phone networks. Once the Russians began forcing everybody to switch to Russian SIM cards, which they could track much more easily, it became extremely dangerous. Kostya, a volunteer, recalled that so long as they could safely send data to the Ukrainian forces, 'we controlled the city in that way'. But once they switched off Ukrainian mobile operators, the groups dwindled because the Russians could easily access the messages.[188] But information gathering continued. Residents in the occupied areas could supply information through different channels including secure bots, such as the 'Yevorog' bot created by the Ukrainian Ministry of Digital Transformation. This information was fed into Ukraine's increasingly successful campaign of long-range artillery and missile attacks on Russian forces behind the lines.[189]

Armed resistance had begun almost as soon as the invasion began. In February 2022 a National Resistance Center of Ukraine (NRC) was established, with the slogan: 'Together we will turn the lives of the occupiers into hell'.[190] According to its website, the NRC 'was created by the Special Operations Forces for the purpose of training, coordinating and scaling movements against the occupation of Ukraine'. Its official mission included teaching non-violent resistance, helping partisans, collecting information about the Russian presence and providing information on what was happening in the occupied territories. According to one report, Western intelligence agencies may have provided training and advice.[191]

The NRC had a YouTube channel and an active Telegram channel, @sprotyv.official, which called for information from those who 'have information about Kremlin agents or collaborators and want to see news about their elimination'. Active operations were carried out by Ukraine's Special Operations Forces, which reportedly backed a group called Rukh Oporu, a partisan resistance movement.[192] It is difficult to tell how much of the resistance stemmed from local groups and networks and how much was run by the Ukrainian military and intelligence agencies. Russian arrests and charges against some detainees on terrorism charges suggested that there were networks of local accomplices, but much of the organisation and logistics was probably managed by Ukrainian special forces and intelligence networks.

Meduza counted nearly twenty attacks in newly occupied territories between March and August 2022.[193] But many more went unreported. In June 2022 Melitopol mayor Fedorov claimed that Ukrainian partisans had already killed up to 100 Russian soldiers.[194] Those locals deemed to be collaborators were also targets. Regional head Vladimir Saldo survived a poisoning attempt. Dmytro Savluchenko, head of the Department of Family, Youth and Sports of the Kherson occupation administration was blown up in a car bomb.[195] In June 2022 local pro-Russian activist Vladimir Rogov claimed that the Ukrainians had shifted from missile attacks to terrorism: 'Ukrainian nationalists will do everything possible to disturb peaceful life, terrorise people and maintain them in fear. This is pure terrorism.'[196]

In September 2022, ahead of the annexation of the territories by Russia at the end of the month, there was an uptick in attacks. Those collaborating with the Russians were primary targets. On 8 September, a bomb blast in Melitopol killed Yury Onyschuk, who was heading the local water supply company; explosions were reported at the homes of two other people accused of working for Russia to prepare a referendum. On 12 September, another blast targeted the rector of Kherson State University, Tatyana Tomilina, leaving her bodyguard dead. On 13 September, a group of partisans reportedly attacked a Russian patrol. On 16 September, presumed Ukrainian partisans shot and killed Oleh Boyko, the deputy head of the Berdiansk city housing division and a former candidate for mayor of Berdiansk, along with his wife Lyudmila. Also on 16 September, in the centre of Luhansk, a bomb blast was reported in the imposing building that housed the LNR General Prosecutor's Office, killing the prosecutor general Sergei Gorenko and his deputy Ekaterina Steglenko.[197] On the same day another bomb explosion was reported in Kherson, apparently aimed at the minister of social policy in the occupation government, Alla Barkhatnova, but instead killing her driver. After his death she promised that 'we will take revenge for everybody who dies here' and 'we will continue to work, however difficult and frightening it may be—and it is really frightening for us—but we came here to ensure that Russia will be here, and Russia will be here'.[198]

This bravado could hardly disguise the fear among Ukrainians collaborating with the Russians, but most of these officials were now trapped. It was difficult for them to resign or to leave—even for Russia—and they were left to live with the consequences of a fateful choice. Russian forces—through the brutal filtration programme and other counterinsurgency measures—clamped down on Ukrainian intelligence networks, but the attacks continued. In December 2022 Vitaly Bulyuk, first deputy head of the Kherson regional administration, survived a car-bomb attack. Two Ukrainians were later sentenced to twenty-three and twenty-four years in prison for the attempt on his life.[199]

There were numerous sabotage attacks. According to Ukrainian sources, 'Melitopol partisans' attacked a train locomotive on 13 October 2023 in Melitopol. Ukraine claimed that this was the tenth successful attack in 2023.[200] A series of attacks also targeted security officials. The assassination attempts continued. In March 2023, Mariupol police chief Mikhail Moskvin survived a car-bomb attack in the city.[201] In May 2023, the LNR interior minister, Igor Kornet, was badly injured in a bomb attack that destroyed a barber's shop in Luhansk.[202] Yury Afanasevsky, formerly head of the LNR customs office, but alleged by Ukrainian sources to be an FSB officer and a close aide of LNR head Leonid Pasechnik, survived an explosion in his house.[203] On 8 November 2023, former policeman and deputy of the LNR regional council, Mikhail Filiponenko, died after a bomb exploded under the seat of his car as he set off for work.[204] Ukrainian military intelligence issued a statement, saying that 'A special operation to eliminate the executioner Filiponenko was implemented together with representatives of the resistance movement', and concluded its press release by promising that 'the hunting continues'.[205] Between December 2023 and January 2024, the scholar Jade McGlynn identified 'more than 73 reported deaths of Russian soldiers, police officers, and occupation officials at the hands of partisan movements' in open source reporting.[206]

As Russian forces continued to consolidate control, there were periods when reports of attacks behind the front line died down. But there were also spikes when Ukrainian intelligence networks were active again and successfully mounted attacks on the military in the occupied territories. On 27 November 2023 Ukrainian media reported a shoot-out with Chechen forces near Melitopol, and the killing of six Russian soldiers in Mariupol. Four bodies were found on the beach, where the soldiers had apparently arranged an impromptu party. Next to the bodies, according to reports, was a portrait of Putin, with the word 'Leave!' written on it in blood. Two other soldiers were reportedly shot in the back of the head on the streets of the city.[207] Russian forces responded with a house-to-house *zachistka* in the villages around Mariupol.[208] Russian officials continued to insist on further repression and surveillance to intercept resistance groups. At a meeting of the Russian interior ministry in April 2024, President Putin warned that 'diversionary groups' were still active in the occupied territories and were using long-standing criminal networks and routes. He called for 'the closest possible control', instructing the security forces 'to literally conduct door-to-door visits to cities and towns. And do everything to prevent, as they say, saboteurs and accomplices of neo-Nazis from being legalised.'[209]

There was almost no public objection to the Ukrainian resistance tactics in the occupied territories, either in Ukraine or in the West. Officials at the NRC claimed to have taken inspiration from the French resistance in World War II.[210] However, attacks on civilians who cooperate with the occupying power are potential war crimes. According to legal scholar Kenneth Watkin, the prohibition of the Geneva Convention on targeting civilians extends also to civilians cooperating with the occupying power. Unless they are directly involved in hostilities, 'the killing of collaborators needs to be investigated as a potential war crime'.[211] This was not a new argument; it had accompanied every resistance movement in World War II. It was unlikely to get much traction in Ukraine, where there was little sympathy for collaborators, whether considered civilians or not. The more complex question was whether it was effective. It probably dissuaded some locals from active public support for the Russians, but thousands of Ukrainians still cooperated with the Russians in local institutions. Over time, a sustained resistance movement might begin to wear down Russia's ability to maintain control. But when I met a former member of the resistance network from the south, he seemed uncertain about the future. 'I don't think we'll ever get the left bank of the Dnipro back again', he told me.[212]

The resistance was not only about sabotage and assassination. Non-violent activists worked to display Ukrainian symbolism in the occupied territories. In effect, all Ukrainian symbols—the flag, the national coat of arms, or anything related to Ukrainian culture or history—were viewed as suspect. Displaying any of them was dangerous. The 'Yellow Ribbon' movement, set up in April 2022, was a civil movement of non-violent resistance, which used the yellow ribbon as a symbol to show that Ukrainians remained in the territories and opposed the occupation. The volunteers took photographs of small yellow ribbons in the occupied territories, left flags on buildings or wrote anti-Russian graffiti. As with the NRC, a major aim of the Yellow Ribbon movement was to provide information. The movement called for Ukrainians to become 'The eyes of Ukraine', and to send: '1) Photos and videos of Russian military personnel and collaborators [...]; 2) Photos of campaign products (newspapers, announcements, billboards); 3) Photos and videos of streets, administration buildings, banks, etc.' The Yellow Ribbon movement called on Ukrainians to boycott Russia and everything Russian, including pensions and passports.[213]

The Yellow Ribbon resistance movement won the European Parliament's Sakharov Prize for Freedom of Thought in 2022 for its non-violent campaign against Russian occupation. Similar movements included 'Zla Mavka', a group of women based in Melitopol.[214] These groups involved brave volunteers who aimed to keep alive the idea that Ukraine would still return to the occupied territories. Their activities were inspiring for many and no doubt were serious irritants for the FSB, but their wider impact was uncertain: the audience for these resistance groups was largely limited to other pro-Ukrainian activists and supporters. Along with the National Resistance Center and other government-backed resistance initiatives, they did not have any communications in Russian, thus losing part of their potential audience.

Perhaps as significant as these state-backed resistance movements was what the social scientist James C. Scott calls 'everyday forms of resistance', which he argues were historically much more common among societies opposing repression than outright revolt. Scott points to a range of tactics, such as 'foot-dragging, evasion, false compliance, pilfering, feigned ignorance, slander and sabotage' as typical ways to resist oppressors when outright opposition appears futile.[215] Russian visitors to the occupied territories sometimes complained that they were not welcomed, that they felt in danger, that they were not served in gas-stations, or were snubbed in bars and restaurants. In this context, Scott points to the 'transcripts' of the oppressed, the ways in which societies delegitimise dominant transcripts by using things such as 'rumour, gossip, disguises, linguistic tricks, metaphors, euphemisms, folktales, ritual gestures, anonymity' as ways of undermining the oppressor's narrative.[216] These approaches are safer than challenging the discourse outright but can be highly effective at destabilising the public narrative imposed by oppressive governments—in this case an occupation regime obsessed with propaganda and ideology.

Conclusion: Systemic violence

The scale and extent of Russian violence was shocking. By September 2023 the Ukrainian authorities had recorded 108,904 potential war crimes committed by Russian forces.[217] The International Criminal Court launched an investigation and indicted President Putin and five other officials, but it would take years to uncover all the individual acts of violence against Ukrainian civilians in the occupied territories. Although there was widespread reporting of cases of torture and killing, many people passed through the Russian detention centres and did not talk about the violence they experienced. This was especially true in cases of sexual violence. Many tried to forget what they had endured.

VIOLENCE

The violence was systemic and deliberate. A culture of violence underpinned the Russian presence, evident in the egregious brutality and indiscipline of many soldiers. Yet the violent acts were not aberrations, but part of a systemic use of coercion through targeted repressions and mass filtration methods that had the strategic goal of quelling any actual or potential resistance in the occupied territories. This was a system of violence that built on decades of experience of repression and coercion dating back to the Soviet period. But it was also interlinked with the modern political, ideological and economic aspects of the occupation to form a systemic, holistic approach to political control.

The violence was ongoing. Hundreds of Ukrainian civilians continued to experience the lawlessness of the Russian regime in the most direct way, incarcerated in Russian jails two years after the war began. Everyday violence or the threat of violence continued to underpin Russia's political control in the occupied territories. Ukrainian armed resistance networks mounted a serious challenge to the occupation authorities, but Russia's extensive surveillance and informer network began to dull their ability to infiltrate the territories and stage attacks on military targets. But an occupation based only on violence would never be sustainable. In the longer term, Russia could only maintain control of the territories if the occupation authorities were able to persuade a large part of society that resistance was futile and that it was better to adapt to the Russian occupation than to resist. That required policies beyond violence—in the sphere of propaganda and persuasion, education and culture, where a mass programme of indoctrination would attempt to ensure compliance without the need to resort to mass repressions.

5

PROPAGANDA

Violence was only one instrument in Russia's occupation toolbox. Like many other modern authoritarian states, Russia understood that relying solely on repression to maintain power was expensive and ultimately unsustainable. Even the most violent and repressive state also requires control of the media, of language, symbols and narratives—or what is sometimes called a hegemonic discourse— 'the dominant ideas, tropes, narratives and syntax that circulate in a society in ways that constrain the possibility of articulating alternatives to the political status quo'.[1] The idea is to inculcate the beliefs and values of the political elite in the rest of society through control of the media, education, culture and symbolism. The aim is to achieve a society where overt political opposition is viewed as inappropriate, unpatriotic or destructive, and where a majority of people either willingly support the regime or believe that any resistance is useless.

Post-Soviet Russian thinkers were obsessed with the political significance of language and discourse. Russian conservatives believed they were in an information war with the West, a 'war of meanings' and a struggle to interpret the world in ways that differed radically from Western liberal thinking.[2] The primary theorist of Putinism, Vladislav Surkov, called for Russian culture to be an 'organism of meaning-formation and ideational influence' that would be involved in the 'production of meanings and images'.[3] Russia wanted to define the world on its own terms and not to be dependent on what Russian officials liked to call the 'Anglo-Saxon media'. This attempt to achieve 'discursive control' became a central concern of the Putinist regime, which invested huge sums in the broadcaster RT, the radio stations and websites run by Sputnik, and a host of other international propaganda platforms, to challenge the West's influence in the global media.[4]

Information was also central to Russian military doctrine, sometimes referred to as *informatsionnoye protivoborstvo*, or 'information confrontation'.[5] Many officials believed that Russia had lost the first Chechen war in 1995 at least partly because damning pictures of death and destruction showed nightly on Russian television.[6] There would be no repeat under Putin. In all of Russia's subsequent military campaigns—the second Chechen war, the Russian military intervention in Syria, the wars in Ukraine, Russian military missions in Nagorno-Karabakh and in several African states—control of information was central to Russian strategy.[7] In each mission, Russian forces harassed and detained independent journalists and blocked alternative media, while Russian outlets ran a raft of positive messaging across social media, TV, radio and the press.

Immediately after the invasion in February 2022, Russia's media management was initially crude and at times confused. War planning in Moscow had been so secretive that key media managers were apparently left out of the loop. But Moscow quickly began to catch up. Russia's intelligence agencies and the Presidential Administration had vast experience in information management and propaganda and had a network of media outlets, journalists and polemicists ready to promote Moscow's version of the war. By 2023, according to leaked secret internal budgets analysed by an Estonian website, the Presidential Administration alone was spending up to US$631 million annually on what it called 'information warfare'.[8]

It was in the occupied territories that the information challenge was greatest. Here Russia's information campaign was much more wide-ranging than simply trying to justify its war or compete with Western and Ukrainian media. Russia was intent on a 'cognitive occupation', a deliberate policy to transform the consciousness of people now living under Russian rule. Russian officials often claimed that Ukrainians had been brainwashed into rejecting a Russian identity and internalising a Ukrainian version of their history. This helped them to explain why so few Ukrainians had welcomed the invading Russian army. Foreign ministry spokesperson Maria Zakharova accused the Ukrainian government of 'recoding the consciousness of millions of Ukrainians, indoctrinating them with the ideas of national exclusivity and superiority'.[9] In response, Russia's information and educational policies sought to unravel what it viewed as three decades of Ukrainian propaganda, and explicitly aimed to 're-educate' the population of the occupied territories.

Russia's propaganda campaign was all-embracing. The occupation authorities set out to transform the entire discursive landscape—all the symbolism that people saw around them, the monuments, the flags, the place names, the media they watched and read, the lessons their children were taught at school. Everything would be changed: the movies in the cinema, the exhibits in museums, the playlists at the theatre and the books on the shelves of libraries. Across the newly occupied territories, Russian officials set out on a campaign to obliterate the Ukrainian past and install a very different, Russian, future.

Symbols

Initially, there were only hints at this grand ambition. During the first few weeks of the invasion there was confusion. The first flag raised by Russian forces on the Kherson administration building was the banner of Russian neo-monarchists, known as the Khorugv, a red flag incorporating the head of Christ and the inscription 'For Faith, Tsar and Holy Triune Rus'.[10] In other places, Ukrainian flags remained up for several weeks. The Soviet Victory banner was everywhere, the same flag that Soviet soldiers had raised on the Reichstag on 1 May 1945. In April 2022 the BBC reported that on the central square in Nova Kakhovka the Russian flag, the flag of the USSR and the Victory banner were all flying outside the Russian Military-Civilian Administration.[11]

In one sense, this cacophony of banners reflected Russia's own identity crisis and the uncertainty of the goals of its military campaign. But the main goal—the destruction of all things Ukrainian—soon became clear. Across the occupied territories, Russian forces destroyed Ukrainian symbols such as the distinctive Ukrainian *tryzub*, the golden trident on a blue background, adopted as Ukraine's coat of arms by the Ukrainian People's Republic in 1918, and taken up again by the modern Ukrainian state in 1992. The Ukrainian colours—yellow and sky-blue—began to be replaced everywhere with Russia's red, white and blue. Huge billboards were erected along city streets, congratulating people on the Russian 'liberation'. Other placards quoted Alexander Pushkin, a poet strongly associated with Russian imperialism, or celebrated eighteenth-century Russian conquerors of this land: Catherine the Great, the military leader Alexander Suvorov and Prince Grigory Potemkin.[12]

The occupation authorities destroyed numerous monuments that commemorated the Holodomor famine.[13] In October 2022 Russian troops dismantled a striking monument in the middle of a quiet square off University Street in Mariupol. This square pedestal of black and red granite was divided down the middle and capped with strands of barbed wire, a symbol of the Gulag. It was dedicated to victims of the Holodomor and to victims of Soviet political repressions. A local pro-Russian activist told Russian media: 'We are not dismantling a monument but a symbol of political disinformation. In the teaching of Ukrainian history, we had these ideas of "genocide" and "Holodomor" forced on us.'[14] Russian historians largely reject the claim that the Soviet-made famine of 1932–33 was an intentional genocide directed at Ukrainians, whereas in Ukraine the collective memory of the Holodomor as a genocidal act against the Ukrainian people has become central to modern Ukrainian national identity.[15]

There was a further battle over street art. In September 2018 a huge portrait of a young girl was revealed on the wall of a high-rise building on Prospekt Myru in central Mariupol. The picture was of Milana Abdurashytova, whose mother died in Mariupol in January 2015 while protecting her child with her own body from Russian shelling. Milana survived and became a symbol of Ukrainian resilience. Now, under occupation, the authorities quickly painted over the mural, along with other street art that celebrated Ukrainian themes. Instead, they commissioned their own artwork, including one by Italian street artist Jorit Ciro Cerullo, better known simply as Jorit, who drew a crying girl's face against a background of a falling bomb, with the label 'NATO'.[16] This in turn was later dismantled, perhaps because it was still too reminiscent of the horrors of war for the new urban environment that Russia wanted to build.

The occupation authorities set about renaming streets, villages and other place names. This was only the latest wave in a history of politicised place-naming in Ukraine that stretched back to the 1917 Russian revolution. Most recently, a decommunisation law in May 2015 had ordered the removal of all Soviet and Communist symbols in Ukraine. Thousands of streets, villages and towns reverted to their historic pre-Soviet names, or were renamed in honour of prominent Ukrainian historical figures. These changes were not always popular. In a 2016 poll, only 35% of respondents nationally supported the renaming of Soviet-era streets and towns; in the east, support dropped to under 20%. Big majorities in a 2018 poll in the south (79%) and east (64%) agreed with the statement: 'Decommunisation is not needed'.[17] For most people, there were simply much more important priorities, such as the failing economy; but for many in an older generation, these symbolic changes appeared to be a condemnation of their own lives, memories and careers.

Now the Russian authorities reversed these changes in the occupied territories, reinstating Soviet-era place names. Suddenly a string of Karl Marx streets and Lenin streets reappeared on the map. In Mariupol, Freedom Square became Lenin Square once again, and Heroes of Ukraine Street became Marshal Zhukov Embankment, after the Soviet war hero. Even the apparently innocuous Morksoy Bulvar (Seaside Boulevard) would once again be known as Komsomol Boulevard, after the long-forgotten Soviet youth movement. Meotida Boulevard, at the heart of the devastated left-bank district of the town, close to the Azovstal factory site, returned to the awkward Soviet-era name, 50th Anniversary of the October Revolution Street.[18]

Not only were the Russians reintroducing Lenin streets, they were also busy re-erecting statues of the Soviet leader. During the 2015–16 decommunisation campaign, the Ukrainian authorities had dismantled over 1,000 statues of Lenin across the country. This policy had also not been popular in parts of the east. In Mariupol, fewer than 7% of respondents in one poll supported tearing down the statues, with 66% opposed.[19] Now the Russians began putting them back up. A Lenin statue was restored on 18 April 2022 in Henichesk and in Nova Kakhovka on 20 April. Through 2022 more Lenin statues were returned to their plinths, including in Melitopol on 5 November. When Lenin was restored to the centre of Svitlodarsk, in Donetsk region, on 3 December 2022, the new Russian-appointed local head said: 'Historical justice is being restored here. Here not only is cultural heritage being preserved, but one of the symbols of equality and social justice is honoured.'[20]

The re-erection of Lenin statues was particularly paradoxical since Putin had made clear on repeated occasions that he blamed Lenin for the break-up of the Russian empire and for a Soviet nationalities policy that led to the creation of a separate Ukrainian Soviet republic. On the eve of the war, he had blamed Lenin for the creation of the modern Ukrainian state, calling him 'its author and architect'.[21] But the aim of these symbolic changes was not to honour Lenin, but to reverse time, to start from 1991 all over again and to destroy any evidence that these territories had ever been part of an independent Ukraine.

In April 2023 more than 400 streets in Melitopol were renamed. Some changes were particularly provocative. University Street was renamed Darya Dugina Street, after the daughter of Russian ultra-nationalist philosopher Alexander Dugin. Like her father, Darya Dugina was also an anti-Ukrainian polemicist. She was assassinated by a car bomb in Moscow in August 2022, allegedly by the Ukrainian secret service.[22] In a symbolic shift, Intercultural Street now became Catherine the Great Street. And Ukraine Street became Soviet Street, which neatly summed up the historical time-shift in the minds of the occupiers. Izrail Dagin, a Melitopol native and a high-ranking NKVD officer under Stalin, also had a street named after him.[23] Dagin was executed in 1940 during purges of the NKVD. Soviet prosecutors refused to rehabilitate Dagin because of his well-documented involvement in mass repressions in the North Caucasus in the 1930s.[24]

The name of one street in Melitopol sums up the political battle over the history of Ukraine in the twentieth century. During the Soviet period and up until 2016 it was called Profintern Street, named after the Russian abbreviation for the Red International of Labor Unions. In 2016 it was renamed as part of the 'decommunisation' campaign as Dmytro Dontsov Street, after a native of Melitopol who went on to become one of the key ideologues of interwar Ukrainian nationalism. An antisemite and an admirer of Hitler and Mussolini, Dontsov was an ideological inspiration for the Organisation of Ukrainian Nationalists (OUN), the far-right Ukrainian nationalist movement established in 1929.[25] The definitive biography of Dontsov by Trevor Erlacher leaves the reader in little doubt that his views aligned with the general tenets of interwar European fascism.[26] The promotion of Dontsov was part of the much wider rehabilitation of 1930s Ukrainian nationalists, many of whom were irredeemably tainted by their association with European fascism and collaboration with the Nazis.

Russia manipulated this aspect of Ukraine's nation-building project into a false casus belli that claimed that the Ukrainian regime was run by 'neo-Nazis' and that it required a campaign of 'denazification'. In an interview with American journalist Tucker Carlson, Putin argued that Ukrainian nationalists such as OUN leaders Stepan Bandera and Roman Shukhevych, who had collaborated with the Nazis, 'have been turned into national heroes in Ukraine', and that 'monuments to these people have been erected, they are displayed on flags, their names are shouted by crowds that walk with torches, as it was in Nazi Germany'. Putin concluded by saying that 'It is necessary to stop this practice and prevent the dissemination of this concept.'[27] But whatever the historical record of Ukrainian nationalist movements and despite the presence of a small minority of far-right groups, modern Ukraine was a pluralistic, multi-ethnic state, not the mono-ethnic authoritarian polity advocated by some 1930s Ukrainian nationalists, and certainly not the grotesque neo-Nazi regime conjured up by Russian propaganda.

Not surprisingly, Dontsov Street was immediately targeted by the Russians as part of their 'denazification' campaign. In June 2022 the street was renamed Sudoplatov Street, to commemorate the memory of General Pavel Sudoplatov, a notorious Stalinist spy and assassin. A plaque of Sudoplatov was unveiled with the tag line: 'The Sword of Vengeance for the Traitors of the Motherland'. Sudoplatov was a Ukrainian, born in Melitopol in 1907. After a spell in the Red Army, he joined the Soviet security services. In 1938 Stalin ordered him to assassinate Yevhen Konovalets, then the leader of the OUN and a follower of Dontsov's ideas. Sudoplatov killed Konovalets in Rotterdam on 23 May 1938 with an exploding chocolate box. He also claimed to have organised the murder of Leon Trotsky in Mexico in 1940, and he was a key figure in the Soviet counterinsurgency campaign in western Ukraine against Ukrainian nationalists after 1945.[28] After Stalin's death, Sudoplatov spent fifteen years imprisoned in the Gulag for his role in the Stalinist repressions. His symbolic resurrection in Mariupol was a remarkable historical comeback.

Sudoplatov's return was not limited to a new street name. He was also rewarded with a new monument. On 7 July 2022 the RIA Novosti news agency issued a report that began: 'In Melitopol, at the intersection of Kirov and Karl Marx streets, a monument was unveiled to a native of this city, Pavel Sudoplatov, a legendary employee of the Soviet special services, a fighter against Ukrainian nationalism.'[29] This new monument on the renamed streets represented an almost surreal time-shift back in history, not just to Soviet times, but to the Stalinist period.[30] At its unveiling, Russian-installed governor Yevgeny Balitsky said: 'Today historical justice has been achieved [...]. No more Banderas or Shukhevyches will desecrate our streets. Monuments to real heroes will stand here.'[31]

In September 2022 Balitsky established a 'Sudoplatov Battalion', led by Yevgeny Gorlachev, reportedly a friend of Balitsky who was also installed as head of the local museum.[32] On 1 October 2023, perhaps in response, President Zelensky named the 131st Separate Reconnaissance Battalion of the Ground Forces in honour of Yevhen Konovalets, the Ukrainian nationalist leader murdered by Sudoplatov.[33] This competitive historicisation of the conflict on both sides of the war only served to further deepen the ideological divide between Moscow and Kyiv.

Media

Cities like Mariupol and Kherson had lively local media scenes before the invasion. By contrast, Russian-controlled areas of Ukraine in the DNR, LNR and Crimea had suppressed any semblance of independent journalism after 2014. In 2023 the US think-tank Freedom House awarded the DNR and LNR the lowest possible scores for media freedom, noting that 'No free and independent media have operated in the occupied Donbas since 2014.'[34] Anybody who wrote critical articles faced severe reprisals. The writer Stanislav Aseyev spent two and a half years in a dire prison in Donetsk known to its inmates as 'Isolation'. His interrogators told him that even his habit of placing inverted commas around the acronym 'LNR' was an extremist act.[35]

A similar fate awaited Ukrainian journalists in the newly occupied territories under Russian rule. Initially, the FSB hoped to persuade Ukrainian journalists to switch sides and start producing pro-Russian content. A few media outlets did work with the Russians. A local television channel, MTV+, controlled by Balitsky, was soon broadcasting pro-Russian material. In Kherson, the VTV+ channel initially broadcast pro-Ukrainian news, but by the end of April it had begun showing interviews with pro-Russian regional head Vladimir Saldo, and had evidently been persuaded to go over to the side of the occupiers. But most journalists refused to work with the Russians, and many fled the occupation as soon as possible.[36]

In Melitopol, Russian soldiers detained Mikhail Kumok, the publisher of local newspaper *Melitopolski vidomosti*, and several of his staff, and asked him to provide 'favourable coverage of events' in town. They even offered financial support. When he refused, they published a fake version of his newspaper anyway.[37] Svetlana Zalizetskaya, editor-in-chief of local news site RIA-Melitopol, was also offered a chance to cooperate by local pro-Russian mayor Galina Danilchenko, who offered her 'a brilliant career' if she collaborated. Instead, she left the city and her news site became one of the main sites for reports on Russian war crimes and collaboration in the city.[38] RIA-Melitopol continued to operate in exile, but the Russians began to round up its contributors and journalists in the occupied territories. The journalists Anastasia Hlukhovska and other colleagues from RIA-Melitopol and the site *Melitopol tse Ukraina* ('Melitopol is Ukraine') were arrested in Melitopol on 20 August 2023. The campaigning organisation Reporters Without Borders commented that '[t]he Russian-occupied Ukrainian territories are lawless zones for independent journalists'.[39]

Almost the first thing Russian forces did when they arrived in any town was to seize the local television tower and to reorient broadcasting from Ukrainian television and radio channels to Russian programming. At the digital terrestrial provider Zeonbud, in Kherson, Russian channels had already replaced Ukrainian broadcasts on 25 February.[40] When they arrived in Berdiansk, Russian forces seized Azovska Khvylia radio station and began broadcasting as 'Svobodnyi Berdiansk' (Free Berdiansk). By March, television in Melitopol had also switched to Russian channels. Probably few locals watched them, although the Russian-imposed mayor Galina Danilchenko told RT that 'many people are happy, here people missed the Russian language'.[41] By June 2022 Russia had seized all seven television towers across Kherson region and recalibrated them to broadcast twenty-four Russian channels around the clock.[42]

Alongside Russian national channels, the authorities needed new local channels offering local content, if only to publicise local instructions and regulations from the occupation authorities. The channel Krym-24 from Crimea began making special broadcasts to the occupied territories on the programmes 'Kherson-24' and 'Zaporozhe-24', which provided upbeat Soviet-style news from the occupied territories. For example, on 30 April 2022, Krym-24 had a segment with the tagline, 'Liberated and Peaceful', showing a wedding in Berdiansk.[43] Over time, new local channels were launched, such as Za!TV, and many, including Luhansk 24 and Soyuz, were included in a new free satellite package, launched for the occupied territories in December 2022, called Russian World.[44] It included twenty national television and radio channels and ten local channels, plus a package of entertainment channels.⁴⁵ It gained 155,000 subscribers in 2023, and was intent on replacing the unlicensed satellite dishes used by some people in the occupied territories that still gave access to Ukrainian television.⁴⁶

Television was important, but the internet was the key information source for most local people. Russian forces quickly seized the transmitters and masts of Ukrainian mobile networks, such as Kyivstar. Local mobile phone networks were forced to switch to Russian operators from Crimea. To make calls, people had to buy new SIM cards that worked with Russian networks.⁴⁷ The DNR company, Phoenix, moved into Mariupol and newly occupied areas of DNR, while the Russian authorities used a Crimean internet provider, Miranda-Media (branded as Mirtelekom), to take over both cellular and internet provision in Russian-controlled areas of Kherson and Zaporizhzhia regions.⁴⁸ On 3 February 2023 Miranda-Media took control of Mediana, the biggest local internet provider in Mariupol, in what appeared to be a 'raider attack', the term used in Russia for a hostile and illicit takeover of a company.⁴⁹ Russian control of the internet allowed them to block Ukrainian news channels using the extensive internet controls already used in Russia. As in Russia, Facebook, Instagram and numerous international and Ukrainian sites were banned, and there were severe legal consequences for any critical posts on social media.

The Russian authorities promoted the main Russian social media platform, VK, but most people still used Telegram, which was also widely used in Ukraine. Telegram was popular because it lacked the moderation of other social media, allowing Russian polemicists (and anybody else) to broadcast their narratives unhindered. And it also had much better performance than other social networks or websites when the internet was not reliable—as was often the case in wartime Ukraine. The Russian military appears to have been behind a Telegram network that appeared on 5–7 March 2022, covering multiple localities and reproducing the same messages about Russian humanitarian aid.⁵⁰ A further set of channels— slightly less identikit—was set up in the days following, such as 'Novyi Melitopol' (New Melitopol) or 'Berdiansk ZaVtra' (Berdiansk

Tomorrow). But the most popular pro-Russian channels were those run by individuals and those termed war correspondents, who were more ideological cheerleaders than proper journalists. Russian officials also launched their own personal channels, including Vladimir Saldo, Yevgeny Balitsky and others. The occupation authorities also mimicked popular Ukrainian sites. There were now two sites called 'Mariupol Now', one pro-Russian and one pro-Ukrainian. The Ukrainian one was much more popular, with over 147,000 subscribers, while only 32,600 followed the Russian site in mid-2024.

Russian state media and other agencies played a role in establishing new media, but the Presidential Administration preferred to outsource this work to specialists, such as Alexander Malkevich, a media entrepreneur who had previously been linked to Yevgeny Prigozhin, head of the Wagner group. Malkevich had first shot to fame with an ill-fated attempt to set up a media outlet in Washington called 'USA Really', backed by Prigozhin. It was a flop, but it got Malkevich included in a US government sanctions list and won him notoriety at home. Back in Russia, he took up a post as head of St Petersburg TV, while also running the Foundation for the Protection of National Values, a platform for all kinds of influence operations, including in Africa alongside Wagner. Malkevich was far from being just a freelancer. He was also a member of the Civic Chamber in Russia, a kind of consultative chamber full of pro-government civil society groups.[51]

In June 2022 Malkevich turned up in Melitopol to establish a new media holding company, ZaMedia, which ran a 24-hour television channel, Za!TV, and a radio station, Za!Radio. He also set up Tavriya TV, which began broadcasting in Kherson in August but was forced to evacuate from the city when Russian forces withdrew. He started a new Television of the New Regions channel and promoted Z-FM—also known as Frontline Radio—as a station aimed at military personnel.[52] In January 2023 Malkevich received an award at a ceremony from the Russian prime minister Mikhail Mishustin for 'organising television broadcasting in the liberated territories'.[53] Malkevich was also active on social media. His Telegram channels 'Malkevich Live' and 'Media Malkevich' had

PROPAGANDA

tens of thousands of followers. He set up a new journalism department at Kherson University and published a textbook titled *Real Russian Journalism for the New Regions*, designed to combat what he called 'total Ukrfascist propaganda'.[54] Another school, Mediatopol, was founded in November 2022, headed by a young pro-Russian activist called Aleksandr Gurov.[55] The idea was simple: to train a new generation of local journalists, using the latest production techniques and media technologies, while also ensuring complete political loyalty to Russia.

Russia did not ignore old-fashioned media. Print newspapers appealed to pensioners and those without the internet. In July 2022, a new free sheet appeared in Kherson called *Naddniepryanskaya pravda*, 'The Truth over the River Dnipro', a deliberate revival of a Soviet-era newspaper of that name. Its layout, font and content all offered unthinking Soviet nostalgia. The USSR's Order of Labour medal even appeared on its front page. When Russian troops fled Kherson, *Naddniepryanskaya pravda* disappeared with them, but journalist Maxim Edwards managed to read some copies. It was a mix of crass propaganda and adverts for jobs for teachers, administrators, doctors and all the other professions that needed to fill posts after thousands had fled the occupation. The front pages were full of dire warnings against 'propagandising terrorism' or 'disseminating false information'. Anti-Ukrainian propaganda filled the inside pages, with one headline calling Kherson a land of 'Russian people with Ukrainian passports', neatly summing up the view in Moscow that Ukrainian nationality was an artificial construct. Then there were the Nazis who had taken over Kyiv, who were accused of 'excis[ing] everything Russian: monuments, culture, language'. As Edwards concluded, the whole content of the newspaper was 'not so much about winning Ukrainians' hearts and minds as restoring them to supposed factory settings'.[56] But the core identity that they appealed to was more Soviet then Russian.

As the occupation consolidated, the media landscape became more sophisticated. A new approach was to encourage YouTube vloggers to post videos claiming to show the positive side of Russian rule. 'Masha from Mariupol' gave a glossy, upbeat view of the reconstruction of Mariupol.[57] The 'Walk&Talk' channel was pro-Russian, but also broadcast many complaints from local people about housing and social problems in Mariupol.[58] YouTube channels benefited from the credibility of a genre that was supposedly independent; but in practice their aim was to normalise the occupation and demonstrate that—despite some everyday problems—Russian rule was here to stay and was benefiting the local population. Generous government budgets continued to encourage other new media initiatives in the occupied territories, such as *Novoe Media* (New Media), a well-funded outfit with high production values that appeared in April 2024.[59]

Initially there was limited take-up among the local population of these new Russian media. In 2022 there was 'a fundamental refusal to consume Russian media', according to a report by Internews Ukraine. But as the occupation continued, this principled stance began to wane. The report concluded that one reason was a 'lack of moral strength to search for reliable Ukrainian information and navigating blocked access'. Perhaps it was just fatigue and the need to survive. More practically, Russian sources gave people 'current, useful information about daily life and solving everyday issues'.[60] Russian television packages also had plenty of entertainment channels and programmes for children. Russian propaganda certainly had an effect on some people. One Kherson resident spoke of a couple who had left to live in Volgograd with relatives. The woman's husband had initially been detained and tortured by the Russians. 'When the war began', the Kherson resident told journalists, 'his wife beat her chest and said that she would no longer utter a Russian word, and then she began to watch TV and two months later she changed beyond recognition—like a different person.'[61]

Part of the problem was that Ukrainian media were losing trust among many people in the occupied territories. According to the Internews survey, interviewees noted 'a discrepancy between what is presented in the news and the realities they see in their cities'. They criticised 'exaggerated optimism' in the Ukrainian news, in which 'victory is said to be imminent'.[62] Ukraine's attempts to maintain a positive news agenda were probably effective in the first months of the war, but its top-down control on news reporting risked being out of touch with the reality of Russia's occupation regime. Its unified news show, the Telemarathon, had lost viewers across the rest of Ukraine too, with critics calling it state propaganda.[63] The other problem was that much of Ukraine's media—on television or on the internet—had switched to Ukrainian-language broadcasting that had less take-up among Russian speakers in the east. The lack of a popular, pro-Ukraine, Russian-language media platform for the occupied territories left the information space open for Russia to exploit.

Heritage

The Russian occupation was also an attack on cultural heritage. In November 2023 UNESCO verified damage to 329 cultural sites across Ukraine since February 2022. Some of the damage was the result of the intense fighting, but Russia was also pursuing deliberate policies to destroy Ukrainian heritage. There were numerous deliberate attacks on cultural institutions, such as the infamous Russian strike on Mariupol's Drama Theatre. Less well-known historical sites, such as Zaporizhzhia's Popov Manor House Museum, a fantastical nineteenth-century Moorish and Gothic brick-built mansion, complete with an astronomical observatory, were also damaged in the fighting and looted. One remarkable cultural site, the house-museum of the naive artist Polina Raiko, in Oleshky, was completely destroyed in the floods that followed the destruction of the Kakhovka dam. One of her famous motifs, a white dove on a blue background, became a symbol of the Kherson resistance movement.[64] In other places, churches and monasteries were caught in the crossfire, such as the golden-domed Sviatohirsk (Holy Mountains) Lavra in Donbas, that was first occupied by Russian forces and then retaken by Ukraine in September 2022.

Wherever Russian forces occupied towns in the south, they quickly seized control of museums and art galleries. Across southeastern Ukraine, there were valuable archaeological and artistic collections in regional historical and ethnographic museums. Few escaped damage, destruction or looting as the fighting raged around them. Museum staff often stayed in their museums in the first weeks of the war to try to hide or protect their collections. Sometimes they hid exhibits in basements or in their homes in an attempt to preserve them from Russian looting. Museum workers were threatened or even abducted to force them to reveal the whereabouts of hidden artefacts.

At first glance, there was little that seemed worth looting in Melitopol's ethnographic museum. One room was full of stuffed animals and ancient pottery. Another hosted a classic Soviet-era diorama of the 'Breakthrough of the German Defence on the River Molochnyi' in October 1943. Old carts, furniture and historical costumes were scattered through the rooms and yard. Like many other Ukrainian museums, there was also a new exhibition dedicated to the 'Anti-Terrorist Operation' after 2014, which had a clear political message. But beyond this normal paraphernalia of any local museum, Melitopol's collection was also famous for its archaeological finds, including a hoard of Scythian gold artefacts discovered by Soviet archaeologists in 1957. As Russian forces advanced on Melitopol, museum workers hid the gold treasures. Images from a surveillance camera in March 2022 show Russian soldiers forcing their way through the entrance of the museum, hunting for the hidden gold.[65]

The Scythians, a nomadic Eurasian people who occupied what is now Ukraine and southern Russia in the seventh to third centuries BCE, were famous for their remarkable gold jewellery, often incorporating animal figures and known as the 'Animal style'. This Scythian gold had a strange cult-like hold on the Russian imagination. Art critic Konstantin Akinsha wrote that 'the Scythian artefacts have become the symbol of a war of identities' between Russia and Ukraine.[66] Russia and Ukraine had been fighting in the courts over who owned a collection of Scythian art from Crimea that had been on exhibition in the Netherlands when Russia annexed Crimea in 2014. After a lengthy legal battle, hundreds of striking items of Scythian jewellery and decoration, including a golden helmet, were transported back to Kyiv, to the great chagrin of Russia's culture warriors.[67]

The imagery of the Scythians has often been used in Russian culture as a metaphorical challenge to Europe, as in the famous

PROPAGANDA

1918 poem, 'The Scythians', by Alexander Blok, which asserted that Russia had a different, Eastern identity that would not be subdued by Europe and the West:

> You are millions, but we are hordes and hordes and hordes.
> Just try to fight us!
> Yes, we are Scythians, we are Asians
> With our slanted, hungry eyes.[68]

This image of Russia as a marauding, ancient people fighting against the West appealed to Russian polemicists. A couple of weeks after the Russian invasion, Dmitry Rogozin, the nationalist politician who later became a 'senator' from Russian-occupied Zaporizhzhia, posted a video of himself reciting Blok's poem, apparently as an accompanying anthem to the ongoing Russian invasion.[69]

Unable to find the Scythian gold in the Melitopol museum, Russian forces abducted the museum director Leila Ibrahimova in an attempt to force her to give up its hiding-place, but she refused to divulge its whereabouts.[70] The authorities only found the 198 precious artefacts when the uncooperative Ibrahimova was ousted as director of the museum and replaced by Yevgeny Gorlachev, a crony of Russian-installed regional head Yevgeny Balitsky, in April 2022. Gorlachev had no apparent qualifications for the role, except, perhaps, his penchant—like Balitsky—for historic battle reenactments. He ran a 'historical-patriotic society' named 'Confrontation', which every year liked to reenact the 1943 Soviet offensive that broke through German defences near Melitopol.[71] The Russian media immediately turned the story of the Scythian gold on its head, claiming that the Russian military had foiled a plot to smuggle the gold out of occupied Melitopol to Kyiv or to Europe.[72]

With Gorlachev in charge, the museum began to see changes. It even had a new address. From being 18 M. Hrushevsky Street, named after eminent Ukrainian historian Mikhailo Hrushevsky, it now became 18 Karl Marx Street, the Soviet-era name. Then there were the exhibitions. The stuffed animals and ancient pots were still there; but alongside long-standing shows of historical sweet wrappers and children's toys, the museum now hosted an exhibition of photographs dedicated to the 'History of the Deoccupation of South-western USSR from the German-Fascist Invaders'. Gorlachev announced that exhibitions about the revolution, the civil war and the 1930s of the Soviet period would be revived, and also promised an exhibition dedicated to the 'liberation of the town during the special military operation'. He was later awarded a medal for his efforts.[73]

At least the beautiful mansion house that housed the Melitopol museum survived. The regional museum in Mariupol was severely damaged in the Russian attack and many exhibits were destroyed in a fire. Russian media showed some 2,000 exhibits being evacuated to Donetsk, but many more may have been destroyed or stolen in the violence and the confusion of the fighting. When Russian-backed mayor Oleg Morgun visited the ruins of the museum in December 2023, he was pictured staring at a few old busts of Lenin in the courtyard. Nothing more remained.[74] Among the treasures taken from Mariupol's museum were reported to be a number of paintings by Ivan Aivazovsky, such as *By the Banks of the Caucasus*, and at least two original works by Arkhip Kuindzhi, a famous nineteenth-century artist from Mariupol's Greek community. A museum of Kuindzhi's work had opened in 2010 in Mariupol, but it was badly damaged by a Russian bomb on 21 March 2022.[75]

There were confused accounts about why the Mariupol Museum's collection was not evacuated before the Russian attack. There were no clear orders from Kyiv, some said, or local staff were reluctant to carry out an evacuation, or perhaps there was just no time to react to the fast-moving situation around the city.[76] But after Russia consolidated control of the city, long-standing political divides came to the surface. Local pro-Ukrainian activists had long been critical of the Mariupol Museum's leadership for their conservatism and their unwillingness to embrace new ideas. Younger people complained that museum guides conducted long, boring, Soviet-style tours, as they always had done. But the new generation in Mariupol—which had a growing student population—wanted modern exhibitions and European-style late night openings and events.[77] Politically, the museum was criticised for being unwilling to stage exhibitions about the Maidan events.[78]

Now, with the Russians in charge, Ukrainian media claimed that museum director Natalia Kapustnikova had willingly handed over the most valuable exhibits to the Russian authorities. In an interview on Russian television, Kapustnikova blamed the Azov Brigade for burning down the museum and for looting its treasures.[79] She later left for Russia, and if there were any doubt about her loyalties, they became clear when she staged an exhibition in Rostov about the Azov fighters, titled 'Ordinary Fascism'.[80]

Kherson's regional museum was not damaged in the fighting, but the Russians seized many of its exhibits when they left the city. Ukrainian media showed pictures of forlorn empty shelves, looted pedestals and empty archives after the Russian withdrawal. The Russians reportedly used trucks and buses to ship away at least 10,000 artefacts as they withdrew, including Greek sculptures and Scythian jewellery, assisted by Russian art specialists.[81] A Human Rights Watch investigation concluded that it was a potential war crime.[82] The Russians appear to have been helped by several museum staff members. The Ukrainian prosecutor general's office charged the director of the museum, Tatyana Bratchenko, with collaboration after she openly supported the Russian invasion.[83] The Russians also looted items from the regional archive in Kherson, including a rare and valuable 'Code of Laws of the Russian Empire'.[84]

Just opposite the Kherson regional museum was the regional art museum (also known as the Shovkunenko Museum). The gallery held one of Ukraine's finest regional art collections, with notable works by artists Oleksii Shovkunenko, Ivan Aivazovsky and Mikhail Vrubel and the locally born painter Ivan Pokhitonov.[85] An eyewitness reported paintings being loaded onto trucks by Russian troops in early November 2022, 'without any packaging, simply like some kind of garbage ... the occupants were more careful with stolen washing machines than with the heritage of world art'.[86] The collection was reported to have been transferred to the Central Museum of Tavrida in Simferopol in Crimea. The Tavrida Museum director, Andrei Malgin, told journalists that he had been 'instructed to take the exhibits of the Kherson Art Museum for temporary storage and ensure their safety until they are returned to their rightful owner'.[87] Some 10,000 valuable paintings, sculptures and icons were seized. One of the few things they left behind was a huge portrait of Lenin.[88]

OCCUPATION

The director of the Kherson art museum, Alina Dotsenko, had built up the collection over a 45-year career. She told journalists that she cried for two weeks when she returned to see the empty building. 'No', she said, 'I didn't cry, I sobbed. I bit the walls. I gnawed.'[89] Dotsenko escaped from Kherson in May, a day after she refused to mount an art exhibition for the occupation administration.[90] The Russians replaced her as director with Natalya Desyatova. She appears to have had few qualifications in the arts, except for regular singing slots in the cafe 'Teatralnoe' in Kherson, but Desyatova told journalists that she took the job because nobody else wanted to do it.[91] The US government sanctioned Desyatova in February 2023, claiming that she 'oversaw the theft of approximately 10,000 items from the museum's collection'.[92]

As the Russians withdrew from Kherson, they took almost everything they could with them. They even exhumed the body of Prince Grigory Potemkin, who had founded the city during Russia's conquest and played a leading role in the creation of eighteenth-century Novorossiya. They removed his remains from a vault under St Catherine's Cathedral in Kherson, where he had lain undisturbed under Soviet rule (when the cathedral was used as Kherson's Anti-Religious Museum) and under successive Ukrainian governments. It took the Russian invasion to end Potemkin's connection with the city that he founded.[93]

Russia's cultural revolution

Russia's cultural campaign did not only involve seizing Ukraine's cultural and historical heritage. Russia began to propagate its own historical narratives and neo-imperialist cultural discourses. It began with history. After 2012 the Russian state began to increase control over history education, publishing new school textbooks and promoting patriotic films and exhibitions. This view of history glossed over difficult periods in Russia's past, glorified its wars and legitimised its empire. As part of this educational campaign, Russia built more than twenty so-called 'history parks' across the country. These were multimedia exhibitions presented in a user-friendly, high-tech format, much of it inspired by the ultra-conservative

PROPAGANDA

Metropolitan Tikhon (Shevkunov) of the Russian Orthodox Church (often rumoured to be Putin's spiritual advisor) and funded by the largesse of Gazprom and the Foundation for Humanitarian Projects.[94] Now this network of history parks would be expanded to the occupied territories.

On 7 September 2023 a new multimedia history park was opened in Luhansk, promoting the official, nationalist version of Russian history. Sergei Kiriyenko was on hand to conduct the opening ceremony and to show off the Russian version of a history of Donbas, 'from ancient Rus to the present day'. Later in September, he appeared again at the opening of a new history park in Melitopol, housed in a former warehouse. He told a scattering of local officials that 'here on Zaporozhian land for 30 years they tried to completely destroy any memory that this was once Novorossiya'.[95] Now the Russian museum aimed to erase any memory of Ukraine.

Museums in Russia were also constructing their own version of the history of south-eastern Ukraine. A new multimedia exhibition entitled 'Russian Azov' toured Russia's history parks, complete with 'real pebbles from the Azov shore'.[96] Glossy exhibits took viewers on a historical tour of a region that included both Russian and Ukrainian territory around the Sea of Azov, from the Scythians to Peter the Great and the Soviet Union. The point was obvious—to legitimise Russian conquest with a historical narrative that emphasised continuity with the Russian imperial past. As the blurb from the exhibition put it: 'The "Russian Azov" project is a historical bridge from the past to the present, showing historical and cultural continuity, [and] the role of Russia in the exploration and development of the region.'[97]

Pride of place in this propaganda extravaganza was reserved for some of the looted artworks from Ukraine's museums. Or—as the project itself claimed—materials from 'the miraculously saved collection of the Mariupol Local History Museum bombed by the Ukrainian Nazis'. These included an original sketch for Kuindzhi's striking painting *Red Sunset* (the full version of which is in the Metropolitan Museum of Art, New York) and Kuindzhi's *Rainbow*, which had been taken by the Russians from its home in the Isaac Brodsky Art Museum in Berdiansk.[98]

OCCUPATION

A selected array of 'acceptable' Azovians were celebrated in the exhibition. Anton Chekhov, whose grandmother was Ukrainian and who attended a Greek school in Taganrog, was included, as was Arkhip Kuindzhi, the artist whose museum had been hit by a Russian bomb. Rudolf Samoilovich, a Soviet-Jewish polar explorer who was executed by Stalin's NKVD in March 1939, was honoured alongside the NKVD assassin Pavel Sudoplatov.[99] It was a contradictory and confused list that nevertheless served the purpose of creating a narrative of 'Russian' Azov that denied any Ukrainian claim to this land. This was history deliberately deployed in information warfare. As the head of the Russian history parks, Ivan Yesin, explained, 'We are embarking on the same path with the fighters of the information front in defending historical truth and returning the good name to Peter's, Catherine's, Alexander's, and Nicholas's victories on this primordially Russian land.'[100] Another organiser said that one goal of the exhibition was to return the name Azov from the 'odious Ukrainian fighter-bandits and neo-Nazis', referring to the Azov Brigade that had played a major role in the defence of Mariupol.[101]

Russia launched a full-scale campaign to use film, music and theatre to legitimise the occupation, although here there was often less overt propaganda and more emphasis on promoting exclusively Russian forms of cultural production. The Russian Ministry of Culture and the Cinema Foundation (*Fond kino*), which funds much of the Russian film industry, announced that a network of new cinemas would open across the occupied territories. The Ministry of Culture planned twenty-eight cinemas in the DNR alone.[102] By the Christmas season in December 2023, the big Savona cinema had reopened in Mariupol. There was little propaganda on the bill, just mindless family entertainment—hit Russian comedies such as 'Serf 2'—and plenty of popcorn. This was cinema as normalisation, not as propaganda. But the effect was potentially powerful—to draw the audience back into the world of Russian popular culture.

Performers from Russia flooded into the occupied territories. For some, this was an ideological visit to support the war. For others, the visits became a strange pilgrimage of penance, an attempt to remove themselves from the Russian Ministry of Culture's unofficial 'black lists' of performers whose political loyalties were suspect. The ability of Russian artists to organise concerts or release music depended on Russia's unofficial censorship system, reported to be overseen by Sergei Novikov, a senior official in the Presidential Administration.[103] Those who opposed the war faced an unofficial ban on their performances. Famous rock band DDT reportedly refused an offer to 'support the special operation' in 2022 and subsequently found that all their concerts had been cancelled.[104] To get a ban lifted, performers had to negotiate with the Presidential Administration and agree to either perform in the occupied territories or fund charities for Ukrainian children from the Donbas. Roman Bilyk, leader of the popular band Zveri, who had initially opposed the Russian invasion in February 2022, performed in the Russian-occupied Donbas for the Russian military in the summer of 2023, after the authorities cancelled a high-profile concert in St Petersburg.[105] The singer Yaroslav Dronov (Shaman), whose hits were full of nationalist zeal, was persuaded to perform in Donetsk and Mariupol after he was criticised by nationalists for not having visited the occupied territories.[106]

Local artists were deeply divided by the occupation, like the rest of society. The cast of Mariupol's Drama Theatre, destroyed by a Russian aerial attack, reflected the pre-invasion and post-invasion cleavages in society. Like many provincial theatres in the post-Soviet world, the Donetsk Regional Academic Russian Drama Theatre in Mariupol was a bastion of cultural conservatism, preferring a traditional Russian-language repertoire to any new or politically controversial productions. That all changed in the spring of 2016, when the word 'Russian' was removed from the theatre's name and a new director, Anatoliy Levchenko, began staging modern Ukrainian-language plays, beginning with a controversial drama by Pavlo Arie, *Glory to the Heroes*. Although the content was a nuanced play about competing Ukrainian memories of World War II, for many locals the title was seen as controversial: 'Glory to the Heroes' was the traditional salute of the wartime Ukrainian Insurgent Army (UPA), widely viewed by older generations in Mariupol as 'Banderovtsy' and 'fascists', although the phrase was used in modern Ukraine without those historical connotations.

This new generation of Ukrainian directors and playwrights ran up against a thoroughly conservative theatre administration, who saw themselves as part of a Russian theatrical tradition and disliked the new Ukrainian plays. Audiences also dwindled for Ukrainian-language productions, which tended to be more experimental and political. Sharp conflicts emerged.[107] The playwright Arie complained to journalists that 'it's very surprising that such a centre of "vatnik" separatism exists and thrives at the expense of Ukrainian taxpayers',[108] using a derogatory term for those viewed as pro-Russian.[109] Many actors also resisted the changes. One actor, Serhii Zabahonskiy, later told the *Wall Street Journal* that 'Almost everybody was against removing the word "Russian" from the name of the theater—including me', although he would later change his mind after the invasion.[110] The new director Levchenko was dismissed from the theatre at least partly, it was suggested, because of his pro-Ukrainian position. He set up his own independent Ukrainian theatre in Mariupol.

Russia's attack on Mariupol transformed these backstage theatrical squabbles into questions of life and death. Serhii Zabahonskiy survived the bomb attack on the Mariupol theatre on 13 March, but the experience transformed his view of Russian culture. 'Now my opinion is absolute', he told journalists in 2022, 'Russia is our enemy.'[111] The Russians detained Anatoliy Levchenko in the filtration process as he tried to leave the city in May 2022. He spent the next ten months in captivity in Donetsk before being released on a legal technicality.[112] But while Levchenko sat in prison, some of his former colleagues began to revive the theatre, with its name changed to the Mariupol Republican Academic *Russian* Drama Theatre. A reduced cast performed Chekhov's one-act plays, the Vaudevilles, in the Philharmonic in Mariupol, while the theatre was being rebuilt.[113]

Another group of actors from the Mariupol Drama Theatre escaped the city and reformed in Uzhhorod, in western Ukraine, under its artistic director Liudmyla Kolosovych. They performed plays such as *The Cry of the Nation*, a new work about anti-Soviet Ukrainian poet and dissident Vasyl Stus, on the theme of suffering to defend Ukrainian language and culture. Levchenko, meanwhile, revived his independent theatre in Kyiv, but appears to have had no illusions about returning to Mariupol. For Levchenko, Mariupol now was a 'dead town'. Indeed, he told the media that 'in fact Ukrainian Mariupol had never existed'.[114]

St Petersburg governor Alexander Beglov promised to rebuild the theatre building, which the Russian military had destroyed with the loss of so many lives.[115] Even the idea of reconstructing a Soviet-era building was divisive. The building itself was a typical provincial theatre in the style of Soviet neo-classicism, built in 1960, which had been declared an architectural monument.[116] Petro Andryushchenko, an advisor to the Ukrainian mayor of Mariupol, said that the theatre 'does not have either historical or architectural value ... like all typical constructions of the Soviet period'. He went on to argue that 'the only historical value arose at the moment when two bombs fell. And it is exactly that historical value that the occupiers are now attempting to hide through their reconstruction.'[117] In this way, the deep divides about the past came to the surface once again: on the one hand, a rejection of the Soviet past, even in its architectural and cultural forms. And on the other hand, by contrast, a Russian campaign to restore continuity with the Soviet period while erasing the evidence of Russia's destructive assault on Ukrainian culture.

Education

Schools were the experimental workbenches in Russia's laboratory of occupation. The Russian authorities were convinced that imposing a new school programme could 'recode' Ukrainian youth to be loyal young Russians. The Russian government had already transformed schools and higher education in Crimea to align with Russian education after 2014. Schools in the DNR and the LNR had also moved closer to the Russian model. The occupation authorities used this experience to move towards a full Russification of the educational system in the newly occupied territories. Russian officials quickly imposed the full Russian national curriculum in Ukrainian schools when the new school year began in September 2022. They sent teachers on retraining courses, and packed

Ukrainian schoolchildren off on 'educational' tours and summer camps in Russia. The goal was simple and comprehensive: to 'de-Ukrainianise' education and produce a new generation who identified not with the homeland that they had lost, but with the country that had attacked them.

The first few months were chaotic. For the first two weeks of the war, schools were closed across Ukraine. In areas of fighting, education was less important than staying alive. Parents huddled with their children in bomb shelters or tried desperately to escape to safer territory. Many places had no electricity, heating, phone or internet communications. Where there was no active fighting, schools resumed in March in the newly occupied territories, with classes mainly taking place online, still working to the Ukrainian curriculum and with the same cohort of Ukrainian teachers—some now working from government-controlled areas or even from abroad. That all began to change between April and June 2022, when teachers in different areas received instructions from the new Russian-appointed education authorities to switch to the Russian curriculum.[118]

In Nova Kakhovka, the Russian-imposed head of the town, Vladimir Leontiev, a local businessman, called in school directors in April 2022 and informed them that they would now be teaching according to the Russian curriculum. Nobody agreed to switch, and they were left largely in peace for the next few weeks.[119] It was a similar story in Kherson city, where schoolteachers also initially resisted any changes. But during the summer, as the beginning of the new school year approached, school directors were replaced if they refused to implement the changes. On 19 June a new director arrived at School No. 28 in Kherson, and quickly began to impose the new Russian curriculum. Many teachers refused to implement the new rules and left, leaving just twenty teachers on the payroll by August. In Nova Kahkovka, the director of Lyceum No. 3, Irina Dubas, held out against any changes. But in August she and her teachers were expelled from the school, and she was arrested for five days while the Russians tried to persuade her to cooperate. She refused, and was finally released and escaped to Ukrainian-controlled territory, where she restarted the school in online mode.[120]

'Education ministries' were set up under the occupation authorities, with new officials drafted in. In Melitopol, Galina Danilchenko appointed Elena Shapurova, the head of the local technical college, as a new director of education.[121] But in many cases more senior officials arrived from Russia and Crimea. On 4 July 2022 Mikhail Rodikov was appointed minister of education in Kherson region's occupation administration. He had already worked during 2015–18 to convert Sevastopol's schools to the Russian system.[122] Now he set about doing the same for Ukrainian schools.

Through the summer of 2022 Russian officials rushed to make new appointments, retrain teachers and introduce the new curriculum: deputies stepped up to replace school heads, or teachers were drafted in from Russia or Crimea. Teachers faced a choice. The illegal Russian education authorities pressured them to sign new contracts agreeing to introduce the Russian curriculum. Otherwise, they would face dismissal. On the other hand, according to Ukrainian law, they faced prosecution for collaboration if they agreed to cooperate with the Russians.

Many pupils were still studying via online education—the experience of the Covid pandemic turned out to be equally useful in wartime. According to Irina Dubas, her school in exile had 618 pupils, 249 of them still living in the occupied territories and only 70 in the rest of Ukraine, while all the remainder were abroad. At least some of those in the occupied territories were also attending Russian schools.[123] Studying online was not easy. The internet was often unreliable in the occupied territories. Teachers who remained under Russian rule feared being caught and interrogated for teaching using Ukrainian textbooks.[124]

Parents were pressured to send their children to Russian schools. Some claimed to be schooling their children at home (which is legal in Russia) or told the school that they were planning to leave the region, to avoid attention. There were reports of parents being pressured at work, threatened with fines or even with losing custody of their children if they did not send them to the Russian schools.[125] Others were persuaded by the 10,000-rouble (US$111) payment that the Russians promised to pay for each pupil who went to school. Sometimes pupils themselves preferred to attend school. One mother told journalists that although her friends were joining the online school, her daughter had 'categorically refused' to study in that format and so would be going to the Russian school.[126] For others, there were more pragmatic reasons for sending their children to school: lack of childcare, free school meals, or being persuaded by familiar teachers to let their children attend.[127]

Whatever the motivations, on 1 September 2022 the occupation authorities reopened some schools, although with many pupils absent.[128] In Kherson region, according to Russian sources, there were only 15,500 pupils left in 91 schools.[129] This was a big drop from numbers before the war, when there were 424 schools in Kherson region and 35,000 students just in Kherson city.[130] At School No. 28 in Kherson, for example, enrolment was sharply down from 937 pupils before the war to just 235 on 1 September 2022.[131] In total, Russian official sources reckoned that some 300,000 children were registered in schools across the four regions in the 2022–23 school year.[132] By the beginning of the next school year in September 2023, some more schools had been repaired and reopened, but numbers of pupils remained low. In Mariupol, in September 2023, Ukrainian authorities reported that the pre-war school population of 40,000 pupils in Mariupol had declined to about 15,000 (of which 3,600 were the children of migrants from Russia) studying in 22 schools, only one third of the numbers before the war.[133]

Despite the big drop in pupil numbers, there was a shortage of teachers, particularly in the key 'political' subjects of Russian language and history.[134] Many teachers had fled the occupation, refusing to teach the new curriculum. At Gymnasium No. 1 in Berdiansk, only five teachers out of sixty were left.[135] In one school, pro-Russian parents complained that Russian language classes were being taught in Ukrainian.[136] Many schools did not have sufficient textbooks or equipment. Teachers had often removed laptops and other equipment to enable them to work from home and to prevent the occupation authorities from using them. The Russians tried to attract teachers to come to work from Russia and Crimea, and by June 2022 there were more than 200 Russian teachers employed in the occupied territories from different Russian regions, with around one third from the region of Dagestan in the North Caucasus.[137]

To teach the Russian curriculum, Ukrainian teachers had to undergo retraining. The Russians did not publish details of these courses—and Ukrainian teachers were often reluctant to admit that they had taken part. An enterprising journalist from the Rostov news site '161.ru' dug around on Russian state procurement websites to work out that at least 1,375 teachers from the DNR and the LNR went to Rostov for retraining courses, and 750 or more directors and deputy directors of schools were bussed to Moscow for training. Teachers from Kharkiv region were sent to Kursk, while others had to take online courses.[138] From July 2022, teachers from Kherson and Zaporizhzhia regions were reportedly dispatched to Yevpatoria in Crimea for retraining courses: at least 746 Ukrainian teachers were expected on these courses between 10 July and 28 August 2022. In total, there were plans for at least 13,000 teachers and school leaders from DNR, LNR, Kherson and Zaporizhzhia to have undergone retraining in 2022, although it is not clear how many actually completed the courses.[139]

The retraining was a mix of straightforward propaganda and learning about the more mundane details of Russia's educational and exam system, all packed into one week of classes. In addition to the classes, teachers who retrained in Rostov were taken on a compulsory excursion to the local 'Russia is My History' park in Rostov, one of the multimedia museums set up across the country to promulgate the official version of Russian history. There they were forced to sit through a lecture on the 'History of Anti-Russian Propaganda' by Alexander Myasnikov, a former Soviet journalist who had ended up as the chief content editor of the history parks across the country. According to those at the lecture, he told the teachers from Ukraine that the 'main global enemy' was 'the Anglo-Saxons'.[140]

These training courses must have felt surreal. The Russian propaganda was one thing. Simply living outside the war zone was a major step for many. Even Rostov seemed a world away from the war zone. Teachers from Mariupol attended week-long courses at

School No. 80 in Rostov, named after Soviet spy Richard Sorge. There were misunderstandings with the locals. A teacher walking down the corridor of the school complimented a guest from Mariupol on her suntan. 'Where did you get so brown?', she asked, assuming she had been on holiday. The answer was unexpected: 'First, by the fire cooking food. Then at the vegetable patch, where [I live instead] of my completely destroyed home', replied the visiting teacher.[141]

Although many teachers left or refused to work with the Russians, the occupation authorities claimed that thousands of teachers continued to work in the schools.[142] About 1,000 teachers were estimated to be working in Mariupol's schools in November 2022.[143] Relations between those who stayed and those who left—or who refused to work under the new system—were fraught. There were numerous reasons for teachers to continue working. Some—probably a minority—had always been pro-Russian or at least opposed the Ukrainianisation of education. Others had elderly relatives or could not leave town for financial reasons. Many were probably persuaded by the prospect of promotions and better salaries. The salaries for teachers offered by the Russians were low, but still slightly higher than in Ukraine. Teachers in Mariupol were reportedly receiving a monthly salary of 25,000–44,000 roubles (around US$280 to US$500),[144] while in government-controlled Ukraine average salaries in 2024 were 10,000–16,000 hryvnia (US$245–400). A few claimed they could mitigate the worst aspects of Russian propaganda—as Russian teachers inside Russia were often doing—and wanted to stay and support their students. Others claimed there was little difference teaching a technical subject like physics in Ukrainian or in Russian.[145]

These various positions produced sharp disagreements. In one school, the 27th Gymnasium in Mariupol, the school director Maryna Yizhakovska refused to work with the Russians and her place was taken by her deputy. She later told journalists:

> Teachers in the occupied territory understand very well that they have betrayed the country, and they do not want to discuss it. [...] They do not want to talk to us, and we do not want to talk to them either. You know, it's like a couple who decided to separate. We

used to live and work together, and now we decided to live our lives separately. And every day this split between us only grows.'[146]

The new director, who had been her friend and colleague for many years, called on teachers to return to work, and reportedly many did so, with some even returning from abroad.[147]

Inevitably, history and language were the key battlegrounds in education. Schools in the south and east of Ukraine had been shifting to Ukrainian-language education since 2013. Now they shifted overnight back to Russian. Almost all pupils understood Russian very well and many spoke it as their native language, but some had problems coping with a full curriculum in Russian. One teacher in Donetsk explained that children who had been to school in Ukrainian-controlled Mariupol all spoke Russian, but because 'all subjects at school were taught in Ukrainian, that creates some problems in understanding certain terms'.[148] Schools in the DNR and LNR had already shifted to Russian-language education after 2014.[149] In some schools in the DNR and the LNR, Ukrainian had initially been retained as an optional, minority language, but eventually it was abolished entirely in schools in the LNR and DNR, despite pleading from parents for it to remain an option.[150]

Initially, Russian minister of education Sergei Kravtsov promised that the Ukrainian language would continue to be taught in schools in the occupied territories: 'Ukrainian language is very rich and interesting. So there certainly can't be any ban [on Ukrainian].'[151] In newly occupied areas, however, Ukrainian appears to have been at best reduced to an optional class—everything else was taught in Russian. Under the new Russian curriculum, every school had a subject known as 'Native language and literature' (*Rodnoi yazyk i literatura*), which gave an hour or two each week for teaching a minority language. In June 2023, a decree in Kherson region declared that there were three official languages in the province: Russian, Ukrainian and Crimean Tatar (the latter in two districts close to Crimea).[152] Consequently, parents were given the right to choose which of the three languages their children would learn as a minority language, according to a Russian-appointed minister of education of Kherson region, Aleksei Galchenkov.[153]

Olga Karpenko, director of School No. 3 in Henichesk, told the press that only ten out of 500 children chose to study Russian in the optional language class, while the rest opted for Ukrainian. Karpenko explained that 'we teach Ukrainian, so that children do not forget their Slavic roots. Schoolchildren should remember their nationality. [...] Children should remember that they are Ukrainians. But not forget that now we are a subject of the RF [Russian Federation] and are part of a big multi-national state.'[154] Across Russian-occupied areas of Kherson region, 64% of children in junior classes took Ukrainian as a second ('native') language and 46% in Zaporizhzhia.[155] Paradoxically, School No. 3 was one of those that had also resisted a shift to Ukrainian-only education when it was introduced in 2017, because parents also wanted their children to learn Russian.[156] Many parents had always wanted both languages to be taught in school.

Even the Russian media admitted that there was widespread opposition to the Russian schools. One parent told Russian media that 'many parents ... secretly teach their children in online courses in Ukrainian schools. And refuse to take them to pro-Russian schools, saying that "our guys [Ukrainian military] will come soon and deal with us for collaborationism".' Other parents reportedly threatened teachers, saying that they would one day pay for working for the Russians.[157] According to Ukrainian officials cited in a 2024 report, around 62,000 children in the occupied territories were still studying online in Ukrainian secondary schools.[158] One school director told a Russian newspaper that teachers constantly received threatening messages, such as 'we are following you, we know where you walk'. She claimed that teachers received threats from 'former [school] directors, former city education officials, former friends and colleagues'. One day somebody approached her on the street and said: 'Either refuse [to work with the Russians], or work for us, otherwise you are sentenced.'[159]

History was inevitably the most sensitive subject. One school director told the Russian press that this was the only subject that would be completely revised.[160] The history curriculum in Ukrainian schools had already been extensively rewritten after 2014, with a strong slant towards nationalist narratives. According to a study by

Georgiy Kasianov, '[v]irtually all school textbooks on the history of Ukraine that have been published since 2018 depict the Soviet period almost exclusively in dark tones as a time of oppression, mass repressions, deportations, famines, and national humiliation', while 'the history of the OUN and the UPA is described exclusively in exalted, glorifying tones, presenting Ukrainian nationalist guerrillas as a part of the European Resistance movement'.[161] Some parents rejected this new history. One told Russian media that 'They taught the children that Russia is the worst enemy [...] And the Banderites are the heroes of Ukraine. They constantly talked about the Holodomor, Euromaidan, the "heavenly hundred".'[162] Now Russia would set about reversing this trend and replacing Ukrainian history textbooks with its own, even more nationalist history, which ignored many of the horrors of Stalinism, denied Ukraine's own history—or even existence—and glorified the Russian empire.

The DNR and LNR had proved useful testing grounds. After 2014 the authorities in the two republics abolished Ukrainian history lessons. They packed the curriculum with Soviet-friendly versions of history and pro-Russian narratives. In a study of School No. 5 in Luhansk, Ivan Posylnyi tracked how history classes became dominated by two key historical themes: first, the unification of Russia and Ukraine in the so-called Russian World; and second, and most importantly, an obsessive focus on the Great Patriotic War, including a local myth about anti-Nazi partisans in eastern Ukraine, dubbed the *Molodaya Gvardiya* (Young Guard) in a 1946 book by Soviet novelist Alexander Fadeev.[163] LNR head Leonid Pasechnik proclaimed 2022 the 'Year of Molodaya Gvardiya', resulting in even more emphasis on the Young Guard story in local media and curricula. Even extra-curricular events had a war theme, from an art exhibition with the title 'Thank You, Grandpa, for the Victory!' to an 'Open basketball tournament, devoted to the Great Victory'.[164]

Now all the teachers in occupied areas of the Donbas had to plan for a new set of classes to fit with the Russian curriculum. Ihor Boiko, a history teacher in a village near Donetsk, told journalists in Rostov that this was the third change in his subject title in a few years. Before 2014 he taught Ukrainian and world history, then the DNR's own 'History of the Fatherland' course. Now he was retraining to teach 'History of Russia and its regional components'.[165] The Russian retraining courses discussed the ways in which to teach pupils about the war in Ukraine—or, more accurately, to provide one-sided propaganda about the conflict. As Boiko explained to a Russian website, 'we say that this is not a [war] against the Ukrainian people, it is a [war] for the denazification and demilitarisation of Ukraine. For the unification of the Slavs. For unification, in other words. Not for the seizure of the Ukrainian state.'[166] According to Boiko, this propaganda eventually paid off. In 2014 and 2015, he recalled teachers arguing with their pupils about politics, 'but now children no longer object'.[167] Russia was betting that given another few years of occupation, the same process of socialisation would produce a loyal, pro-Russian generation of schoolchildren.

Teachers of physics or maths might be able to teach almost the same lessons in a Russian school, but in history it meant teaching openly discredited claims that contradicted everything they believed. One Ukrainian history teacher who went into hiding rather than teach the warped Russian view of history, told Amnesty International: 'I taught the history of Ukraine all my life, real history, not those lies Russia told. How could I go and look my students in the eyes and tell them everything we knew was wrong?'[168] In August 2023 schools in the occupied territories received the new standard Russian history textbook, which was in use in schools throughout the country. Russian minister of education Kravtsov confirmed that schoolchildren in the 10th and 11th classes (senior years) in the LNR, the DNR, Kherson and Zaporizhzhia regions were studying with the new textbook, which he claimed ensured that 'children from every region of Russia will be able to have reliable information'.[169] The textbook was an amateur affair, comprising all the well-worn tropes of Russian propaganda and often outright disinformation. It taught children that the West was seeking the 'dismemberment of Russia and control over its resources'. In Ukraine, an 'aggressive minority' from western Ukraine was said to have repressed Russian language and culture after a 'military coup' in 2014. NATO advisors were 'training Kyiv for an attack on Donbas', the US was setting up secret biolaboratories in Ukraine, and Ukraine was said to be trying to develop nuclear weapons. In this context the 'special military operation' against Ukraine was a justified response to the threat from Ukraine and the West.[170] The textbook celebrated the annexation of the newly occupied territories in 2022, and asked students to 'Show on the map the territories which became part of Russia in 2022.'[171]

This propaganda was not confined to history lessons, but was evident across the school curriculum. Leaked documents from the Russian Ministry of Education in 2024 appeared to be instructions to teachers in Russia on how to deal with pupils from refugee families from Ukraine. They warned that such pupils might be vulnerable to a 'destructive ideology' and so teachers should be engaged in the 'reorientation and formation of the Russian identity of the younger generation of the Donetsk and Lugansk People's Republics, Zaporozhye and Kherson regions'. This re-education should be based on 'the spiritual-moral values, the historical and nation-cultural traditions of the Russian Federation'. The aim was simple: 'to form a Russian identity' among children from Ukraine.[172]

As part of this onslaught on Ukrainian culture and identity, the occupation authorities also began purging libraries of what the Russian-installed mayor of Melitopol, Danilchenko, called 'pseudo-historical books propagating nationalist ideas'. Even *Ukraine Is Not Russia*, a book written by former Ukrainian president Leonid Kuchma, with whom Putin once had good relations, was anathema.[173] In May 2022 the DNR Ministry of Culture ordered the removal of 'extremist literature' from libraries. An official at the ministry, Viktoria Kamynina, told journalists that specialists from the Donetsk republican library were travelling to dozens of libraries in newly seized territories and raiding their bookshelves. According to Kamynina, by May they had confiscated around 2,000 volumes, which included books devoted to

> the history, politics, and activities of the 'Organisation of Ukrainian Nationalists', 'Ukrainian Insurgent Army' [...], state symbols of Ukraine, political and religious figures, Hitler, as well as collections of poems about Bandera, the publication 'History of the

People's Movement of Ukraine', [and] the book series 'Library of the Azov Regiment'.[174]

On 20 January 2023 the LNR education and science ministry also instructed schools and universities to remove from their libraries any 'literature of an extremist nature, expressing the ideology of Ukrainian nationalism'. The ministry compiled a list of 365 books to be banned, including a series of biographies for young people called 'Famous Ukrainians'. Any books about the Holodomor, the Soviet-induced famine that killed millions of Ukrainians, or anything about Ukraine since 2014, were banned, along with any literature 'propagandising European gender "values"'.[175] Russian security forces also targeted the libraries of religious communities. In June 2022 the entire library of the Cathedral of Petro Mohyla in Mariupol was reportedly burned in the yard outside.[176]

Youth propaganda

On 4 November 2023, during the official celebrations of Russia's Day of National Unity in Red Square, a 19-year-old girl from Melitopol, Yulia Klimenko, was on hand to thank Vladimir Putin personally for launching the 'Special Military Operation'. 'Thank you for returning us home, to our historical lands', she told the president, 'we completely support your governance and all your decisions.' According to a report by *Verstka* media, six years earlier, when Yulia Klimenko had been a young pupil at the Lyceum No. 16 in Melitopol, she was commended for taking part in an essay competition to celebrate the centenary of the Ukrainian People's Republic, in which participants had to write an essay about Ukrainian history or create a patriotic piece of work. By 2023, Yulia had become head of a local pro-Russian youth group, 'Youthful South' (*Yug molodoi*) and was frequently cited in the media praising Putin and thanking Russia for the annexation.[177]

This was the kind of transformation of patriotic Ukrainians into loyal Russians that the occupation authorities sought to achieve through a massive campaign of youth indoctrination. A myriad of youth organisations began working in the occupied territories, combining crude propaganda with useful life skills and opportunities for young people to get ahead in education and in their careers.

PROPAGANDA

The new Russian youth organisations offered a form of social mobility and career opportunities in an environment that otherwise offered few prospects of advancement.

The youth programme was overseen by the Presidential Administration, which set up ministries of youth policy in each of the four regions. The Federal Agency for Youth Affairs (Rosmolodezh) played a key role. The deputy head of Rosmolodezh, Denis Ashirov, visited the region several times with first deputy head of the Presidential Administration, Sergei Kiriyenko. Rosmolodezh supported several youth organisations, including Klimenko's Youthful South, the 'Volunteers of Victory' network, and the Molodaya Gvardia organisation (the youth wing of Russia's ruling party, United Russia). Many of these overlapped—Klimenko was heading both Youthful South and Molodaya Gvardiya in Zaporizhzhia region, perhaps because there were few other volunteers.[178] Younger children were encouraged to join the 'Movement of the First' (*Dvizhenie pervykh*) group, which had been set up in Russian in 2023 as a modern-day version of the Soviet 'Pioneer' movement. In March 2023 it opened branches in Zaporizhzhia and Kherson regions. The movement was explicitly designed to ensure that children were protected from 'foreign influences' and 'brought up as patriots'.[179]

Rosmolodezh worked almost like any grant-giving agency in a Western country. Youth groups would submit applications for funding and the agency would pick the winners. Applicants from the four regions won nearly 340 million roubles (US$3.7 million) in grants in June 2023 in one of Rosmolodezh's regular grant competitions.[180] Rosmolodezh was also busy setting up youth centres: ten were due to open by the end of 2024, including two major centres in Zaporizhzhia and Kherson regions. This was part of a much bigger national project that President Putin had announced in February 2024, focusing on building infrastructure for youth and inculcating 'patriotic values'.[181] Russia was using the war as the backdrop for a far-reaching programme to transform Russian youth through lessons in patriotism and the promotion of anti-Western and anti-Ukrainian values.

Youth from the occupied territories were quickly drawn into Russia's national programme of youth education and training.

Activists and teachers were invited to Russia's youth training centres in Senezh (Moscow region), Tavrida in Crimea and a brand-new centre 'Mashuk' in Pyatigorsk. The Mashuk centre was also involved in retraining Ukrainian teachers to work with the new Russian curriculum. When the centre celebrated the arrival of its 15,000th participant in December 2023, it turned out to be Yulia Yefimova, a teacher from Zaporizhzhia region.[182]

A new programme called *Universitetskie smeny* (University Exchanges) took about 15,000 teenagers from the occupied territories to Russian universities in 2023, where they took part in special summer schools, tried out different study options and were effectively socialised into Russian higher education. Russian television showed children from Donetsk region sitting in a classroom in the Russian city of Tambov with the motto of Tambov State University displayed proudly on the wall above them: 'To understand science and be loyal to Russia'. This summed up the goal of the Russian education programme. Russian minister of education Sergei Kravtsov told the Russian media that 'the kids admit that … there are many facts that they did not know. They thought that Russia was the enemy. But they return to their region, share their impressions with friends, and the effect of this new and truthful knowledge is further enhanced.'[183] The propaganda was leavened by entertainment. Day-time training and seminars were followed by performances in the evenings. At one event in Berdiansk in August 2023, 150 youth workers watched a performance by the hardline anti-Ukrainian rapper Akim Apachev, author of one of the hits of Russia's military campaign, the pro-Wagner song, 'Leto i arbalety' (Summer and crossbows).[184]

The problem for the authorities was that not all teenagers followed their script. Videos from Mariupol often showed vandalism and graffiti on new buildings and playgrounds. At least some young people engaged in pro-Ukrainian underground movements. A special Russian agency began monitoring young people's mobile phone use to check their loyalty. The Centre for the Study and Network Monitoring of the Youth Environment (TsISM) was given a budget of 1.7 billion roubles for their work, including opening 'Information Security Centres' in the occupied territories.[185] The

TsISM had legitimate concerns—tackling dangerous content or the Russian online youth phenomenon known as 'trash-streaming'—but the bulk of its work focused on checking for any signs of political or social discontent. According to a Meduza investigation, TsISM used a monitoring programme known as 'Profilaktika', which monitored millions of social accounts of young people.[186] Through the programme, they were able to access content on individual phones and compile detailed profiles of each child based on a set of risk indicators—including engaging with opposition media. The programme gave each child a rating—what was referred to as a 'coefficient of destructiveness' or a 'coefficient of oppositionness'. This Orwellian idea was all designed, according to one Russian source, 'to help our [security] organs uncover activists in the resistance'.[187] According to leaked documents, they were instructed to monitor at least 85% of social media accounts of children and young people in the occupied territories.[188]

Another active youth organisation was the Federal Centre for the Development of Programmes for the Socialisation of Teenagers (FTsRPSP), more often known as the 'Federal Teenager Centre'. It was opened in 2022 to implement youth programmes across the country and to try to instil patriotism in young people. It had a special role to 'help' 'young people, located in the zone of the Special Military Operation'.[189] A director of one of the youth centres that worked with FTsRPSP explained that Ukrainian teenagers often 'do not fully understand why this war began', and that 'many support Ukraine, and many tend to be against the head of state [i.e. Putin]. We invite specialists from the competent organs, who explain [everything] to them.' The FTsRPSP opened centres in the occupied territories, including in Mariupol and Donetsk, tasked with monitoring the situation and 'implementing programmes for the integration of children from new regions'.[190]

Universities

Universities were early targets for takeover by the Russian occupation authorities. But the new authorities were often left only with control over half-empty buildings, as staff and students fled the occupied territories and transferred their universities to new sites in government-controlled areas. This was not easy: they left behind buildings, laboratories, dormitories and sometimes priceless collections in libraries and archives. Mariupol State University was forced to relocate to Kyiv, leaving behind its damaged building in the city but retaining many of its educational programmes online and establishing a new home in the capital.[191] Meanwhile, back in Mariupol, the Russians rebuilt Mariupol State University; it was officially reopened by Deputy Prime Minister Marat Khusnullin in September 2023.[192] They claimed that around 3,000 students were studying there in 2024, now working to a Russian curriculum.[193]

In Melitopol, there was a similar split. Natalia Falko took over as rector of the Bogdan Khmelnitsky Melitopol State Pedagogical University and successfully re-established the university in Zaporizhzhia with most of the staff and students.[194] Back in Melitopol, about 125 staff out of 500 remained and a few hundred students.[195] They were now attending a new 'Melitopol State University', with teachers brought in from Russia, including a new rector from St Petersburg, Nikolai Toivonen.[196] The events left a bitter taste. Natalia Falko told journalists: 'When we now hear that people had no choice, that they wrote an application at gunpoint—this is all untrue. Because they were given a choice.'[197] The choice—as she later explained it—was clear: either remaining loyal to Ukraine or cooperating with the occupiers.[198]

Berdiansk State Pedagogical University also relocated to Zaporizhzhia, with staff and students forced to endure the long drive and a nervous wait at the Russian checkpoint at Vasylivka to escape from Russian occupation. As of the end of 2022, 57% of university staff from Berdiansk had left for territories controlled by Ukraine, while 43% remained under Russian occupation. Most staff continued to work online. Only 6% of academics and 14% of non-academic staff at Berdiansk university had agreed to work in the new Russian-controlled college, which had been set up as a branch of the Russian-controlled Melitopol State University.[199]

In each case, the Russians seized university buildings, laboratories, libraries and other assets and re-registered them as belonging to Russia. The occupation authorities seized Kherson University in June 2022 and replaced the rector, Alexander Spivakovsky, with

Tatyana Tomilina, who was already notorious before the war for her pro-Russian position.[200] A former student recalled her as 'a pretty standard representative of the Russian World idea', one of those 'people for whom Pushkin is more important than Shevchenko, for whom the sun rises in the north, [who...] remain part of empire'.[201] Ukrainian prosecutors issued her with a 'notice of suspicion' on 6 April 2023, claiming that she had cooperated with the occupation administration 'to seize the premises of Kherson State University' and had registered the university as a Russian institution in violation of Ukraine's laws on collaboration.[202]

A new Russian federal law was adopted on 17 February 2023 that integrated all the higher education institutions in the four annexed regions into the Russian higher education system. In 2023 the Russian Ministry of Science and Higher Education counted twenty-nine higher education establishments in the four occupied regions and twenty-two scientific organisations. They reckoned that there were 103,000 students and 8,000 teachers,[203] although that was likely an overestimate: other reports claimed that it was difficult to attract students even with free places and no entrance exams. In any case, they put together a budget of some 70 billion roubles (US$778 million) for the annual spend, but also attracted funding for the reconstruction of universities damaged in the fighting.[204]

Universities were a key site for Russian socialisation and indoctrination of youth. In the occupied territories, as in the rest of Russia, students studied a new 'patriotic' course, 'Foundations of Russian Statehood', which told them that the end of the Soviet Union was a 'genuine tragedy' for Russians and Russian speakers, because newly independent states began 'an aggressive nationalist policy against our country, which became a genuine tragedy for the whole Russian world'. They would be taught false information that most Ukrainians preferred to speak Russian (as judged by dubious statistics on internet searches) and that Russian speakers faced repression in independent Ukraine. In the course materials, Russia's occupation of Ukrainian territory was referred to as the 'return of territories lost during the collapse of the USSR', described as one of the markers of Russia's return as a 'world leader'.[205]

How much of this had an impact is hard to say. Students had experienced similar pro-Russian teaching in the DNR since 2014, but it was not always effective. A former student at Donetsk State University recalled:

> What I am sure of is that any patriotic movement in the DPR since 2014 was considered [among my classmates] ridiculous and shameful. Even those who joined the 'Young Republic' or the fucking 'Youth Parliament' [pro-government student movements] always made excuses that they weren't serious and they didn't believe in the DNR.[206]

Yet this cynicism did not translate into political opposition. The multiple levers of control that the regime exerted through universities made it difficult for students to be outright opponents of the regime. Whatever they thought privately, many students in the occupied Donbas went along with the propaganda and articulated the right opinions to ensure that they remained enrolled and were allowed to pass their examinations. Russia's cultural and educational strategy did not aim to produce mobilised patriots, but to enforce a cloying discursive hegemony over society and to exclude even the thought that one day these territories might return to Ukraine.

Conclusion: Discursive control

Russia's media, culture and education offensive in the occupied territories aimed to turn a temporary military presence into a permanent, self-sustaining annexation, supported—passively or actively—by a majority of residents. At one level, Russia's narrative used historical and cultural claims to legitimise its presence.[207] Turning back the clock to Soviet-era place names and monuments was part of a campaign to remove the period of Ukrainian independent statehood from regional history and to claim a continuity of Russian control of the region since the Tsarist and Soviet periods. Russia's narrative constantly denigrated Ukrainian history and used attacks on the Ukrainian nationalist movement of the 1930s and 1940s to discredit the concept of Ukraine as an independent state and undermine Ukrainian claims, not only to these territories but to statehood as such. The Russification of education and culture was presented as a return to an era, prior to Kyiv's Ukrainianisation programme, when cultural and educational institutions largely operated in Russian. But the Russians went further—even in the Soviet period, there had been some Ukrainian-language education. Now they set about eradicating almost all traces of Ukrainian culture and history from schools and universities.

For anybody not convinced by Russia's flawed historical and cultural narrative, there was an even simpler message. Russia was here to stay so it was best to adapt and accommodate—and even to take advantage of new opportunities. This strand of Russian propaganda claimed that life under Russian rule would be significantly better than under Ukrainian governance. Salaries would be higher, welfare and pension payments more generous. More investment would boost infrastructure and the economy. Cities would be rebuilt and jobs would be plentiful. Students and schoolchildren would have the chance to go to Russia, to learn new skills and to gain a university education.

The problem with this two-level propaganda campaign is that it had obvious weaknesses on both levels. Although a small minority welcomed the Russification campaign, the region had always had a pluralistic culture and Russia's heavy-handed propaganda struggled to gain traction with locals. On the material front, Russia did win some support from those who found that the new welfare and pension payments boosted their incomes. But—as discussed in the next chapter—the promises made by the Russians of new housing and better jobs were often unfulfilled.

The Russification project reflected an extreme version of Russian nationalism, which denied the existence of a Ukrainian nation. People in south-eastern Ukraine had previously managed cultural and political differences through a constant process of blurring, silencing and mixing in language, culture and art. Now Russia made a determined attack on Ukrainian heritage, forcing Ukrainian citizens in the occupied territories to identify as Russian and to reject everything associated with Ukrainian language and culture. The longer the occupation continued, the more this Russification campaign deepened and hardened, and the greater the emerging divide between occupied and government-controlled Ukraine. From a hybrid, borderland culture, south-eastern Ukraine was transformed into competing and polarised cultural spaces which diverged further and further from each other. With the war, all the cultural and linguistic compromises that had characterised the Russian-Ukrainian borderlands appeared to be at an end.

6

MONEY

Governance, violence and propaganda were the first three pillars of Russia's occupation regime. The fourth was control of the economy. Under President Putin, Russia's entire political economy had evolved into a system that prioritised political control over economic prosperity; it rewarded loyalty and punished rebellion through a system of financial incentives and severe deterrents. Businesspeople who challenged the Kremlin could end up in prison or in exile—or as victims of a mysterious poisoning or defenestration. Loyal cronies of Putin flourished, winning lucrative state contracts and benefiting from the corruption that was endemic throughout the system. This system was refined and adapted during the conflict in Chechnya, and then deployed in Russia's wars in Syria and parts of Africa.[1] Russia channelled money to loyal elites, co-opted poorer parts of society with welfare and humanitarian aid, and punished potential rebels by expropriating their assets, seizing their businesses or blocking their access to humanitarian supplies. It was a simple and brutal system, and in Chechnya this corrupt, patronal order was effective at stabilising society after the war. More than US$14 billion was invested in reconstruction, with much of the expenditure personally controlled by the Chechen political leadership to fund an extensive patronage network based on loyalty.[2] In this system corruption was a feature, not a bug—it was a way, as the scholar Yuliya Zabyelina puts it, of 'buying peace'.[3]

A similar hierarchical and corrupt form of political economy was introduced in Crimea after Russia's annexation in 2014. The Crimean 'State Council' issued a decree on 30 April 2014 which nationalised property belonging to the Ukrainian state, any 'ownerless' property and any other property that the Crimean authorities considered attractive.[4] Many of these nationalised enterprises were later sold—often at knock-down prices—to Putin's cronies. According to media reports, companies associated with Putin's close friend and banker Yuri Kovalchuk bought the famous Massandra winery and the Novy Svet champagne factory. Another close Putin associate, Arkady Rotenberg, was linked to privatisations of luxury health resorts in Crimea.[5] In February 2023 the Crimean authorities announced a further expropriation of some 700 assets belonging to Ukrainian businesses.[6] The Crimean authorities claimed that they would not seize the property of ordinary Ukrainians but only those who 'were responsible for crimes against the Russian army and peaceful population', but the criteria were highly arbitrary.[7]

The process in the DNR and LNR was slower because Russia still formally recognised them as part of Ukraine until 2022. After 2014 some major enterprises initially continued functioning in the DNR and LNR—including those owned by Rinat Akhmetov, the biggest business owner in the east and one of the most powerful oligarchs in Ukraine. After the Kyiv government imposed an economic blockade on the territories in 2017, the DNR authorities 'nationalised' many of Akhmetov's enterprises, and rerouted exports—mainly coal and metals—to Russia and onwards through an opaque network of companies to Turkey and Europe. The DNR leadership set up a holding company, Vneshtorgservis, which took control of over forty major enterprises—primarily in coal and metals—and used a bank from South Ossetia to avoid sanctions.[8] In 2021 this complex scheme was wound up and seven of the region's big metal factories were amalgamated into a single holding company, the Southern Mining and Metallurgical Complex (YuGMK), headed by Yevgeny Yurchenko.[9] Analysts interpreted the move as another step in asserting Moscow's control over the statelets, 'moving on from the wild days of economic piracy to more orderly exploitation schemes'.[10]

As both Crimea and the DNR/LNR showed, the Kremlin and its proxies were ultimately in charge, but on the ground there was fighting over assets and battles over turf among businesses, political figures, Russia's security agencies and criminal groups. The same would prove to be true in the newly occupied territories, where a toxic mix of locals on the make, Russian officials and corporates, security and intelligence networks, Chechen militias and organised crime, all fought over the ruins of the local economy. The occupation authorities oversaw a large-scale expropriation of Ukrainian businesses and properties, re-registering more than 30,000 Ukrainian legal entities in the Russian corporate register.[11] The vast metals plants of Mariupol, Zaporizhzhia's fertile agricultural fields and the Sea of Azov ports of Berdiansk and Mariupol, were taken over by a mix of Russian private business and state officials. Russia initiated a multibillion-dollar reconstruction programme that was central to its propaganda campaign. This huge reconstruction budget offered big profits for well-connected construction companies linked to Russian regional authorities, the Ministry of Construction and the Ministry of Defence.[12]

Although often chaotic, Russia's economic occupation was planned as a mechanism to enhance Russian control of the occupied territories. Three features stand out. First, the occupation regime—in violation of international law—seized private assets from any individuals who were viewed as disloyal or likely to challenge Russian rule. This involved a rapid programme of expropriation of Ukrainian property and businesses and their transfer to loyal locals or to incomers from Russia. Second, the introduction by the Russian Central Bank and the Ministry of Finance of the Russian currency and a Russian banking system ensured that local people had to work within the Russian financial and legal system to survive. Third, Russia's huge spending in the territories provided a way to co-opt some local people—whether local business leaders or teachers and pensioners—who could see some material advantage in not opposing the Russian takeover. Local elites saw opportunities to make money by seizing rival businesses under the cover of war, reorienting their business towards Moscow and feeding from the government spending bonanza. These features all enabled Russia to consolidate its hold on the region and make any future Ukrainian reintegration of the territories more difficult.

Plunder and theft

Pillage (or plunder) is defined as 'the forcible taking of private property by an invading or conquering army from the enemy's subjects'.[13] Plunder and expropriation of private property during an occupation are outlawed under international law.[14] According to Article 46 of the 1907 Hague Regulations, 'Private property cannot be confiscated', while Article 47 notes that 'Pillage is formally forbidden.'[15] The Rome Statute of the International Criminal Court (ICC) considers that 'pillaging a town or place, even when taken by assault' constitutes a war crime.[16]

In Russia's invasion in 2022, Russian forces paid no attention to this aspect of international law. Everything was up for grabs. Russian troops stole everyday items from houses and apartments. They stripped shops and companies. Armed men turned up at a premium kitchenware company in Melitopol in May and seized its entire stock.[17] Tractors and combine harvesters worth nearly US$5 million were looted from the Agrotek dealership in Melitopol. They were later spotted in Chechnya.[18] Soldiers had virtual impunity to steal and rob. It was best not to show any outward signs of wealth. Businessmen faced detentions, shakedowns and informal 'taxes'. Troops took over sanitoriums or apartments for their own use. It was no use complaining. It was all too easy to end up 'in the basement' if you were seen as a 'troublemaker'.

Some looting was just theft by ordinary soldiers. In other cases, it was clearly organised by the military, militias and security agencies. The mass theft and export of materials from major metals plants—including its unimpeded export across the Russian border—could only have been done by groups with links to senior officials. Even according to Russian official customs figures (collected before Russia formally annexed these territories in September

2022), almost US$2 million worth of metal was taken from the Azovstal plant in Mariupol to Russia and a further 400 tonnes of steel worth some US$380,000 from the MMK Ilyich metallurgical plant, also in Mariupol.[19] This was only the amount officially recorded. Metinvest, which owned these metals plants, reckoned that Russian groups had stolen as much as US$600 million worth of products from its metallurgical factories.[20] There were also huge coal stocks in many of these plants—these also disappeared into the Russian black market.

The other quick way to make money was through kidnap for ransom. As discussed in Chapter 4, the GSB, the ad hoc security agency set up in Kherson in 2022, was notorious for kidnapping and torturing businesspeople until they paid ransoms for their release.[21] Newspaper owner Mikhail Kumok told the BBC that businessmen in Melitopol were being detained either to persuade them to pay informal taxes of 10% or 20%, or 'to force them to reopen their business or on the contrary to try to seize it from them'.[22] There were numerous reports of businessmen being kidnapped—either for ransom or to persuade them to do deals with the new authorities. Any sign of social activity by business was particularly discouraged. In Kherson region, the businessman Aleksei Postol was reportedly detained after he set up a humanitarian food network.[23]

Multiple reports claimed that Russian security agencies played a role in these criminal deals, although there is very limited direct evidence of how these informal systems worked. The Ukrainian security officials at the GSB allegedly worked closely with the FSB in this process of violent extraction, concentrating on easily liquidated assets such as grain, cars and agricultural machinery, according to Ukrainian officials. A police source cited by journalists said that 'this was all coordinated with the FSB. The plunder worked like a single mechanism. There was no competition between the GSB, the FSB, the military and Rosgvardiya. Everybody was making money.'[24] Other sources suggested there was infighting among different groups over control of assets and business. For example, Ukrainian sources alleged that there had been a struggle for influence in Mariupol between two different political factions and their patrons in the security services. Both groups sought more control over the economy of Mariupol.[25]

Into this chaotic situation, organised crime gangs also made inroads. The market for drugs among soldiers and workers in the occupied territories provided an attractive opportunity for organised crime. Criminal groups had already played a significant role in the Russian occupation regimes in Donbas and in Crimea prior to 2022.[26] Criminal networks were also useful to the Russian occupation authorities as an instrument of control, a way to augment its military and security forces, building on long-standing ties between criminal groups and Russian intelligence agencies. Reports surfaced of racketeering and extortion of business, drug trafficking and prostitution.[27] Locals complained about criminals from the 1990s coming out of the woodwork and running extortion rackets. Reports in Ukrainian media claimed that there were frequent clashes among gangs and armed groups in Mariupol, including shoot-outs.[28] In August 2023 Ukrainian sources published a video of two dead men, one slumped over his steering wheel, the other falling out of the door of a bullet-ridden car, in the town of Urzuf in Mariupol district. Media reports claimed there had been a clash between a Chechen militia and the Russian military.[29]

President Putin admitted in April 2023 that 'purely criminal elements, including organised crime, drug-traffickers, financial fraudsters and so forth, are attempting to take advantage of the current situation in DNR, LNR, Zaporozhye and Kherson oblasts'.[30] Putin went on to argue, without irony, that Russian law enforcement and security forces 'should do everything to guarantee the secure life of the local population, to defend people [...] and their property from crime, lawlessness and violence, including providing support to local entrepreneurs'.[31] Putin noted a rise in serious crimes in the regions, including 'attempts to seize other people's property'.[32]

Gradually, some sort of order emerged from this 1990s-style chaos, although there were still occasional reports of shoot-outs and disputes among armed gangs. But most businesspeople willing to cooperate with the authorities soon found themselves 'patrons' or 'roofs' (*krysha*) in the classic Russian style, in which powerful officials or security agencies provided protection in exchange for a cut of the business. Those who refused to cooperate with the

Russians left for Ukraine, Europe or Russia. A few returned from Europe to try to hold onto their property or business, or appointed proxies in an attempt to retain or sell their assets. Others could only look on from exile as Russians and their local supporters stole their houses, their businesses and their livelihoods. Meanwhile, the entire Russian bureaucratic and administrative regime began to transform economic life in the occupied territories.

Funding the occupation

Occupation is expensive. Russian media sometimes tried to present the occupation as a boost to Russia's economy, counting up the businesses and assets that Russia had seized in these territories. In reality, the occupation was a black hole into which Russian federal funds disappeared at a rapid rate. Russia's costs in running the territories far outstripped any potential economic benefits—and that was unlikely to change in the near future. In December 2023 President Putin claimed that every year more than 1 trillion roubles (approximately US$11 billion) would be spent from the federal budget 'for the development of these regions and their gradual incorporation into the economic and social life of Russia'. Plus, he claimed another 150 billion roubles was transferred directly from other regions in 2023, with a further 100 billion to come from various regional twinning arrangements in the future.[33] This spending negated any national economic benefit from the occupation for Russia, but it was not such a burden as to make the occupation unsustainable. It amounted to less than 0.5% of Russia's GDP of US$2.2 trillion in 2022.

Working out how much was being spent and where it was being spent was difficult. Putin's figures combined several different pots of spending. First, there was a budget mechanism to provide subsidies to poorer regions—the same funding mechanism that many Russian regions enjoyed. Less developed and politically sensitive regions received the bulk of this regional spending—places such as Dagestan (133 billion roubles in 2023) or Crimea (162 billion). The budget spending announced in 2023 for the occupied territories was bigger—but in the same ballpark. In April 2023 the four regions together were allocated 410.7 billion roubles (approximately US$4.6 billion), most of which was expected to go on social payments and salaries. The biggest slice of funding—196.4 billion roubles—went to the DNR.[34] In the end, funding was even higher. At the end of 2023, Forbes calculated that the overall direct budget subsidies to the regions amounted to some 513 billion roubles, although the government hoped to reduce this to 303 billion roubles in 2024 as the regions' economies were supposed to rebound.[35]

Second, a whole range of other federal spending went directly to the regions. This included very large military and security budgets, but there were also significant sums in the budget for cultural and educational programmes. For example, according to budget plans announced in September 2023, the budget for 2024 would include 776 million roubles for libraries, music schools and 'virtual concert halls' in the occupied territories, and other funding for cultural programmes and schools. One budget line provided an annual payment of 9.3 billion roubles for security of educational institutions in the regions. A new sports programme would receive 2 billion roubles in 2024–26, while 334 million roubles was set aside for 'cultural-educational' school visits in 2023, in other words propaganda tours for Ukrainian schoolchildren.[36]

Third, government funding was allocated to a 'State Programme for the Rehabilitation and Socio-Economic Development of the Donetsk People's Republic, the Lugansk People's Republic, Zaporozhye region and Kherson regions', adopted by the Russian government on 22 December 2023. This programme aimed to raise socio-economic indicators in these regions to the Russian average by 2030, primarily through construction, improved transport infrastructure and encouragement of private enterprise. The funding for this state programme—according to the draft budget in September 2023—amounted to 653.5 billion roubles in 2024–26 (around US$7.1 billion), including 232.9 billion roubles in 2024. The regions themselves were supposed to pay 62.3 billion roubles of this overall spending plan, with the remainder amounting to federal subsidies.[37] This was effectively the budget for reconstruction, channelled through the Department for Implementation of the Special Infrastructure Project of the Ministry of Construction and a network of related companies, as discussed below.

There were other channels for funding that did not come from the federal budget. The *shefstvo* twinning system, discussed in Chapter 3, encouraged Russian regions to 'adopt' towns and districts across the occupied territories.[38] The idea was partly to shift the costs of reconstruction away from the federal budget, but also to mobilise local and regional support for the war—to include more of the Russian political and business elite in the business of occupation. Moscow took on Donetsk and Luhansk as partner cities, while St Petersburg 'adopted' Mariupol. More distant regions picked smaller cities or districts. Khabarovsk Krai—some seven time zones and 8,500 kilometres away in Russia's Far East—was partnered with the small town of Debaltseve in Donetsk region.[39] By April 2023 at least fifty-six regions were providing assistance to the occupied regions.[40]

Leningrad region was twinned with Yenakieve, a depressed mining town about 55 kilometres north-east of Donetsk. The town was dominated by the Yenakieve metallurgical factory, once owned by Rinat Akhmetov's Metinvest, but in terminal decline since Yenakieve ended up in the DNR after 2014. The Leningrad regional government claimed to have spent 870 million roubles on reconstruction work in 2022 and planned a further 2.5 billion roubles in 2023.[41] But these investments could hardly turn around the local economy, which had few prospects under Russian rule. Whatever happened, these Soviet-era industrial towns in occupied eastern Ukraine faced a difficult future as young people left and businesses closed.[42] This reconstruction work was not without its dangers. The optimistically named Hotel Paradise in Yenakieve, where visitors from Leningrad region often stayed, was destroyed by a Ukrainian missile on 29 September 2023, probably aimed at a meeting of local and Russian officials that had just ended.[43] But the twinning programme did provide cheap propaganda opportunities for regional officials. There were regular news segments on the regional LenTV about life in Yenakieve. In August 2023 LenTV showed groups of children from Yenakieve travelling to summer camps in the Leningrad region.[44]

OCCUPATION

The reality of these partnerships was often much less impressive than the glossy propaganda around them suggested. People in the occupied territories complained that the equipment they received was old, that the assistance was substandard, or that regional officials were pocketing some of the money. The *shefstvo* system was very vulnerable to everyday bureaucratic corruption of the type typical throughout Russia: skimming contracts, embezzling budgetary funds, or receiving kickbacks on contracts. The funding systems themselves were opaque. Some regions were digging into their reserve funds, while others expected to get sponsorship from local businesses, using the informal off-the-books budgets—the so-called 'black accounts' (*chernaya kassa*)—that many regions maintained.[45] St Petersburg—twinned with Mariupol—was one of the most active.[46] The city found money in its reserve budget and then diverted funds into the 'Pobeda [Victory] Foundation'. The Pobeda Foundation was a non-transparent and unaccountable funding mechanism, raising concerns among opposition politicians about how these funds were being spent.[47] In April 2023 the Pobeda Foundation did announce that it had raised 11.8 billion roubles for the reconstruction of Mariupol, but revealed no details on how the money was being spent.[48]

This lack of transparency made it difficult to assess how much the regions were spending. In 2023, according to the Russian Minster of Construction, Irek Faizullin, the regions spent a total of 115 billion roubles on reconstruction projects in the occupied territories.[49] In December Putin put the figure higher—at 140–150 billion roubles—with future spending of 100 billion still to come.[50] Moscow was the most generous, setting aside 95 billion roubles over three years in its 2024–26 budget to spend on Donetsk and Luhansk regions, with 35 billion roubles coming in 2024.[51] Moscow could afford it. For other regions, the political requirement to fund the occupation was an unwelcome extra burden. Regional governors wanted the political kudos of 'helping' the occupied territories, but were also wary of local discontent if people believed that money was being diverted from local needs. Polls showed that they were right to be concerned. In a November 2023 survey, 53% of Russians believed that aid to the new regions was at the right level, but 28% said it was too much; only 7% believed it was insufficient.[52]

A final chunk of substantial spending came in the form of new pension payments. I discuss the introduction of these pensions below, but they were a major expense for Russia. In 2023 the pension fund reportedly allocated 369 billion roubles (US$4.1 billion) for pension payments in the occupied territories, rising to 386 billion in 2024 and 406 billion in 2025.[53]

A billion here, a billion there, and the costs of occupation started to add up. In 2023 the budget spending probably came to more than 1,100 billion roubles, or roughly US$12.2 billion, not including spending on the military or security services. In the context of Russia's overall annual budget of around 25.1 trillion roubles in 2023 (US$279 billion), it looked manageable at around 3.5% of annual spending. The occupation would not bankrupt Russia. But it inevitably meant less money for the rest of Russia, where the need for new housing, roads, schools and hospitals was often acute. The Russian government was hoping that the regions' economies would quickly rebound. But local revenues were tiny and were unlikely to increase while the war continued.[54] The Russian invasion had driven more than half of the population into exile, closed many businesses and trade routes, and prompted the US and its allies to impose sanctions on almost any economic activity in the occupied territories. It was hard to imagine a genuine revival of these regions' economies without an end to the war.

Money and banks

Even before the formal annexation in September 2022, the Russian Central Bank and Ministry of Finance had taken charge of all treasury functions in the occupied territories—the issuing and circulation of currency, financial transactions, the regulation of credit institutions and banks. The first step was the currency. Russia was already beginning a shift away from the Ukrainian hryvnia to the Russian rouble in the occupied territories as early as May 2022.[55] National currencies are part of what Michael Billig calls 'banal nationalism', the everyday symbols that are hardly noticed but nevertheless reinforce nationalist myths and a sense of belonging.[56]

OCCUPATION

The circulation of the rouble offered a constant reminder of Russia's claims to sovereignty over the occupied territories, and the Ukrainian resistance often used pictures of defaced or fake roubles in their anti-Russian memes and posts.[57] Ukrainian banks in the occupied territories were forced to close, and the occupation authorities announced that from 1 January 2023 the hryvnia would no longer be in legal use.

Ukrainian banks had done their best to avoid handing over any cash to the Russians. On 24 February, as reports emerged of Russian tanks crossing the border, bank employees at the branch of Oshchadbank in Kherson rushed down to the vaults and began making stacks of banknotes before drilling holes in them, to make sure they could not be used by the occupation forces.[58] For a couple of months these drilled notes sat in the bank, apparently useless. But in June the bank was raided by the occupation authorities and security forces. They allegedly stripped the vaults of jewellery and valuables and any money they could find, and then stumbled across the damaged banknotes. According to media reports, they later found a way to reintroduce the damaged banknotes into circulation in the rest of Ukraine.[59]

Major Russian banks were still nervous about setting up in the occupied territories for fear of even more stringent sanctions, so a state-owned bank, Promsvyazbank (PSB), took the lead in providing banking services. PSB had already been sanctioned by Western countries in February 2022 and disconnected from the SWIFT network that enabled international financial transactions. PSB had many links to the security establishment—its head was Petr Fradkov, son of a former head of Russian external intelligence, Mikhail Fradkov, who was well connected in all the offices in Moscow that mattered.[60] PSB, in effect, was a merger of banking with the Russian security state in one highly effective package.

In April 2022 PSB began working in Crimea as a retail bank, and in June it expanded its operations into the LNR, the DNR, Kherson and Zaporizhzhia regions.[61] It was very quick to open new branches, but it was also forced to abandon newly opened banks when Ukrainian forces liberated areas of Kharkiv and Kherson regions. Nevertheless, its expansion across the rest of the occupied territories continued.⁶² In April 2023 Russian prime minister Mishustin announced that PSB would be the primary financial institution in the occupied territories.⁶³ It proceeded to open dozens of branches in Kherson and Zaporizhzhia regions, and in Donetsk and Luhansk.⁶⁴

PSB was not the only Russian bank working in the occupied territories. A more mysterious entity was the Centre for International Settlements Bank (CMR Bank). CMR had taken over the operations of a murky bank called the International Settlement Bank (*Mezhdunarodnyi raschetnyi bank*; MRB), registered in South Ossetia, which had opened a branch in LNR in 2015 and in DNR in 2018. The MRB made use of a legal loophole prior to 2022 that enabled Russian banks to transfer money to the LNR and DNR via the unrecognised territory of South Ossetia, to avoid sanctions. In 2022 CMR Bank began opening branches across the occupied territories.⁶⁵ Just twelve months after the invasion, in February 2023, Russian banks had opened a total of 194 branches in the LNR and DNR, thirty-three in Zaporizhzhia region and twenty-three in Kherson region, and the numbers continued to expand rapidly.⁶⁶ Despite this swift expansion of Russian financial institutions, local people often complained in social media about frequent queues in banks and insufficient ATMs.

Access to banking was a highly effective mechanism of control. Although many residents were still receiving salaries or pensions from the Ukrainian government, it was hard to access these funds. Enterprising entrepreneurs offered ways to get cash from Ukrainian accounts for a cut, but for many residents, having access to a Russian bank account quickly became a necessity. From 1 January 2023, salaries, social welfare payments and bank transfers were paid to a personal bank account in one of the new Russian banks. The authorities demanded that businesses work only in roubles, open Russian bank accounts and register with the Russian tax service and Russian corporate register.⁶⁷ It became difficult to survive without a Russian bank account. But residents usually needed a Russian passport and Russian registration documents to open an account. In this way, banking became a highly effective mechanism to ensure compliance from the population.

OCCUPATION

Welfare

General David Petraeus, commander of US forces in Iraq in 2007–08, once wrote that 'Money is my most important ammunition in this war.' The US military spent millions of dollars in Iraq to support countless small projects to try to win over hearts and minds.[69] Much of the spending was ineffective, because US commanders had little idea where the money was going. Russian officials agreed on the importance of money as a weapon of war. But they had a much more ruthless approach: money and aid went to friends and proxies; enemies faced starvation and siege. Russia used this dual approach to devastating effect against rebels in Syria.[69]

There was a similar logic to Russia's control of the economy in Ukraine. Although there was little threat of starvation in this agriculturally prosperous land, Russia used humanitarian aid and welfare to generate compliance from a very vulnerable population whose livelihoods had been destroyed by the Russian invasion. Russian television showed regular pictures of desperate queues of pensioners lining up to receive assistance from Russian soldiers to demonstrate Russia's 'humanitarian mission'. Many Ukrainians initially refused to accept this Russian aid, but not everybody was able to take a principled stand. As shops emptied in the spring of 2022, foodstuffs and money were in short supply. Russia played on a very simple instinct—that of survival.

The military and the Russian Ministry of Emergency Situations (MChS) took the lead in distributing humanitarian aid, assisted by 'volunteers', such as those from the Molodaya Gvardiya youth wing of the United Russia (ER) party. This activity was largely cynical, designed to ensure a role for United Russia as a political player in the occupied territories. No international organisations were permitted to deploy in the occupied territories. Anybody who tried to provide independent humanitarian aid was immediately targeted by the Russians as a threat. In Melitopol in April 2022, the Russians detained a food-store owner after he distributed free food.[70] Churches who tried to provide humanitarian aid also faced reprisals.

The Russian authorities began providing what was initially a one-off payment of 10,000 roubles (US$111) to residents. The

MChS transported the money into the occupied territories in cash and distributed it to pensioners directly.[71] This was later converted to a monthly payment to local pensioners and families. For poorer parts of the population, this was potentially a boost to incomes and an obvious attempt by Russia to win over some parts of local society. Along with this monthly stipend, Russian officials distributed a monthly food package—bags of pasta, some tins of food. The food and the money provided a very basic survival package for the poorest in society.[72]

From 1 March 2023 residents in the occupied territories were able to apply to receive Russian pensions and welfare payments. Since there were many pensioners living under occupation, a new pension system was an important part of Russia's economic policy. Russia's Social Fund produced a hybrid system that guaranteed that any Russian pension would not be lower than an existing Ukrainian pension. The main outcome was that many poorer pensioners were usually better off under the Russian system. The average pension in the territories would be 18,235 roubles (around US$203), according to figures from the Ministry of Labour in July 2023.[73] These pensions were still extremely low, but for many this was a bigger monthly pension than they had received in Ukraine, where the average pension was closer to US$150.

By the end of 2023 more than a million residents of the four regions were receiving Russian pensions, according to figures from the Russian Social Fund.[74] Other welfare payments also became available, such as child benefit. The prerequisite for receiving the relatively generous child benefit payments was that both mother and child had to be Russian citizens.[75] In other words, to access Russian welfare systems, residents in the occupied territories had to accept a Russian passport.

Russian propaganda made much of these welfare payments. Deputy Prime Minister Marat Khusnullin argued that the figures showed that attempts to intimidate people by the Ukrainian authorities, who warned that people 'should not take money from Russia', had been thwarted, with these social payments becoming one of the most important sources of funding in the 'new regions'.[76] In reality, people had little choice. Russia's ability to control the flow of funds to all parts of society—from the poorest to local business elites—was designed to ensure dependency on Moscow and therefore engineer compliance from the population.

Expropriation

Many entrepreneurs left in the early months of the occupation, forced to abandon their businesses and start again in government-controlled Ukraine or in Europe. It is not clear how many stayed. In 2023 Ukrainian officials suggested that around 30% of Ukrainian businesspeople had remained in Mariupol.[77] Those entrepreneurs who did not leave faced an impossible choice. If they refused to cooperate, their business was likely to be seized by the occupation authorities and re-registered under new management.[78] But if they agreed to register with the Russian tax authorities, Ukrainian businesses risked crossing a line, resulting in 'not just co-existence but cooperation' with the occupation authorities, as one resident phrased it. This left them open to the threat of prosecution by the Ukrainian authorities on charges of collaboration.[79]

Even before the annexation in September 2022, the new authorities began an inventory of the entire property stock of the newly occupied territories. By December 2022 the Russian Federal Tax Service had re-registered more than 30,000 Ukrainian organisations and companies in the Russian corporate register, the Unified State Register of Legal Entities (EGRYUL), which lists all Russian companies and organisations. The Russian tax authorities appear to have simply copied the equivalent Ukrainian register, regardless of whether Ukrainian companies agreed or not. Companies now listed in the Russian register had until the end of 2023—or mid-2024 for Kherson and Zaporizhzhia—to update all their paperwork in accordance with Russian laws and regulations.[80] An investigation by the Russian independent newspaper *Novaya gazeta Evropa* identified over 1,000 major companies in the cities of Melitopol, Berdiansk, Mariupol, Lysychansk and Severodonetsk that had been re-registered as Russian entities in this way.[81]

In Zaporizhzhia the occupation authorities set up a new 'Ministry of Property and Land Relations' in August 2022.[82] The ministry began to publish lists on an almost daily basis of what they claimed were 'ownerless' or 'abandoned' properties. Legal owners had only three days to report their ownership—together with a list of documents—to the Russian authorities, before the property was liable to be registered with the local authorities as 'abandoned' and therefore subject to de facto nationalisation. Most of these owners had been forced to flee and leave their property behind, so complying with these demands was very difficult. The exact criteria for declaring a property 'abandoned' were completely opaque. One farmer who retained control of his lands by re-registering them with the Russians, called the process 'corrupt' and said 'there are no clear rules [that set out] the criteria by which property enters these registers'.[83]

According to one investigation, the authorities in Zaporizhzhia registered some 4,000 businesses and assets as 'abandoned', and therefore liable to de facto 'nationalisation'.[84] The lists included businesses, apartments, houses and cars.[85] By December 2022, according to the head of the Russian-appointed regional government, Anton Koltsov, some 400 businesses in Zaporizhzhia region had been taken over by the occupation authorities. Koltsov claimed that these takeovers were only aimed at ensuring that enterprises continued working, and that they were not being transferred to new owners but remained on the books of the regional administration.[86] In practice, this looked very much like a process of illegal expropriation by the occupying power. In June 2023 the Russian-appointed 'Senator' from Zaporizhzhia region in Russia's Federation Council, Dmitry Vorona, was more candid: 'a decision was made to nationalise all property that was left behind by the people who owned it previously', he told a conference in Moscow. 'Those who did not go through re-registration in Zaporozhye oblast … [and] who have not got their enterprise up and running, creating jobs—all that property has been nationalised.'[87]

The regional commission appears to have taken charge of expropriating local shops, apartments, cars, smaller factories and petrol stations, but the ownership of major enterprises was almost certainly decided in Moscow. In October 2022 the Russian government set up a special commission to arrange external management of 'abandoned' enterprises in the newly occupied regions. Deputy Prime Minister Khusnullin oversaw the new commission, with Minister of Construction Irek Faizullin as his deputy.[88] Russian industrial defence giant Rostec was reportedly among those looking to take over some of these enterprises. The proposed list of companies included an iron ore plant in Berdiansk, which provided raw material for the Azovstal and MMK Ilyich metallurgical plants; Mariupol port; Severodonetsk Azot chemical factory (belonging to Dmitry Firtash's Group DF); the salt mines at Soledar; several coal-fired power stations; and the Zaporizhzhia Nuclear Power Plant (ZNPP).[89]

The most dangerous case was the takeover of the ZNPP at Enerhodar by Russia's nuclear power corporation Rosatom. After Russian forces took control of the ZNPP in March 2022, Russian officials simply informed staff that they were now working for Rosatom.[90] On 3 October 2022 Rosenergoatom—the Rosatom subsidiary that runs Russia's nuclear power plants—set up a new company, the 'Zaporozhye NPP Operating Organisation, Joint Stock Company', to run the plant under a new director, Oleg Romanenko.[91] On 5 October President Putin signed a decree that instructed the government to take over the ZNPP and to set up a company that would manage the property.[92] The situation inside the plant must have been almost unbearable, with staff working under extreme pressure to maintain the safety of the plant, with fighting going on around them, while also having to deal with the Rosatom takeover. As noted in Chapter 4, there were credible reports of torture against staff and constant pressure on them to accept Russian citizenship and sign contracts with Rosatom.

Not far from Enerhodar, in the town of Dniprorudne, the Russians also took over the Zaporizhzhia Iron Ore Plant (ZZRK) in June 2022. According to media reports, thousands of tonnes of iron ore were stolen.[93] A new director was installed, reported to be a former Russian military officer. In August 2022 the plant was re-registered in the Russian corporate database as the Dneprorudny Iron Ore Plant.[94] The Ukrainian authorities claimed in March 2023 that ore from ZZRK was being exported through Mariupol port and sold by 'structures related to the FSB', although it was impossible to corroborate these claims.[95]

Mines were potentially lucrative businesses, requiring little investment and fast returns. The Tokmak granite quarry was also seized in June 2022 after the management refused to cooperate with Russian forces.[96] In November 2022 the quarry appeared in the Russian corporate register with new owners from Crimea.[97] Another mining company, 'Mineral' in Zaporizhzhia, was also re-registered with a new owner and director.[98] Crimean companies were active in the takeover of Ukrainian companies. They had the local knowledge and the connections to benefit from the expropriation before companies from Russia could get involved.

In Mariupol before the war, some 35,000 people worked for Rinat Akhmetov's Metinvest group, which owned the vast Azovstal steel plant and the MMK Ilyich metals plant. Azovstal had been devastated by the fighting, and it was unlikely it would ever be rebuilt. Its ruins fuelled a lucrative scrap metal business in the region. The MMK Ilyich plant was less badly damaged and there were plans to resume production. Two enterprising Americans had founded the plant in 1898 before it was nationalised by the Bolsheviks and renamed after Vladimir Ilyich Ulyanov, the Bolshevik revolutionary better known as Lenin. In 2016, under Ukraine's decommunisation programme, the plant kept the Ilyich name, but the management rather craftily announced that it was now named after a scientist called Zot Ilyich Nekrasov.[99] Under Russian rule it remained the Ilyich plant, but instead of being emblazoned with portraits of the Soviet leader, its entrance now proudly displayed the faces of Vladimir Putin, Chechen leader Ramzan Kadyrov and DNR head Denis Pushilin, a line-up that neatly symbolised the strange new political hierarchy of the occupied territories.[100]

Chechen networks appear to have been given control of the plant as reward for their role in the siege and capture of Mariupol. Initially, according to a BBC report in January 2023, Chechen businessman Valid Korchagin had registered as co-owner of a company in the DNR called MMK Ilyich, together with Yury Muray, a local businessmen connected to the authorities in the DNR.[101] Korchagin later appears to have bowed out of the deal, with Alash Dadashov, a Chechen businessman and head of a

Moscow fight-club, taking a 50% stake in the company.[102] A report in the *Wall Street Journal* in October 2024 confirmed that companies and individuals linked to Chechnya were in control of the plant.[103] Initially, it seemed that the plant would just be plundered for scrap metal, but in December 2023 the Russian press reported that there were plans to resume production.[104]

The fate of these huge metals plants was decided in Moscow, but local players had plenty of opportunities to win a stake in this distribution of looted property. Groups of businesspeople gathered around the four regional heads—Balitsky, Saldo, Pushilin and Pasechnik—to take advantage of a bonanza of stolen property. As in other areas of the occupation, the expropriation was also a way of continuing pre-existing rivalries and expanding control over a business sector. A local entrepreneur who owned a fuel sales company expanded his business by seizing control of petrol stations from the Ukrainian chains Okko-Light and West Petrol Market after the occupation. According to Ukrainian officials, he shared the profits with the local administration.[105] Ukrainian media accused local officials of involvement in takeovers of Ukrainian companies, such as the Melitopol Tractor Parts Factory in Obilnoe, near Melitopol, in April 2022.[106] According to the new management, by February 2023 the Tractor Parts Factory was producing automobile and tractor parts for Russian and Belarusian buyers.[107]

The occupation authorities took control of any food production companies early in the war, aware that their closure could lead to a humanitarian disaster. The occupation authorities seized bread factories belonging to Boris Shestopalov's HD Group in Berdiansk and Melitopol.[108] On 1 February 2023 the Melitopol Bread Plant was re-registered in the Russian corporate register with a new director.[109] In May 2022 Ukrainian media reported that the local Melitopol Meat Factory had been taken over by armed men.[110] Similar takeovers took place in other regions where owners refused to pay informal taxes to the occupation authorities or register under the new Russian tax system. New retail chains opened, selling food products from Russia and Crimea, a source of constant complaint from local people. Not only were the new shops often much more expensive, but customers complained that the quality of products was lower than in Ukrainian shops.

Resisting a hostile takeover was dangerous and futile. Well-known Berdiansk businessman Oleksandr Ponomarev was detained in March 2022 by Russian forces for ten days; in protest, workers at his factories reportedly went on strike.[111] Ponomarev was an influential figure in Berdiansk—some people called him an informal governor—and he also served as a parliamentary deputy from the 'Opposition Platform - for Life' party, often viewed as 'pro-Russian'. His detention was a shock—if Russia could not work with Ponomarev, their chances of co-opting other local elites seemed slim. The Zaporizhzhia occupation authorities seized Ponomarev's companies—Agrinol, Azmol and the machine-building company Berdiansk Harvesters.[112] According to Russian sources, the reason was the 'misconduct' of the owner, who had allegedly refused to resume production and pay taxes to Russia.[113] By May 2023 Berdiansk Harvesters, marketed under the brand 'John Greaves', was exhibiting at an agricultural fair in Krasnodar Krai in Russia.[114] Representatives of the company, selling their bright yellow combines and other farm equipment, told journalists that their factory was 'fully functioning' and that 'we have resolved all the logistical problems in supply chains that we faced last year'.[115]

Initially, the Ponomarev story seemed a major boost for Ukraine, a sign that even those local elites with strong connections to Russia were resisting the occupation. Having lost control of his enterprises, Ponomarev left for Kyiv in early 2023. But in July 2023 the story turned on its head when he was arrested by the Ukrainian authorities on charges of treason. Ponomarev denied the charges and told the press that he had been offered everything by the Russians: '[senior] positions; resources; contracts ... just so long as I agreed [to work with them]. But I did not agree, and because of that I was arrested.' Ponomarev was shocked by his reception in Kyiv. 'I expected that I would be welcomed with joy, but in response I received a series of allegations that I allegedly collaborated', he told journalists.[116] The details of the investigation remained unclear, but it showed how murky the environment was in the occupied territories, and how thin the line could be between collaboration and resistance.

Even when the Russians seized factories, it was not clear how productive they might be. Many were in poor condition even before the war. Industrial plants were often badly damaged in the fighting. Specialist workers had fled. Supply chains were badly disrupted, and it was hard to access any finance. The Azovmash plant, which had exported thousands of railway wagons to Russia prior to 2012, had been stagnating for almost a decade. Its legal owner lived in Monaco and different Russian and local groups struggled to control what was left of it. The Russian truck-maker KAMAZ showed an interest, the DNR authorities set up a new company called Mariupoltyazhmash in late 2023 to relaunch production, and the RosKapStroi agency also planned a project on the site.[117] In reality, these Soviet-era plants had few prospects. Instead of being a thriving industrial city, Mariupol became the centre of a lucrative business in scrap metal. Even before the war, scrap metal was a semi-criminalised business in Mariupol and other parts of the Donbas. Now it became one of the easiest ways for businesses, officials and criminal groups to make money, stripping and selling the wrecked industrial assets of the city.

Agriculture and grain exports

Russia's newly occupied territories in Zaporizhzhia and Kherson contain some of Ukraine's prime agricultural land. This is the heart of the famed black-earth region that was the breadbasket of the Soviet Union and the centre of Ukraine's successful grain export business. After February 2022, Russian companies and their accomplices moved quickly to seize this prime agricultural land and to control grain exports. According to research by the Kyiv School of Economics, the agricultural sector suffered some US$10.3 billion in damages in the first two years of the war, including US$1.97 billion in damaged or stolen agricultural goods and inputs in the occupied territories.[118] Swathes of land along the front line were uncultivated, covered in mines and fortifications. Despite the fighting, some 88% of winter crops planted in occupied areas in 2022 were still harvested, but farmers had little choice now but to sell to new Russian monopoly buyers, who then exported it to Russia or abroad.[119]

Chief executive officer of Ukrainian agribusiness HarvEast, Dmitry Skornyakov, told Bloomberg that 'Everything that was harvested on our fields was stolen and exported from Ukraine.'[120] One investigation concluded that Russian proxies harvested more than 10 million tonnes of grain on newly occupied territories of Ukraine in the first two years of the occupation.[121] Another report suggested that Russia may have earned over US$2 billion from the harvest in occupied parts of Zaporizhzhia and Kherson regions in 2022 and US$1.25 billion in 2023.[122]

Initially, there were numerous reports of straightforward theft by Russian looters and marauding troops. Farmers reported that their farms had been seized by groups of armed men, including Chechen forces, DNR militias and regular Russian military. In April 2022, according to Andrii Chorniy, owner of Agrokoin, a vegetable producer, armed men turned up on his farm accompanied by a local pro-Russian official and seized his horticultural greenhouses. His company was 'nationalised' and Chorniy lost control over the business.[123] A local farmer, Andrian Khablenko, told journalists that he was detained and tortured in September 2022 by armed men from the unofficial GSB security outfit, and forced to sign a blank piece of paper transferring his farm to cronies of the occupation regime.[124] The company Agroton claimed that some 350,000 tonnes of crops—some in storage, some still in the ground—were stolen. In many places farmers were forced to rewrite contracts, sometimes at gunpoint, and to register their farms in accordance with Russian law. There were reports that in some places different Russian militias faced off against each other, as they fought for control of farmland.[125]

Many big Russian companies were wary of investing in the occupied territories. Sanctions risks, war risks and the threat of losing everything in a military reversal made major corporates cautious. But agriculture was different. Here at least one major Russian company did show interest. Three major Ukrainian companies, HarvEast, Nibulon Ltd and Agroton Public Ltd, accused a Russian company, Agrocomplex, of seizing their lands, totalling some 400,000 acres.[126] Agrocomplex, one of Russia's biggest farm operators, was run by former Russian agriculture minister and Krasnodar governor Alexander Tkachev.[127] Tkachev gained a reputation as one of the most successful businesspeople in Russian agriculture, and developed a taste for the high life along the way.[128] His company was also reported to be developing a food distribution network in the occupied territories in 2023.[129]

Everybody wanted a share in the grain export business. In May 2022 a new company, the State Grain Operator (GZO), was set up in Melitopol.[130] The company took over large parts of the grain production and logistics chain; by 2023 they were employing some 1,300 people.[131] In 2023 GZO was reported to have exported 212,000 tonnes of Ukrainian grain worth some US$46 million. A large part of it was channelled through shell companies and sold to buyers in Turkey and to offshore corporations.[132] Initially, most of the illicit grain export appears to have been routed via Crimea or mainland Russia. Yevgeny Balitsky admitted in June 2022 that grain from Zaporizhzhia was being exported through Crimean ports.[133] A major export market was Syria, which was in desperate need of grain. According to Reuters, wheat exports to Syria from Sevastopol rose more than seventeen times in 2022 to over 500,000 tonnes, using Russian-flagged ships and three sanctioned Syrian ships.[134] In other cases, the grain was shipped to Russia first. In such cases, Ukrainian grain became indistinguishable from Russian grain, which could be exported without any sanctions.

As local ports in the occupied territories were repaired, they were also used for grain exports. Russian officials were proud of their role in this trade. Yulia Maksimova, the head of RosKapStroi, the Ministry of Construction agency that took over Mariupol port, could be seen in one of her official videos celebrating the loading of grain into a ship.[135] 'Ghost' fleets emerged to transport illicit cargoes of grain out of the occupied territories. A *Financial Times* investigation tracked shipments across the Black Sea to Turkey on a Syrian-flagged vessel, the *Pawell*. Despite the Syrian flag, the ship was owned by a UK-based partnership, the Pawell Shipping Company, registered in Bloomsbury, London.[136]

Other officials were also deeply involved in the trade. Ukrainian prosecutors claimed that in Kherson region, the Russian-installed governor Vladimir Saldo was implicated in the illegal export of grain.[137] A company called Grainholding Ltd was registered in November 2022 at UK Companies House, with a company director

MONEY

by the name of 'Volodymyr Saldo', the same name as the Russian-appointed Kherson governor.[138] Whether it was really his company or not remained unclear, but everybody with influence in the occupied territories wanted a part of the lucrative grain business.

Reconstruction

In early March 2024, a delegation of Ukrainian exiles from Mariupol travelled to Hull, England, to discuss the future reconstruction of their city. Hull was the most bombed city in the UK during World War II and had extensive experience of how to rebuild a city after war. Although the delegation was discussing what a future Mariupol might look like, Professor Mykola Trofymenko, the rector of Mariupol University, sounded a gloomy note in an interview:

> I don't believe all [the] people will come back after what they faced out there. Mariupol is now a huge cemetery. We'll have discussions about whether to rebuild it totally or partly, or if we will create a memorial to human stupidity, when the ruler of one country decided to destroy and kill so many people.[139]

As the war continued, the prospect of return to Mariupol became more distant. Nevertheless, Vadym Boychenko, mayor of Mariupol, continued to develop new visions of urban reconstruction, drawn up by international and Ukrainian architects, which projected a new city built on the ruins of the old.[140] The problem was obvious: Ukraine did not control Mariupol, and in the city under Russian occupation a quite different vision was being promoted. In August 2022 the Russian Ministry of Construction had developed a glossy 'Master Plan' for Mariupol, which envisaged a futuristic Russian city by the sea, with plans for schools, business and housing for up to 500,000 people by 2035.[141] Even this upbeat brochure admitted that the population of Mariupol had shrunk to 212,000, less than half of the pre-war population of more than 431,000. It seemed evident that the planned population increase would rely on immigration from Russia.

It was hard to imagine the glossy pictures in the city plan coming to fruition from the grim ruins of Mariupol. But Russia had considerable experience in building these mega-construction projects. Former Russian prime minister Sergei Stepashin, now head of a public council under the Ministry of Construction, openly compared Mariupol to Grozny, the Chechen capital that had been razed to the ground by Russian attacks but was then reconstructed in a modern Middle Eastern style, all glass skyscrapers and soaring minarets. The Grozny reconstruction campaign was an attempt to bury the memory of the war in modern architecture under the slogan 'No traces of war'.[142] Now the Russians sought to repeat the experience in Mariupol, both obscuring the memory of the war and also obliterating any traces of the city's Ukrainian history.

As people emerged from the basements, where some had spent weeks hiding from Russian missiles and shelling, they often found their apartments uninhabitable. Almost no building in Mariupol had survived completely unscathed. A detailed investigation of the video evidence concluded that 'munitions have left their mark on nearly every building across its 166 square kilometers'.[143] Much of the downtown area was destroyed, with the dead buried in makeshift graves in apartment yards amid the ruins. The Azovstal site was a post-apocalyptic nightmare, and large parts of the district around it in the east of the city (left-bank Mariupol) were flattened. Tens of thousands of people were homeless or living in severely damaged apartments and houses. Power, water, heating and communications were all severely damaged.

Even while the fighting was going on, Andrei Turchak, secretary of the United Russia party, had announced that rebuilding would begin: 'Russia will rebuild everything. First, we must conclude the operation. Then, builders and everyone will pile in and get it done. Everything will be restored', he promised.[144] A major reconstruction programme began after Russian troops finally seized full control of the city in May 2022. Thousands of workers were shipped in from Russia to start clearing the debris, to demolish dangerous buildings, to restore power and water and to start construction of new homes. Russian engineers also worked to set up new gas networks independent of the Ukrainian network, and to repair or replace energy systems ahead of the winter of 2022–23. Government ministers claimed that over 4,000 pieces of energy infrastructure had been repaired by April 2023.[145] Russian water engineers built a new 200-kilometre water pipeline from the Don River to Donetsk in just five months.[146] Despite all the hype, residents continued to report serious problems with power, water and other utilities. The electricity grid had been disconnected from Ukraine's grid but would not be fully integrated with Russia's until 2028, leaving the region with frequent power outages.[147] The supply of water was a problem across the region, despite the new infrastructure, with many people in Donetsk and Mariupol experiencing shortages.

Many people were still homeless in the winter of 2022–23, despite Russia's promises to rehouse them. Those who had left the city could only watch and hope that their houses or apartments were still intact. In many cases other people moved into empty homes, squatting because they had nowhere else to live, or—less charitably—because they wanted to take advantage of the forced exile of so many people. One Mariupol resident in exile told me that she wished her apartment had been destroyed rather than taken over by strangers. She had no way of returning to assert her right to the property, although she had all her documents intact.[148]

People whose houses had been destroyed or were damaged beyond repair were promised new housing. Some received new apartments, but many were disappointed. A government decree in 2022 promised new housing in the same reconstructed building or at least in the same district. In August 2023 they changed the rules, now promising only new housing in the same town or within the DNR. According to local figures, by September 2023 more than 13,000 Mariupol residents had applied for new housing. But more than 4,000 of these applications were rejected for various reasons.[149] One loophole used by the authorities was the stipulation that compensation would only be given to people with no other accommodation. As a result, applicants were often turned down because they had an unheated shed on their suburban allotments or some other uninhabitable building. Probably tens of thousands more were unable or unwilling to apply for compensation—they had left for Europe or other parts of Ukraine, their parents or relatives had died, their documents had been lost in fires or in the chaos, or children did not have a will or faced other legal obstacles.

OCCUPATION

Thousands of people died, but it was not easy to prove the right to inherit property. Unless there was a dead body, the Russian procuracy refused to provide any certificate of death, leaving relatives in legal limbo.[150] In some cases, local officials and lawyers seem to have conspired to deceive people. Irina barely escaped with her life when her apartment was bombed. Her husband died, but when she tried to claim compensation, she gave her documents to a lawyer who disappeared. When she complained to the authorities and threatened to write to President Putin, a local official reminded her that 'you are in the DNR, not in Russia. We decide here, not Putin.'[151] It was a stark reminder that whatever the grand schemes dreamt up in Moscow, local elites often had the power to subvert and adapt policies in ways that suited their own interests.

Even those whose applications were approved struggled to get a new apartment. By September 2023, according to Russian figures provided by a vlogger on YouTube, only 2,427 out of the more than 13,000 applicants had been rehoused, while others remained in a very long, slow queue, living with friends or renting rooms in other people's houses. The report calculated that despite all the rebuilding, the city would be short of at least 10,000 apartments, leaving many people homeless.[152] An alternative scheme gave residents financial compensation, but the payouts were too small to allow people to buy a new property. There was not much you could buy in Mariupol's booming real estate market for the 1–2 million roubles (US$11–22,000) compensation that most people received.[153] Prices for apartments in Mariupol went from US$40,000 upwards. Even renting a flat cost 20–30,000 roubles (US$220–330) a month. Many local people could not afford it.

The reason for this disregard for the local homeless was simple: money. Russian property developers could make significant profits if they sold their apartments privately, rather than giving them away to local residents. Private developers wanted to build apartments for sale to people who could qualify for a mortgage. Local people were mostly too poor to qualify, so sales went mainly to Russian incomers and a few local businesspeople or officials. Registering ownership and applying for compensation was made as difficult as possible: applicants had to wait for hours in queues to provide documents or give in forms. These were 'eternal queues', said one pensioner, 'and people treated us like cattle, with inhuman rudeness'. Small protests broke out and slogans appeared on the fences around building sites: 'Give us our home back' or 'No to mortgages, [give] homes to people'.[154]

An apartment building at 82 Nakhimova Street was almost completely destroyed in the fighting. The location was enviable. Across the road was a large green park that stretched down to the seaside. Seeing an opportunity, a company called YugStroiInvest demolished the old building and built a brand-new luxury apartment block, offering 'apartments filled with fresh air and sunlight, and beautiful views of a green courtyard'. They were soon sold out.[155] But the former residents of 82 Nakhimova Street were left on the street outside holding small protests. One recorded a video clip, complaining that: 'the residents of the apartment block, which was here, have been thrown out on the street. And now they are building apartments for sale. We worked half our lives for this apartment and lived in it for more than 30 years. And we have lost everything!'[156] The house was even given a new official address, 1b Chernomorsky Lane. It was as though their home had never existed. This was not some shadowy builder breaking the rules: Marat Khusnullin gave the project the official seal of approval when he visited the building site in July 2023.[157]

This is what scholars mean by the term 'urbicide': not only the deliberate destruction of cities, but their reconstruction in ways that make them unrecognisable to their original communities. During this reconstruction, the city as historical entity, as a community, ceases to exist and is replaced by a new form of spatial ordering that has profound demographic, political and social consequences. Nurhan Abujidi and Han Verschure, in a study of urbicide in the occupied territories of Palestine, distinguished 'design by destruction'—the razing and bulldozing of neighbourhoods—from 'design by construction', in which spaces are transformed by new infrastructure and housing projects that deliberately exclude Palestinian communities.[158] In Mariupol, both modes of urbicide were evident: Russia first destroyed the city, and then rebuilt it as an exclusionary urban space that aimed to erase all traces of its Ukrainian history and culture.

Martin Coward argues that urbicide goes beyond the initial destruction of buildings. It is an attack on the shared spaces, the heterogeneity and pluralism that are characteristic of city life, 'a killing of urbanity' itself.[159] The Russian reconstruction campaign in Mariupol completed the destruction of the old Mariupol, a place of complex and contested identities, and imposed a new order that attacked any sense of pluralism. The old community was destroyed. Tens of thousands were dead, many more were exiled. Among those who remained in Mariupol, the divisions were not only between occupier and occupied; there was also a stark division between those who had lost everything and those who were profiting from the occupation.

Some of those who suffered homelessness were people who had genuinely believed that Russia would restore the city. Ella, a pensioner, told a Russian journalist that she had 'so believed in Russia, and believed that they would not abandon me'. She concluded that 'It is all built on lies … We were so critical of people who left for Europe. And now it turns out to be a monstrous deception.'[160] The Russian authorities were not even working to win over pro-Russian citizens, let alone those Ukrainians who completely rejected the occupation.

In October 2023 the authorities announced that they would be carrying out a 'comprehensive inventory' of the residential properties in the city. They demanded that owners prove their property title by showing the inspectors their property documents. For residents who had left the city, going back to secure their properties was not usually feasible. Some could afford to hire a lawyer, but many could not—or did not trust them. Many did not want to engage with the Russian authorities at all. If owners were unable to present their property documents within thirty days, they would 'lose the right to use such residential premises', according to the decree from the city's mayor.[161] This looked like another property grab by the local authorities, who would then be able to reallocate apartments to cronies, the military or incomers from Russia.

Even as fighting continued, some Russian citizens started looking at the occupied territories as an investment opportunity, a chance to snap up a seaside home on the cheap. Irina, from the Siberian city of Krasnoyarsk, wanted to live by the sea in a city with 'good ecology'. Mariupol offered cheap housing and potentially a high salary for her husband, she told journalists. Olesya, also from Siberia, from the city of Omsk, believed property in Mariupol would be a promising investment. She was confident about the future—'under the wing of Russia it has a great future ... it will become a popular place for recreation and tourism'. Eldar, also from Krasnoyarsk, was looking for an apartment. He wasn't afraid that the town would get caught up in fighting again, because 'our armed forces reliably guard our borders'.[162] The cheapest apartments were on the market for 3 million roubles (US$33,000) and houses (usually detached one-storey houses with a yard) for 4.8 million roubles (US$53,000).[163] In August 2023 a 100-square-metre house with 1,500 square metres of land, situated 'on the banks of the warm Sea of Azov', was advertised on the Russian real estate site Avito for 10 million roubles. An apartment in the city centre, in an 'undamaged house' with a new lift, cost 3 million roubles.[164] By 2024 prices had risen, even for war-damaged property. A two-bedroom apartment 'in the historical centre', just '15 minutes' walk to the sea', was on offer for 5.8 million roubles. But the photographs on the real estate website showed a scene of internal devastation, the walls, ceilings and windows destroyed in the war.[165]

The war profiteers

Who was making money from this buzzing real estate market? The rebuilding of one of Mariupol's most famous buildings gives some insights. The Clock House was the local name for an apartment block with a clock spire in central Mariupol. In March 2022 a Russian shell destroyed much of the building and killed two residents. A Russian company, RKS-Development, was awarded a contract to build a new version of this much-loved monument on the site, but none of the residents were to be rehoused in the new apartment block. Instead, the apartments were sold off-plan at prices none of the residents could afford: around 8.5 million roubles (US$94,000) for a two-bed apartment.[166] Who were these property developers? According to corporate records, RKS-Development had only been set up in May 2023. RKS-NR (also known as RKS-Novorossiya) owned 98% of the company, while Konstantin Lopukhov, a former minister of construction from Tula region in central Russia, owned the other 2% and ran the company.[167] RKS-NR was set up by RosKapStroi, an agency of the Ministry of Construction, which began to crop up as the key contractor on almost every billboard outside a building site in Mariupol.

The Clock House deal was just a small part of a classic Russian patronage pyramid. At the very top was Marat Khusnullin, the deputy prime minister put in charge of reconstruction by President Putin. It was Khusnullin who became the point-person for the whole reconstruction process, reporting directly to Putin on progress, and sitting in the passenger seat while Putin drove around Mariupol at night-time during his visit to the city in March 2023. This gave Khusnullin an important profile in the occupied territories, overseeing a multibillion-dollar budget and taking responsibility for hundreds of construction projects.

Khusnullin was an economist by profession, a graduate of Kazan University in the Republic of Tatarstan in central Russia. He made his career as minister of construction in Tatarstan from 2001 to 2010. But his big break came with a move to Moscow in 2010. He oversaw all construction in the capital during a period when Moscow mayor Sergei Sobyanin had launched a hugely expensive reconstruction programme. In 2020 Khusnullin went further up the political ladder, appointed as deputy prime minister in the federal government, in charge of construction and housing. He had a reputation as somebody who could oversee complex, high-profile construction projects, but he also had plenty of detractors. Transparency International alleged a series of conflicts of interest as companies run by his associates snapped up state contracts.[168] In 2023 an investigation by the Dossier Center uncovered properties in France and Cyprus allegedly belonging to members of his family.[169] Khusnullin denied any wrongdoing.

As deputy prime minister, Khusnullin oversaw the Ministry of Construction, Housing and Utilities, led by his ally from Tatarstan, Irek Faizullin. The deputy minister of construction, Valery Leonov, headed the ministry's Department for Implementation of the Special Infrastructure Project, which had been set up in May 2022 to oversee the reconstruction programme. Leonov directly oversaw the huge reconstruction budget and was reportedly deployed almost full-time in the occupied territories.[170] The ministry ran construction projects through a state holding company, the so-called 'Single Contractor in the Construction Sphere' (EZSS). EZSS hired thousands of workers and by August 2024 claimed to have built forty-six apartment complexes in Mariupol and numerous other buildings.[171] EZSS in turn contracted another agency of the Ministry of Construction, RosKapStroi, tasked with rather vague powers of project management and headed by an energetic head, Yulia Maksimova, who became a regular visitor to the Donbas. In May 2022 RosKapStroi set up a construction company, RKS-NR (or RKS-Novorossiya), which took on numerous construction contracts in Mariupol. Finally, at the end of the chain, RKS-NR established RKS-Development, which took on the contract to build the new apartment block in the destroyed Clock House. This was the kind of complex patronage pyramid that was typical of Russia's occupation regime, characterised by apparent conflicts of interest and a very blurred division between the private and public sectors. The important point for Mariupol's residents was that the billions of dollars flowing through these contracts often ended up not with new housing for the homeless, but with luxury apartments for sale on the open market.

Nobody was better placed to take advantage of the reconstruction programme than Timur Ivanov, a deputy defence minister. When Defence Minister Sergei Shoigu paid a flying visit to Mariupol in March 2023, a news clip showed Timur Ivanov by his side, as the delegation visited a new set of apartment blocks in the Nevsky district built by the defence ministry's construction company, VSK.[172] The Nevsky complex became a central image in Russia's propaganda about Mariupol and was visited by Putin during his March 2023 visit. Ivanov had his own patronage system in the vast Ministry of Defence construction sector. VSK contracted work to its favoured companies, chief among them Olimpsitistroy, which built the Nevsky apartment complex.[173] Olimpsitistroy was founded in 2006 by two well-connected businessmen with military ties, Alexander Fomin and Dmitry Khavronin, and had become one of the Ministry of Defence's favoured contractors.[174] Ivanov's family appears to have become very wealthy. According to leaked emails, photographs and receipts, analysed by Alexei Navalny's Anti-Corruption Foundation (FBK), the Ivanov family used to spend at least US$200,000 every year on their annual summer holiday in the south of France, where they kept a Rolls-Royce just for their vacations.[175]

On 23 April 2024 this life of luxury imploded. Ivanov was arrested in Moscow and the next day he appeared at Basmanny court, standing in full military uniform in a glass cage, listening to the charge: receiving a bribe on an 'especially large scale'.[176] Police also arrested Alexander Fomin, the head of Olimpsitistroy, the company involved in building the Nevsky apartment block in Mariupol.[177] The reconstruction in Mariupol was not mentioned in the charges against Ivanov, but one report claimed that VSK paid out 130 billion roubles (US$1.3 billion) more to contractors in 2022 than in the previous year, and most of this was likely spent in Mariupol. Olimpsitistroy reported a huge boost to its profits in 2023, increasing by 283% to 11 billion roubles.[178]

Despite all the corruption and profiteering and the exclusion and ill-treatment of so many local people, Russian officials viewed the reconstruction programme as a success. Although often portrayed in Western media coverage as a 'Potemkin village', the programme did achieve at least a partial reconstruction of central Mariupol. Khusnullin was an effective manager, who knew that his career depending on delivering some level of success in restoring Mariupol. By March 2024 officials claimed that almost all the apartment blocks in Mariupol, most of which had been badly damaged, had been restored. Public transport was running again. Schools were working. Visitors reported that restaurants, bars and shops were opening up again. People were coming back to the city, according to Russian officials. In March 2024 Khusnullin claimed that the population had risen to 270,000, from 170,000 a year earlier; now there were even traffic jams in the city centre.[179]

Ukrainian officials believed that any population increases were down to in-migration from Russia, part of a long-term plan to transform the demographics of the occupied territories. Ivan Fedorov, the governor of Zaporizhzhia region, claimed that Melitopol's population had increased by almost 100,000 because of migration from Russia.[180] It was impossible to establish accurately the extent of migration from Russia itself or to distinguish it from local people returning from Russia and elsewhere. There had been a big influx of construction workers. As many as 50,000 workers were deployed in the occupied territories, many of them from Central Asia, the North Caucasus or from among other ethnic minorities in Russia. The import of thousands of workers at times created tensions with some local residents, but these construction workers also became part of this traumatised community. Some of the workers told the media that they would like to stay, raising the prospect of demographic change in the region. Other Russians had arrived to work in the local administrations, in schools and hospitals, or in the security forces, while a few were on the lookout for cheap property investments.

Neighbouring military occupations—as discussed in the Introduction—are often accompanied by population in-transfers, in violation of international law.[181] Israel in the West Bank and Turkey in Northern Cyprus are both examples of attempts to settle occupied territory with loyal citizens both for security reasons and to effect long-term demographic change. Russia almost certainly had similar intentions, following the pattern in Crimea, where at least 200,000 Russian citizens were estimated to have settled since 2014.[182] Russian State Duma deputy Aleksei Zhuravlev drafted a law that would give an 'East Ukrainian hectare' to Russian soldiers, saying that 'Russia has increased by more than 100 million hectares and after our victory this land will have to be cultivated by somebody', overlooking the obvious point that millions of people already lived there and owned this land.[183] This was a typical colonial mental map that still saw 'Novorossiya' as 'the Wild Lands' needing to be colonised and conquered. In truth, Russia's own demographic crisis meant that it would struggle to find hundreds of thousands of potential settlers to move to a war zone. But the Russian intent was clear: the economic occupation was designed to make the annexation irreversible, through economic control, new infrastructure projects and ultimately demographic change.

OCCUPATION

Mariupol was Russia's showcase of occupation. It featured in all Russia's propaganda videos about the war. There was less attention paid to the other parts of the occupied territories, although there were smaller reconstruction projects under way in each of the regions. Sergei Kiriyenko and Vladimir Saldo talked up the prospects for a new town on the Arabat Spit, south of Henichesk in Kherson region.[184] However, any investment in Kherson region appeared even more vulnerable than in Mariupol—the loss of Kherson city in November 2022 had a major impact on the psyche of officials in the region. Only the bravest investors would build a new town within range of Ukrainian missiles. In April 2024 Denis Pushilin claimed that the DNR would also reconstruct Avdiivka, the town that Russian forces had destroyed almost completely in their conquest in the winter and spring of 2023–24. But almost everybody in Avdiivka was either dead or had fled long ago. Officials talked of rebuilding the city's schools, but the DNR education minister, Olga Koludarova, admitted that the Russian assault had reduced the city's population of schoolchildren to just two teenagers.[185] Russian television reports in October 2024 showcasing a reconstruction project in Avdiivka merely emphasised the almost complete destruction of the town; as long as Russia continued the war, it was not clear who might want to return to live in this urban wasteland.[186]

Transport

One of Russia's main strategic goals in the war was to create a land corridor to Crimea. If Russia could establish a reliable rail and road link to Crimea through the Donbas and along the northern coast of the Sea of Azov, its strategic position in Crimea would be hugely strengthened.

In early June 2022 Defence Minister Sergei Shoigu announced that Russia had restored road links across the mainland from Russia to Crimea, but these were often in poor repair and delays were common. Roads were wrecked by the heavy military traffic. The delays and security challenges all added to the costs. Truck deliveries to the four regions cost four times as much as to regions inside

Russia, pushing up consumer prices for residents.[187] But Russian companies soon began widening the main road from the Russian border to Mariupol and on towards Crimea. Videos showed a four-lane highway being built in 2024, part of a major road modernisation project that was designed to cope with a three-fold increase in traffic, including heavy truck traffic in and out of the occupied territories. A ring road around Mariupol was planned to be completed in 2026, part of the Russian plan for an R-280 Highway 'Novorossiya', running from Rostov-on-Don, through Mariupol to Melitopol and Simferopol in Crimea.[188]

Addressing the Moscow Urbanist Conference in August 2023, Marat Khusnullin told the audience about an ambitious plan to build a new road network dubbed the 'Azov Ring'. A network of new and upgraded roads would form a 1,400-kilometre-long road to link Rostov-on-Don and Taganrog in Russia to towns in the occupied territories—Mariupol, Melitopol and Henichesk. It would then travel down the east coast of Crimea, and back across the 19-kilometre Crimean Bridge into Russia. The new road network was expected to cost upwards of 400 billion roubles, leading some Ukrainian experts to suggest that this was just an empty announcement for Putin's pre-election campaign.[189] But Russian officials like Khusnullin were very effective at completing these strategically important mega-projects. The Crimean Bridge, completed in 2019, was a demonstration of how quickly Russia could implement high-profile projects when there was pressure from the Kremlin.

The other transport priority for Russia was to establish reliable rail links in the occupied territories. A Soviet-era railway had been designed to link the coalfields and industry of the Donbas to the ports on the Sea of Azov—Taganrog, Mariupol and Berdiansk. But the line to Mariupol had been severed after the 2014 war. An east-west line travelled around 80 kilometres inland, too close to the front line to be a safe resupply route for Russia. Now Russia set about building new lines and repairing old ones to create a viable rail land corridor that could transform its military supply chain. It also rebuilt the railway station in Mariupol, which was planned as a logistics hub for the whole region.

Signs of rail construction first appeared in 2022, but the Russian authorities were tight-lipped about their plans. In a meeting with Pushilin in April 2023, President Putin promised new transport links through the Donbas, including new roads and railways.[190] Then, on 29 May 2023, Prime Minister Mikhail Mishustin signed a decree creating a 'Railways of Novorossiya' state company, which would unite all the different railways of the four regions but keep them separate from the national carrier, Russian Railways, presumably to avoid further sanctions pressure.[191]

Russian companies began repairing the old line from Mariupol to Donetsk, via Volnovakha, but this route still strayed close to the front line. By October 2023 Ukrainian journalists were spotting new construction in satellite pictures. British Defence Intelligence posted that 'Russia … is constructing a new railway line to Mariupol which will reduce travel times for supplies to the Zaporizhzhia front', while making the coy suggestion that the railways were still 'within the notional range of Ukrainian long-range precision strike'.[192] This new line was a spur designed to link Mariupol to Taganrog and Rostov in Russia via a route that ran much further away from Ukrainian missile strikes. Another route was being built between Mariupol and Berdiansk, running alongside the M14 main road before linking up with the Mariupol–Donetsk route. The plan envisaged the eventual completion of a reliable rail route to Crimea at some distance from the front line.

The railway was a key strategic asset for Russia. In November 2023 Balitsky commented that 'by building a railway branch, at least one track … we will solve the problem of the military … and, most importantly, the issue of exporting grain to the continent, exporting iron ore, scrap metal, coal'. He argued that 'driving across the Crimean Bridge is not only far, but today the bridge is an object of increased danger'.[193] The vulnerability of the Crimean Bridge—it had been hit twice by Ukrainian attacks—made the land bridge strategically vital for Russia. There was even talk of a tunnel being built by Russian and Chinese companies to link Russia and Crimea, although that plan seemed far-fetched.[194] More likely, Russia would continue to invest in the key routes across Donbas and the occupied territories. The strategic importance of the transport corridor was one more reason why Russia would be reluctant to give up this territory in any negotiations.

Meanwhile, for most people the only viable public transport was by bus, taxi or minivan. There were a couple of rail passenger services linking Luhansk and Donetsk regions, but no passenger train across the border to Russia. Long-distance bus services linked the occupied territories to Crimea and to Russia. Operators advertised passenger services from Mariupol to Warsaw and beyond, including to Kyiv. These trips involved a long and arduous journey through Russia and tickets cost up to US$500, prohibitive for many locals. Occasionally the authorities clamped down on these routes. On 1 December 2023 Ukrainian SBU officers claimed to have arrested businesspeople running a bus service between Kyiv and the occupied territories via Russia. They told the press that it was a way for collaborators to escape from justice, but interfering with these routes appeared to be counterproductive, blocking a way for Ukrainians to maintain contact with their families and relatives in the occupied territories.[195]

Travelling to Ukraine directly from Russia was extremely difficult, but one border crossing remained open in Sumy region, until it too was forced to close in August 2024. In December 2023 a traveller from Mariupol paid US$250 for a minivan ride for herself and her two cats to reach the Ukrainian border. She had to walk the last 2 kilometres across an uneasy no man's land.[196] It was even more difficult to travel from Ukraine to the occupied territories. The only viable route in 2024 was via Sheremetyevo airport in Moscow. As discussed in Chapter 4, that route involved an exhausting interrogation with a risk of deportation. As the war continued, the lack of transport links or economic ties across the front line drove a sharp wedge between the two societies, between those living under Russian occupation and those who had left. Russia's transport and infrastructure plans were aligned with the geopolitics of occupation, reinforcing the divide between Russian- and Ukrainian-controlled territory by creating transport networks that consolidated ties with Russia and with Crimea.

Russia also invested heavily in reviving the ports on the Sea of Azov. Mariupol port began working again in late 2022, after being damaged in the fighting. In March 2023 the Russian Ministry of Transport reported that it had included the Ukrainian ports of Mariupol and Berdiansk in the Russian register of national ports.[197] A new shipping route was developing between Mariupol, Azov and Rostov across the Sea of Azov. As discussed above, grain was being exported from Mariupol (twenty-four grain ships left Mariupol port in the first seven months of 2023).[198] A Russian television report showed a local official explaining that the port was also being used for transporting construction materials into the city as well as for the grain trade.[199] A large part of the trade was being managed by RosKapStroi, which set up a logistics centre at the port and took over most of its operations.[200] It even began running its own cargo shipping line, comprising foreign ships that had been expropriated during the war. A Ukrainian report dubbed this a 'Pirate Fleet', which illegally transported grain, kaolin clay, coal and scrap metal out of the occupied territories. The ships then returned to Mariupol port with thousands of tonnes of construction materials for the reconstruction programme.[201]

Conclusion: The economics of occupation

The whole occupation project was run through opaque and murky patronage systems, in which kickbacks, side-payments and off-the-books deals were the norm. Patrons at the top of the system needed results, and they achieved them by distributing benefits to companies and individuals down the chain. This system—characterised by corruption and a lack of rule of law—is what Vladimir Gelman, a scholar of Russian politics, describes as 'bad governance'. For Gelman, bad governance is 'a distinctive politico-economic order that is based on a set of formal and informal rules, norms, and practices quite different from those of good governance'.[202] Although bad governance is not the best way to ensure prosperity or to spread wealth, it still enables states to get things done. Moreover, as Gelman argues, 'bad governance' can be a useful mechanism to 'reduce the risk of breakdown of hierarchical power pyramids'.[203] Corrupt payments up and down the pyramid are what prevent Russia's political system from collapsing.

Bad governance turns out to be a highly effective system for running an occupation regime. It gives the occupation regime a near-monopoly of economic power, unconstrained by law or markets. The regime can distribute assets and funding to co-opt key local players or to incentivise involvement by major Russian corporations. The system allowed powerful patronage networks around the Ministry of Construction and Ministry of Defence to manage much of the reconstruction, a system that both incentivised officials and business to work in the occupied territories and also gave officials leverage to get things done quickly. Russia also used its dominance of the economic system to structure incentives and punishments for local elites and local society. Its monopoly of banking and welfare systems forced almost every resident to adopt a Russian passport, while the threat of expropriation persuaded local businesses either to align with Russian strategies or to abandon their enterprises and leave the occupied territories. In short, this highly corrupt and highly exploitative form of political economy played a vital role in the Russian occupation.

The system also encouraged accommodation by at least some part of local society. In Bohdan Logvinenko's account of the liberation of Russian-occupied territories, Vitaly Ovcharenko, an activist from Lyman in Donetsk region, tried to convey the mentality of his former classmates in the Donbas: 'they say "we don't really like Ukraine, but we understand that it has prospects. We live quietly, have a small business, everything suits us. But if the Russians come, they will steal everything. We don't want that".'[204] This combination of political scepticism and economic pragmatism was typical of many people in eastern and southern Ukraine. It partly explains Russia's failure to engender more support from people in the region, despite their instinctive suspicion of aspects of Ukraine's nation-building project. Whatever their views on the politics of history or language or wider geopolitics, for many ordinary people Ukraine was a much freer environment in which to live and run a business or to bring up children. Ukraine had many governance problems, but at least there was no heavy-handed Russian state that could steal your business or leave you lingering in prison. Its European orientation offered a viable future for a younger generation.

OCCUPATION

However, this economic pragmatism also encouraged part of the population to adapt to the occupation in order to survive. Some people were even better off under Russian rule. Salaries and welfare payments boosted incomes for at least part of the population, ensuring that the Russian occupation authorities co-opted a minority of locals. In business, some of those who stayed also managed to adapt, making the most of the money flooding in from Moscow, alongside a class of local pro-Russian officials on the make. This economy of occupation was often corrupt and chaotic, and failed to address the social or economic needs of large parts of society. But the ability of Russia to co-opt local elites and to project a sense of permanence made the economy a powerful pillar of the occupation regime.

7

LIBERATION

When Viktoria Dovhoborodova, a lecturer at Kherson medical college, heard that Ukrainian troops had arrived in Kherson city in November 2022, she did not believe it at first. She went to the city's Freedom Square to see for herself. A Ukrainian flag was on the pedestal and people were singing Ukrainian songs. 'I'm not a sentimental person, but I burst into tears', she told a Ukrainian writer.[1] Kherson residents who had been forced into exile also found it hard to take in the news. Iryna Panchenko, a maritime law lecturer who had escaped from Kherson in July, heard the news in Kyiv, but initially she could also hardly believe it.[2] Another local resident, who had remained in Kherson, had a similar reaction: 'For four or five days, everyone just walked around in a state of ecstasy.'[3]

Jubilation was widespread as Ukraine's counteroffensive pushed back Russian troops in 2022. But initial euphoria soon turned to a sober assessment of the problems that occupation left in its wake. For many, it was difficult simply to deal with the immediate aftereffects. When Vitaly Ovcharenko arrived in Lyman after it was liberated, he felt as though his parents' house had been violated: 'The blankets in your own room smell of strangers. Other people's things are lying about everywhere, and half of our property had been looted.'[4] Everywhere was filth, looting and destruction. The police station in Lyman had been turned into 'a warehouse of plunder', clogged from top to bottom with stolen goods and junk.⁵ The clean-up everywhere was endless, truckload after truckload of garbage had to be taken away after eight months of Russian occupation. That was before any rebuilding could begin.

In most liberated areas to the north and north-east of Kyiv, residents could return and begin rebuilding in relative safety. In the two years after the Russian withdrawal from Bucha, Irpin and other towns near Kyiv, there was a remarkably successful effort to begin to reconstruct homes and the infrastructure around them, even if the psychological scars and memories ran deep. In the south and east, the situation was much more precarious. Even after Russia withdrew from Kherson, Russian artillery continued to fire across the Dnipro River. On some days artillery would open up without warning every fifteen minutes. In the year after Ukrainian troops liberated the city, Russian fire killed 397 people and injured more than 2,000, according to the local authorities.⁶ The pre-war population of 280,000 had shrunk to under 70,000 by May 2024.⁷ It was too dangerous for most people to return except for short visits, to visit relatives, to repair a house. Those who stayed in the city played a deadly game of Russian roulette. So inured were most people to the bombings that they hardly flinched when new rounds of artillery crashed around them.⁸

Much of the land liberated by Ukrainian troops was littered with mines and unexploded ordinance. Ukrainian officials predicted that clearing agricultural land of mines could take a decade. The World Bank estimated that demining and clearing explosives would cost US$ 34.6 billion over the period to 2033, but Ukraine had insufficient funds and too few certified demining companies for such an extensive programme.⁹ Without access to demined agricultural land, southern towns would struggle economically. Moreover, much of the agricultural land on which Kherson's economy depended was on the east bank of the Dnipro, occupied by Russian troops. Kherson had always been famous for its watermelons and other fruits, but when journalists visited the city in May 2023, there were no fresh fruit or vegetables, and no cafes or ordinary shops working—just a few grocery stores with the bare necessities.[10] Volunteer groups worked miracles on the ground, fixing people's houses, providing meals for the elderly and evacuating those who could not take the constant firing any more.[12] But only 5% of Kherson's businesses had returned by mid-2024.[12] Meanwhile, as the Russians left, prosecutors and war crimes investigators arrived. By November 2023, a team of prosecutors in Kherson had documented 19,000 potential war crimes since the outbreak of the war.[13] But documenting and prosecuting these cases was a huge burden on an under-resourced and weak criminal justice system.

Ukraine's successful counteroffensives in 2022 regained control of some 19,000 square kilometres of territory. The liberation of Kherson city and large parts of Kharkiv region in September–November 2022 raised hopes that the occupation of other parts of Kherson and Zaporizhzhia regions would also be short-lived. But gradually the momentum faded. In 2023 the Ukrainian counteroffensive failed to make headway. Many of those living under occupation lost hope of early liberation and either escaped to government-controlled Ukraine or adapted to the new realities under Russian rule. Those in exile—in other parts of Ukraine, in Russia or in Europe—began to put down roots in their new homes.

Living as displaced people was not easy. Internally displaced people (IDPs) did receive some government help, but monthly payments of 2,000 hryvnia (US$50) for an adult and 3,000 hryvnia (US$74) for children were hardly sufficient to survive on for long. Some IDPs felt unwelcomed in other parts of Ukraine, where not everybody understood the trauma of living on the front line or under occupation.[14] Some began to drift back to their home towns. People returned to the dangers of living in Kherson because they could not cope with life in exile. There were reports of small numbers of people returning to the occupied territories because they had struggled to find jobs and housing in government-controlled Ukraine.[15]

Meanwhile, the spatial scar of the front line divided Ukraine into government-controlled and Russian-occupied territory. Fighting remained intense, but significant territorial changes were rare. Opinion polls confirmed that the majority of Ukrainians opposed any territorial concessions to end the war. In mid-2024 only 22%

supported a suspension of hostilities and a freezing of the conflict at the current front line. By contrast, 96% supported an outcome in which Russia withdrew all its troops from Ukrainian territory. In 2024 there was some evidence that public opinion was shifting, as the enormity of the challenge of regaining control of the occupied territories became clearer. Among young people aged 18–25, only 40% believed that Ukraine should continue fighting until it liberated its entire 1991 borders.[16] In Kyiv, in private conversations, there was more talk of a Korea-style solution, in which a semi-permanent armistice would end the fighting, but not resolve the wider conflict. Many Ukrainians were exhausted, and wanted to try to salvage what was possible from the war and get on with their lives. But officially Ukraine continued to promote a strategy that envisaged a complete end to the occupation by military means. On 24 February 2024 President Zelensky said: 'We can end this war on our Ukrainian terms. We can return our land and people from the occupation. We can bring Russia to justice for what it has done. But for this to happen, we must fight.'[17] However, as the situation at the front worsened during 2024, this reliance on military force to liberate the occupied territories looked increasingly unrealistic.

Deoccupation strategies

Ukraine's liberation of occupied territory in 2022 was achieved by military force. Its strategy for regaining control over the rest of the occupied territories also relied primarily on regaining control of territory through a military offensive, although many officials also admitted that a final end to the war could only come through negotiations and a peace treaty.[18] On one level, this reliance on military force made sense. Russia showed no sign that it would withdraw from the occupied territories unless Ukraine had the military advantage. On the other hand, the emphasis on military victory at times made Ukrainian diplomacy one-dimensional and constrained Kyiv's ability to use a wider range of diplomatic, economic, political and other tools to counter the occupation.

The continued rhetorical commitment to military victory also risked distracting from the challenging political work that deoccupation would also entail. In territories where Russia had been in control for a long time, a military victory would only be the start. In Crimea, where more than 60% of the population were ethnic Russians and most residents were Russian speakers even before the annexation, any attempt to reintegrate the peninsula into the Ukrainian state would face enormous social, political and security challenges. Apart from the politics, even the legal work of undoing ten years of property transactions or confirming marriages, births and deaths would be difficult: only one in ten children born in Crimea after 2014 had a Ukrainian birth certificate.[19] The longer the Russian occupation continued, the harder it would be to unravel, not least because it involved addressing issues that were often too politically sensitive for Ukrainian politicians to consider in public. As a result, the various strategies that Ukraine promoted under the headings of 'deoccupation' or 'reintegration' were often criticised for being out of touch with reality. A coalition of civil society groups claimed in 2023 that a 'national overall vision for reintegrating these territories into the legal, educational, cultural, and information spaces of Ukraine does not exist'.[20]

The problem was two-fold. First, there was a lack of consensus among Ukrainian officials on how people should behave under occupation. In August 2022 the Ministry for Reintegration published 'Seven rules for life in the Temporarily Occupied Territories', which ordered people not to cooperate with the enemy, not to take a Russian passport, and to evacuate at the first opportunity.[21] This might have been realistic if Ukraine had been in a position to retake the territories quickly. However, as the occupation lingered from months into years, it was no longer viable for people living under occupation to avoid applying for a Russian passport or engaging in activities that might be interpreted as cooperation. And if everybody had evacuated, it would surely have served Russia's unspoken goal of expelling the pro-Ukrainian population out of the territories. Dmytro Lubinets, the Ukrainian ombudsmen, contradicted the ministry, saying that he 'would advise Ukrainians in the temporarily occupied territories to take a Russian passport. We understand that now it is a matter of survival. […] Therefore, take a passport, survive and wait for us to liberate the territory.' He added that taking a Russian passport under duress would not be considered a crime by the Ukrainian state.[22] But Iryna Vereshchuk, deputy prime minister and minister for reintegration of the temporarily occupied territories, maintained her ministry's recommendations 'not to take Russian passports, not to cooperate with the occupiers, to leave if possible and wait for the Armed Forces'.[23] This left Ukrainians living under occupation with a lack of clarity—but few had a choice. If they wanted to survive, they were forced to take a Russian passport and work within Russia's rules and laws.

Second, there was no clear political strategy for long-term reintegration. Even after 2014, Kyiv had struggled to find a workable policy that would maintain links to its citizens under occupation, while not normalising Russia's annexation of Crimea or its de facto control of the DNR and the LNR. An economic blockade imposed by Kyiv on the DNR and LNR in 2017 was counterproductive, making the breakaway republics fully dependent on Russia and severing ties with the rest of Ukraine. The Ukrainian government's refusal to pay pensions to residents of the DNR and LNR unless they travelled to government-controlled territory deepened the divide across the front line and made the prospects for reintegration even more distant.[24] Limiting economic ties with Crimea in the same period also appears to have helped Russia to consolidate its control.

In 2021 Ukraine set up an international 'Crimea Platform', which sought to remind the world of the serious human rights abuses under Russian rule and to highlight Russia's violations of international law. According to Amnesty International, during the decade of occupation after 2014, Russia had 'suppressed Ukrainian and Crimean Tatar identities through restrictions on education, religion, media, representative institutions, judicial system, and cultural celebrations'.[25] As part of this refocus on Crimea, in 2021, President Zelensky launched a Strategy for De-occupation and Reintegration of the Temporarily Occupied Territory of the Autonomous Republic of Crimea (Qirim) and the City of Sevastopol (Aqyar). These strategies focused on building diplomatic pressure on Russia, but were often pitched at an abstract level, with the emphasis on marshalling international condemnation rather than developing a political campaign to win over hearts and minds among Russian speakers inside Crimea.

As the Ukrainians shifted to counterinsurgencies during the second half of 2022 and 2023, officials in Kyiv started thinking about what to do if they made a military breakthrough and were able to regain control of Crimea or Donbas. An updated reintegration strategy was issued in 2023 by the office of the Permanent Representative of the President of Ukraine in the Autonomous Republic of Crimea headed by Tamila Tasheva, a strong advocate for Crimean Tatar rights. The new version envisaged the establishment of military administrations in Crimea and new measures to tackle the complex bureaucratic aftermath of occupation, but it still lacked detail on key political, legal and cultural issues.[26] There was no similar strategy for the other occupied territories, although activists advocated the development of a single strategy for all the occupied territories, not just Crimea.[27]

One Ukrainian official proposed a list of more concrete ideas, including dismantling the Crimean Bridge, renaming the home of the Black Sea Fleet, Sevastopol, as 'Object No. 6', nullifying property transactions made under Russian rule, and introducing forms of lustration that could see many people lose the right to vote.[28] Ukraine also proposed new measures to correct the historical repression and expulsion of Crimean Tatars from Crimea, including education in Crimean Tatar and measures to provide cultural autonomy for Tatar communities, and other communities considered to be 'indigenous peoples'. This was an important breakthrough after centuries of marginalisation of Crimean Tatars. However, there were no such proposals to provide autonomy for Russian culture or language, despite ethnic Russians making up at least 60% of the population and most residents being Russian speakers. Instead, in November 2023, the Mission of the President of Ukraine in the Autonomous Republic of Crimea published a new strategy for 'cognitive deoccupation' of Crimea, which proposed 'a gradually progressive Ukrainianization of the public sphere in Crimea'.[29] This initiative had a legitimate aim: to counter the indoctrination and militarisation of youth experienced in Russian schools and media. But it went much further, aiming to change 'the beliefs, emotions and other humanitarian and social characteristics of the population that were formed before the Russian occupation', a much more troubling concept that sounded like a mass re-education programme of Russians in Crimea.[30] These strategies were politically unrealistic and sharply at odds with Ukraine's wider goal of becoming a European liberal democracy.

Ukraine's official reintegration strategies underestimated the challenge of regaining political control over territories that had been under Russian control for a decade, and where there was strong attachment to the Russian language and culture, reinforced by years of Russian indoctrination and propaganda. The reintegration of Crimea and the territories held by the DNR and LNR prior to 2022 into Ukraine would open up a huge set of legal, humanitarian and political challenges. As Russia consolidated control in the newly occupied territories, the same challenges would develop over time in occupied Kherson and Zaporizhzhia. In private conversations in Kyiv, sober-minded analysts admitted that Ukrainian forces would not be welcomed in parts of Donbas or in Crimea, and argued that rapid reintegration of these territories back into the Ukrainian polity could destabilise Ukrainian politics if it happened too quickly. However, understandably, a large part of the Ukrainian public was in no mood for compromise after two years of full-scale war against Russia.

Divisions

Russian defence minister Sergei Shoigu announced the 'liberation' of the town of Sviatohirsk on 7 June 2022.[31] After more than three months of fighting, Ukrainian troops regained control of the city on 12 September. The Ukrainian military posted that 'units of the National Guard, the Armed Forces of Ukraine and the Territorial Defense entered the town of Sviatohirsk. Step by step, meter by meter, we are liberating our land from the occupier'.[32] Many local people welcomed the return of Ukrainian troops. But not all. Pro-Russian sentiments were common here. The mayor of Sviatohirsk, Volodymyr Bandura, had switched sides to align with the Russians.

LIBERATION

This was the home of a famous Orthodox monastery, or *lavra*, still loyal to the Moscow Patriarchate, and viewed as one of the Russian Orthodox Church's five holiest sites. A monk told the *New York Times* that 'Western Ukraine is thinking in its own way, and Donbas is thinking in a different way', and compared those from western Ukraine to 'occupiers'. Other pro-Russian residents had the same sentiment, seeing the victory of Ukrainian forces not as a liberation but as an 'occupation'.[33]

As people returned to Sviatohirsk, it became clear that many had quite different experiences and memories of occupation. One resident told journalists that 'things weren't too bad. It was summer. The Russians were distributing humanitarian aid. The only problem was that they were drunk too often.' But others had a different view. 'I don't understand those who stayed when the Russians arrived', said one local official, who had left.[34] The different experiences of those who stayed and those who left occupied areas would emerge as a major cleavage in post-occupation society. Resentments ran deep. Some pro-Ukrainian residents claimed that their neighbours had informed on them to the Russians. Others reported that their businesses and houses had been looted, even by neighbours and people that they had considered to be friends.[35]

Both sides blamed the other for the shelling between the two armies across the Siverskyi Donets river that had damaged the Sviatohirsk monastery and killed forty people, including several monks.[36] Reports at the time appeared to indicate that it was mainly reckless Russian bombardments that hit the monastery, but many monks seem not to have believed this version.[37] The Ukrainian authorities viewed the Lavra with suspicion. According to reports in the media, the head of the Sviatohirsk Lavra, Metropolitan Arsenii, had his Ukrainian citizenship revoked in January 2023.[38] He was then arrested in April 2024 on charges of 'covertly leaking' the position of Ukrainian checkpoints to the enemy, accusations that seemed far-fetched, based on the public evidence cited by the SBU.[39]

During the war, political differences came to the surface in the starkest possible way in places such as Sviatohirsk. Across the occupied territories, only a small minority became open supporters of the Russian occupation regime. Others initially tried to maintain a principled position that avoided adopting Russian citizenship and kept their children out of Russian schools. But as time wore on and the prospect of liberation became more distant, this position became harder to maintain. Most people did their best to avoid outright collaboration but went along with new Russian regulations and strictures when they had little choice—opening bank accounts, taking up Russian passports and working wherever possible to earn a wage. For those who maintained a principled position, it was galling to see neighbours openly collaborating with the Russians. Those who left the occupied territories and saw their property or businesses being taken over by those loyal to the occupiers, were also understandably unforgiving towards those labelled as collaborators. This made the return of internally displaced people and refugees potentially highly traumatic and contested. Similar challenges had been experienced in the aftermath of the war in Bosnia-Herzegovina and in many other conflicts.[40]

The arrest of Metropolitan Arsenii in Sviatohirsk was a reminder that the SBU and Ukrainian prosecutors were actively searching for alleged collaborators and war criminals whenever the Ukrainian military regained control of territory. The SBU had a dubious reputation among human rights activists. It had been accused of maintaining a network of unofficial prisons in 2015 and in the first months of the 2022 war.[41] But few in Ukraine questioned its legitimacy during wartime. Its counter-intelligence operation after Russia's invasion in February 2022 was remarkably effective. Russia struggled to achieve any major sabotage operations behind Ukrainian lines, despite a network of sympathisers. In late 2022, as Russian forces retreated from Kherson and Kharkiv regions, the SBU and the Ukrainian police were active in identifying and prosecuting people who were accused of collaboration. In this they were often helped by local activists and journalists, who worked to identify those who had collaborated with Russian forces.

Deep-seated social and political divisions went wider than active collaboration with the Russians. In a city such as Kherson, many locals reported that the number of their friends and acquaintances who had actively collaborated with the Russians was relatively small.[42] Nevertheless, when Russian troops withdrew from the city in November 2022, thousands of people left the city and other parts of Kherson region for other Russian-controlled territories or Russia itself.[43] Some probably left involuntarily or because of a fear of being caught in the crossfire. But many had worked in the Russian administration or in Russian-led schools or hospitals or had cooperated with the Russians in other ways. Journalists from the *Washington Post* came across mounds of documents in an office in Kherson that were full of long lists of residents who had applied for passports, asked for work or requested to send their children to a summer camp in Crimea.[44] In the most serious cases, documents seized from the occupation authorities would later serve as the basis for prosecutions under Ukraine's collaboration laws.

Collaboration

It is hard to think of a more emotive word in modern European history than 'collaboration'. It conjures up images of Vichy France and its collaborator-in-chief, Philippe Pétain, or Vidkun Quisling, the Norwegian wartime leader who lent his name to the role he so enthusiastically embraced. It is a history clouded in silence, quiet violence and murky and morally dubious compromises, a history that many European states even now have never been able fully to address. Ukraine itself is part of this history. The collaboration of many members of the Ukrainian nationalist movement with the Nazis remains an episode in Ukraine's history that continues to cause divisions in society.

Not surprising, then, that collaboration with the invading Russians in 2022 would produce a legal and moral dilemma, a topic in Ukrainian society that threatened to create even deeper divisions as the war dragged on. The problem was not new. Between 2014 and 2022, Ukrainian citizens had worked with the Russian occupying powers in Crimea and engaged in different forms of cooperation with the de facto authorities in the DNR and the LNR. Millions of Ukrainians lived under Russian rule, directly or indirectly, and had cooperated with the occupation regime. For many years, the Ukrainian parliament had discussed criminalising collaboration but had struggled to come up with a working definition of such a slippery concept.

On 3 March 2022, with Russian troops on the outskirts of Kyiv, the Verkhovna Rada finally decided that the situation was too urgent to delay any longer. A new law on collaboration was adopted without discussion. The situation was critical, as parliamentary deputy Andrii Osadchuk later recalled: 'the occupiers were not only in the suburbs of Kyiv but on the territory of eight oblasts. There were people who were helping them, and there was no distinct, clearly written punishment for them.'[45]

The law added new articles to the Ukrainian Criminal Code on 'Collaboration activity' (Article 111–1) and 'aiding and abetting the aggressor state' (Article 111–2).[46] Lawyers were quick to identify problems with the wording of the law. According to the UN, 'the vagueness and overly broad terminology in the legal provisions raise concerns with respect to the principle of legality and have led to arbitrary detention in a number of cases'.[47] Instead of defining 'collaboration', the law simply set out a series of activities that were considered criminal offences, including conducting 'propaganda in education establishments or occupying posts in the occupation administration', or any 'economic activities in cooperation with the aggressor state'. It also outlawed providing material support for the occupation force.[48] These provisions criminalised a very broad range of activities. For example, as discussed in Chapter 6, anybody who wanted to conduct business under occupation had little choice but to pay taxes to the Russian authorities, but this potentially constituted grounds for prosecution under the law.

Moreover, some activities that were now criminalised might be either permitted or required under international humanitarian law. A legal analysis concluded that Article 111–1 might criminalise 'perfectly legitimate activities', including humanitarian aid, medical services or running a grocery store. The government drafted a new law to deal with some of these questions, but it lingered in a parliamentary committee. Ukrainian civil society and legal experts produced their own analysis, which concluded that 'the residents of the occupied territory [...] are at risk of being held criminally liable for acts that are not socially dangerous but may fall under the provisions of Art. 111–1'.⁴⁹ Under this new law, as of August 2023, more than 6,000 cases had been opened in Ukraine involving alleged collaboration.⁵⁰

Vague drafting allowed a range of different approaches to be taken by prosecutors. The same activities could be defined under different articles of the Criminal Code with different sentencing. One person who took a post as manager of the Kherson branch of Russia's Promsvyazbank was charged under Article 111–2 ('aiding and abetting the successor state'), with a potential sentence of ten to twelve years in prison and lustration for ten to fifteen years. But another banker, appointed head of a branch of the 'State Bank of the LNR', was charged under Part 5 of Article 111–1 ('collaboration activity'), which meant a lesser punishment of five to ten years in prison. Meanwhile, a woman from Mariupol who shouted pro-Russian slogans was sentenced to five years in prison, with all her property confiscated. In other cases such crimes received much more lenient sentences.⁵¹

Many cases were decided through plea bargains, giving the impression of a conveyor of cases, ticking statistical boxes for prosecutors and policemen. Lviv judge Kateryna Kotelva criticised this practice, pointing out that properly argued court cases could play an important role in beginning a public dialogue around collaboration, helping society understand what had happened and ensuring that the public believed that justice had been done.⁵² Others argued for motive to be taken into account, distinguishing between those who willingly cooperated with the Russians for material or ideological reasons and those who were forced to operate in accordance with Russian laws in order to run enterprises for the good of the community, such as food shops or local utility companies.⁵³ This distinction was an important one. Under certain interpretations of international law, the local population was obliged to cooperate with the occupying power to ensure the provision of food, medical assistance, heating and utilities. A UN assessment concluded that 'The law on collaboration activities adopted on 3 March 2022, which introduced criminal liability for collaborating with an "aggressor State", criminalizes a wide range of conduct, potentially including conduct which can be lawfully compelled by the occupying power under IHL [International Humanitarian Law].'⁵⁴

OCCUPATION

A special investigation by the website Graty reported on collaboration cases that the Ukrainian authorities initiated after Russian forces were forced to withdraw from Lyman, a town in the north of Donetsk region. Russian forces took control of Lyman on 27 May 2022 but retreated from the town on 1 October. When the Russians withdrew, Ukrainian security services sought out alleged collaborators. Many had left with the Russians, but among those investigated by the SBU were Valentyna Tkach and Tetiana Potapenko, who had remained in their homes throughout the occupation.

The two women held voluntary posts in Lyman before the war as street wardens. Tkach was also deputy head of her local district, called 'Northern'. Potapenko had the same role—deputy head of the Komunalny district. These were not government positions, but unpaid posts. As the Russians approached, many officials fled, including the heads of the local districts. Tkach remained behind, living on her street with mainly elderly residents who could not afford to leave or did not want to abandon their smallholdings. She cooked and distributed food in between artillery attacks. She buried three of her neighbours who died in the fighting. 'We thought it was the end of the world', she later told reporters.[55]

After the Russians took over, the women continued to deal with urgent humanitarian problems. The main counterpart for them was not the mayor's office, but an ad hoc organisation, the Social Movement 'Donetsk Republic' of Denis Pushilin, which had set up a 'help centre' headed by a Viktoria Zinchuk. Zinchuk had apparently once been a Ukrainian patriot, who ran a local cultural centre and was often seen wearing the Ukrainian national dress, the embroidered shirt known as *vyshyvanka*, and singing Ukrainian folk songs on national holidays. For reasons that remain unclear, by July 2022 she had begun to work for the DNR and even received an award.[56]

Zinchuk asked the two women to take over as heads of their districts. They spent most of their time delivering humanitarian aid to their communities, getting pensions for old people from the Russians and trying to sort out everyday problems. When the Russians were pushed out and Ukrainian forces retook the town in October 2022, the two women continued their work, only now they were delivering Ukrainian aid to the same elderly residents. The SBU questioned them soon after Ukrainian forces seized control of the town, but then released them. But in November, Tkach was taken to Dnipro and arrested. Potapenko followed in January 2023, charged with collaboration under Article 111–5, which prohibited 'occupying leading positions in the occupation administration'.

When Tkach was arrested, the SBU issued a press release accusing her of turning in members of the resistance and helping the occupiers organise a fake referendum. None of these serious allegations emerged on the eventual charge sheet, however, which confined the charges to holding 'a leading position' in the occupation administration. Neither woman could understand why they had been arrested. Tkach told journalists that 'they made me out to be an enemy of the people … But I gave my soul to the people.' Potapenko was equally unbelieving, telling reporters: 'I do not think I did anything wrong. I can't understand why they arrested me. […] What did I do wrong for the country of Ukraine?'[57]

At the court hearing on 15 August 2023, Tetiana Potapenko was sentenced to five years in prison. In a concession, the state did not confiscate her small brick house with its makeshift corrugated-sheet fence, which would have left her elderly husband and son homeless. Potapenko could not understand the prison sentence. She later told reporters: 'According to that logic you can take everybody after the occupation and arrest them. Including a grandmother who received their [Russian] pension, and those who got the one-off [Russian] welfare payments.'[58]

These and similar cases raised hard questions about how people should act under occupation. The unclear legal framework left almost anybody who had worked in some way with the occupation administration potentially liable to arrest and prosecution. During Russia's occupation of Lyman, Dmytro Herasymenko stayed in the city to look after his elderly relatives, and he ran the local electricity company. He was arrested in December 2022 after Ukrainian troops had liberated the town. The SBU claimed that he had cut energy to the city and supplied it instead to the Russian base.[59] However, any cases that involved providing essential utilities were difficult, because under international law, the occupying power is required to maintain energy supplies, and to do so inevitably necessitates local people continuing to work in utility companies.

When the case went to trial, Herasymenko claimed that he had little choice: 'We were all left without any money, without work, with nothing. I had to work, at least to earn some money for food, for medicine for my father and so on … We had to survive, that's why I went [to work].'[60] His father told reporters that he believed the accusations were unjust, and complained that '[j]ust as in the Soviet Union they stuck labels on people, so they are doing the same now'.[61] In any case, there were others more worthy of punishment, he claimed: 'I look around and see somebody who informed on people, someone who held a [pro-Russian meeting], somebody who did propaganda.' His points seem to have ultimately had an impact on the court. Herasymenko was initially sentenced to three years in prison at a court in Dnipro, but he was later released on appeal.[62]

Working in local utilities companies was one of the most common types of collaboration that the Ukrainian authorities prosecuted. Another alleged collaborator in Lyman ran the local gas company and was charged under Part 4 of Article 111–1, which outlawed 'implementation of economic activities in cooperation with the aggressor state'.[63] The main accusation in each of these cases was not only that these workers had cooperated with the Russians, but that they had prioritised providing heat or power to Russian military facilities.[64] Another elderly man, Petr Muravlev, was sent to prison for restarting a railway repair shop. Muravlev was initially given a prison sentence, but it was reduced to a conditional sentence on appeal. The judiciary—at least in these cases—often had a more lenient approach than the prosecution. Initial severe sentences were often reversed or reduced on appeal. In other cases, charges of economic cooperation with the occupation authorities tended to attract a non-custodial sentence.[65]

Another difficult case involved the prosaic activity of rubbish collection. In March 2023 a court ordered the detention of Olena and Dmytro Dubrovsky, whose company, Khersonavtokomunservis, had been collecting the rubbish in the city of Kherson for the past twenty years. They were also charged with 'economic activities in cooperation with the aggressor state', after their company opened Russian bank accounts, took payments in roubles and was re-registered in the Russian tax system—all requirements of the Russian occupation authorities to allow a business to continue operating. The court ordered the confiscation of their refuse trucks, forcing the city to collect the rubbish using tractors while the trucks sat idle.[66]

After the liberation of Kherson, numerous collaboration cases came to light. The motivations for collaboration were often difficult to discern. In the Kherson Maritime College, most staff did not cooperate with the Russians and the college evacuated to Odesa. However, according to media reports, fifty-one out of 178 staff stayed in Kherson, and their rouble salaries tripled.[67] Maryna Ivanovka, head of the college, refused to work with the Russians and was replaced not by a pro-Russian ideologue, but by a teacher of Ukrainian history and 'patriotic education'. When the Russians left Kherson, the Russian-appointed head left with them.[68] More than ideology, money and promotion prospects seem to have been powerful drivers of collaboration in these cases.

By July 2023 the prosecutor's office in Kherson had opened 1,088 cases involving charges of collaboration and another 234 cases with charges of assisting the aggressor state.[69] A local Telegram channel, the 'Database of Traitors', also listed numerous alleged collaborators, many of them teachers and local officials involved in organising elections, and local people who had voted in Russian elections or promoted pro-Russian propaganda on social networks. The channel administrator claimed to have around 2,000 names in the database.[70] There were other similar initiatives. The Media Detector group began a project in August 2023 to highlight 'collaborators' in the media, to write what they called 'a history of those who were broken or seduced, and those who did not agree to cooperate with the enemy'.[71]

By August 2023 fifty court cases had been completed in cases of collaboration in Kherson. Most of those prosecuted had occupied low-level positions in the local authorities or had issued some statements interpreted as pro-Russian. Usually, they ended with relatively lenient sentences, such as a form of lustration, including a ban on occupying public positions for a number of years. However, pensioners who had carried voting urns around a village as part of the Russian referendum campaign in September 2022 often ended up being given five-year prison sentences. Joining the Russian police earned an eight-year sentence.[72] Taking up any kind of decision-making position in the local administrations—the positions regularly labelled by Ukrainians as 'Gauleiter', using the word for an official in Nazi occupation regimes—earned long sentences. Yury Petukhov, who ran the occupation administration in the village of Novovoskresenske, was sentenced to twelve years in prison. According to the court, he organised propaganda meetings, helped the Russians to track down pro-Ukrainian activists and supported the introduction of the Russian educational system in schools.[73]

Few Ukrainians disagreed with long sentences for those who willingly filled posts at the top of the occupation administration. But not all cases were so clear-cut. The role of teachers was controversial. Many teachers refused to work in schools, as discussed in Chapter 5, but those who did faced serious repercussions, although in most cases the maximum sentence of three years in prison was not imposed. A teacher in Kherson who introduced the Russian curriculum was sentenced to three months in prison and a ten-year teaching ban.[74] In August 2023 the mayor of Mariupol, Vadym Boychenko, promised that none of the teachers working in Mariupol's schools would be employed after it was liberated: 'After deoccupation, only those teachers who chose the Ukrainian future will remain in schools. And we will make every effort to return such teachers to the city. Those who have pro-Russian views will be deprived of the opportunity to work in Mariupol schools.'[75]

In some cases, collaboration was accidental—or the result of an impossible choice. In Chapter 2 we met Illia Karamalikov, the local businessman in Kherson who organised citizen patrols in the chaos of occupied Kherson. This activity was already controversial since it inevitably meant some level of cooperation with the Russian military, since they were operating after curfew.[76] But when a lost Russian helicopter pilot was captured by one of his patrols, Karamalikov contacted his Russian liaison—a Russian colonel—to arrange the pilot's handover to Russian forces. Ukrainian forces were many miles away, there was no Red Cross representative in the area, and Karamalikov was not the type to kill an enemy soldier in cold blood. But when Karamalikov left Kherson in mid-April for Odesa, he was detained by Ukrainian officials at a checkpoint. According to his lawyer, he was badly beaten, cut with sharp objects and administered drugs while being interrogated in Kryvyi Rih. He was eventually charged with collaboration for handing over the Russian pilot to the enemy. His lawyer posed the question: 'to this day we have asked a question that no one can answer: What else, in those circumstances, in that city, at that time, was he supposed to do?'[77] In 2024 Karamalikov was still held in prison in pre-trial detention.[78]

Regardless of how the law was implemented, the question of who collaborated with the Russians would remain a source of tension in liberated communities. How would people who had chosen different paths live and work together in the future? Many of those who remained under Russian rule complained that it was impossible to convey the psychological difficulties of living under occupation. Posts during an online question-and-answer session with former mayor of Melitopol Ivan Fedorov were full of mutual recriminations between those who remained under occupation, who were often accused of collaboration or cooperation with the Russians, and those who had left.[79]

Oleksiy Arestovych, a maverick former advisor to President Zelensky, laid out what he expected to happen in territories where Ukraine regained control. He divided the population into three categories. The first, people who had 'clearly collaborated with the enemy', would run away: 'Nobody is going to wait for the SBU, who will ask what you did the last nine years.' The second, middle category, 'people who could have not cooperated, but did cooperate [with the enemy]', would face lustration ('ten years without the vote, something like that [...] fines, arrests'). A third category included, for example, pensioners who took Russian passports to get medical help. For such people there would be a 'total amnesty'.[80] Arestovych was not an official and had become increasingly marginalised from power. His views reflected one potential response to the problem, but there was still little clarity from the authorities, and there was no guarantee that there would be a political consensus around ideas such as an amnesty in the event of a Ukrainian military victory.

The collaboration law had been designed as a short-term response to a critical situation as Russian forces advanced across the country in March 2022. It was designed to deter people from voluntarily helping the Russians, politically or economically. The law was less appropriate for situations of long-term occupation, because it effectively criminalised most of the population. In Crimea, according to Ihor Ponochovnyi, head of the Ukrainian prosecutor's office responsible for Crimea, 99.9% of the residents of Crimea could fall foul of Article 111–1 of the Criminal Code, even though—as he argued—the majority of those who remained in Crimea were not traitors. For Ponochovnyi, the law was designed to address a short-term challenge in the newly occupied territories, but was poorly suited to the occupation of Crimea.[81] Tamila Tasheva, permanent representative of the President of Ukraine in the Autonomous Republic of Crimea, admitted that the challenge was particularly acute in Crimea, where the new law would potentially require hundreds of thousands of prosecutions.[82] As human rights defenders pointed out, Article 111–1 would potentially criminalise many Crimean residents for teaching, serving in local administrations or carrying out any business. It was evident that these laws were hardly likely to make Crimeans welcome the prospect of a successful Ukrainian military campaign to take back the peninsula.[83] Some Ukrainian officials began to argue for a more nuanced approach, pointing out that Russia was using the threat of Ukrainian prosecutions to boost support for the Russian occupation.[84] The lack of clarity over potential collaboration prosecutions in Ukraine became another mechanism that Russia used to consolidate its hold over the population.

Conclusion: The challenge of deoccupation

'Deoccupation' is an ugly word, but it represented a life-transforming moment for those liberated from Russia's occupation regime during Ukraine's 2022 counteroffensives. There was no blurring of lines between occupation and deoccupation: you were in one world or the other. Yet the transition from occupation to deoccupation did not guarantee security or prosperity. The physical withdrawal of Russian troops was just the beginning. The liberated territories faced an uncertain economic future, huge reconstruction costs and a massive challenge to demine the land. There was also a demographic crisis. Many people had left for other locations in Ukraine or for Europe. It was not clear how many would eventually return.

The liberation of territory also uncovered divisions in society that partly predated the war but had been deepened under occupation. In some ways the war had united Ukrainian society as never before, in opposition to the Russian invasion. But it did not overcome completely the long-standing divisions in parts of the south and the east of the country. Indeed, occupation accentuated some of these cleavages as people reacted in diverse ways to the Russian occupation. While most Ukrainians hoped for liberation of their lands from Russian occupation, a small minority welcomed the Russian invasion. The number of overt pro-Russian voices was tiny in most areas. But some residents began to adapt to the occupation regime and became fearful of what a return to Ukrainian political control might involve—the loss of a job or an income, or, worse, prosecution under collaboration laws, lustration or even imprisonment. Local economic elites could certainly expect to lose their assets and their businesses. Others faced even more serious reprisals, including arrest, imprisonment or even assassination.

The problem of collaboration was much more than simply a question about how laws should be designed or implemented. It was also a question about what kind of Ukraine would emerge from the war, and what political strategy would best enable Ukraine to regain control of the occupied territories and successfully reintegrate them into a reunited country. A reliance solely on military victory overlooked the difficulties that Ukraine would face in reintegrating the occupied territories without resorting to mass prosecutions or ethnic cleansing. Ukraine's deoccupation strategy was premised on a quick military victory. It needed a different strategy to challenge a long-term Russian occupation, with a strong political component, including mechanisms to address divergent views and identities in the south and east of Ukraine. Ukraine's reintegration strategies glossed over these complex political questions too readily, leaving many of those living under occupation in an increasingly uncertain limbo. Many waited for liberation, but others feared what it might entail.

CONCLUSION

FUTURES

As discussed in the introduction, the concept of occupation in international law always implies a temporary status. There can be no permanent, legal status of occupation. Yet by 2024, parts of Ukraine had been under Russian occupation for more than a decade. More than two years had passed since Russian troops first entered southern towns such as Mariupol and Melitopol. Time plays an important role in the politics of occupation. The term *zhduny*—those who wait—was used by both sides to criticise those who were waiting either for the Russians to arrive or for Ukrainian liberation. Waiting was integral to the experience of occupation. Many waited in exile, dreaming of a future in which they could return home. Others remained living under occupation, waiting patiently for change, but slowly losing hope.

Russia's policies were designed to extinguish any hope that the occupation might end and instead ensure that the occupation became permanent. Moscow rushed through rigged referendums and changed the Russian Constitution to make it difficult for any future Russian leader to consider withdrawing from the territories. Russia imposed its political and legal systems on the occupied territories in an attempt to preclude the possibility of any future change. The occupation authorities even attempted to fix the future identities of those living under occupation through mass passportisation and a Russification programme. Some Russian citizens also moved into the occupied territories, raising the prospect of long-term demographic change. Yet despite Russia's efforts to predetermine the course of events, the occupation represented a profoundly uncertain and ambivalent future, not only for those who lived in the occupied territories, but also for the states and societies of Ukraine and Russia—and even for the international order more widely.

By 2024 Russia had developed a highly effective occupation regime that relied on a set of mechanisms designed to ensure that Russian control would be sustainable over the long term. As discussed in previous chapters, Russia had successfully combined Michael Mann's two different concepts of state power—infrastructural power and despotic power—in its occupation regime. Moscow's willingness to resort to despotic power—brutal violence—lay at the heart of the occupation. Yet it was also able to saturate the occupation zone with its political institutions, cultural and educational programmes, and financial and economic policies that it used to co-opt local elites and buy off some local communities. The four pillars of Russian occupation—governance, violence, propaganda and money—all worked together to produce a space in which resistance was extremely difficult and the costs of occupation for Russia—in terms of security threats and financial costs—appeared sustainable. Moreover, Russia's investments in education and propaganda seemed likely to pay off in the future, producing a more pro-Russian populace that would make any future return to Ukrainian rule extremely difficult.

This model of Russian rule represented a potential blueprint for further Russian occupations elsewhere, but there were three important caveats. First, the south-east of Ukraine offered Russia unique geographical benefits. The geography—at least after Russia retreated behind the Dnipro River—offered defensive advantages. Russia had an extensive border with the occupied territories and benefited from pre-existing Russian or proxy administrations in Crimea and the DNR and LNR that made expansion into the newly occupied territories relatively easy. As Russian forces moved further to the west in Ukraine, imposing an occupation regime became more difficult, as Russia discovered in Kherson region, where its supply lines became over-extended and its defensive lines vulnerable to Ukrainian counteroffensives.

Second, Russia benefited from a minority of people in these south-eastern regions who were either openly sympathetic to Russia or at least sufficiently ambivalent about their identity and political views to not actively resist Russian occupation. In the previous chapters, I discussed how important it was for Russia to co-opt local elites and ordinary people in society. Russia was unable to impose its rule directly without a mediating elite of collaborators—these networks were critical to Russian success, as they had been throughout much of Russia's imperial history. It was extremely difficult to assess whether Russia would be able to find sufficient people willing to do its bidding in other areas of Ukraine, but opinion polls and the experience of previous Russian incursions into northern Ukraine suggested that it was unlikely.

Finally, occupying less than 20% of Ukrainian territory was affordable for Moscow in the first two years of the war, but any territorial expansion of Russian control would lead to mounting economic costs and an over-extended security apparatus, as Russian forces faced more resistance and sabotage. Maintaining an extended occupation of a much greater expanse of Ukrainian territory would become much more costly for Russia. A highly authoritarian regime in Moscow might still be able to impose those costs on its own population, but the risks of the occupation backfiring on stability inside Russia would increase.

The risk of the occupation destabilising Russian domestic politics in the future was real. The occupation regime was also a lens into the realities of Russian politics in the late Putinist period. Indeed, the occupation represented one of Russia's potential futures, in which an atomised society existed under a lawless security regime. The occupation zone was a space of exception, a land where the law recedes and another more violent, lawless order takes its place. In the occupation zone, anything could happen. People disappeared, children were abducted, property was stolen. There was no way to achieve justice or recompense. Some Russian radicals welcomed this neo-Stalinist future for Russia. But the Russian government attempted to maintain a sense of normality in

Russian society even amidst increasing domestic repression and the carnage of the war. While arguing that the occupied territories were an integral part of Russia, the Russian government attempted to draw clear boundaries between the Russian Federation and Ukrainian territories, which were viewed as a source of danger and instability. They introduced special zones along the border and maintained an exhaustive filtration process for Ukrainians entering Russia. In this way Moscow retained a sense of ambiguity and blurredness in Russia's frontiers—something only accentuated by Ukraine's occupation of part of Kursk region inside Russia in August 2024. This sense of the occupied territories being both part of Russia and also simultaneously not belonging is typical of spaces of exception. According to the theorist Giorgio Agamben, 'the state of exception represents the inclusion and capture of a space that is neither outside nor inside.'[1] The occupied territories were destined never to be fully a part of Russia, and yet Russia refused to allow them to return to their homeland.

This problem was not new for Russia. Chechnya had also become just such a lawless space of exception in the 1990s and 2000s. Michaela Pohl wrote that 'the entire republic of Chechnya … [was] turned into a special off-limits zone, a place where disappearances, torture, and violent death are commonplace experiences'.[2] Jeffrey Kahn called it a 'legal blackhole in a geographic territory that, ironically, Russia claimed to be an integral part of the Russian Federation'.[3] Yet the exceptional practices that had turned Chechnya into a space of unconstrained violence were never contained within Chechnya. They also spilled over onto the streets of Moscow, and ultimately into Ukraine too. Chechen forces took part in the brutal siege of Mariupol. The 'filtration' system and the house-to-house '*zachistki*' designed to flush out Ukrainian partisans were all perfected in the lawless zone of Chechnya. Just as the wars in Chechnya had fatally undermined Russian politics in the 1990s and 2000s, so the Russian occupation regime in Ukraine risked further corroding Russia's political system at home. Unless Russia could change course and find a way to withdraw from Ukraine, its own future would be permanently blighted by the occupation.

CONCLUSION

The occupation was also a lens through which to consider different futures for Ukraine. The election of President Zelensky had raised hopes for a new era of civic nationalism in Ukraine, in which allegiance to the state and to democratic values would triumph over the narrow politics of language and ethnicity.[4] This initiative had been at best only a partial success. Prior to the war, Zelensky had gradually shifted to a more nationalist stance that had fuelled Russia's false narratives about Ukrainian politics. During the war, the space for political compromise further narrowed, and the public tolerance of any hint of pro-Russian tendencies was understandably close to zero. In a poll in July 2024, 94% of respondents in Ukraine said that the word Russia evoked only negative associations, while 80% reported that the phrase 'ordinary Russians' was associated with highly negative words and phrases, such as 'zombies' or 'nonhumans'.[5] As Russia continued to bomb and kill civilians in Ukrainian cities, it was difficult to argue for cultural pluralism or a more nuanced approach to Ukrainian history. Yet, if Ukraine were ever to end the occupation, it would also have to find mechanisms to reintegrate the occupied territories into a reunited Ukraine. Reclaiming the occupied territories would require not only a military victory, but also a political campaign to win back segments of a population often estranged from Kyiv and from the Ukrainian state-building project.

Ukraine's best option for future reintegration of the occupied territories into its polity remained the power of attraction, as a modernising European state with a powerful and inclusive vision of the future. Tetyana Malyarenko and Borys Kormych have argued that Russia's policies in the occupied territories constituted a form of rapid demodernisation, as businesses were looted, specialists fled the region, and any international ties were made almost impossible by lack of recognition and sanctions.[6] The Russian cultural campaign emphasised this strange temporal shift, which seemed to promote a return to the Soviet period, renaming streets and reintroducing Soviet-style youth organisations, censorship and propaganda. On a much wider scale, Alexander Etkind makes the same case against Russia, that it is a state struggling against modernity, characterised by its overlapping reliance on energy resources and state violence.⁷ Russia lacked any vision of the future likely to appeal to a new generation, unless it was one of spiralling war and expanding repression. By contrast, Ukraine's aspirations to join the European Union offered a different future, defined in terms of economic, social and political modernisation. A future Ukraine could hope to reintegrate the occupied territories, not on the basis of an exclusivist nation-building agenda, but as part of a pluralist and inclusive vision that rejected the polarising territorial nationalisms of the past.

Finally, the occupation was a lens into the future of global order. The occupation was a profoundly local endeavour, extending across a territory about the size of Iceland. In 2024 any significant expansion of Russian territorial control seemed unlikely, with both sides bogged down in a brutal war of attrition. Yet many portrayed the Russian invasion as only the prelude to a future Russian offensive, threatening the Baltic States, Poland and other NATO states. A comparison with Nazi Germany was often explicit: 2022 is 1938, Ukraine is Czechoslovakia, Donbas is Sudetenland.⁸ In June 2024 Polish prime minister Donald Tusk warned that Europe was in 'a pre-war phase' in which 'literally any scenario is possible'.⁹ Russian hardliners echoed much of this rhetoric, calling for further occupation of Ukrainian lands, and even the complete destruction of the Ukrainian state, as part of a radical challenge to the West.¹⁰

This argument about the occupation as a dangerous precedent for further conquests also had a global version. If Russia were able to normalise its territorial conquests, the entire normative basis of the international order would be thrown into doubt. Western officials such as Jens Stoltenberg, NATO secretary-general, argued that it would be a signal to China 'that when they use military force, they get what they want. So what happens in Ukraine today can happen in Taiwan tomorrow.'¹¹ Russia's occupation would set a precedent, went the argument, undermining long-standing international norms against conquest and starting a pattern of irredentist wars around the world.

The rhetoric was at times exaggerated but Russia's intervention in Ukraine did have serious global implications. Other major powers also aspired to spatial orders larger than the boundaries of the nation-state. Turkey had resurrected a neo-Ottoman vision and extended its influence into Syria, Iraq and North Africa. China also aspired to a geopolitical space that extended deep into the disputed seas off its coast, including control of Taiwan. Iran used its proxies to extend a sphere of influence across parts of the Middle East, in ways that refracted historical Persian imperial power. As Jeffrey Mankoff claimed in a major comparative work, this wave of expansionist foreign policies threatened to create a future 'world safe for empires'.[12] States often cited security concerns as drivers of expansionist foreign policies, but the deeper motivations were in the realms of ideas, identity, status and international order. Where Western commentators feared an unravelling of the old order, Russian commentators saw this as a welcome and radical challenge to the status quo. Pro-Russian activists talked of an 'axis of resistance' from Donbas to Gaza, united by the aim of 'overthrowing the unipolar hegemon that has quashed their national aspirations'.[13]

Such grand strategic thinking often seemed overblown. In reality, Russia had failed to make the territorial gains it had hoped for in 2022. Its occupation of south-eastern Ukraine was presented in Russian propaganda as a victory, but in many ways it represented a major strategic defeat. In 2024 Russian forces were even struggling to expel Ukrainian troops from their own soil. Nevertheless, as discussed in Chapter 1, what was important was the underlying ideology of Russian aggression. Russia's occupation seemed to open up the prospect of a reordering of the world through geopolitics in a primordial, violent sense of the word, in which the *geo*— from the Greek word for 'earth'—is dug into the ground as trenches, tunnels, walls and fortifications that divide two worlds. The *politics* describes the construction of different forms of political order on either side of the divide and the deep-rooted enmity that defines the line of occupation. This was occupation as division, effectively defining the lines of a new Iron Curtain through south-eastern Ukraine, with different political systems—different philosophies—on either side of the divide.

The risk of the war leading to growing instability in the international system prompted different policy responses. One approach sought to prevent a wider escalation of the war by localising and containing the conflict through a negotiated pause in the fighting—effectively accepting the de facto Russian occupation, at least temporarily. But Ukraine sought to challenge any proposal under which the occupation could become permanent and normalised through a ceasefire or a 'frozen conflict'. This view was echoed in a report from the London-based think-tank Chatham House, which concluded that 'Russia's wider threat to the rules-based international order' was 'insufficiently acknowledged', and that a ceasefire 'will do no more than reward the aggressor while punishing the victim'. Instead, Western support should be increased to ensure 'a convincing Ukrainian victory'.[14] Ukrainian policymakers also argued for a decisive defeat of Russia, both to ensure their own territorial integrity and to prevent a future resurgence of Russian aggression. Some Western commentators went further, calling not just for the defeat of Russia, but its decolonisation and break-up, effectively pushing the 'deoccupation' agenda deep inside Russian territory.[15]

Yet was unlikely that Ukraine—even with Western support—could achieve these maximalist goals in the near future. Nor would military victory necessarily result in a Russia that withdrew willingly from occupied territories and accepted its defeat. The more likely outcome was an ongoing war, in which continued losses of territory by either side did not end the overarching conflict, and in which neither side was able to achieve a decisive victory. To avoid this scenario, realist thinkers argued that in the short term, the divisions created by Russia's invasion and occupation should be temporarily accepted in a ceasefire or armistice as the best option to avoid escalation and contain the fallout from the conflict. New policy initiatives should focus on guaranteeing the security of the rest of Ukraine, for example by extending NATO membership to a Ukrainian state that temporarily excluded the occupied areas.[16] This view aimed to contain Russia, not to overthrow its regime or roll back its temporary conquests. The question became how to mitigate the occupation, while ensuring that it was not legitimised—and leaving open the hope that it might one day be reversed. Other military occupations had also continued for decades despite international opposition: Turkish forces had been occupying North Cyprus since 1974 and had been in northern Syria since

CONCLUSION

2016. Israel had occupied the West Bank, East Jerusalem, the Golan Heights and the Gaza Strip since 1967, despite international censure. In this view, Russia's occupation might also join a list of intractable conflicts that remained a serious threat to international security, but did not risk a complete breakdown in the international system.

These debates about different policies focused on grand strategy and international relations. There was little attention among analysts to the lived reality of life under occupation or to the lives of those who had lost their businesses and homes and been forced into exile. Realists too easily glossed over the grim facts of life under occupation in their enthusiasm for ending the fighting in the name of wider strategic goals. Those who advocated a more active counteroffensive by Ukraine to take back control of the occupied territories spent little time considering what a military campaign would mean for residents of occupied areas, or how they would be reintegrated into the Ukrainian state after a military victory. Discussions about a war fought to end the occupation too often failed to incorporate the views of people directly affected by the occupation. The people who were waiting—for changes on the front line, for a chance to return home, or simply to hear news from relatives in a Russian prison—were seldom included in these debates.

The occupation was the locus for radically different futures for those people who were waiting for change. And it was also the harbinger of different futures in Ukraine, in Russia and in the international order. Mapping these different trajectories underlined the radical uncertainty that the state of occupation entailed. It was impossible to predict how events might unfold around these territories. But the significance of these different scenarios was clear. The story of occupation was critical to the future of Ukraine, Russia and the international system. International attention often focused on other aspects of the war, but whatever the significance of the wider geopolitical dynamics, it was also a conflict about territory, about concrete geographical places, streets, villages and towns, occupied by Russian forces. This book has offered an early account of the first years of the occupation, but it will be followed by numerous other writings, including by those who lived under occupation, who will tell their own stories. These accounts may one day contribute to a process of rebuilding and reconciliation in Ukraine—and potentially, in a very distant future, between Ukraine and a transformed Russia. But that will only happen if the recording of historical facts, the painstaking work by war crimes investigators and the accounts by witnesses of these traumatic events eventually produce some form of justice and a reckoning for what happened after 24 February 2022 under Russian rule in south-eastern Ukraine.

NOTES

INTRODUCTION: OCCUPATION

1. Early accounts of the war include: Luke Harding, *Invasion: Russia's Bloody War and Ukraine's Fight for Survival* (London: Guardian/Faber, 2022); Yaroslav Trofimov, *Our Enemies will Vanish* (London: Penguin, 2024); Samuel Ramani, *Putin's War on Ukraine: Russia's Campaign for Global Counter-Revolution* (London: Hurst, 2022); Jade McGlynn, *Russia's War* (London: Polity, 2023). Christopher Miller's *The War Came to Us* (London: Bloomsbury, 2023) offers particularly valuable insights from a long-term foreign correspondent in Ukraine. The URLs cited in the following notes were last accessed June–August 2024.
2. Recent accounts that reference the complex histories of Russian-Ukrainian relations include Maria Popova and Oxana Shevel, *Russia and Ukraine: Entangled Histories, Diverging States* (London: John Wiley & Sons, 2023) and Serhii Plokhy, *The Russo-Ukrainian War: The Return of History* (London: Penguin, 2023). For a more journalistic account, see Mikhail Zygar, *War and Punishment: The Story of Russian Oppression and Ukrainian Resistance* (London: Weidenfeld & Nicolson, 2023). Paul D'Anieri's *Ukraine and Russia: From Civilised Divorce to Uncivil War* (Cambridge: Cambridge University Press, 2023) is the most thorough academic work on the relationship after 1991. For an account that places Russia's war against Ukraine in the context of Russia's other post-Soviet wars, see Mark Galeotti's engaging *Putin's Wars: From Chechnya to Ukraine* (London: Osprey Publishing, 2022).
3. Sergei Guriev and Daniel Treisman, *Spin Dictators: The Changing Face of Tyranny in the 21st Century* (Princeton, NJ: Princeton University Press, 2022).
4. This argument derives from a model of authoritarian conflict management developed in David Lewis, John Heathershaw and Nick Megoran, '"Illiberal Peace?" Authoritarian Modes of Conflict Management', *Cooperation and Conflict* 53, no. 4 (2018): 486–506; see also David G. Lewis, 'Varieties of Authoritarianism in

Central Asia', in *Routledge Handbook of Contemporary Central Asia*, ed. Rico Isaacs and Erica Marat (New York: Routledge, 2022), 73–86.

5. Michael Mann, *The Sources of Social Power*, Vol. II: *The Rise of Classes and Nation-States, 1760–1914* (Cambridge: Cambridge University Press, 1993), 58–59.
6. 'Putin zayavil, chto v plany Rossii ne vkhodit okkupatsiya Ukrainy', *RIA Novosti*, 24 February 2022, https://ria.ru/20220224/plany-1774620742.html.
7. President of Russia, 'Meeting with Foreign Ministry Senior Officials', *President of Russia*, 14 June 2024, http://en.kremlin.ru/events/president/news/74285.
8. President of Russia, 'Meeting of Pobeda (Victory) Organising Committee', *President of Russia*, 15 November 2022, http://en.kremlin.ru/events/president/news/69836.
9. Maria Zakharova, 'Briefing by Foreign Ministry Spokeswoman Maria Zakharova, Moscow, March 13, 2024', *Ministry of Foreign Affairs of the Russian Federation*, 13 March 2024, https://mid.ru/en/foreign_policy/news/1938362/.
10. President of Russia, 'Vladimir Putin Congratulated the Russian Military on the Liberation of Artemovsk', *President of Russia*, 21 May 2023, http://en.kremlin.ru/events/president/news/71172.
11. Tyler Hicks and Mark Santora, 'Bakhmut is Gone: An Aerial Look at the War's Destruction', *The New York Times*, 22 May 2023, https://www.nytimes.com/2023/05/22/world/europe/bakhmut-ukraine.html.
12. Eliav Lieblich and Eyal Benvenisti, *Occupation in International Law* (Oxford: Oxford University Press, 2022), 9.
13. Lieblich and Benvenisti, *Occupation in International Law*, 9.
14. Marco Longobardo, *The Use of Armed Force in Occupied Territory* (Cambridge: Cambridge University Press, 2018), 4.
15. RULAC, 'Military Occupation of Ukraine by Russia', *RULAC*, 2023, https://www.rulac.org/browse/conflicts/military-occupation-of-ukraine.
16. Kenneth Watkin, 'Occupation: Treachery, Treason and Ukraine's War in the Shadows', *Texas International Law Journal* 58, no. 3 (2022): 1–32.
17. Watkin, 'Occupation: Treachery, Treason and Ukraine's War', 6.
18. Hague Convention (IV) Respecting the Laws and Customs of War on Land and its Annex: Regulations Concerning the Laws and Customs of War on Land, The Hague, 18 October 1907, Article 42, 36 Stat. 2277, https://ihl-databases.icrc.org/en/ihl-treaties/hague-conv-iv-1907/regulations-art-42.
19. Constitutional Court of the Russian Federation, 'Postanovleniye konstitutsionnogo suda Rossiiskoi Federatsii ot 2 Oktyabrya 2022 goda No. 36-p "po delu o proverke konstitutsionnosti ne vstupivshego v silu mezhdunarodnogo dogovora mezhdu Rossiiskoi Federatsiei i Donetskoi Narodnoi Respublikoi o prinyatii v Rossiiskuyu Federatsiyu Donetskoi Narodnoi Respubliki i obrazovanii v sostave Rossiiskoi Federatsii novogo subyekta"', 2 October 2022, https://rg.ru/documents/2022/10/02/ks-post36-site-dok.html.
20. According to the 1926 Soviet census, ethnic Ukrainians formed a majority in most districts of the Ukrainian Soviet Socialist Republic (UkSSR), and com-

prised 80% of the population. Russians (9%) and Jews (5%) were the largest minorities.

21. Constitutional Court of the Russian Federation, 'Postanovleniye konstitutsionnogo suda'.
22. RULAC, 'Military Occupation of Ukraine by Russia'.
23. Yoram Dinstein, *The International Law of Belligerent Occupation* (Cambridge: Cambridge University Press, 2019), 35.
24. In July 2024 the International Court of Justice (ICJ) ruled that Israel's occupation of Palestinian territory was illegal. See 'Legal Consequences Arising from the Policies and Practices of Israel in the Occupied Palestinian Territory, including East Jerusalem', *International Court of Justice*, 19 July 2024, https://www.icj-cij.org/case/186.
25. A study by Gilad Ben-Nun of twenty-two Neighbouring Military Occupations (NMO) since 1945 concludes that when states occupy neighbouring land, they typically advance territorial claims (unlike remote occupiers) and frequently import their own civilian populations into the occupied territory and expel existing populations. Such occupations, unfortunately, also 'run the long-term risk of irreversibility—thus effectively morphing into de facto territorial conquests'. Gilad Ben-Nun, 'Neighboring Military Occupation: Modern Surrogate to Conquest', in *The Palgrave Handbook of Diplomatic Thought and Practice in the Digital Age*, ed. Francis Onditi et al. (Cham: Springer, 2023), 379–97 (383).
26. Ben-Nun, 'Neighboring Military Occupation', 383–84.
27. Lieblich and Benvenisti, *Occupation in International Law*.
28. Bryan A. Garner, *Black's Law Dictionary*, Fifth edition (St Paul, MN: West Publishing, 1979).
29. This situation holds even when the occupying power does not agree that it is an occupying power. John Dugard explains: 'In cases of de facto or de jure annexation the international community persists in holding the annexing power accountable under the law of occupation, as in the case of Western Sahara, the TRNC, the Crimea, Golan and East Jerusalem. This approach persists despite the fact that the annexing power refuses to have regard to either the Hague Regulations or the Geneva Conventions governing the law of occupation, refuses to see the situation as temporary and has no intention of negotiating a peace treaty with the occupied power.' See John Dugard, 'Preface', in *The Legality of Economic Activities in Occupied Territories: International, EU Law and Business and Human Rights Perspectives*, ed. Antoine Duval and Eva Kassoti (New York: Routledge, 2020), ix–xiv (xi).
30. Christine de Matos and Rowena Ward, *Gender, Power, and Military Occupations: Asia Pacific and the Middle East Since 1945* (New York: Routledge, 2012), 3.
31. De Matos and Ward, *Gender, Power*. 3.
32. For further discussion, see Volodymyr Artiukh, Taras Fedirko, Maryna Hrymych, Tina Polek and Ana Ivasiuc, 'Ukraine, One Year On: Listening to Ukrainian Anthropologists', *Conflict and Society* 9, no. 1 (2023): 173–85.

33. Reporters Without Borders, 'More than 100 Journalists Victims of Russian Crimes During Two Years of Covering War in Ukraine', *RSF*, 12 February 2024, https://rsf.org/en/more-100-journalists-victims-russian-crimes-during-two-years-covering-war-ukraine.
34. Olga Baysha and Kamilla Chukasheva, 'Silencing Alternative Voices in Times of War in Ukraine and Russia', in *Media, Dissidence and the War in Ukraine*, ed. Tabe Bergman and Jesse Owen Hearns-Branaman (New York: Routledge, 2024), 101–18.
35. Interviews with journalists, Kyiv, February 2024.
36. CPJ, 'CPJ Calls for Transparent Investigation into Ukraine Surveillance of Bihus. Info Journalists', *Committee to Protect Journalists*, 9 February 2024, https://cpj.org/2024/02/cpj-calls-for-transparent-investigation-into-ukraine-surveillance-of-bihus-info-journalists/.
37. For example, Stanislav Aseyev, *In Isolation* (Cambridge, MA: Harvard Ukrainian Research Institute, 2022); Bohdan Logvinenko, *Deokupatsiya: Istorii Oporu Ukraintsiv* (Kyiv: Ukrainer, 2023); Tetyana Malyarenko and Borys Kormych, 'New Wild Fields: How the Russian War Leads to the Demodernization of Ukraine's Occupied Territories', *Nationalities Papers* 52, no. 3 (2024): 497–515.
38. Alexander Vorbrugg and Jevgeniy Bluwstein, 'Making Sense of (the Russian War in) Ukraine: On the Politics of Knowledge and Expertise', *Political Geography* 98 (2022): 102700.
39. Julia Buyskykh, 'Beyond Epistemic Violence: Un-Silencing Diverse Ukrainian Voices', *Etnografia Polska* 67, no. 1–2 (2023).
40. Buyskykh, 'Beyond Epistemic Violence'.
41. On this debate over the politics of knowledge production, see Olga Burlyuk and Vjosa Musliu, 'The Responsibility to Remain Silent? On the Politics of Knowledge Production, Expertise and (Self-) Reflection in Russia's War against Ukraine', *Journal of International Relations and Development* 26, no. 4 (2023): 605–18.
42. Olesya Khromeychuk, 'Where is Ukraine?: How a Western Outlook Perpetuates Myths about Europe's Largest Country', *RSA Journal* 168, no. 2 (5589) (2022): 26–31.
43. Tereza Hendl et al., '(En)Countering Epistemic Imperialism: A Critique of "Westsplaining" and Coloniality in Dominant Debates on Russia's Invasion of Ukraine', *Contemporary Security Policy* 45, no. 2 (2024): 171–209.
44. James Forsyth, *A History of the Peoples of Siberia: Russia's North Asian Colony, 1581–1990* (Cambridge: Cambridge University Press, 1994).
45. Dominic Lieven, *Empire: The Russian Empire and its Rivals* (New Haven, CT: Yale University Press, 2002).
46. David Lewis, *Stalinism and Empire: Soviet Policy in Tuva, 1921–1953*, Doctoral Thesis (London School of Economics and Political Science, University of London, 2002).

NOTES

47. See Andy Byford, Connor Doak and Stephen Hutchings, 'Decolonizing the Transnational, Transnationalizing the Decolonial: Russian Studies at the Crossroads', *Forum for Modern Language Studies*, 60, no. 3 (2024), 339–357.
48. Buyskykh, 'Beyond Epistemic Violence', 12.
49. Volodymyr Ishchenko, 'Ukrainian Voices?', *New Left Review* 138 (2022), 3.
50. Ishchenko, 'Ukrainian Voices?'

1. IDEAS

1. Eric Carlton, *Occupation: The Policies and Practices of Military Conquerors* (London: Routledge, 1992), 177.
2. Karen Dawisha, *Putin's Kleptocracy: Who Owns Russia?* (London: Simon & Schuster, 2015).
3. Mikhail Suslov, *Putinism—Post-Soviet Russian Regime Ideology* (London: Routledge, 2024); David Lewis, *Russia's New Authoritarianism: Putin and the Politics of Order* (Edinburgh: Edinburgh University Press, 2020).
4. President of Russia, 'Signing of Treaties on Accession of Donetsk and Lugansk People's Republics and Zaporozhye and Kherson Regions to Russia', *President of Russia*, 30 September 2022, http://en.kremlin.ru/events/president/news/69465.
5. President of Russia, 'Signing of Treaties'.
6. RFE/RL, 'After Putin Blames West for War, Biden Says Kremlin Leader's "Lust for Land and Power" Doomed', *Radio Free Europe/Radio Liberty*, 22 February 2023, https://www.rferl.org/a/putin-russia-speech-ukraine-war-biden-kyiv/32280708.html.
7. Constitutional Court of the Russian Federation, 'Postanovleniye konstitutsionnogo suda Rossiiskoi Federatsii ot 2 Oktyabrya 2022 goda'.
8. The term 'coloured revolutions' refers to political unrest in Georgia in 2003, Ukraine in 2004 and Kyrgyzstan in 2005, and subsequent protest movements in Moscow and throughout the Arab Spring, many of which resulted in changes in government. See Graeme P. Herd, 'Colorful Revolutions and the CIS: "Manufactured" versus "Managed" Democracy?', *Problems of Post-Communism* 52, no. 2 (2005): 3–18.
9. On Russian messianism, see Alicja Curanović, *The Sense of Mission in Russian Foreign Policy: Destined for Greatness!* (New York: Routledge, 2021) and Lewis, *Russia's New Authoritarianism*, ch. 9.
10. On Russia as a 'state-civilisation', see F. Linde, 'State Civilisation: The Statist Core of Vladimir Putin's Civilisational Discourse and its Implications for Russian Foreign Policy', *Politics in Central Europe* 12, no. 1 (2016): 21–35.
11. For a review of civilisationism, see Gregorio Bettiza, Derek Bolton and David Lewis, 'Civilizationism and the Ideological Contestation of the Liberal International Order', *International Studies Review* 25, no. 2 (2023), viad006.

12. Ben-Nun, 'Neighboring Military Occupation'.
13. Carl Schmitt, 'The Großraum Order of International Law with a Ban on Intervention for Spatially Foreign Powers: A Contribution to the Concept of Reich in International Law (1939–1941)', in *Writings on War*, ed. and trans. T. Nunan (Cambridge: Polity, 2011), 75–124.
14. Carl Schmitt, *Staat, Großraum, Nomos: Arbeiten aus den Jahren 1916–1969* (Berlin: Duncker & Humblot, 1995), 259–60.
15. Jan-Werner Müller, *A Dangerous Mind: Carl Schmitt in Post-War European Thought* (New Haven, CT: Yale University Press, 2003); Brendan Sims, *Die Rückkehr des Großraums?*, Carl-Schmitt-Vorlesungen, Band 6 (Berlin: Duncker & Humblot, 2023).
16. Alexander Dugin, *Osnovy Geopolitiki: Geopoliticheskoe Budushchee Rossii* (Moscow: Arctogeia, 1997), 110.
17. Dugin, *Osnovy Geopolitiki*, 348.
18. John B. Dunlop, 'Aleksandr Dugin's "Neo-Eurasian" Textbook and Dmitrii Trenin's Ambivalent Response', *Harvard Ukrainian Studies* 25, no. 1–2 (2001): 91–127 (91).
19. Vladimir Putin, 'Vladimir Putin Meets with Members of the Valdai Discussion Club. Transcript of the Plenary Session of the 20th Annual Meeting', Valdai Club, 5 October 2023, https://valdaiclub.com/events/posts/articles/vladimir-putin-meets-with-members-of-the-valdai-club-transcript-2023/.
20. Alexander Dugin, 'Multipolarity: The Era of the Great Transition' [Translation of speech, 26 February 2024], *Arktos* 8 (22 March 2024), https://arktos.com/2024/03/24/multipolarity-the-era-of-the-great-transition/.
21. Alexander Dugin, 'Mnogopolyarnoe chelovechestvo: Vystuplenie Aleksandr Dugina na forume Multipolyarnosti, Moscow, 26 February 2024' [video], *Paideuma* (February 2024), https://paideuma.tv/video/mnogopolyarnoe-chelovechestvo-vystuplenie-aleksandra-dugina-na-forume-multipolyarnosti-moskva.
22. Ben-Nun, 'Neighboring Military Occupation', 386.
23. Brook Gotberg, 'The End of Conquest: Consolidating Sovereign Equality', in Wayne Sandholtz and Kendall W. Stiles, *International Norms and Cycles of Change* (Oxford: Oxford University Press, 2009), 55–83 (55).
24. Steven Pinker, *The Better Angels of Our Nature: The Decline of Violence in History and Its Causes* (London: Penguin, 2011), 211.
25. President of Russia, 'Zasedaniye Mezhdunarodnogo diskussionnogo kluba "Valdai"', *President of Russia*, 28 October 2014, http://kremlin.ru/events/president/news/46860.
26. Dmitri Trenin, 'Russia is Undergoing a New, Invisible Revolution', *RIAC*, 3 April 2024, https://russiancouncil.ru/en/analytics-and-comments/comments/russia-is-undergoing-a-new-invisible-revolution/.
27. Taras Kuzio, 'Imperial Nationalism as the Driver behind Russia's Invasion of Ukraine', *Nations and Nationalism* 29, no. 1 (2023): 30–38.

28. Andrew Osborn and Andrey Ostroukh, 'Putin Rues Soviet Collapse as Demise of "Historical Russia"', *Reuters*, 12 December 2021, https://www.reuters.com/world/europe/putin-rues-soviet-collapse-demise-historical-russia-2021-12-12/.
29. Even in largely Russophone Donetsk region, in the east of the country, 83% of voters opted for independence. In Crimea, only a bare majority of voters approved independence on a low turnout. Identities and votes were in flux that year. A few months earlier, over 70% of Ukrainians had voted to preserve a reformed version of the Union of Soviet Socialist Republics.
30. 'Bolshaya igra', RuTube [video], uploaded by Russian Channel 1, 12 March 2024, 00:31:32, https://rutube.ru/video/8cfe588415963dd7819147305c88e874/.
31. Katya Arenina, 'Putevoditel po Putinskim ekspertam', *Proekt*, 19 December 2023, https://www.proekt.media/en/guide-en/putin-advisers/.
32. Marlene Laruelle, 'The Izborsky Club, or the New Conservative Avant-Garde in Russia', *The Russian Review* 75, no. 4 (2016): 626–44.
33. Laruelle, 'The Izborsky Club', 639.
34. M. Laruelle, 'Conceiving the Territory: Eurasianism as a Geographical Ideology', in *Between Europe and Asia: The Origins, Theories, and Legacies of Russian Eurasianism*, ed. M. Bassin, S. Glebov and M. Laruelle (Pittsburgh, PA: University of Pittsburgh Press, 2015), 68–83 (70).
35. E. Vinokurov, 'Pragmatic Eurasianism: Prospects for Eurasian Integration', *Russia in Global Affairs* 11, no. 2 (2013): 87–96.
36. S. Glebov, 'N. S. Trubetskoi's *Europe and Mankind* and Eurasianist Antievolutionism: One Unknown Source', in *Between Europe and Asia: The Origins, Theories, and Legacies of Russian Eurasianism*, ed. M. Bassin, S. Glebov and M. Laruelle (Pittsburgh, PA: Pittsburgh University Press, 2015), 48–67 (48).
37. Mikhail Suslov, 'Mapping "Holy Russia": Ideology and Utopia in Contemporary Russian Orthodoxy', *Russian Politics and Law* 52, no. 3 (2014): 67–86.
38. I. Zevelev, 'The Russian World Boundaries', *Russia in Global Affairs* 12, no. 2 (2014), https://eng.globalaffairs.ru/articles/the-russian-world-boundaries/.
39. Arenina, 'Putevoditel'.
40. 'Bolshaya igra', RuTube [video], uploaded by Russian Channel 1, 12 March 2024, 00:30:23, https://rutube.ru/video/8cfe588415963dd7819147305c88e874/.
41. Alexander Solzhenitsyn, *Rebuilding Russia* (New York: Harvill Press, 1991).
42. Alan Ingram, '"A Nation Split into Fragments": The Congress of Russian Communities and Russian Nationalist Ideology', *Europe-Asia Studies* 51, no. 4 (1999): 690–91.
43. Dmitri V. Trenin, *Post-Imperium: A Eurasian Story* (Washington, DC: Brookings Institution Press, 2011), 100.
44. Gerard Toal, *Near Abroad: Putin, the West and the Contest over Ukraine and the Caucasus* (Oxford: Oxford University Press, 2017), 248.

45. Anna Arutunyan, *Hybrid Warriors* (London: Hurst, 2022).
46. President of Russia, 'Direct Line with Vladimir Putin', *President of Russia*, 21 April 2014, http://en.kremlin.ru/events/president/news/20796.
47. Willard Sunderland, *Taming the Wild Field: Colonization and Empire on the Russian Steppe* (Ithaca, NY: Cornell University Press, 2019), 71.
48. Olivia Irena Durand, '"New Russia" and the Legacies of Settler Colonialism in Southern Ukraine', *Journal of Applied History* 4, no. 1–2 (2022): 58–75 (60).
49. Durand, '"New Russia" and the Legacies of Settler Colonialism', 60.
50. Sunderland, *Taming the Wild Field*, 70.
51. Sunderland, *Taming the Wild Field*, 77.
52. On the fate of the Greek community, see the lecture by Tetiana Liubchenko, Associate Professor of Greek Linguistics at Kyiv National Linguistic University, at the Jordan Center for the Advanced Study of Russia, New York University, 'The War and Ukraine's Nadazov Greeks', YouTube [video], uploaded by @NYUJordanCenter, 13 November 2023, https://www.youtube.com/watch?v=v7BTgB2jea0.
53. Serhii Plokhy, *The Gates of Europe: A History of Ukraine* (New York: Basic Books, 2015), 142.
54. 'The DPR Became a Legal Successor of the Donetsk-Krivoy-Rog Republic', *Novorossia Today*, 5 February 2015, http://novorossia.today/the-dpr-became-a-legal-successor-of-the-donetsk-krivoy-rog-republic/.
55. President of Russia, 'On the Historical Unity of Russians and Ukrainians', *President of Russia*, 16 July 2021, http://en.kremlin.ru/events/president/news/66181.
56. Gerard Toal and Carl T. Dahlman, *Bosnia Remade: Ethnic Cleansing and its Reversal* (Oxford: Oxford University Press, 2011), 5.
57. Frol Vladimirov, 'Tak chto zhe s Novorossiei? Ona utonula?', *Zavtra*, 10 August 2014, https://zavtra.ru/blogs/tak-chto-zhe-s-novorossiej-ona-utonula.
58. Toal, *Near Abroad*, 258.
59. See, inter alia, Gwendolyn Sasse, 'The "New" Ukraine: A State of Regions', *Regional and Federal Studies* 11, no. 3 (2001): 69–100.
60. Gerd Hentschel and Tilmann Reuther, 'Ukrainisch-Russisches und Russisch-Ukrainisches Code-Mixing. Untersuchungen in Drei Regionen Im Süden Der Ukraine', *Colloquium: New Philologies* 5, no. 2 (2020): 105–132.
61. Olga Onuch and Henry E. Hale, 'Capturing Ethnicity: The Case of Ukraine', *Post-Soviet Affairs* 34, no. 2–3 (2018): 84–106 (100).
62. President of Russia, 'Expanded Meeting of Defence Ministry Board', *President of Russia*, December 2023, http://en.kremlin.ru/events/president/news/73035.
63. Volodymyr Kulyk, 'Shedding Russianness, Recasting Ukrainianness: The Post-Euromaidan Dynamics of Ethnonational Identifications in Ukraine', *Post-Soviet Affairs* 34, no. 2–3 (2018): 119–38 (128).

64. Kulyk, 'Shedding Russianness', 133.
65. Kulyk, 'Shedding Russianness', 121.
66. Pew Research, 'Despite Concerns about Governance, Ukrainians Want to Remain One Country', *Pew Research Center*, Global Attitudes Project, 8 May 2014, https://www.pewresearch.org/global/2014/05/08/despite-concerns-about-governance-ukrainians-want-to-remain-one-country/.
67. Toal, *Near Abroad*, 263.
68. The south-east in this case refers to six regions, from Odesa in the west through Kherson and Zaporizhzhia regions in the south, and Donetsk, Luhansk and Kharkiv regions in the east. John O'Loughlin, Gerard Toal and Vladimir Kolosov, 'Who Identifies with the "Russian World"? Geopolitical Attitudes in Southeastern Ukraine, Crimea, Abkhazia, South Ossetia, and Transnistria', *Eurasian Geography and Economics* 57 (2017): 1–34.
69. In 2004 voters in the east overwhelmingly backed Viktor Yanukovych, whose political heartland was Donetsk region. Only Kherson region was divided, with about half the votes going to the pro-Western candidate, Viktor Yushchenko. This trend continued even after 2014, with the Moscow-leaning Opposition Bloc sweeping local elections in 2015. Kherson was again the exception, with districts on the western bank of the river voting for the party of President Poroshenko, while towns in the Donbas often still returned the more pro-Russian parties. See Mykhaylo Shtekel, 'Why War-Torn East Ukraine Votes for Pro-Russian Parties', *Atlantic Council*, 5 November 2020, https://www.atlanticcouncil.org/blogs/ukrainealert/why-war-torn-east-ukraine-votes-for-pro-russian-parties/; also, Paul D'Anieri, 'Ukraine's 2019 Elections: Pro-Russian Parties and the Impact of Occupation', *Europe-Asia Studies* 74, no. 10 (2022): 1915–36.
70. On Zelensky's rise and his popular appeal, see Olga Onuch and Henry Hale, *The Zelensky Effect* (London: Hurst, 2022). For insights into his wartime presidency, see Simon Shuster, *The Showman* (London: William Collins, 2024).
71. President of Ukraine, 'Volodomyr Zelenskyy's Inaugural Address', Kyiv, *President of Ukraine*, 20 May 2019, https://www.president.gov.ua/en/news/inavguracijna-promova-prezidenta-ukrayini-volodimira-zelensk-55489.
72. D'Anieri, *Ukraine and Russia*, 262.
73. In March 2020 many pro-European NGOs signed demands for Kyiv to refuse to negotiate with representatives of the breakaway states of DNR and LNR. See Ukraine Crisis Media Center, 'Priamyi dialoh Ukrainy z predstavnykamy ORDLO – neprypustymyi. Zaiava hromadskykh orhanizatsii', Press-release, 3 March 2020, https://uacrisis.org/uk/75229-pryamij-dialog-ordlo?fbclid=IwAR0-tSAsPyYz0CpqyeQVhE0ofQbPIVFON7BNsGhJ1ZqLt3Ufli_jukPeqsg.
74. Shuster, *Showman*, 176.
75. Onuch and Hale, *The Zelensky Effect*, 260.
76. RFE/RL, 'Council of Europe's Experts Criticize Ukrainian Language Laws', *Radio Free Europe/Radio Liberty*, 7 December 2019, https://www.rferl.org/a/council-europe-criticizes-ukrainian-language-laws/30312541.html.

77. Rachel Denber, 'New Language Requirement Raises Concerns in Ukraine', *Human Rights Watch*, 19 January 2022, https://www.hrw.org/news/2022/01/19/new-language-requirement-raises-concerns-ukraine.
78. 'Ukraintsy otvetili, kak otnosyatsya k obsluzhivaniyu na ukrainskom yazyke', *Ukrainskaya pravda*, https://www.pravda.com.ua/rus/news/2021/02/3/7282144/.
79. Ukrainskaya pravda, 'Ukraintsy otvetili, kak otnosyatsya k obsluzhivaniyu na ukrainskom yazyke'.
80. Georgiy Kasianov, *Memory Crash: Politics of History in and around Ukraine, 1980s–2010s* (Budapest: Central European University Press, 2022), 23. Kasianov contrasts an exclusivist approach which 'affirms and imposes a homogeneous version of historical memory', with an 'inclusivist' approach, which accepts a pluralist framework in which different variants of historical memory can coexist, 'unified by the idea of civic patriotism'.
81. Figures vary, but most historians conclude that between 3 and 4 million people died in Ukraine from the famine in 1932–33, the result of the Soviet Communist Party's violent campaign to collectivise agriculture and extract as much grain as possible from peasant farmers. The authorities did almost nothing to alleviate the famine. More than thirty states and the European Parliament have recognised the Holodomor as a genocide against the Ukrainian people. Independent scholars remain divided over this interpretation, with continuing disputes over whether there was genocidal intent behind the famine. See Anne Applebaum, *Red Famine: Stalin's War on Ukraine* (Toronto: Signal, 2017) for a balanced discussion of the different viewpoints. On the Ukrainian debate, see Olga Andriewsky, 'Towards a Decentred History: The Study of the Holodomor and Ukrainian Historiography', *East/West: Journal of Ukrainian Studies* 2, no. 1 (2015): 17–52. John-Paul Himka offers a critical view in 'Encumbered Memory: The Ukrainian Famine of 1932–33', *Kritika: Explorations in Russian and Eurasian History* 14, no. 2 (2013): 411–36 (429–30).
82. The UPA was the armed wing of the Organisation of Ukrainian Nationalists (OUN-B), the more radical branch of the Organisation of Ukrainian Nationalists (OUN), a far-right nationalist movement founded in 1929 that shared similar views to European fascist parties of the period. The OUN-B, led by Stepan Bandera, initially collaborated with the Nazis in 1941, before turning against the Germans in their fight for an independent Ukraine. Members of Bandera's OUN and the UPA were accused of involvement in the massacre of between 60,000 and 90,000 Poles in 1943–44 and were also implicated in violence against Jews during the Holocaust in Ukraine. The UPA continued to fight an insurgency against the Soviets in western Ukraine until the late 1940s. The law adopted in Ukraine in 2015 made it illegal to deny the 'legitimacy' of the struggle of the OUN for Ukrainian independence or to express 'public contempt' towards Ukrainian nationalist fighters of that period. For a critical view of Ukraine's politics of history, see Per A. Rudling, *Tarnished Heroes: The*

Organization of Ukrainian Nationalists in the Memory Politics of Post-Soviet Ukraine (Hannover: Ibidem, 2024).

83. David R. Marples, 'Decommunization, Memory Laws, and "Builders of Ukraine in the 20th Century"', *Acta Slavonica Iaponica* 39 (2018): 1–22 (7).
84. 'Law of Ukraine. On the Legal Status and Honoring the Memory of Fighters for Ukraine's Independence in the Twentieth Century', 2 March 2020, https://uinp.gov.ua/dokumenty/normatyvno-pravovi-akty-rozrobleni-v-instytuti/zakony/law-of-ukraine-on-the-legal-status-and-honoring-the-memory-of-fighters-for-ukraines-independence-in-the-twentieth-century.
85. Kasianov, *Memory Crash*, 312.
86. 'Suspilno-politychni nastroi naseleniia', *Rating Group*, 27 July 2021, http://ratinggroup.ua/research/ukraine/obschestvenno-politicheskie_nastroeniya_naseleniya_23–25_iyulya_2021.html.
87. The survey was conducted in the regions of Odesa, Mykolaiv and Kherson. Jan Patrick Zeller, 'Attitudes on Languages, Identities and Politics at the Ukrainian Black Sea Coast in 2020/21', *Russian Linguistics* 46 (2022): 291–311.
88. Anton Alekseev, 'ERR v Mariupole: zhiteli goroda po-raznomu otnosyatsya k Rossii', *ERR.ee*, 31 January 2022, https://rus.err.ee/1608484613/err-v-mariupole-zhiteli-goroda-po-raznomu-otnosjatsja-k-rossii.
89. Michael Gentile, 'The "Elephant" in Mariupol: What Geopolitical Moods Prevail in the City', *Vox Ukraine*, 23 November 2020, https://voxukraine.org/en/the-elephant-in-mariupol.
90. Cited in Ivan Posylnyi, 'The Soviet Pillar of Belonging: How Donbas Schools Construct the Reality in Occupation', *Communist and Post-Communist Studies* 57, no. 2 (2024): 112–34 (121).
91. Posylnyi, 'The Soviet Pillar of Belonging', 113.
92. Posylnyi, 'The Soviet Pillar of Belonging', 121.
93. Olga Malinova, 'Political Uses of the Great Patriotic War in Post-Soviet Russia from Yeltsin to Putin', in *War and Memory in Russia, Ukraine and Belarus*, ed. Julie Fedor et al. (London: Palgrave, 2017), 43–70 (46).
94. Tatiana Zhurzhenko, 'Russia's Never-Ending War against "Fascism"', *Eurozine*, 7 May 2015, https://www.eurozine.com/russias-never-ending-war-against-fascism/.
95. Gentile, 'The "Elephant" in Mariupol'.
96. Olga Vasilyeva, 'Zagnannye kryshi. Sbezhavshiye v Rossiyu zhiteli Khersona poluchayut millionnye sertifikaty na zhile. Kto-to pokupayet doma v provintsii, no mnogiye ikh prosto pereprodayut', *Novaya gazeta Evropa*, 7 September 2023, https://novayagazeta.eu/articles/2023/09/07/zagnannye-kryshi.
97. Gentile, 'The "Elephant" in Mariupol'.
98. Michael Gentile, 'Pax McDonaldica Before the Storm: From Geopolitical Fault-Line to Urbicide in Mariupol, Ukraine', *Transactions of the Institute of British Geographers* 48, no. 3 (2023): 665–70 (669).
99. Gentile, 'The "Elephant" in Mariupol'.

100. RFE/RL, 'Zelenskiy Defends Decision to Block TV Channels Controlled by Russia-Linked Magnate', *Radio Free Europe/Radio Liberty*, 4 February 2021, https://www.rferl.org/a/ukraine-medvedchuk-tv-channels-zelenskiy-defends-ban/31085877.html.
101. There was no reason why the law should have included Russians. It was designed to enhance the rights only of three indigenous peoples, the Crimean Tatars, the Krymchaks and the Karaites. It did not include Ukrainians or other minorities such as Hungarians. However, it had a clear political aim to delegitimise Russian claims to Crimea. For an explainer, see Konstantin Skorkin and Dmitry Kartsev, 'Why Ukraine's Legislation on "Indigenous Peoples" Doesn't Include Russians', *Meduza*, 9 July 2021, https://meduza.io/en/cards/why-ukraine-s-legislation-on-indigenous-peoples-doesn-t-include-russians.
102. 'Putin sravnil ukrainskii zakon o korennykh narodakh s ideyami natsistskoi Germanii', *Izvestiya*, 9 June 2021, https://iz.ru/1176702/2021-06-09/putin-sravnil-ukrainkii-zakon-o-korennykh-narodakh-s-ideiami-natcistskoi-germanii.
103. President of Russia, 'On the Historical Unity of Russians and Ukrainians'.
104. President of Russia, 'On the Historical Unity of Russians and Ukrainians'.
105. V. Shulgin, *Ukrainstvuyushchie i My* (Belgrade, 1939).
106. Andrei Prakh, '"Ukrainiskii vopros" postavili rebrom', *Kommersant*, 29 February 2024, https://www.kommersant.ru/doc/6535309.
107. Denys Azarov, Dmytro Koval, Gaiane Nuridzhanian and Volodymyr Venher, 'Understanding Russia's Actions in Ukraine as the Crime of Genocide', *Journal of International Criminal Justice* 21, no. 2 (2023): 233–64.
108. Oleg Roi, 'Ukrainstvo—splav natsizma i manipulyatsii', *Vzglyad*, 7 April 2022, https://vz.ru/opinions/2022/4/7/1152532.html.
109. 'Mikhalkov vystupil protiv prepodavaniya na ukrainskom yazyke v shkolakh Donbassa', *RIA Novosti*, 25 August 2022, https://ria.ru/20220825/mikhalkov-1812187241.html. These attacks on Ukrainian language and culture had begun before the 2022 invasion. In 2018 the Russian authorities finally closed the Library of Ukrainian Literature in Moscow. Its director Natalya Sharina had been convicted in 2017 on trumped-up charges of 'inciting national enmity or hatred'. See Andrew Osborn, 'Disappearing Books: How Russia is Shuttering its Ukrainian Library', *Reuters*, 15 March 2017, https://www.reuters.com/article/world/disappearing-books-how-russia-is-shuttering-its-ukrainian-library-idUSKBN16M0PU/; Ukrainska pravda, 'Library of Ukrainian Literature Destroyed in Moscow', *Euromaidan Press*, 23 April 2018, https://euromaidanpress.com/2018/04/23/library-of-ukrainian-literature-destroyed-in-moscow/.

2. ATTACK

1. Katarina Tishchenko, 'V Khersonskoi oblasti proshli ucheniya, Zelenskii

NOTES

nablyudal', *Ukrainskaya pravda*, 12 February 2022, https://www.pravda.com.ua/rus/news/2022/02/12/7323753/.

2. Ben Hall and Roman Olearchyk, 'Ukrainian Frontier City Weighs Threat of Renewed Russian Aggression', *Financial Times*, 27 January 2022, https://www.ft.com/content/9f527a39-3750-453b-9fdc-9215aa683c77.

3. Vlasta Lazur, '"Nikhto ne kazav, shcho bude viina, a prezydenta ya ne zapytav". Mer Boichenko pro te, yak Mariupol (ne) hotuvaly do viiny. Interviu', *Radio Svoboda*, 14 April 2024, https://www.radiosvoboda.org/a/mer-mariupolya-boychenko-chy-hotuvaly-misto-do-viyny/32360469.html.

4. Yaroslava Volvach, 'Izmena i predateli v SBU. Kuda i pochemu bezhali podchinennyye Bakanova 24 fevralya', *Hromadske*, 4 September 2023, https://hromadske.ua/ru/posts/izmena-i-predateli-v-sbu-kuda-i-pochemu-bezhali-podchinennye-bakanova-24-fevralya.

5. Human Rights Watch, '"Our City Was Gone": Russia's Devastation of Mariupol, Ukraine', *Human Rights Watch*, 8 February 2024, https://www.hrw.org/feature/russia-ukraine-war-mariupol/report.

6. 'Chongar Demining: Bridges on Chongar Were Not Blown Up Because of Sabotage Group of Russian Federation or Wires Damaged by Mortar,—Soldier Sestryvatovsky, Who Could Not Activate Explosives', *Censor.net*, 6 July 2023, https://censor.net/en/news/3429244/bridges_on_chongar_were_not_blown_up_because_of_sabotage_group_of_russian_federation_or_wires_damaged.

7. Joshua Yaffa, 'A Ukrainian City Under a Violent New Regime', *The New Yorker*, 23 May 2022, https://www.newyorker.com/magazine/2022/05/23/a-ukrainian-city-under-a-violent-new-regime.

8. Censor.net, 'Chongar Demining'.

9. Olga Besperstova, '"My za zhodnykh obstavyn ne pidemo na postupky rosii"—Mykhailo Podolyak', *Fakty.ua*, 29 August 2022, https://fakty.ua/406508-my-ni-pri-kakih-obstoyatelstvah-ne-pojdem-na-ustupki-rossii---mihail-podolyak.

10. Michael Schwirtz and Richard Pérez-Peña, 'First Ukraine City Falls as Russia Strikes More Civilian Targets', *The New York Times*, 2 March 2022, https://www.nytimes.com/2022/03/02/world/europe/kherson-ukraine-russia.html.

11. Sevgil Musaeva, 'Ihor Kolykhaev: Ne zabivaete o Khersone. Nam seichas ochen slozhno', *Ukrainskaya pravda*, 5 April 2022, https://www.pravda.com.ua/rus/articles/2022/04/5/7337193/.

12. Geoff Brumfiel, 'Video Analysis Reveals Russian Attack on Ukrainian Nuclear Plant Veered near Disaster', *NPR*, 11 March 2022, https://www.npr.org/2022/03/11/1085427380/ukraine-nuclear-power-plant-zaporizhzhia.

13. Yaffa, 'A Ukrainian City'.

14. Luis de Vega, 'Mayor of Mariupol Vadym Boychenko: "We Should Have Done More. We Didn't Ask Kyiv for Help"', *El País English*, 6 March 2023, https://english.elpais.com/international/2023-03-06/mayor-of-mariupol-vadym-boychenko-we-should-have-done-more-we-didnt-ask-kyiv-for-help.html.

15. Yuliia Tkach, 'Heneral Marchenko rozpoviv, iak vdalosia zakhystyty Mykolaiv: "Meni 8 raziv davaly komandu pidirvaty Varvarivskyi Mist"', *NikVesti*, 23 May 2022.
16. Andrew Harding, 'Battle for Mykolaiv: "We Are Winning This Fight, but Not This War"', *BBC News*, 11 March 2022, https://www.bbc.com/news/world-europe-60711659.
17. Igor Burdyga, 'Kherson: Surviving 100 Days under Russian Occupation', *openDemocracy*, 9 June 2022, https://www.opendemocracy.net/en/odr/kherson-ukraine-russian-occupation/.
18. 'Rossiiskie voennye soobshchili o vzyatii Khersona pod polnyi kontrol', *Interfax*, 2 March 2022, https://www.interfax.ru/world/825656.
19. Marfa Smirnova, 'Chto mozhet byt khuzhe? Oni menya ubyut? Oni uzhe', *Verstka*, 15 May 2023, https://verstka.media/reportazh-iz-hersona-kotoriy-s-noyabria-2020-goda-obstrelivayut-bezhavshie-iz-goroda-rossiyskie-voennye.
20. Halyna Liashevska (@liashevska.galina), Facebook post, 7 March 2023, https://www.facebook.com/share/p/HzUD3hH7eagG5z5C/.
21. Musaeva, 'Ihor Kolykhaev'.
22. Jeffrey Gettleman, 'He Returned a Dazed Soldier to the Russians. Ukraine Calls it Treason', *The New York Times*, 5 December 2022, https://www.nytimes.com/2022/12/03/world/europe/ukraine-kherson-treason.html.
23. Gettleman, 'He Returned a Dazed Soldier'.
24. Musaeva, 'Ihor Kolykhaev'.
25. Online interviews, May 2024.
26. Gettleman, 'He Returned a Dazed Soldier'.
27. Yevgenii Maslov, 'Bandit ili Robin Gud. Khersontsu za spasennogo pilota svetit pozhiznennoe', *AiF*, 9 December 2022, https://aif.ru/politics/world/bandit_ili_robin_gud_hersoncu_za_spasennogo_pilota_svetit_pozhiznennoe.
28. Yaffa, 'A Ukrainian City'.
29. Yevhenia Drozdova, Yuliia Dukach and Nadja Kelm, 'Telegram Occupation. How Russia Wanted to Breed a Media Monster, but Ended up with a Paper Tiger', *Texty.Org.Ua*, 15 November 2015, https://texty.org.ua/projects/108161/telegram-occupation-how-russia-wanted-breed-media-monster-ended-paper-tiger/.
30. Andrei Zakharov, Anastasia Lotareva and Olesya Gerasimenko, '"Skoro perestroites". Kak Rossiya zakreplyaetsya na okkupirovannykh ukrainskikh territoriyakh', *BBC News Russian Service*, 29 April 2022, https://www.bbc.com/russian/features-61257099.
31. The Donetsk People's Republic (DNR) and the Lugansk People's Republic (LNR) proclaimed independence on 11 May 2014. After Russia recognised the DNR and LNR on 21 February 2022, they were also recognised by Syria on 29 June 2022 and North Korea on 13 July 2022. No other state recognised them, including Russia's closest ally Belarus.
32. Volvach, 'Izmena i predateli v SBU'.

33. Artem Budrin, 'Mer Kupianska, predavshii Ukrainu, arestovan Rossiyanami i soderzhitsya pod strazhei', *Unian.Net*, 7 July 2022, https://www.unian.net/society/mer-kupyanska-predavshiy-ukrainu-arestovan-rossiyanami-i-soderzhitsya-pod-strazhey-novosti-ukrainy-11894487.html.
34. 'Military Intelligence: Collaborant Ex-Mayor of Kupiansk in "Critical Condition" after Assassination Attempt in Russia', *The Kyiv Independent*, 8 June 2024, https://kyivindependent.com/ukraines-military-intelligence-claims-kupiansks-ex-mayor-in-critical-condition-after-assassination-attempt-in-russia/.
35. Halyna Liashevska (@liashevska.galina), Facebook post, 7 March 2023, https://www.facebook.com/share/p/HzUD3hH7eagG5z5C/.
36. Ihor Kolykhaev (@kolykhaev.igor), Facebook post, 2 March 2022, https://www.facebook.com/kolykhaev.igor/posts/4999567616803299.
37. '"He bylo vremeni na strakh". Rasskaz mera Melitopolya, pobyvavshego v plenu', *BBC News Russian Service*, 25 March 2022, https://www.bbc.com/russian/media-60877926.
38. Anastasia Lotareva and Andrei Zakharov, 'Eks-"regional", bukhgaltersha i gornyi inzhener: kto stal novoi vlastiu na okkupirovanykh ukrainskikh territoriyakh', *BBC News Russian Service*, 1 April 2022, https://www.bbc.com/russian/news-60948087.
39. 'Galina Danilchenko, i o mera ot okkupatsionnoi vlasti Melitopolya', YouTube [video], uploaded by @yuliiayuliia4123, 12 March 2022, https://www.youtube.com/watch?v=0Of0uZPdfIY.
40. Ilya Vasyunin, 'Zdes skuchali po russkomu yazyku: i. o. mera Melitopolya—o vozvrashchenii goroda k mirnoy zhizni', *RT*, 27 March 2022 [https://russian.rt.com/ussr/article/981819-melitopol-vlasti-vosstanovlenie-goroda-ukraina]; accessed at https://web.archive.org/web/20220327132227/https://russian.rt.com/ussr/article/981819-melitopol-vlasti-vosstanovlenie-goroda-ukraina.
41. Alla Konstantinova, 'Tretya "respublika". Chto proiskhodit v Khersone—edinstvennom oblastnom tsentre Ukrainy, zakhvachennom Rossiei posle 24 fevralya', *Mediazona*, 2 May 2022, https://zona.media/article/2022/05/02/kherson.
42. Ganna Kamlach, '"Prosnutsya, syadut na svoi beteerchiki, priedut, s oruzhiem razdadut gumanitarku, blokposty postavyat i uedut". Razgovor s dvumya khersonkami o zhizni pod okkupatsiei', *Mediazona-Belarus*, 29 April 2022, https://mediazonaby.com/article/2022/04/29/kher-a-ne-kherson.
43. Kamlach, 'Prosnutsya'.
44. Zakharov, Lotareva and Gerasimenko, 'Skoro perestroites'.
45. Online interview, Kherson resident, May 2024.
46. Kamlach, 'Prosnutsya'.
47. Kamlach, 'Prosnutsya'.
48. 'My Wonderful Kyrylivka', *Voice of America*, 12 May 2024, https://learningenglish.voanews.com/a/my-wonderful-kyrylivka/7600398.html.
49. 'The Vasylivka Survival Path in Zaporizhzhia: The Toll of Escaping to Freedom', *Euromed*, 12 August 2022, https://www.euromed-f.com/en/news/doroga-zhizni-vasilevka-zaporozhe-kakova-tsena-svobody/.

50. Kamlach, 'Prosnutsya'.
51. Ihor Kolykhaev (@kolykhaev.igor), Facebook post, 25 April 2022, https://www.facebook.com/kolykhaev.igor/posts/5142515045841888.
52. Zakharov, Lotareva and Gerasimenko, 'Skoro perestroites'.
53. Lotareva and Zakharov, 'Eks-"regional", bukhgaltersha i gornyi inzhener'.
54. Ekaterina Reznikova, 'Kto rukovodit okkupirovannymi territoriyami Ukrainy', *Proekt*, 29 September 2022, https://war-proekt.media/chinovniki-iz-rossii-v-ukraine/person/.
55. 'Polkovnik Bedrik: Propagandisty "zasvetili" veroyatnogo okkupatsionnogo komendanta Khersonskoi oblasti', *Center of Journalistic Investigations*, 23 April 2022, http://investigator.org.ua/en/news-2/242154/.
56. 'Okkupatsionnyi "mer" Khersona Kobets sluzhil v KGB-SBU, zanimalsya biznesom v Kieve i imeet dolgi', *Center of Journalistic Investigations*, 29 April 2022, http://investigator.org.ua/en/news-2/242332/.
57. Zakharov, Lotareva and Gerasimenko, 'Skoro perestroites'.
58. Reznikova, 'Kto rukovodit okkupirovannymi territoriyami Ukrainy'.
59. Reznikova, 'Kto rukovodit okkupirovannymi territoriyami Ukrainy'.
60. Roman Petrenko, 'Regional Military Administration: Janitor Appointed "Deputy Mayor" in Occupied Berdiansk', *Ukrainska pravda*, 20 April 2022, https://www.pravda.com.ua/eng/news/2022/04/20/7340907/.
61. Yaffa, 'A Ukrainian City'.
62. Marus News, 'Lolita Milyavskaya v Kherson uzhe ne priedet i Saldo po pole ne nashlepaet', *Marus News*, 27 November 2016, http://marusnews.com/uncategorized/lolita-milyavskaya-v-herson-uzhe-ne-priedet-i-saldo-po-pope-ne-nashlyopaet; Elena Kostyuchenko, 'Kherson. Reportazh spetskora "Novoi gazety" Eleny Kostiuchenko', *Meduza*, 30 March 2022, https://meduza.io/feature/2022/03/30/herson-reportazh-spetskora-novoy-gazety-eleny-kostyuchenko.
63. Burdyga, 'Kherson: Surviving 100 Days'.
64. Olga Vasilyeva, 'Traits of a Traitor. What Happened to the Head of the Kherson Region Installed by Russia and What Residents Think about His Sudden "Illness"', *Novaya gazeta Europe*, 8 September 2022, https://novayagazeta.eu/articles/2022/08/09/traits-of-a-traitor.
65. Burdyga, 'Kherson: Surviving 100 Days'.
66. Mikhail Khomchenko, '"Komitet spaseniya": Khersonskie kollaboranty sygrali eshche odin spektakl dlya rossiiskikh propagandistov', *Depo.ua*, 16 March 2022, https://herson.depo.ua/rus/herson/komitet-spaseniya-khersonski-kolaboranti-zigrali-shche-odnu-vistavu-dlya-rosiyskikh-propagandistiv-202203161434338.
67. Burdyga, 'Kherson: Surviving 100 Days'.
68. Halyna Liashevska (@liashevska.galina), Facebook post, 28 June 2022, https://www.facebook.com/liashevska.galina/posts/pfbid02nnrKV6X2TvrjkRJmxWUpPLoBWzQZctcjAUDr13KybyNx5Qf4NmzxQnAHDMYzXuz7l.
69. Online interview, Svyatoslav Kolykhaev, June 2024; Politika strany (@stranaua), Telegram post, 17 September 2023, https://t.me/stranaua/122976.

NOTES

70. Michael Schwirtz and Ivor Prickett, 'A Ukrainian Mayor Disappeared, but Questions of His Loyalty Did Not', *The New York Times*, 2 March 2023, https://www.nytimes.com/2023/03/02/world/europe/ukraine-kherson-mayor-russia.html.
71. Halyna Liashevska (@liashevska.galina), Facebook post, 7 March 2023, https://www.facebook.com/share/p/HzUD3hH7eagG5z5C/.
72. Denis Rafalsky, 'Sdacha Khersona, sotni millionov i mashina ot pokrovitelya', Strana.ua, 19 September 2023, https://ctrana.news/articles/analysis/445648-hennadij-lahuta-chto-privelo-k-samoubijstvu-byvsheho-hlavy-khersonskoj-oblasti.html.
73. Konstantinova, 'Tretya "respublika"'.
74. IWPR, 'Occupied Energodar, as Quiet as a Graveyard', *Institute for War and Peace Reporting*, 13 June 2022, https://iwpr.net/global-voices/occupied-energodar-quiet-graveyard.
75. For an overview of the rise of Azov and its links to the European and international far right, see Michael Colborne, *From the Fires of War: Ukraine's Azov Movement and the Global Far Right* (Hannover: Ibidem, 2022).
76. Gentile, 'Pax McDonaldica Before the Storm'.
77. Harding, *Invasion*, 121.
78. Human Rights Watch, 'Our City Was Gone'.
79. Online interview, Liudmyla Chychera, May 2024. Liudmyla reestablished Halabuda as a voluntary organisation in Cherkasy. See 'Supporting Ukrainian Civil Society Heroes: Liudmyla Chychera', *CEELI Institute*, https://ceeliinstitute.org/news/supporting-ukrainian-civil-socity-heroes-liudmyla-chychera.
80. 'Yuriy Butusov, Chomu zvilnyly sodolya i shcho zminytsia?', YouTube [video], uploaded by @ButusovPlus, 25 June 2024, https://www.youtube.com/watch?v=TFnmQGKZCpQ.
81. Butusov, 'Chomu zvilnyly sodolya i shcho zminytsia?'.
82. 'Mariupol: Key Moments in the Siege of the City', *BBC News*, 17 May 2022, https://www.bbc.com/news/world-europe-61179093.
83. Msytslav Chernov, '20 Days in Mariupol: The Team that Documented City's Agony', *AP News*, 22 March 2022, https://apnews.com/article/russia-ukraine-europe-edf7240a9d990e7e3e32f82ca351dede.
84. María R. Sahuquilloluis and Luis De Vega, 'Russian Forces Exert Stranglehold on Mariupol after Failure of Ceasefire', *El País English*, 6 March 2022, https://english.elpais.com/international/2022-03-06/russian-forces-exert-stranglehold-on-mariupol-after-failure-of-ceasefire.html.
85. Human Rights Watch, 'Our City Was Gone'.
86. Human Rights Watch, 'Our City Was Gone'.
87. Human Rights Watch, 'Our City Was Gone'.
88. 'Azovstal Evacuee Tells of Russian Bombardment of Mariupol Steel Plant', YouTube [video], uploaded by @NBCNews, 2 May 2022, https://www.youtube.com/watch?v=h71tEnXla6A. See also the full interview at 'Azovstal evacuee Natalia Usmanova claims she was held captive by Azov forces at the

Steel works', YouTube [video], uploaded by @SubjectAccess, 10 May 2022, https://www.youtube.com/watch?v=jbz4JvGvONo.

89. Amnesty International, 'Ukraine: Ukrainian Fighting Tactics Endanger Civilians', *Amnesty International*, 4 August 2022, https://www.amnesty.org/en/latest/news/2022/08/ukraine-ukrainian-fighting-tactics-endanger-civilians/. In Severodonetsk, the BBC reported that some residents were angry when Ukrainian artillery was set up in the central yards by their houses. Arif, a Ukrainian activist, told the BBC that he responded to the objectors by asking if they wanted just to give up the city: 'it's not the military hiding behind us, but we are hiding behind them'. See '"Vidimo, mir soshel s uma". Chto govoryat i kak zhivut protivniki i storonniki Rossii v Severodonetske i okrestnostyakh', *BBC News Russian Service*, 27 June 2022, https://www.bbc.com/russian/features-61909686.

90. Human Rights Watch, 'Our City Was Gone'.

91. Amnesty International, 'Deadly Mariupol Theatre Strike "a Clear War Crime"', *Amnesty International*, 30 June 2022, https://www.amnesty.org/en/latest/news/2022/06/ukraine-deadly-mariupol-theatre-strike-a-clear-war-crime-by-russian-forces-new-investigation/.

92. Lori Hinnant, Msytslav Chernov and Vasilisa Stepanenko, 'AP Evidence Points to 600 Dead in Mariupol Theater Airstrike', *AP News*, 4 May 2022, https://apnews.com/article/Russia-ukraine-war-mariupol-theater-c321a196fbd568899841b506afcac7a1.

93. 'Russia Jails Anti-War Journalist 6 Years for "Fake News"', *The Moscow Times*, 15 February 2023, https://www.themoscowtimes.com/2023/02/15/russia-jails-anti-war-journalist-6-years-for-fake-news-a80230.

94. Human Rights Watch, 'Our City Was Gone'.

95. Daniel Boffey, 'Ukrainian Who Walked 140 Miles to Safety Fears for His Canine Companion', *The Guardian*, 15 May 2022, https://www.theguardian.com/world/2022/may/15/ukrainian-who-walked-140-miles-to-safety-fears-for-his-canine-companion.

96. Human Rights Watch, 'Our City Was Gone'.

97. Human Rights Watch, 'Our City Was Gone'.

98. Human Rights Watch, 'Our City Was Gone'.

99. Sebastian Shukla, Kosta Hak and Alex Marquard, '"The Heart of the War": Inside the Secret Talks with Putin's Generals that Ended the Siege of Mariupol', *CNN*, 9 March 2023, https://www.cnn.com/2023/03/09/europe/azovastal-mariupol-siege-talks-intl-cmd/index.html.

100. Amnesty International, 'Deadly Mariupol Theatre Strike'; Human Rights Watch, 'Our City Was Gone'.

101. Mikhailo Podolyak (@Podolyak_M), '83 Days of Mariupol Defense Will Go down in History as the Thermopylae of the XXI Century' (tweet), X, 17 May 2022, https://x.com/Podolyak_M/status/1526502875261706250.

102. Butusov, 'Chomu zvilnyly sodolya i shcho zminytsia?'.

103. Butusov, 'Chomu zvilnyly sodolya i shcho zminytsia?'.
104. Isabelle Khurshudyan, 'Amid War Setbacks and Complaints, Ukraine Changes Another Top General', *Washington Post*, 26 June 2024, https://www.washingtonpost.com/world/2024/06/26/ukraine-army-sodol-zelensky-syrsky/.
105. 'V Kharkovskoi oblasti zayavili o stremlenii regiona prisoedinitsya k RF', *Izvestiya*, 6 July 2022, https://iz.ru/1360409/2022-07-06/v-kharkovskoi-oblasti-zaiavili-o-stremlenii-regiona-prisoedinitsia-k-rf.
106. Yaroslav Krechko, 'Rosiia planuvala "referendum" na Kharkivshchyni z 1 po 7 lystopada', *Radio Svoboda*, 19 September 2022, https://www.radiosvoboda.org/a/news-rosiya-psevdoreferendum-kharkivska-oblast/32040467.html.
107. Vladimir Socor, 'Ukraine Evicts Russian Occupation Administration from Kharkiv Region', *Eurasia Daily Monitor*, Jamestown Foundation, 15 September 2022, https://jamestown.org/program/ukraine-evicts-russian-occupation-administration-from-kharkiv-region/.
108. Vitaly Ganchev, @GancheVga, 'Govorit Ganchev', Telegram channel, https://t.me/GancheVga.
109. 'Ganchev rasskazal o situatsii v Kharkovskoi oblasti', *Lenta.ru*, 27 June 2024, https://lenta.ru/news/2024/06/07/ganchev-rasskazal-o-situatsii-v-harkovskoy-oblasti/.
110. Mark Trevelyan, 'Russia Abandons Ukrainian City of Kherson in Major Retreat', *Reuters*, 9 November 2022, https://www.rcuters.com/world/europe/russia-orders-pullout-west-bank-dnipro-kherson-2022-11-09/.
111. Julia Mueller, 'Russia's Retreat from Kherson Divides Putin's Allies', *The Hill*, 13 November 2022, https://thehill.com/policy/international/3733445-russias-retreat-from-kherson-divides-putins-allies/.
112. Nic Robertson and Amy Woodyatt, 'No Water, Power or Internet—Only Euphoria in Newly Liberated Kherson', *CNN*, 12 November 2022, https://www.cnn.com/2022/11/12/europe/kherson-city-ukraine-russia-intl/index.html.
113. Olga Vasilyeva, 'Vsei semei pereselimsia v odnu komnatu i budem dyshat', *Novaya gazeta Evropa*, 4 November 2022, https://novayagazeta.eu/articles/2022/11/04/vsei-semei-pereselimsia-v-odnu-komnatu-i-budem-dyshat.
114. 'My bezhentsy iz Khersona. Evakuirovalis v Rossiyu, spasayas ot obstrelov VSU. U nas bolshe net doma', YouTube [video], uploaded by @OlyaGrace, 21 October 2022, https://www.youtube.com/watch?v=oCO9Dxg4wCg.
115. Olga Vasilyeva, '"My molimsya, chtoby Rossiiskie voennye kak zashli v gorod, tak i vyshli"', *Novaya gazeta Evropa*, 14 November 2022, https://novayagazeta.eu/articles/2022/11/14/my-molimsia-chtoby-rossiiskie-voennye-kak-zashli-v-gorod-tak-i-vyshli.
116. Vasilyeva, 'My molimsya'.
117. Dennis Soltys, 'It is Still Far Too Early to Write off Ukraine's Counteroffensive', *Atlantic Council*, 14 September 2023, https://www.atlanticcouncil.org/blogs/ukrainealert/it-is-still-far-too-early-to-write-off-ukraines-counteroffensive/.
118. Josh Holder, 'Who's Gaining Ground in Ukraine? This Year, No One', *The*

New York Times, 28 September 2023, https://www.nytimes.com/interactive/2023/09/28/world/europe/russia-ukraine-war-map-front-line.html.

3. GOVERNMENT

1. Lotareva and Zakharov, 'Eks-"regional", bukhgaltersha i gornyi inzhener'.
2. Jack Watling and Nick Reynolds, 'The Plot to Destroy Ukraine', *Royal United Services Institute*, 15 February 2022, https://rusi.org/explore-our-research/publications/special-resources/plot-destroy-ukraine.
3. Michael Schwirtz, David E. Sanger and Mark Landler, 'Britain Says Moscow is Plotting to Install a Pro-Russian Leader in Ukraine', *The New York Times*, 22 January 2022, https://www.nytimes.com/2022/01/22/world/europe/ukraine-russia-coup-britain.html.
4. Derk Venema, 'War, Law, Society, and the Courts, 1939–1945: An Introduction', in *Supreme Courts Under Nazi Occupation*, ed. Derk Venema (Amsterdam: Amsterdam University Press, 2023), 13–29 (23).
5. 'Exclusive: As War Began, Putin Rejected a Ukraine Peace Deal Recommended by Aide', *Reuters*, 14 September 2022, https://www.reuters.com/world/asia-pacific/exclusive-war-began-putin-rejected-ukraine-peace-deal-recommended-by-his-aide-2022-09-14/.
6. Konstantinova, 'Tretya "respublika"'.
7. Andrey Pertsev, 'Istochniki "Meduzy" utverzhdaet: v seredine maya v LNR i DNR sobirayutsya provesti referendum o prisoyedinenii k Rossii. A v Khersonskoi oblasti—o sozdanii KHNR', *Meduza*, 27 April 2022, https://meduza.io/feature/2022/04/27/istochniki-meduzy-utverzhdayut-v-seredine-maya-v-lnr-i-dnr-sobirayutsya-provesti-referendum-o-prisoedinenii-k-rossii.
8. 'Glava DNR zayavil o planakh rassmotret vopros o vkhozhdenii respubliki v sostav Rossii', *Meduza*, 29 March 2022, https://meduza.io/news/2022/03/29/glava-dnr-zayavil-o-planah-rassmotret-vopros-o-vhozhdenii-respubliki-v-sostav-rossii.
9. Pertsev, 'Istochniki "Meduzy" utverzhdayut: v seredine maya'.
10. Andrey Pertsev, 'Vitse-korol Donbassa. "Meduza" rasskazyvaet, kak Sergei Kiriyenko za vremya voiny popal v "blizhnii krug" Vladimira Putina, a teper gotovit prisoyedineniye Donbassa i "obraz budushchei Rossii"', *Meduza*, 8 June 2022, https://meduza.io/feature/2022/06/08/vitse-korol-donbassa.
11. Natalia Galimova and Aleksandr Atansuntsev, 'Sergey Kiriyenko stal kuratorom vzaimodeystviya s LNR i DNR v Kremle', *RBC*, 27 April 2022, https://www.rbc.ru/politics/27/04/2022/626713529a7947c57f2a80f8.
12. Reuters, 'Exclusive: As War Began'.
13. '"Ona stala babushkoi dlya vsei Rossii". Kiriyenko vystupil na tseremonii otkrytiya pamyatnika "babushke s flagom" v Mariupole', *Meduza*, 5 May 2022, https://meduza.io/news/2022/05/05/ona-stala-babushkoy-dlya-vsey-rossii-kirienko-vystupil-na-tseremonii-otkrytiya-pamyatnika-babushke-s-flagom-v-mariupole.

14. Andrey Pertsev, 'Stantsuyem vals bolshoi voiny', *Meduza*, 9 June 2022, https://meduza.io/feature/2022/06/09/stantsuem-vals-bolshoy-voyny.
15. Ilya Kukulin, 'Alternativnoye sotsialnoye proyektirovaniye v Sovetskom obshchestve 1960–1970-kh godov, ili pochemu v sovremennoi Rossii ne prizhilis levye politicheskiye praktiki', *Polit.ru*, 29 February 2008, https://polit.ru/article/2008/02/29/kukulin/.
16. Ilya Kukulin, 'Alternativnoye sotsialnoye proyektirovaniye'.
17. Igor Kastyukevich, 'Pro vizit', *Telegraph*, 7 June 2022, https://telegra.ph/Pro-vizit-06–07.
18. 'Galina Danilchenko, vozglavivshaya Melitopol posle okkupatsii Zaporozhskoi oblasti, zayavila o nachale podgotovki k referendumu', *Meduza*, 7 June 2022, https://meduza.io/news/2022/06/07/galina-danilchenko-vozglavivshaya-melitopol-posle-ego-zahvata-armiey-rf-zayavila-o-nachale-podgotovki-k-referendumu.
19. 'Odin iz liderov ER zayavil, chto Rossiya navsegda ostanetsya v Khersone', *Interfax*, 6 May 2022, https://www.interfax.ru/world/839724.
20. Marina Dulneva, '"Kak s Krymom": Kreml prokommentiroval ideyu prisoyedinit Khersonskuyu oblast k Rossii', *Forbes*, 11 May 2022, https://www.forbes.ru/society/465187-kak-s-krymom-kreml-prokommentiroval-ideu-prisoedinit-hersonskuu-oblast-k-rossii.
21. 'Na okkupirovannykh territoriyakh Ukrainy 23–27 sentyabrya provedut "referendumy o prisoyedinenii k Rossii"', *Meduza*, 20 September 2022, https://meduza.io/feature/2022/09/20/na-okkupirovannyh-territoriyah-ukrainy-23–27-sentyabrya-provedut-referendumy-o-prisoedinenii-k-rossii-glavnoe.
22. Andrey Pertsev, 'Kreml "postavil na stop" referendumy o "prisoyedinenii" okkupirovannykh territoriy k Rossii, utverzhdayut istochniki "Meduzy". Ikh "otlozhili na neopredelennyi srok" iz-za uspeshnogo ukrainskogo kontrnastupleniya', *Meduza*, 11 September 2022, https://meduza.io/feature/2022/09/11/kreml-postavil-na-stop-referendumy-o-prisoedinenii-okkupirovannyh-territoriy-k-rossii-utverzhdayut-istochniki-meduzy.
23. Ukrainian intelligence claimed there had been a plan to hold a vote in Kharkiv region. Leaked documents seemed to show that Russia was planning a referendum campaign centred on the slogan 'Say Yes to Russia' and with a pre-planned outcome: 75% in favour on a 70% turnout. See Krechko, 'Rosiia planuvala "referendum" na Kharkivshchyni z 1 po 7 lystopada'.
24. Pavel Polityuk, 'Russia Holds Annexation Votes; Ukraine Says Residents Coerced', *Reuters*, 24 September 2022, https://www.reuters.com/world/europe/ukraine-marches-farther-into-liberated-lands-separatist-calls-urgent-referendum-2022–09–19/.
25. 'V samoprovozglashennykh DNR i LNR i na okkupirovannykh territoriyakh Ukrainy obyavleny rezultaty "referendumov". Vy ne poverite: za vkhozhdeniye v sostav Rossii yakoby progolosovali pochti 100%', *Meduza*, 27 September, https://meduza.io/feature/2022/09/27/v-samoprovozglashennyh-

dnr-i-lnr-i-na-okkupirovannyh-territoriyah-ukrainy-ob-yavleny-predvaritelnye-rezultaty-referendumov.

26. 'Vysokaya yavka v pustykh selakh. Kak prokhodyat "referendumy" na zakhvachennykh territoriyakh Ukrainy', *BBC News Russian Service*, 27 September 2022, https://www.bbc.com/russian/features-63040911.

27. 'Ukraine War: Kyiv Forces Accused of Killing Two in Kherson Hotel Strike', *BBC News*, 25 September 2022, https://www.bbc.com/news/world-europe-63027205.

28. UN General Assembly, 'General Assembly Resolution ES-11/4. Territorial Integrity of Ukraine: Defending the Principles of the Charter of the United Nations', 12 October 2022, *UN*, https://documents.un.org/doc/undoc/gen/n22/630/66/pdf/n2263066.pdf.

29. Vicky Stark, 'Ukrainians in South Africa Slam ANC Youth League for Endorsing Russian Referendums', *Voice of America*, 28 September 2022, https://www.voanews.com/a/ukrainians-in-south-africa-slam-anc-youth-league-for-endorsing-russian-referendums/6767304.html.

30. UN General Assembly, 'General Assembly Resolution ES-11/4'.

31. Peter Fabricius, 'SA Abstains on a UN General Assembly Resolution Condemning Russia … Again', *Daily Maverick*, 12 October 2022, https://www.dailymaverick.co.za/article/2022-10-13-sa-abstains-on-a-un-general-assembly-resolution-condemning-russia-again/.

32. President of Russia, 'Federal Constitutional Law on the Accession of the Kherson Region to the Russian Federation and the Establishment of a New Constituent Entity of the Russian Federation, the Kherson Region', *President of Russia*, 20 October 2022, http://en.kremlin.ru/acts/news/69516.

33. Viktor Poliakov, 'Chto oznachaet slovo "goida", kotoroe tak lyubit Ivan Okhlobistin?', *Argumenty i fakty*, 23 February 2023, https://aif.ru/society/education/chto_oznachaet_slovo_goyda_kotoroe_tak_lyubit_ivan_ohlobystin.

34. 'Konflikt s Ukrainoi: sentyabr 2022 goda', *Levada*, 29 September 2022, https://www.levada.ru/2022/09/29/konflikt-s-ukrainoj-sentyabr-2022-goda/.

35. 'Obshchestvennoye mneniye o budushchem Khersonskoi i Zaporozhskoi oblastei Ukrainy', *Levada*, 2 September 2022, https://www.levada.ru/2022/09/02/obshhestvennoe-mnenie-o-budushhem-hersonskoj-i-zaporozhskoj-oblastej-ukrainy/. Levada was considered Russia's leading independent pollster, but it was difficult to assess the reliability of opinion polls in Russia's authoritarian wartime state. For a discussion of the challenges in interpreting polls in Russia, including self-selection bias and social desirability bias, see Maxim Alyukov, 'In Russia, Opinion Polls are a Political Weapon', *openDemocracy*, 9 March 2022, https://www.opendemocracy.net/en/odr/russia-opinion-polls-war-ukraine/.

36. President of Russia, 'Federal Constitutional Law on the Accession of the Donetsk People's Republic to the Russian Federation and the Establishment of a New Constituent Entity of the Russian Federation, the Donetsk People's Republic', *President of Russia*, 19 October 2022, http://en.kremlin.ru/acts/news/69513.

37. 'Russia Vows to Keep Consulting People in Kherson, Zaporozhye Regions Over Their Borders', *TASS*, 3 October 2022, https://tass.com/politics/1517135.
38. 'Donbass ukreplyayut rossiiskimi kadrami', *Kommersant*, 13 June 2022, https://www.kommersant.ru/doc/5408803.
39. 'Koltsov vozglavil pravitelstvo Zaporozhskoi oblasti', *RIA Novosti*, 18 July 2022, https://ria.ru/20220718/koltsov-1803330519.html.
40. 'Byvshii ministr zdravookhraneniya Tuvy vozglavil Minzdrav Khersonskoi oblasti', *TASS*, 28 March 2023, https://tass.ru/politika/17391011.
41. Andrey Pertsev, '"Almost Impossible to Turn Down." How Working in Ukraine's Occupied Territories Has Become Some Russian Career Officials' Best Shot at Upward Mobility', *Meduza*, 6 September 2022, https://meduza.io/en/feature/2022/09/07/almost-impossible-to-turn-down.
42. Andrey Pertsev, '"I'm Not Your Boss, I'm Your Commander": Russian Officials Are Picking up Bad Habits in Occupied Ukraine, Where Corruption and Impunity Reign', *Meduza*, 2 February 2024, https://meduza.io/en/feature/2024/02/02/i-m-not-your-boss-i-m-your-commander.
43. Andrey Pertsev, 'The Kremlin Promised Career Growth in Exchange for Work in Occupied Ukraine. That Didn't Happen—and Officials Are Catching On', *Meduza*, 1 May 2024, https://meduza.io/en/feature/2024/05/01/the-kremlin-promised-career-growth-in-exchange-for-work-in-occupied-ukraine-that-didn-t-happen-and-officials-are-catching-on.
44. Pertsev, 'The Kremlin Promised Career Growth'.
45. Anastasia Tenisheva, 'Russian Towns Get Ukrainian "Twins" in PR Drive, Political Deflection Tactic', *The Moscow Times*, 8 July 2022, https://www.themoscowtimes.com/2022/07/08/russian-towns-get-ukrainian-twins-in-pr-drive-political-deflection-tactic-a78195.
46. President of Russia, 'Zasedanie Soveta Bezopasnosti', *President of Russia*, 10 April 2023, http://kremlin.ru/events/president/news/70870.
47. Alina Ampelonskaya, 'Vitse-gubernator Lenoblasti Sergey Kharlashkin vernulsya—i otpravlyayetsya v DNR', *Fontanka*, 23 October 2023, https://www.fontanka.ru/2023/10/23/72839567/; Pertsev, 'I'm Not Your Boss, I'm Your Commander'.
48. Reznikova, 'Kto rukovodit okkupirovannymi territoriyami Ukrainy'.
49. Aleksei Belyanin, 'Sledstvie ukhvatilos za ruzhe', *Kommersant*, 22 December 2021, https://www.kommersant.ru/doc/5142461.
50. Reznikova, 'Kto rukovodit okkupirovannymi territoriyami Ukrainy'.
51. President of Russia, 'Zasedanie Soveta Bezopasnosti'.
52. Henry E. Hale, 'Russian Patronal Politics Beyond Putin', *Daedalus* 146, no. 2 (2017): 30–40 (30–31).
53. 'Chto izvestno o glave pravitelstva DNR Yevgenii Solntseva', *TASS*, 30 March 2023, https://tass.ru/info/17408973.
54. President of Russia, 'Zasedanie Soveta Bezopasnosti'.
55. Arutunyan, *Hybrid Warriors*, 81–82.

56. Yulia Tarapata, 'Deputat Gosdumy Dmitrii Sablin: My otstroim Mariupol zanovo', *Vechernaya Moskva*, 31 August 2022, https://vm.ru/society/992755-deputat-gosdumy-dmitrij-sablin-my-otstroim-mariupol-zanovo.
57. 'Demidov Anton Vyacheslavovich', *Edinaya Rossiya*, https://er.ru/person/f303d124-59c2-4033-8391-04484788d75f.
58. UK Ministry of Defence (@DefenceHQ), 'Latest Defence Intelligence Update on the Situation in Ukraine—22 April 2024' (tweet), X, 22 April 2024, https://x.com/DefenceHQ/status/1782318421436514503.
59. Interviews, Kyiv, May 2024.
60. Ernst Fraenkel, *The Dual State: A Contribution to the Theory of Dictatorship* (Oxford: Oxford University Press, 2018).
61. Richard Sakwa, 'Systemic Stalemate: *Reiderstvo* and the Dual State', in *The Political Economy of Russia*, ed. N. Robinson (Plymouth: Rowman & Littlefield, 2013), 69–96 (70).
62. 'Kherson Clan a Driving Force Behind Danone Russia Takeover', *Intelligence Online*, 25 July 2023, https://www.intelligenceonline.com/international-deal-making/2023/07/25/kherson-clan-a-driving-force-behind-danone-russia-takeover,110006915-art.
63. 'Kadyrov rasskazal o vosstanovlenii Mariupolya, mobilizatsii i "satanizme" Zapada', *RTVI*, 18 May 2022, https://rtvi.com/news/kadyrov-rasskazal-o-vosstanovlenie-mariupolya-mobilizatsii-i-satanizme-zapada/.
64. Reznikova, 'Kto rukovodit okkupirovannymi territoriyami Ukrainy'.
65. Michael E. Miller and Samantha Schmidt, 'In Kherson City, Sympathies for Russia Complicate Reintegration into Ukraine', *Washington Post*, 22 November 2022, https://www.washingtonpost.com/world/2022/11/22/kherson-city-sympathies-russia-complicate-reintegration-into-ukraine/.
66. Isobel Koshiw, '"What Life is This?": Fleeing Ukraine's Occupied Territories', *openDemocracy*, 7 December 2023, https://www.opendemocracy.net/en/odr/ukraine-russia-occupied-territories-life-war-luhansk/.
67. 'Kadrovyi konkurs "Lidery vozrozhdeniya, Luganskaya narodnaya respublika"', *Lidery vozrozhdeniya*, 2023, http://xn--k1aej.xn--b1adbccegehv4ahbyd6o2c.xn--p1ai.
68. Reznikova, 'Kto rukovodit okkupirovannymi territoriyami Ukrainy'.
69. 'V LNR vozbudili ugolovnoye delo protiv zamglavy Krasnodona po podozreniyu v poluchenii vzyatki', *TASS*, 24 March 2023, https://tass.ru/proisshestviya/17360617.
70. 'Vremennym rukovoditelem Luganska naznachena Yana Pashchenko', *Bloknot*, 9 November 2023, https://bloknot-lugansk.ru/news/vremennym-rukovoditelem-luganska-naznachena-yana-p-1667733.
71. 'Chelyabinskiye chinovniki osvaivayut novye territorii', *Kommersant*, 27 June 2024, https://www.kommersant.ru/doc/6791917.
72. Ghanna Mamonova, Yuliana Skibitska and Kateryna Kobernyk, 'Oleksandr Yakymenko, Head of the SBU during Yanukovych's Time, Created a Local FSB

in Kherson, Set up a Torture Chamber and Robbed Businessmen. This is How This System Worked', *Babel*, 7 September 2023, https://babel.ua/en/texts/98223-oleksandr-yakymenko-head-of-the-sbu-during-yanukovych-s-time-created-a-local-fsb-in-kherson-set-up-a-torture-chamber-and-robbed-businessmen-this-is-how-this-system-worked.

73. Sonya Savina and Katya Bonch-Osmolovskaya, 'Eto vy ne so mnoi razgovarivaete. Ego netu', *Vazhnye istorii*, 28 August 2023, https://istories.media/stories/2023/08/28/eto-vi-ne-so-mnoi-razgovarivaete-yego-netu-kogo-rossiya-prodvigaet-v-zaksobraniya-anneksirovannikh-territorii/.
74. Interviews, Kyiv, May 2024.
75. Reznikova, 'Kto rukovodit okkupirovannymi territoriyami Ukrainy'.
76. 'Rukovodil pivzavodom i byl pod sanktsiyami RF: chem izvesten glava Zaporozhya Yevgenii Balitskii', *Kommersant*, 5 October 2022, https://www.kommersant.ru/doc/5594938.
77. Lotareva and Zakharov, 'Eks-"regional", bukhgaltersha i gornyi inzhener'.
78. President of Russia, 'Meeting with Central Election Commission Chairperson Ella Pamfilova', *President of Russia*, 4 July 2023, http://en.kremlin.ru/events/president/news/71576.
79. 'Izbirkomy novykh regionov ne publikuyut spiski kandidatov v deputaty zaksobranii', *Vedomosti*, 10 August 2023, https://www.vedomosti.ru/politics/articles/2023/08/10/989383-izbirkomi-novih-regionov-ne-publikuyut-spiski-kandidatov-v-deputati.
80. Savina and Bonch-Osmolovskaya, 'Eto vy ne so mnoi razgovarivaete. Ego netu'.
81. Savina and Bonch-Osmolovskaya, 'Eto vy ne so mnoi razgovarivaete. Ego netu'.
82. Savina and Bonch-Osmolovskaya, 'Eto vy ne so mnoi razgovarivaete. Ego netu'.
83. Igor Burdyga, 'Why did Russia Hold so-called "Elections" in Occupied Ukraine?', *openDemocracy*, 20 September 2023, https://www.opendemocracy.net/en/odr/russia-occupied-ukraine-pseudo-elections-kherson-donetsk-luhansk-zaporizhzhia/.
84. US Department of the Treasury, 'Treasury Sanctions Over 40 Individuals and Entities Across Nine Countries Connected to Corruption and Human Rights Abuse', Press release, US Department of the Treasury, 9 December 2022, https://home.treasury.gov/news/press-releases/jy1155.
85. Savina and Bonch-Osmolovskaya, 'Eto vy ne so mnoi razgovarivaete. Ego netu'.
86. Andrei Prakh, 'Novyye regiony golosuyut dolshe', *Kommersant*, 7 February 2024, https://www.kommersant.ru/doc/6494380.
87. Burdyga, 'Why did Russia Hold so-called "Elections"?'.
88. 'Kak v DNR, LNR, Khersonskoi i Zaporozhskoi oblastyakh proshli vybory deputatov', *Rossiiskaya gazeta*, 13 September 2023, https://rg.ru/2023/09/13/kak-v-dnr-lnr-hersonskoj-i-zaporozhskoj-oblastej-proshli-vybory-deputatov.html.
89. '"Edinaya Rossiya" nabrala bolee 70% na vyborakh vo vsekh novykh regionakh', *RBC*, 11 September 2023, https://www.rbc.ru/politics/11/09/2023/64fe32e19a794715dcf4fbae.

90. Jennifer Gandhi and Ellen Lust-Okar, 'Elections under Authoritarianism', *Annual Review of Political Science* 12, no. 1 (2009): 403–22.
91. Diana Kurishko and Ivan Antipenko, '"Prishli s byulletenyami, a ya—v sarai". Kak Rossiya provodila vybory na okkupirovannykh territoriyakh Ukrainy', *BBC News Russian Service*, 11 September 2023, https://www.bbc.com/russian/articles/cll8dzlrpm0o.
92. Burdyga, 'Why did Russia Hold so-called "Elections"?'.
93. Burdyga, 'Why did Russia Hold so-called "Elections"?'.
94. Andrei Prakh and Andrei Vinokorov, 'Pole izbraniya', *Kommersant*, 3 October 2023, https://www.kommersant.ru/doc/6252099.
95. Prakh and Vinokorov, 'Pole izbraniya'.
96. Andrei Prakh, 'Dvazhdy v odnu federatsiyu', *Kommersant*, 5 January 2024, https://www.kommersant.ru/doc/6427059.
97. Anastasia Kornya, 'Prezidentskiye vybory zakrepilis na novykh territoriyakh', *Kommersant*, 12 December 2023, https://www.kommersant.ru/doc/6395285.
98. Anastasia Kornya, 'Osobye vybory', *Kommersant*, 14 December 2023, https://www.kommersant.ru/doc/6397007.
99. 'Bolee 4,5 millionov izbiratelei zaregistrirovany v Donbasse i Novorossii—TsIK', *Donetskoe Novostnoe Agenstvo*, 19 February 2024, https://dan-news.ru/obschestvo/bolee-45-millionov-izbiratelej-zaregistrirovany-v-donbasse-i-novorossii--cik/.
100. Polina Uzhvak, 'Vlasti Rossii zaregistrirovali na vyborakh v okkupirovannykh oblastyakh Ukrainy pochti vdvoye bolshe izbiratelei, chem tam realno prozhivayet', *Vazhnye istorii*, 13 March 2024, https://istories.media/news/2024/03/13/vlasti-rossii-zaregistrirovali-na-viborakh-v-okkupirovannikh-oblastyakh-ukraini-pochti-vdvoe-bolshe-izbiratelei-chem-tam-realno-prozhivaet/.
101. Sergei Gavrilyuk and Aleksandr Tikhonov, 'Pervyye dlya novykh regionov vybory prezidenta Rossii proshli s vysokoi yavkoi', *Vedomosti*, 18 March 2024, https://www.vedomosti.ru/politics/articles/2024/03/18/1025804-perviedlya-novih-regionov-vibori-prezidenta-rossii.
102. Anastasiya Shepeleva, '"Vybory" v okkupatsii. Kak golosovali i pryatalis Ukraintsy', *DW*, 19 March 2024, https://www.dw.com/ru/vybory-na-okkupirovannyh-territoriah-kak-golosovali-i-pratalis-ukraincy/a-68613777.7.
103. Kseniya Sokolianskaya, '"Eti lyudi budut v tyurme". Konsultant glavy ofisa Zelenskogo—o posledstviyakh dlya organizatorov golosovaniya na okkupirovannoi chasti Ukrainy', *Nastoyashchee Vremya*, 18 March 2024, https://www.currenttime.tv/a/32865170.html.
104. Sokolianskaya, '"Eti lyudi budut v tyurme'.
105. Prakh and Vinokorov, 'Pole izbraniya'.
106. Prakh, 'Dvazhdy v odnu federatsiyu'.
107. 'Period po integratsii novykh territorii s Rossiiei prodlitsya do 2026 goda', *Izvestiya*, 2 October 2022, https://iz.ru/1404354/2022-10-02/period-po-integratcii-novykh-territorii-s-rossiei-prodlitsia-do-2026-goda.

108. Lazurnoe TU (@vga_lazurnoe), Telegram post, 10 August 2023, https://t.me/vga_lazurnoe/1594.
109. 'AP Report: Russia Imposes its Passport on Occupied Ukraine, Coercing Hundreds of Thousands into Citizenship', *PBS*, 15 March 2024, https://www.pbs.org/newshour/world/russia-imposes-its-passport-on-occupied-ukraine-coercing-hundreds-of-thousands-into-citizenship.
110. Physicians for Human Rights, 'Coercion and Control: Ukraine's Health Care System under Russian Occupation', *Physicians for Human Rights*, 12 December 2023, https://phr.org/our-work/resources/coercion-and-control-ukraines-health-care-system-under-russian-occupation/.
111. Physicians for Human Rights, 'Coercion and Control', 20.
112. Veronika Shevtsova, 'Kak ukrainskomu bezhentsu poluchit rossiiskii pasport', *Miloserdie.ru*, 21 December 2022, https://www.miloserdie.ru/article/kak-ukrainskomu-bezhenczu-poluchit-rossijskij-pasport/.
113. 'MVD: rossiiskiye pasporta poluchili okolo 90% zhitelei novykh regionov', *Vedomosti*, 31 December 2023, https://www.vedomosti.ru/politics/news/2023/12/31/1013791-rossiiskie.
114. President of Russia, 'Rasshirennoe zasedanie kollegii MVD', *President of Russia*, 2 April 2024, http://kremlin.ru/events/president/news/73770.
115. PBS, 'AP Report: Russia Imposes its Passport on Occupied Ukraine'.
116. 'Russia Paves Way for Deportations from Annexed Ukrainian Regions', *Reuters*, 28 April 2023, https://www.reuters.com/world/europe/putin-signs-law-stripping-naturalised-russians-who-threaten-national-security-2023-04-28/.
117. 'Zhiteli Zaporozhskoi oblasti smogut zamenit prava v lyubom regione', *MK.ru Zaporozhe*, 28 December 2023, https://www.mk-zap.ru/social/2023/12/28/zhiteli-zaporozhskoy-oblasti-smogut-zamenit-prava-v-lyubom-regione.html.
118. Larisa Ionova, 'Novyi ofis MFTs otkrylsya v Khersonskoi oblasti', *Rossiiskaya gazeta*, 20 December 2023, https://rg.ru/2023/12/20/novyj-ofis-mfc-otkrylsia-v-hersonskoj-oblasti.html.
119. Geneva Convention (IV) Relative to the Protection of Civilian Persons in Time of War, Geneva, 12 August 1949, Article 54—Judges and Public Officials, https://ihl-databases.icrc.org/en/ihl-treaties/gciv-1949/article-54.
120. 'Federalnyi zakon ot 3 aprelya 2023 g. N 87-FZ "O sozdanii sudov Rossiiskoi Federatsii na territorii Zaporozhskoi oblasti i o vnesenii izmenenii v otdelnye zakonodatelnye akty Rossiiskoi Federatsii"', *Rossiiskaya gazeta*, 6 April 2023, https://rg.ru/documents/2023/04/06/fz87.html.
121. 'Federalnyi zakon ot 31 iyulya 2023 goda N 395-FZ "O premenenii polozhenii Ugolovnogo-protsessyalnogo kodeksa Rossiiskoi Federatsii na territoriyakh Donetskoi Narodnoi Respubliki, Luganskoi Narodnoi Respubliki, Zaporozhskoi oblasti i Khersonskoi oblasti"', *Rossiiskaya gazeta*, 2 August 2023, https://rg.ru/documents/2023/08/02/fz395-site-dok.html.
122. 'Sudy v DNR, LNR, Khersonskoi i Zaporozhskoi oblastyakh nachnut rabotat 21 sentabrya', *Pravo.ru*, 19 September 2023, https://pravo.ru/news/248755/.

123. Maria Sokolova and Nikolai Kozin, 'Sudy v novykh regionakh budut rabotat po rossiiskim zakonam', *Parlamentskaya gazeta*, 2 November 2023, https://www.pnp.ru/social/sudy-v-novykh-regionakh-budut-rabotat-po-rossiyskim-zakonam.html.
124. 'Kogo Vladimir Putin naznachil v sudy anneksirovannykh territorii', *Verstka*, 21 June 2024, https://verstka.media/sudyi-na-okkupirovannoy-territorii.
125. Verstka, 'Kogo Vladimir Putin naznachil v sudy anneksirovannykh territorii'.
126. Verstka, 'Kogo Vladimir Putin naznachil v sudy anneksirovannykh territorii'.
127. Verstka, 'Kogo Vladimir Putin naznachil v sudy anneksirovannykh territorii'.
128. Verstka, 'Kogo Vladimir Putin naznachil v sudy anneksirovannykh territorii'.
129. Artem Gireev, 'Prigovory mogut oglashat i kukharki: kto stal sudyami na okkupirovannoi chasti Zaporozhskoi oblasti', *ZMINA*, 16 February 2024, https://zmina.info/ru/articles-ru/prigovory-mogut-oglashat-i-kuharki-kto-stal-sudyami-na-okkupirovannoj-chasti-zaporozhskoj-oblasti/.
130. Verstka, 'Kogo Vladimir Putin naznachil v sudy anneksirovannykh territorii'.
131. Gireev, Artem, '"Pravosudiye" vsled za tankami: kto est kto v sudakh pervoy instantsii na okkupirovannoi chasti Donetskoi oblasti', *ZMINA*, 10 April 2024, https://zmina.info/ru/articles-ru/pravosudie-vsled-za-tankami-kto-est-kto-v-sudah-pervoj-instanczii-na-okkupirovannoj-chasti-doneczkoj-oblasti/.
132. Verstka, 'Kogo Vladimir Putin naznachil v sudy anneksirovannykh territorii'.
133. Artem Gireev, 'Sudi, prokurorskiye i proizvoditel spermy: kto "osushchestvlyayet pravosudiye" v okkupirovannoi Luganskoi oblasti', *ZMINA*, 30 April 2024, https://zmina.info/ru/articles-ru/sudi-prokurorskie-i-proizvoditel-spermy-kto-osushhestvlyaet-pravosudie-v-okkupirovannoj-luganskoj-oblasti/.
134. 'Oni khotyat ves gorod prosto kinut', *Kholod*, 1 December 2023, https://holod.media/2023/12/01/kvartiry-v-mariupole/.
135. Artem Gireev, 'S takimi sudyami i prokurory ne nuzhny: kto poshel rabotat v «sudy» na okkupirovannoi Khersonshchine', *ZMINA*, 7 February 2024, https://zmina.info/ru/articles-ru/s-takimi-sudyami-i-prokurory-ne-nuzhny-kto-poshel-rabotat-v-sudy-na-okkupirovannoj-hersonshhine/.
136. 'Sud na okkupirovannoi territorii Donetskoi oblasti prigovoril troikh voyennykh iz "Azova" k 25 i 24 godam kolonii', *Verstka*, 14 November 2023, https://verstka.media/sud-na-okkupirovannoy-territorrii-doneckoy-oblasti-prigovoril-3-voennyh-iz-azova-k-25-i-24-godam-kolonii.
137. Lori Hinnant, Hanna Arhirova and Vasilisa Stepanenko, 'Thousands of Ukraine Civilians Are Being Held in Russian Prisons. Russia Plans to Build Many More', *AP News*, 13 July 2023, https://apnews.com/article/ukraine-russia-prisons-civilians-torture-detainees-88b4abf2efbf383272eed9378be13c72.
138. Vadym Chovgan, Mykhailo Romanov and Vasyl Melnychuk, *"Nine Circles of Hell": Places of Detention in Ukraine Under the Russian Occupation, March 2022–December 2022* (Copenhagen: Danish Institute against Torture—DIGNITY, 2023), 27.
139. Igor Burdyga, 'Revealed: How Russia Stole 2,000 Ukrainian Prisoners', *openDemocracy*, 10 November 2023, https://www.opendemocracy.net/en/odr/ukrainian-prisoners-stuck-in-russia-forced-deportation-kherson-stolen-liberation/.

140. Burdyga, 'Revealed: How Russia Stole 2,000 Ukrainian Prisoners'.
141. 'Ukrainian Ex-Prisoners Deported to Russia Stuck at Border Crossing for Two Weeks as Georgia Refuses to Let Them Enter', *Meduza*, 25 October 2023, https://meduza.io/en/news/2023/10/25/ukrainian-ex-prisoners-deported-to-russia-stuck-at-border-crossing-for-two-weeks-as-georgia-refuses-to-let-them-enter.
142. Lilia Yapparova, '"Nas prevrashchali v zatravlennykh zhivotnykh." Kak ustroyeny tyurmy, v kotorykh rossiiskiye spetssluzhby derzhat mirnykh ukraintsev, zakhvachennykh na okkupirovannykh territoriyakh', *Meduza*, 20 May 2023, https://meduza.io/feature/2023/05/26/nas-prevraschali-v-zatravlennyh-zhivotnyh.
143. 'Prokurorami novykh regionov Rossii stali siloviki s chechenskim opytom', *MK.ru*, 23 December 2022, https://www.mk.ru/politics/2022/12/23/prokurorami-novykh-regionov-rossii-stali-siloviki-s-chechenskim-opytom.html.

4. VIOLENCE

1. Watling and Reynolds, 'The Plot to Destroy Ukraine', 9.
2. Nick Reynolds and Jack Watling, 'Ukraine Through Russia's Eyes', Royal United Services Institute, 25 February 2022, https://rusi.org/explore-our-research/publications/commentary/ukraine-through-russias-eyes.
3. Andrei Soldatov and Irina Borogan, 'The Shadow War: Putin Strips Spies of Ukraine Role', *CEPA*, 9 May 2022, https://cepa.org/article/the-shadow-war-putin-strips-spies-of-ukraine-role/.
4. Shukla, Hak and Marquard, 'The Heart of the War'.
5. Roman Kravets, 'Kyrylo Budanov: My shvydko nablyzhaiemosia do hlobalnoi viiny', *Ukrainska pravda*, 12 October 2023, https://www.pravda.com.ua/articles/2023/10/12/7423740/.
6. Erika Kinetz, '"We Will Find You:" Russians Hunt Down Ukrainians on Lists', *AP News*, 21 December 2022, https://apnews.com/article/russia-ukraine-europe-3ae1bccfb0ef34dbe363f7c289ce7934.
7. Irina Borogan and Andrei Soldatov, 'Pytki, filtratsiya, doprosy: kak menyaetsya rol rossiiskikh spetssluzhb s nachala voiny', *Sapere Aude*, 17 July 2022, https://sapere.online/pytki-filtratsiya-doprosy-kak-menyaetsya-rol-rossijskih-spetssluzhb-s-nachala-vojny/.
8. Mamonova, Skibitska and Kobernyk, 'Oleksandr Yakymenko, Head of the SBU'.
9. Mamonova, Skibitska and Kobernyk, 'Oleksandr Yakymenko, Head of the SBU'.
10. 'Ranshe Donetskiye i Luganskiye mobilizovannye ispolzovalis kak raskhodnye material, a teper—Rossiiskie', *Vazhnye istorii*, 7 March 2023, https://istories.media/news/2023/03/07/ranshe-donetskie-i-luganskie-mobilizovannie-ispolzovalis-kak-raskhodnii-material-a-teper-rossiiskie/.

11. 'Ya proshla kurs denatsifikatsii. Osoznayu svoyu vinu'—zhitelnitsu Khersona zastavili izvinyatsya na kameru pered voyennymi iz Rossii', *The Insider*, 3 March 2022, https://theins.info/news/251420.
12. Petr Ruzavin, '"Batya, chto zhe ty takoye sdelal, chto tebya segodnya zavalyat?". Kak vyzhivayut khersonskiye selyane—pod okkupatsiyei, v plenu i posle begstva v Krivoy Rog', *Mediazona*, 10 June 2022, https://zona.media/article/2022/06/10/kryvyi-rih.
13. For a debate on whether the war can be termed a civil war, see Dominique Arel and Jesse Driscoll, *Ukraine's Unnamed War: Before the Russian Invasion of 2022* (Cambridge: Cambridge University Press, 2023). They argue that 'the dynamics of the armed conflict in Donbas were initially consistent with those of a civil war in the social science meaning of the term—not in how Russia used the term in its state propaganda—and that considering the Eastern Donbas conflict as a civil war had analytical utility in the pre-2022 war period' (p. 2).
14. Aleksei Arunyan, 'Plokhaya energetika. Kak sudy vnachale posadili, a potom otpustili elektrika iz Donetskoi oblasti, kotoryi vosstanavlival elektroseti v okkupirovannom Limane', *Grani*, 28 September 2023, https://graty.me/ru/plohaya-energetika-kak-sudy-vnachale-posadili-a-potom-otpustili-elektrika-iz-doneczkoj-oblasti-kotoryj-vosstanavlival-elektroseti-v-okkupirovannom-limane/.
15. Arunyan, 'Plokhaya energetika'.
16. President of Russia, 'Zasedanie Soveta bezopasnosti'.
17. Eastern Human Rights Group, *Plans of the Russian Federation in the Occupied Territories of Ukraine* (Kyiv: Eastern Human Rights Group, 2023).
18. Eastern Human Rights Group, *Plans of the Russian Federation*, 12.
19. Eastern Human Rights Group, *Plans of the Russian Federation*, 25.
20. Eastern Human Rights Group, *Plans of the Russian Federation*, 25.
21. Kinetz, 'We Will Find You'.
22. Musaeva, 'Ihor Kolykhaev'.
23. Lorenzo Tondo and Alessio Mamo, '"Some Never Came Back": How Russians Hunted down Veterans of Donbas Conflict', *The Guardian*, 2 July 2023, https://www.theguardian.com/world/2023/jul/02/russians-hunted-down-veterans-of-donbas-conflict-ukraine.
24. Tondo and Mamo, 'Some Never Came Back'.
25. On 'stay behind' tactics, see Jade McGlynn, 'Crossing Thresholds: Ukrainian Resistance to Russian Occupation' (Washington, DC: Centre for Strategic and International Studies (CSIS), 18 June 2024), 10, https://www.csis.org/analysis/crossing-thresholds-ukrainian-resistance-russian-occupation.
26. Kinetz, 'We Will Find You'.
27. Yapparova, 'Nas prevrashchali v zatravlennykh zhivotnykh'.
28. Interview, Kyiv, May 2024.
29. 'Ukrainian Journalist Viktoria Roshchyna Dies In Russian Captivity', RFE/RL, 10 October 2024, https://www.rferl.org/a/ukraine-journalist-viktoria-roshchyna-death-russia-captivity/33154122.html

NOTES

30. 'At Least 28 Ukrainian Journalists Are in Russian Captivity. Here Are Some of Their Stories', *Meduza*, 29 May 2024, https://meduza.io/en/feature/2024/05/29/at-least-28-ukrainian-journalists-are-in-russian-captivity-here-are-some-of-their-stories.
31. Konstantin Skorkin, 'Holy War: The Fight for Ukraine's Churches and Monasteries', *Carnegie Politika*, 11 April 2023, https://carnegieendowment.org/russia-eurasia/politika/2023/04/holy-war-the-fight-for-ukraines-churches-and-monasteries?lang=en.
32. Felix Corley, 'Occupied Ukraine: "Disappeared" Clergy, Seized Places of Worship, Library Purge', *Forum 18*, 3 February 2023, https://www.forum18.org/archive.php?article_id=2808.
33. Felix Corley, 'Occupied Ukraine: "'If They Took Russian Citizenship, They Could Return to Donetsk"', *Forum 18*, 19 January 2024, https://www.forum18.org/archive.php?article_id=2886.
34. 'UGCC Priests Ivan Levytsky and Bohdan Geleta Released from Russian Captivity', *Ukrainian Greek Catholic Church*, 28 June 2024, https://ugcc.ua/en/data/ugcc-priests-ivan-levytsky-and-bohdan-geleta-released-from-russian-captivity-1109/.
35. Felix Corley, 'Occupied Ukraine: Religious Leaders Seized, Tortured; Churches, Mosques Closed; No News of Seized Baptist Couple', *Forum 18*, 20 October 2022, https://www.forum18.org/archive.php?article_id=2784.
36. Felix Corley, 'Occupied Ukraine: Zaporizhzhia Priests Still "Disappeared", 4 Churches Banned', *Forum 18*, 20 December 2023, https://www.forum18.org/archive.php?article_id=2882.
37. Halya Coynash, 'Evangelical Deacon and his Son Found Murdered near Nova Kakhovka after Being Abducted by the Russians', *Kharkiv Human Rights Protection Group*, 30 November 2022, https://khpg.org//en/1608811453.
38. Corley, 'Occupied Ukraine: Zaporizhzhia Priests Still "Disappeared"'.
39. 'Russians Abduct 132 Ukrainian Officials: 14 Still in Captivity, 4 Killed', *ZMINA*, 27 September 2023, https://zmina.ua/en/event-en/russians-abduct-132-ukrainian-officials-14-still-in-captivity-4-killed-zmina/.
40. Andrei Sidorchik, 'Vechera na khutore bliz Khersona. Kak mer Mikolayenko s Rossiyei "voyeval"', *Argumenty i fakty*, 27 December 2019, https://aif.ru/society/people/vechera_na_hutore_bliz_hersona_kak_mer_mikolaenko_s_rossiey_voeval.
41. 'Poyavilis kadry iz kvartiry eks-mera Khersona s kollektsiyei vin i serebrom', *Izvestiya*, 1 May 2022, https://iz.ru/1329053/2022–05–01/poiavilis-kadry-iz-kvartiry-eks-mera-khersona-s-kollektciei-vin-i-serebrom.
42. US Mission, Geneva, 'Joint Statement on the Situation of Ukrainian Mayors', *US Mission to International Organizations in Geneva*, 31 March 2023, https://geneva.usmission.gov/2023/03/31/joint-statement-on-the-situation-of-ukrainian-mayors-hrc52/.
43. '"He Was Hard to Deal With": Oleksandr Babych, the Mayor of Hola Prystan,

Has Been Held in the Crimea Pre-Trial Detention Center for Eight Months', *Media Initiative for Human Rights*, 29 November 2023, https://mipl.org.ua/en/he-was-hard-to-deal-with-oleksandr-babych-the-mayor-of-hola-prystan-has-been-held-in-the-crimea-pre-trial-detention-center-for-eight-months/.

44. Media Initiative for Human Rights, 'He Was Hard to Deal With'.
45. 'V Khersonskoi oblasti ubit eks-deputat "Slugi naroda"', pereshedshii na storony Rossii', *BBC News Russian Service*, 29 August 2022, https://www.bbc.com/russian/news-62717841.
46. Stanislav Miroshnichenko, '"Proukrainska aktivistka—ekstremistka"', *Media Initiative for Human Rights*, 9 January 2023, https://mipl.org.ua/proukrayinska-aktyvistka-ekstremistka/.
47. '"My klaly na holovu podushky, aby ne chuty, yak biut khloptsiv"—meshkanka Berdianska pro polon', *Media Initiative for Human Rights*, 20 April 2023, https://mipl.org.ua/my-klaly-na-golovu-podushky-aby-ne-chuty-yak-byut-hlopcziv-meshkanka-berdyanska-pro-polon/.
48. Human Rights Watch, 'Ukraine: Russian Torture Center in Kherson', *Human Rights Watch*, 13 April 2023, https://www.hrw.org/news/2023/04/13/ukraine-russian-torture-center-kherson; Isobel Koshiw, 'Kherson Torture Centres Were Planned by Russian State, Say Lawyers', *The Guardian*, 2 March 2023, https://www.theguardian.com/world/2023/mar/02/kherson-torture-centres-were-planned-by-russian-state-say-lawyers.
49. Chovgan et al., *Places of Detention in Ukraine*.
50. Sam Mednick and Hanna Arhirova, '"I Thought I Was Going to Die": Abuses Widespread in Ukraine', *AP News*, 18 November 2022, https://apnews.com/article/russia-ukraine-europe-government-and-politics-51cc16dff52a642bd33893ae105eca53.
51. 'Torture and Deportations Said to Be Part of Putin's Plan in Occupied Areas', *Bloomberg*, 9 May 2023, https://www.bloomberg.com/news/articles/2023-05-09/torture-and-deportations-said-to-be-part-of-putin-s-plan-in-occupied-areas.
52. OHCHR, 'Detention of Civilians in the Context of the Armed Attack by the Russian Federation against Ukraine 24 February 2022—23 May 2023', UN Office of the High Commissioner on Human Rights, Geneva, 27 June 2023, 2, https://www.ohchr.org/sites/default/files/2023-06/2023-06-27-Ukraine-thematic-report-detention-ENG.pdf.
53. Smirnova, 'Chto mozhet byt khuzhe?'.
54. IICI Ukraine, 'Report of the Independent International Commission of Inquiry on Ukraine. A/HRC/55/66', UN Human Rights Council, Geneva, 18 March 2024, 16, https://www.ohchr.org/sites/default/files/documents/hrbodies/hrcouncil/coiukraine/a-hrc-55-66-aev.pdf.
55. IICI Ukraine, 'Report of the Independent International Commission of Inquiry on Ukraine. A/78/540', UN General Assembly, Geneva, 19 October 2023, 15–16, https://www.ohchr.org/sites/default/files/documents/hrbodies/hrcouncil/coiukraine/A-78-540-En.pdf.

NOTES

56. IICI Ukraine, 'Report of the Independent International Commission of Inquiry on Ukraine. A/78/540', 13.
57. 'Tortures of Civilians and POWs: Testimonies of the Survivors. Summary of the Meeting at the OSCE', *Media Initiative for Human Rights*, 2 May 2023, https://mipl.org.ua/en/event/tortures-of-civilians-and-pows-testimonies-of-the-survivors-summary-of-the-meeting-at-the-osce/.
58. OHCHR, 'Detention of Civilians in the Context of the Armed Attack by the Russian Federation against Ukraine, 24 February 2022—23 May 2023', 2.
59. Media Initiative for Human Rights, 'Tortures of Civilians and POWs'.
60. Smirnova, 'Chto mozhet byt khuzhe?'.
61. Smirnova, 'Chto mozhet byt khuzhe?'.
62. Halya Coynash, '60-Year-Old Kherson Village Head Tortured "for Pleasure" by Russian Invaders', *Kharkiv Human Rights Protection Group*, 22 July 2022, https://khpg.org//en/1608810710.
63. Mamonova, Skibitska and Kobernyk, 'Oleksandr Yakymenko, Head of the SBU'.
64. Kinetz, 'We Will Find You'.
65. The term 'Orc' derives from J. R. R. Tolkien's *Lord of the Rings*, where the orcs are evil, humanoid monsters, notorious for their cruel and brutal behaviour.
66. The Insider, 'Ya proshla kurs denatsifikatsii. Osoznayu svoyu vinu'.
67. Coynash, '60-Year-Old Kherson Village Head Tortured "for Pleasure"'.
68. Human Rights Watch, 'Ukraine: Russian Torture Center in Kherson'.
69. Mamonova, Skibitska and Kobernyk, 'Oleksandr Yakymenko, Head of the SBU'.
70. Oksana Ivanitskaya, '"Kriki takiye, budto razryvayut na kuski zazhivo". Cherez chto prokhodili i prokhodyat rabotniki ZAES', *Hromadske*, 30 September 2023, https://hromadske.ua/ru/posts/kriki-takie-budto-razryvayut-na-kuski-zazhivo-cherez-chto-prohodili-i-prohodyat-rabotniki-zaes.
71. OHCHR, 'Detention of Civilians in the Context of the Armed Attack by the Russian Federation against Ukraine 24 February 2022—23 May 2023', 1.
72. Halya Coynash, 'Russia Abducted, Usually Tortured, over a Thousand Civilians, Including Children in Kherson Oblast Alone', *Kharkiv Human Rights Protection Group*, 6 June 2023, https://khpg.org//en/1608811635.
73. OHCHR, 'Detention of Civilians in the Context of the Armed Attack by the Russian Federation against Ukraine 24 February 2022—23 May 2023', 2.
74. OHCHR, 'Detention of Civilians in the Context of the Armed Attack by the Russian Federation against Ukraine 24 February 2022—23 May 2023', 3.
75. OHCHR, 'Detention of Civilians in the Context of the Armed Attack by the Russian Federation against Ukraine 24 February 2022—23 May 2023', 3.
76. OHCHR, 'Detention of Civilians in the Context of the Armed Attack by the Russian Federation against Ukraine 24 February 2022—23 May 2023', 32.
77. ICRC, 'Russia-Ukraine International Armed Conflict: Your Questions Answered about ICRC's Work', *International Committee of the Red Cross*, 6 April 2022, https://www.icrc.org/en/document/false-information-about-icrc-ukraine.
78. IICI, 'Report of the Independent International Commission of Inquiry on Ukraine. A/HRC/55/66'.

79. OHCHR, 'Detention of Civilians in the Context of the Armed Attack by the Russian Federation against Ukraine 24 February 2022—23 May 2023', 2.
80. US Treasury, 'Treasury Sanctions Over 40 Individuals and Entities Across Nine Countries Connected to Corruption and Human Rights Abuse', 9 December 2022, https://home.treasury.gov/news/press-releases/jy1155.
81. Franziska Exeler, 'Filtration Camps, Past and Present, and Russia's War Against Ukraine', *Journal of Genocide Research* 25, no. 3–4 (2023): 426–44 (435).
82. Exeler, 'Filtration Camps', 438.
83. Emma Gilligan, *Terror in Chechnya: Russia and the Tragedy of Civilians in War* (Princeton, NJ: Princeton University Press, 2009), 1048.
84. Arunyan, 'Plokhaya energetika'.
85. On the role of the *zachistka* in Chechnya, see E. Gilligan, 'Propaganda and the Question of Criminal Intent: The Semantics of the Zachistka', *Europe-Asia Studies* 68, no. 6 (2016): 1036–66.
86. Yale Humanitarian Research Lab (HRL), 'Yale Researchers Identify 21 Sites in Donetsk Oblast, Ukraine Used for Civilian Interrogation, Processing, and Detention', *Yale School of Public Health*, 25 August 2022, https://ysph.yale.edu/news-article/yale-researchers-identify-21-sites-in-donetsk-oblast-ukraine-used-for-civilian-interrogation-processing-and-detention/.
87. Pjotr Sauer, 'Hundreds of Ukrainians Forcibly Deported to Russia, Say Mariupol Women', *The Guardian*, 4 April 2022, https://www.theguardian.com/world/2022/apr/04/hundreds-of-ukrainians-forcibly-deported-to-russia-say-mariupol-women.
88. Embassy of Russia in the USA (@RusEmbUSA), Facebook post, 21 March 2022, https://www.facebook.com/RusEmbUSA/posts/333477265484259.
89. David Kortava, 'Inside Russia's "Filtration Camps" in Eastern Ukraine', *The New Yorker*, 3 October 2022, https://www.newyorker.com/magazine/2022/10/10/inside-russias-filtration-camps-in-eastern-ukraine.
90. Faddei Aleksandrov, 'Ogranicheniya dlya grazhdan Ukrainy na vyezd v RF: zachem nuzhny i kogo kosnutsya', *FederalPress*, 17 October 2023, https://fedpress.ru/article/3274487.
91. Stanislav Miroshnichenko, 'Operatsiia "filtratsiia". Cherez shcho prokhodiat ukraintsi, yaki opynylysia pid rosiiskoiu okupatsiieiu', *Media Initiative for Human Rights*, 23 May 2022, https://mipl.org.ua/operacziya-filtracziya-cherez-shho-prohodyat-ukrayinczi-yaki-opynylysya-pid-rosijskoyu-okupacziyeyu/.
92. Miroshnichenko, 'Operatsiia "filtratsiia"'.
93. Yale Humanitarian Research Lab, 'Yale Researchers Identify 21 Sites in Donetsk Oblast'.
94. Sauer, 'Hundreds of Ukrainians Forcibly Deported'.
95. Gleb Golod, '"Tak strashno mne ne bylo nikogda". "Meduza" rasskazyvayet, kak ustroyena sistema "filtratsionnykh lagerei" dlya ukraintsev, organizovannaya rossiiskimi voyennymi. I chto proiskhodit s temi, kto ne smog proiti "filtratsiyu"', *Meduza*, 12 May 2022, https://meduza.io/feature/2022/05/12/tak-strashno-mne-ne-bylo-nikogda.

96. Sauer, 'Hundreds of Ukrainians Forcibly Deported'.
97. Golod, 'Tak strashno mne ne bylo nikogda'.
98. Golod, 'Tak strashno mne ne bylo nikogda'.
99. Miroshnichenko, 'Operatsiia "filtratsiia"'.
100. Under Russian law, several Ukrainian organisations were designated as 'terrorist organisations', including the Azov movement, the Aidar battalion and the Noman Çelebicihan Crimean Tatar Volunteer Battalion. The listings were highly politicized. The category of 'extremist organisations' in Russia also included media organisations and political opposition groups.
101. Golod, 'Tak strashno mne ne bylo nikogda'.
102. Kortava, 'Inside Russia's "Filtration Camps" in Eastern Ukraine'.
103. Golod, 'Tak strashno mne ne bylo nikogda'.
104. Kortava, 'Inside Russia's "Filtration Camps" in Eastern Ukraine'.
105. Golod, 'Tak strashno mne ne bylo nikogda'.
106. Yevgeny Legalov and Sergei Dobrynin, 'Matrasy v Sheremetyevo. Ukraintsy sutkami zhdut "filtratsii"', *Radio Svoboda*, 9 November 2023, https://www.svoboda.org/a/matrasy-v-sheremetjevo-ukraintsy-sutkami-zhdut-filjtratsii-/32677771.html.
107. Gosavtoinspektsia Zaprozhskoi oblasti (@gibddzp), Telegram post, 24 July 2024, https://t.me/gibddzp/2770.
108. Russia had announced that only two border crossings would be open for Ukrainian citizens: Sheremetyevo airport in Moscow and Vientule on the Latvian-Russian border. The Russian authorities claimed that the restrictions were introduced in response to a ban on cars with Russian numberplates crossing EU borders. The Latvian authorities in turn closed Vientule crossing, claiming that channelling all Ukrainian citizens through one crossing would cause huge queues and create a threat to public order.
109. 'Andryushchenko dal prakticheskiye sovety, kak legche proiti ukraintsam filtratsiyu v Sheremetyevo', *DonPress*, 29 October 2023, https://donpress.com/news/29-10-2023-andryuschenko-dal-prakticheskie-sovety-kak-legche-proyti-ukraincam-filtraciyu-v.
110. DonPress, 'Andryushchenko dal prakticheskiye sovety'.
111. DonPress, 'Andryushchenko dal prakticheskiye sovety'.
112. 'Rostovskaya oblast ustanovila osobuyu zonu na granitse s DNR i LNR', *TASS*, 23 May 2024, https://tass.ru/politika/20882689.
113. Alona Savchuk, 'Death by Jail: What Occupied Crimea Does to Political Prisoners', *openDemocracy*, 15 August 2019, https://www.opendemocracy.net/en/odr/simferopol-detention-centre-crimea-political-prisoners/.
114. Yapparova, 'Nas prevrashchali v zatravlennykh zhivotnykh'.
115. Yapparova, 'Nas prevrashchali v zatravlennykh zhivotnykh'.
116. Yapparova, 'Nas prevrashchali v zatravlennykh zhivotnykh'.
117. Yapparova, 'Nas prevrashchali v zatravlennykh zhivotnykh'.
118. Varuzhan Sargsyan, 'The Gentleman Vanishes. Spanish National Mariano García

Calatayud Has Now Spent a Year and a Half in Russian Detention after Being Abducted from Outside His Home in Broad Daylight', *Novaya gazeta Europe*, 4 October 2023, https://novayagazeta.eu/articles/2023/10/04/the-gentleman-vanishes-en.

119. Sargsyan, 'The Gentleman Vanishes'.
120. IICI, 'Report of the Independent International Commission of Inquiry on Ukraine. A/HRC/55/66', 13.
121. Sargsyan, 'The Gentleman Vanishes'.
122. Yapparova, 'Nas prevrashchali v zatravlennykh zhivotnykh'.
123. Yapparova, 'Nas prevrashchali v zatravlennykh zhivotnykh'.
124. Sargsyan, 'The Gentleman Vanishes'.
125. Halya Coynash, 'Abducted and Tortured Ukrainian Writer and Journalist Serhiy Tsyhipa Sentenced to 13 Years on Surreal Charges', *Kharkiv Human Rights Protection Group*, 9 October 2023, https://khpg.org//en/1608812891.
126. 'Na Zaporozhe budut sudit nesostoyavshuiusya terroristku', *Tsargrad*, 24 November 2023, https://zp.tsargrad.tv/news/na-zaporozhe-budut-sudit-nesostojavshujusja-terroristku_915552.
127. Maria Ivanova, 'Tri bomby potyanuli na 18 let', *Kommersant*, 23 November 2023, https://www.kommersant.ru/doc/6352594.
128. Mikola Mirniy, 'Over 30 Citizens of Ukraine Are Persecuted for Participation in the Noman Çelebicihan Crimean Tatar Volunteer Battalion', *ZMINA*, 10 March 2023, https://zmina.info/en/articles-en/17-citizens-of-ukraine-are-persecuted-for-participation-in-the-noman-celebicihan-crimean-tatar-volunteer-battalion/.
129. 'Over 1.3M Ukrainians Already Deported to Russia—Ombudsperson', *Ukrinform*, 17 May 2022, https://www.ukrinform.net/rubric-society/3485634-over-13m-ukrainians-already-deported-to-russia-ombudsperson.html.
130. US National Intelligence Council, 'Russia's Filtration Operations and Forced Relocations', *United States Department of State*, 6 September 2022, https://www.state.gov/russias-filtration-operations-and-forced-relocations/.
131. Cited in Eastern Human Rights Group, 'Prinuditelnaya deportatsiya detei v RF' (Kyiv: Eastern Human Rights Group, December 2022), 11.
132. ICRC, 'Rule 129: The Act of Displacement', *International Committee for the Red Cross*, https://ihl-databases.icrc.org/en/customary-ihl/v1/rule129.
133. Human Rights Watch, '"We Had No Choice": "Filtration" and the Crime of Forcibly Transferring Ukrainian Civilians to Russia', *Human Rights Watch*, 1 September 2022, 20, https://www.hrw.org/report/2022/09/01/we-had-no-choice/filtration-and-crime-forcibly-transferring-ukrainian-civilians.
134. Christopher Miller, 'The Last Russia-Ukraine Border Crossing', *Financial Times*, 26 January 2024, https://www.ft.com/content/545f37fd-feaa-4066-bdd8-37683cbfcdce.
135. Olga Kanunnikova, 'Rossiiskaya pravozashchitnitsa Svetlana Gannushkina: Govorit, chto "my k etomu neprichastny" nevozmozhno', *Novaya gazeta Baltiya*,

14 April 2023, https://novayagazeta.ee/articles/2023/04/14/rossiiskaia-pravozashchitnitsa-svetlana-gannushkina-govorit-chto-my-k-etomu-neprichastny-nevozmozhno.

136. Pjotr Sauer, 'A Russian Pacifist Helped Ukrainians Flee the Country. Then the Kremlin Caught Him', *The Guardian*, 13 April 2024, https://www.theguardian.com/world/2024/apr/13/a-russian-pacifist-helped-ukrainians-flee-the-country-then-the-kremlin-caught-him.
137. Cited in Eastern Human Rights Group, 'Prinuditelnaya deportatsiya detei v RF', 11.
138. 'Ne zhdali. Kak ukrainskiye bezhentsy vyzhivayut v Rossii bez deneg, dokumentov i raboty', *Vazhnye istorii*, 23 June 2022, https://istories.media/reportages/2022/06/23/ne-zhdali/.
139. Viktoria Safronova, 'Pochemu Ukrainskiye bezhentsy ostayutsya v PVR v Rossii spustya dva goda', *BBC News Russian Service*, https://www.bbc.com/russian/articles/cqvn7zd81ezo.
140. Safronova, 'Pochemu Ukrainskiye bezhentsy ostayutsya v PVR'.
141. 'Za god c Ukrainy i iz Donbassa na territoriyu RF pribylo 5.3 mln bezhentsev', *TASS*, 20 February 2023, https://tass.ru/obschestvo/17091725.
142. Konstantin Troitsky, 'How Many Refugees from Ukraine Are There in Russia?', *Civic Assistance Committee*, 10 March 2023, https://refugee.ru/en/dokladyi/how-many-refugees/.
143. TASS, 'Za god c Ukrainy i iz Donbassa na territoriyu RF pribylo 5.3 mln bezhentsev'.
144. 'Over One Million Refugees from Donbass, Ukraine Receive Help from Russian Red Cross', *TASS*, 15 May 2023, https://tass.com/society/1617889.
145. Vasilyeva, 'Zagnannye kryshi'. This scheme was also in place for people living in other areas, where the Russians were encouraging evacuation because they were fortifying the left bank of the Dnipro River (interviews, Kyiv, May 2024).
146. Vasilyeva, 'Zagnannye kryshi'.
147. Vasilyeva, 'Zagnannye kryshi'.
148. Vasilyeva, 'Zagnannye kryshi'.
149. Vasilyeva, 'Zagnannye kryshi'.
150. Vasilyeva, 'Zagnannye kryshi'.
151. Shaun Walker, 'Deportation and Re-Education: Life in Russian-Occupied Areas of Ukraine', *The Guardian*, 6 March 2024, https://www.theguardian.com/world/2024/mar/06/deportation-re-population-russia-occupied-ukraine-zaporizhzhia.
152. 'Soldaty RF prinuditelno vygonyayut lyudei iz Zaporozhskoi oblasti za otkaz sotrudnichat s RF', YouTube [video], uploaded by @GENDOLHBELIY, 18 September 2022, https://www.youtube.com/watch?v=aah71jw1N6Y.
153. The talk of a 'gay-world' was part of an anti-LGBT agenda that formed a central pillar of Russia's propaganda campaigns, which advocated 'traditional values' as part of its wider anti-Western propaganda. 'Balitskii rasskazal o vyselenii na

Ukrainu tekh, kto ne podderzhival spetsoperatsiyu', *Vedomosti*, 25 February 2024, https://www.vedomosti.ru/strana/new_regions/news/2024/02/25/1022013-balitskii-rasskazal-viselenii; see also Fridrih Show (@FridrihShow), Telegram post, 20 February 2024, https://t.me/FridrihShow/10276.

154. These deportations were almost certainly a violation of international humanitarian law. Article 49 of the fourth Geneva Convention of 1949 prohibits both 'individual' and 'mass forcible transfers'. The Israeli Supreme Court has ruled that Israel's practice of individual deportations from occupied Palestinian territories did not violate international law, claiming that the provision in the Convention does not apply to individual deportations. But most international lawyers reject that interpretation. Yoram Dinstein has argued that, 'In conformity with the ordinary meaning of the words of the first paragraph of Article 49 in their context, every deportation of protected persons from occupied territories is interdicted, regardless of the individual or collective nature of the act or its motive.' See Yoram Dinstein, 'The Israel Supreme Court and the Law of Belligerent Occupation: Deportations', in *Israel Yearbook on Human Rights*, Vol. 23, ed. Yoram Dinstein (Leiden: Brill Nijhoff, 1993), 1–26 (15).

155. ICC, 'Situation in Ukraine: ICC Judges Issue Arrest Warrants against Vladimir Vladimirovich Putin and Maria Alekseyevna Lvova-Belova', *International Criminal Court*, 17 March 2023, https://www.icc-cpi.int/news/situation-ukraine-icc-judges-issue-arrest-warrants-against-vladimir-vladimirovich-putin-and.

156. 'Putin's Children's Envoy Reveals She Adopted Child from Mariupol', *The Moscow Times*, 27 November 2023, https://www.themoscowtimes.com/2023/02/16/putins-childrens-envoy-reveals-she-adopted-child-from-mariupol-a80249.

157. Hillary Andersson, 'Missing Ukrainian Child Traced to Putin Ally', *BBC News*, 23 November 2023, https://www.bbc.com/news/world-europe-67488646.

158. Eastern Human Rights Group, 'Prinuditelnaya deportatsiya detei v RF'.

159. Interview, Ombudsman's office, Kyiv, February 2024.

160. Human Rights Watch, 'Key Recommendations on the Reform of Ukraine's Child Protection and Care System', *Human Rights Watch*, 15 June 2023, https://www.hrw.org/news/2023/06/15/key-recommendations-reform-ukraines-child-protection-and-care-system.

161. Yousur Al-Hlou and Masha Froliak, '46 Children Were Taken from Ukraine. Many Are Up for Adoption in Russia', *The New York Times*, 2 June 2024, https://www.nytimes.com/2024/06/02/world/europe/ukraine-children-russia-war.html.

162. '"A Concentration Camp for Kids:" Journalists Discovered 14 Ukrainian Orphans from Kherson in a Crimean Orphanage with Brutal Conditions', *Meduza*, 27 January 2023, https://meduza.io/en/feature/2023/01/27/a-concentration-camp-for-kids.

163. 'V Khersonskoi oblasti proinspektirovali gotovyashchiisya k otkrytiyu "Dom

rebenka'", *MK.ru*, 28 May 2024, https://www.mk-herson.ru/social/2024/05/28/v-khersonskoy-oblasti-proinspektirovali-gotovyashhiysya-k-otkrytiyu-dom-rebenka.html.

164. Ministry of Labour and Social Protection, Kherson region (@socialpolitics_ks), Telegram post, 6 August 2023, https://web.archive.org/web/20240208104946/https://t.me/socialpolitics_ks/1856.
165. Al-Hlou and Froliak, '46 Children Were Taken from Ukraine'.
166. 'Kastyukevich zhestko otreagiroval na rassledovaniye NYT o khersonskikh detyakh', *Argumenty i Fakty*, 4 June 2024, https://aif.ru/society/law/kastyukevich-zhestko-otreagiroval-na-rassledovanie-nyt-o-hersonskih-detyah.
167. Carlotta Gall et al., 'Ukraine's Stolen Children', *The New York Times*, 27 December 2023, https://www.nytimes.com/interactive/2023/12/26/world/europe/ukraine-war-children-russia.html.
168. Smirnova, 'Chto mozhet byt khuzhe?'.
169. Smirnova, 'Chto mozhet byt khuzhe?'.
170. Smirnova, 'Chto mozhet byt khuzhe?'.
171. Smirnova, 'Chto mozhet byt khuzhe?'.
172. Gall et al., 'Ukraine's Stolen Children'.
173. Interview, February 2024.
174. Al-Hlou and Froliak, '46 Children Were Taken from Ukraine'.
175. Katya Bonch-Osmolovskaya and Anna Ryzhkova, '"I Want to Go Home"', *IStories*, 3 April 2024, https://istories.media/en/stories/2024/04/03/donbas-children/.
176. Geneva Convention (IV) Relative to the Protection of Civilian Persons in Time of War, Geneva, 12 August 1949, Articles 49 and 50, https://ihl-databases.icrc.org/en/ihl-treaties/gciv-1949.
177. Yulia Ioffe, 'Forcibly Transferring Ukrainian Children to the Russian Federation: A Genocide?', *Journal of Genocide Research* 25, no. 3–4 (2023): 315–51.
178. James Glanz et al., 'Why the Evidence Suggests Russia Blew Up the Kakhovka Dam', *The New York Times*, 16 June 2023, https://www.nytimes.com/interactive/2023/06/16/world/europe/ukraine-kakhovka-dam-collapse.html.
179. Christopher Miller and Anastasia Stognei, 'Ukrainians in Flooded Towns under Russian Control Plead for Help', *Financial Times*, 9 June 2023, https://www.ft.com/content/7e6d368a-22bc-4b92-a95f-402db61822d5.
180. 'V zatoplennykh Oleshkakh pogibli desyatki lyudei, MChS RF ne propuskayet v gorod lodki so spasatelyami, opasayas diversionnykh grupp—volonter', *The Insider*, August 2023, https://theins.info/news/262417.
181. Vasilyeva, 'Zagnannye kryshi'.
182. Samya Kullab and Illia Novikov, 'Russia Covered Up and Undercounted True Human Cost of Floodings after Dam Explosion, AP Investigation Finds', *AP News*, 28 December 2023, https://apnews.com/article/russia-ukraine-war-dam-collapse-kakhovka-kherson-daacdc431f42912dfb91548794f03a3c.

183. Izolda Drobina, 'Voda uidet, ostanetsya tolko gryaz', *Novaya gazeta*, 10 June 2023, https://novayagazeta.ru/articles/2023/06/10/voda-uidet-ostanetsia-tolko-griaz.
184. 'Situatsiya v zone zatopleniya (levyi bereg Dnepra)', *BBC News Russian Service*, 10 June 2023, https://www.bbc.com/russian/live/news-65849028?page=44.
185. Kullab and Novikov, 'Russia Covered Up and Undercounted'.
186. Olga Voitovych, 'Zelensky Says Russians Shooting at Rescuers in Flooded Areas', *CNN*, 8 June 2023, https://www.cnn.com/2023/06/08/europe/ukraine-rescue-efforts-nova-kakhovka-dam-intl-hnk/index.html.
187. Smirnova, 'Chto mozhet byt khuzhe?'.
188. Smirnova, 'Chto mozhet byt khuzhe?'.
189. Kateryna Zakharchenko and Chris York, 'The Secretive Ukraine Partisan Center Causing Havoc Behind Enemy Lines', *KyivPost*, 30 August 2023, https://www.kyivpost.com/post/21087.
190. 'Khto my', *National Resistance Center*, https://sprotyv.mod.gov.ua/hto-my/.
191. McGlynn, 'Crossing Thresholds', 10.
192. 'Inside Ukraine's Assassination Programme', *The Economist*, 5 September 2023, https://www.economist.com/europe/2023/09/05/inside-ukraines-assassination-programme.
193. 'Collaborationist Officials Targeted and Killed in Ukraine's Occupied Territories', *Meduza*, 30 August 2022, https://meduza.io/en/feature/2022/08/30/collaborationist-officials-targeted-and-killed-in-ukraine-s-occupied-territories.
194. Yaffa, 'A Ukrainian City'.
195. Anhelina Sheremet, 'In Kherson, the Car of Collaborator Dmytro Savluchenko Was Blown Up. He Died on the Spot', *Babel*, 24 June 2022, https://babel.ua/en/news/80450-in-kherson-the-car-of-collaborator-dmytro-savluchenko-was-blown-up-he-died-on-the-spot.
196. 'Ukraina pereshla k terrorizmu v Zaporozhskoi oblasti, soobshchili vlasti regiona', *RIA Novosti*, 13 June 2022, https://ria.ru/20220613/terror-1794977183.html.
197. Olesya Pavlenko, 'Genprokuror LNR pogib pri vzryve v Luganske', *Kommersant*, 16 September 2022, https://www.kommersant.ru/doc/5569158.
198. Mariana Migal, 'U Khersoni zahynuv vodii "ministerky sotspolityky", kolaboranty vidreahuvaly smikhom', *Glavcom*, 16 September 2022, https://glavcom.ua/country/incidents/vibukhi-u-budivli-sudu-okupovanoho-khersona-poranena-mistseva-kolaborantka--875728.html.
199. Savina and Bonch-Osmolovskaya, 'Eto vy ne so mnoi razgovarivaete. Ego netu'.
200. 'Sprotyv' (@sprotyv_official), Telegram post, 13 October 2023, https://t.me/sprotyv_official/3183.
201. 'Car Bomb Goes off in Assassination Attempt on Russian-Appointed Mariupol Police Chief', *Meduza*, 27 March 2023, https://meduza.io/en/news/2023/03/27/car-bomb-goes-off-in-assassination-attempt-on-russian-appointed-chief-of-mariupol-police.

202. 'Interior Minister of Self-Declared "LNR" Igor Kornet Seriously Injured in Explosion', *Meduza*, 15 May 2023, https://meduza.io/en/news/2023/05/15/interior-minister-of-self-declared-lnr-igor-kornet-seriously-injured-in-explosion.
203. 'V "LNR" podorvali byvshego nachalnika tamozhni', *The Moscow Times, Russian Service*, 5 September 2023, https://www.moscowtimes.ru/2023/09/05/v-lnr-podorvali-bivshego-nachalnika-tamozhni-a105922.
204. 'Chto izvestno o gibeli deputata Filiponenko v Luganske', *TASS*, 5 September 2023, https://tass.ru/proisshestviya/19230867.
205. HUR [Ukrainian military intelligence] (@DIUkraine), Telegram post, 8 November 2023, https://t.me/DIUkraine/3038.
206. McGlynn, 'Crossing Thresholds', 18.
207. Irina Pogorelaya, 'Vo vremenno okkupirovannom Mariupole likvidirovali shest okkupantov', *Unian*, 27 November 2023, https://www.unian.net/war/novosti-mariupolya-vo-vremenno-okkupirovannom-gorode-likvidirovano-shest-okkupantov-12467811.html.
208. Tatiana Odnoletok, 'Rossiyane prodolzhayut volny zachistok pod Mariupolem: kuda okkupanty dvinulis s raspravami', *Unian*, 1 December 2023, https://www.unian.net/war/rossiyane-prodolzhayut-volny-zachistok-pod-mariupolem-kuda-okkupanty-dvinulis-s-raspravami-12471774.html.
209. President of Russia, 'Rasshirennoe zasedanie kollegii MVD', *President of Russia*, 3 April 2024, http://kremlin.ru/events/president/news/73770.
210. Zakharchenko and York, 'National Resistance Center'.
211. Watkin, 'Occupation: Treachery, Treason and Ukraine's War in the Shadows', 31.
212. Interview, 2024.
213. Yellow Ribbon (Zhovta strichka), https://www.zhovtastrichka.org/.
214. According to its website, the group was established in 2023. See https://zlamavka.com/.
215. James C. Scott, *Weapons of the Weak: Everyday Forms of Peasant Resistance* (New Haven, CT: Yale University Press, 1985).
216. Scott, *Weapons of the Weak*.
217. Andrew S. Bowen and Matthew C. Weed, 'War Crimes in Ukraine', *Congressional Research Service*, 16 October 2023, https://crsreports.congress.gov/product/pdf/R/R47762.

5. PROPAGANDA

1. David Lewis, 'Blogging Zhanaozen: Hegemonic Discourse and Authoritarian Resilience in Kazakhstan', *Central Asian Survey* 35, no. 3 (2016), 422.
2. A. Bartosh, 'Strategiya i kontrstrategiya gibridnoi voiny', *Voennaya Mysl*, 10 October 2018.
3. Vladislav Surkov, 'Natsionalizatsiya budushchego', *surkov.info*, 6 December 2006, https://surkov.info/nacionalizaciya-budushhego-polnaya-versiya/.

4. Stephen Hutchings, Vera Tolz, Precious Chatterje-Doody, Rhys Crilley and Marie Gillespie, *Russia, Disinformation, and the Liberal Order: RT as Populist Pariah* (Ithaca, NY: Cornell University Press, 2024).
5. For a detailed account of information confrontation, see Michelle Grisé, Alyssa Demus, Yuliya Shokh, Marta Kepe, Jonathan W. Welburn and Khrystyna Holnska, 'Rivalry in the Information Sphere: Russian Conceptions of Information Confrontation', *RAND Corporation*, 18 August 2022, https://www.rand.org/pubs/research_reports/RRA198-8.html.
6. Gavin Wilde and Justin Sherman, 'No Water's Edge: Russia's Information War and Regime Security', *Carnegie Endowment for International Peace*, 4 January 2023, https://carnegieendowment.org/2023/01/04/no-water-s-edge-russia-s-information-war-and-regime-security-pub-88644.
7. David Lewis, 'Contesting Liberal Peace: Russia's Emerging Model of Conflict Management', *International Affairs* 98, no. 2 (2022): 653–73.
8. Holger Roonemaa and Marta Vunsh, 'Kremlin Leaks: Secret Files Reveal How Putin Pre-Rigged his Reelection', *VSquare*, 26 February 2024, https://vsquare.org/kremlin-leaks-putin-elections-russia-propaganda-ukraine/.
9. Ministry of Foreign Affairs, Russia (@MID_RF), '#Zakharova: V svoyom stremlenii perepisat istoriyu kiyevskii rezhim gotov na lyubye shagi' (tweet), X, 3 May 2023, https://x.com/MID_RF/status/1653673824460718080.
10. Mykola Homanyuk, 'Reich, Union, Rossija', *Zeitschrift Osteuropa* 72, no. 12 (2022): 13–29.
11. Zakharov, Lotareva and Gerasimenko, 'Skoro perestroites'.
12. Homanyuk, 'Reich, Union, Rossija'.
13. On the Holodomor, see note 81, Chapter 1.
14. 'V Mariupole demontirovali pamyatnik "Zhertvam golodomora"', *Kommersant*, 19 October 2022, https://www.kommersant.ru/doc/5621133.
15. See Andriewsky, 'Towards a Decentred History'.
16. Tondo and Mamo, 'Some Never Came Back'.
17. Georgiy Kasianov, 'In Search of Lost Time? Decommunization in Ukraine, 2014–2020', *Problems of Post-Communism* 71, no. 4 (2024): 326-340 (334). In the south, 73% of residents opposed the changing of Soviet-era place names, and a majority of those in the south and east did not see a need for the decommunisation campaign.
18. Homanyuk, 'Reich, Union, Rossija'.
19. Gentile, 'The "Elephant" in Mariupol'.
20. Homanyuk, 'Reich, Union, Rossija'.
21. President of Russia, 'Obrashchenie Prezidenta Rossiiskoi Federatsii', *President of Russia*, 21 February 2022, http://kremlin.ru/events/president/news/67828.
22. Julian E. Barnes, 'U.S. Believes Ukrainians Were Behind an Assassination in Russia', *The New York Times*, 5 October 2022, https://www.nytimes.com/2022/10/05/us/politics/ukraine-russia-dugina-assassination.html.
23. 'V Melitopole poyavilis ulitsy v chest Dari Duginoi i Aleksandra Zakharchenko', *Kommersant*, 12 April 2023, https://www.kommersant.ru/doc/5927905.

24. Samuel Arthur Casper, *The Bolshevik Afterlife: Posthumous Rehabilitation in the Post-Stalin Soviet Union, 1953–1970*, Doctoral Thesis (University of Pennsylvania, 2018), 198–99.
25. See note 82, Chapter 1.
26. Trevor Erlacher, *Ukrainian Nationalism in the Age of Extremes: An Intellectual Biography of Dmytro Dontsov* (Cambridge, MA: Harvard University Press, 2021).
27. President of Russia, 'Interview to Tucker Carlson', *President of Russia*, 9 February 2024, http://en.kremlin.ru/events/president/news/73411. In 1941–42 Roman Shukhevych commanded auxiliary Ukrainian units under German command (the Nachtigall Battalion and the Schutzmannschaft Battalion 201) and was subsequently the military leader of the UPA, which was implicated in the massacres of tens of thousands of Poles in 1943-44. For a discussion of the rehabilitation of Shukhevych in modern Ukraine, see P. A. Rudling, 'The Cult of Roman Shukhevych in Ukraine: Myth Making with Complications', *Fascism: Journal of Comparative Fascist Studies* 5, no. 1 (2016): 26–65.
28. Andrei Pokrovsky, 'Po stopam Sudoplatova: k chemu prizyvaet Konstantinov v Krymu?', *Krym.Realii*, 21 August 2023, https://ru.krymr.com/a/vladimir-konstantinov-metody-sudoplatova-krym-rossiya-politicheskiye-ubiystva/32557301.html.
29. 'B Melitopole otkryli namyatnik Pavlu Sudoplatovu', *RIA Novosti*, 7 July 2022, https://ria.ru/20220707/melitopol-1801007033.html.
30. The propaganda campaigns in the occupied territories had opened up new opportunities for Russia's ideological entrepreneurs. The monument to Sudoplatov was erected by the Russian Military-Historical Society (RVIO), a formally independent organisation that had been at the forefront of a new wave of 'patriotic' memorialisation across Russia, headed by nationalist former culture minister, Vadim Medinsky. A monument to Sudoplatov was also established in Donetsk in October 2022. 'V Donetske otkryli pamyatnik znamenitomu razvedchiku Pavlu Sudoplatovu', *Rossiiskaya gazeta*, 28 October 2022, https://rg.ru/2022/10/28/v-donecke-otkryli-pamiatnik-znamenitomu-razvedchiku-pavlu-sudoplatovu.html.
31. 'Biust Pavlu Sudoplatovu ustanovlen v Melitopole', *Rossiiskoe voenno-istoricheskoe obshchestvo*, 7 July 2022, https://rvio.histrf.ru/activities/news/byust-pavlu-sudoplatovu-ustanovlen-v-melitopole.
32. 'Khto formue "dobrovolchi zagony" kolaborantiv na pivdni Ukraini', *Center of Journalistic Investigations*, 28 October 2022, https://investigator.org.ua/ua/investigations/248071/.
33. President of Ukraine, 'On the Day of Defenders of Ukraine, the President Presented State Awards and Took Part in the Oath Taking by Military Lyceum Students', *President of Ukraine*, 1 October 2023, https://www.presidcnt.gov.ua/en/news/u-den-zahisnikiv-i-zahisnic-ukrayini-prezident-vruchiv-derzh-86009.
34. 'Eastern Donbas: Freedom in the World 2023 Country Report', *Freedom House*,

35. Aseyev, *In Isolation*.
36. Shaun Walker and Pjotr Sauer, '"Tavriya TV Will Promote Happiness and Love": Russia Opens Station in Occupied Kherson', *The Guardian*, 27 August 2022, https://www.theguardian.com/world/2022/aug/27/tavriya-tv-will-promote-happiness-love-russia-opens-station-occupied-kherson.
37. Zakharov, Lotareva and Gerasimenko, 'Skoro perestroites'.
38. Yaffa, 'A Ukrainian City'.
39. Reporters Without Borders, 'Occupied Territories of Ukraine: RSF Calls on Russia to Release a Ukrainian Journalist and Her Colleagues who Have Been Held in Secret Detention for Nearly Eight Months', *RSF*, 10 April 2024, https://rsf.org/en/occupied-territories-ukraine-rsf-calls-russia-release-ukrainian-journalist-and-her-colleagues-who.
40. 'Analysis: TV in Ukraine's Occupied Kherson, Zaporizhzhya Regions', *BBC Monitoring*, 23 December 2022, https://monitoring.bbc.co.uk/product/c203z73f.
41. Ilya Vasyunin, 'Zdes skuchali po russkomu yazyku: i. o. mera Melitopolya—o vozvrashchenii goroda k mirnoy zhizni', *RT*, 27 March 2022, https://russian.rt.com/ussr/article/981819-melitopol-vlasti-vosstanovlenie-goroda-ukraina.
42. 'Ha vsei territorii Khersonskoi oblasti naladili Rossiiskoe televeshchanie', *TASS*, 21 June 2022, https://tass.ru/armiya-i-opk/14980507.
43. 'Reportery ubedilis, chto rossiiskie voennie i novye vlasti vosstanavlivayut mirnuyu zhizn v Berdianske', *Krym 24*, 30 April 2022, https://crimea24tv.ru/content/reportyori-ubedilis-chto-rossiyskie-v/.
44. Tatyana Badalova, 'Vklyuchaemsya v "Russikii Mir"!', *Komsomolskaya pravda*, 19 February 2023, https://www.donetsk.kp.ru/daily/27467/4722932/.
45. 'Russkii mir', https://rusmirtv.ru/.
46. Aleksei Mikolenko, '"Russkii mir" vyzval na boi "Gorynychei"', *ComNews*, 4 June 2024, https://www.comnews.ru/content/233540/2024-06-04/2024-w23/1007/russkiy-mir-vyzval-boy-gorynychey.
47. Vladislav Skobelev and Irina Yuzbekova, 'Rossiiskii telefonnii kod: kto stroit seti svyazi v Khersonskoi oblasti i Zaporozhye', *Forbes*, 27 May 2022, https://www.forbes.ru/tekhnologii/467029-rossijskij-telefonnyj-kod-kto-stroit-seti-svazi-v-hersonskoj-oblasti-i-zaporoz-e; see also 'Operatory vybirayut mezhdu sanktsiyami i Donbassom, Dzhonson usidel v kresle, bankam razreshat sbrosit zamorozhennye aktivy', *The Bell*, 7 June 2022, https://thebell.io/operatory-vybirayut-mezhdu-sanktsiyami-i-donbassom-dzhonson-usidel-v-kresle-bankam-razreshat-sbrosit-zamorozhennye-aktivy.
48. Nikita Korolev and Yulia Yurasova, '"Miranda-media" raskidyvaet seti', *Kommersant*, 13 March 2023, https://www.kommersant.ru/doc/5873563. Miranda-Media was a company registered in Crimea in 2004 in which Russian state telecoms company Rostelecom had almost 20% of the shares, with the rest

owned by a little-known shipping company called Liukstrans. Anna Ustinova, 'Krymskii operator svyazi "Miranda-media" vsled za DNR zakhodit v LNR', *Vedomosti*, 6 April 2023, https://www.vedomosti.ru/technology/articles/2023/04/06/969710-krimskii-operator-svyazi-miranda-media-vsled-za-dnr-zahodit-i-v-lnr.

49. 'Mediana vse—rashisty v Melitopole priznali, chto provaider prekratil svoyu deytelnost', *RIA-Melitopol*, 7 February 2023, https://ria-m.tv/news/311290/mediana_vse_rashistyi_v_melitopole_priznali_chto_provayder_prekratil_svoyu_deyatelnost.html.
50. Drozdova, Dukach and Kelm, 'Telegram Occupation'.
51. On Malkevich's Ukraine operations, see Reporters Without Borders, 'The Malkevich Propaganda Machine, the Wagner-Allied Network in Ukraine', *RSF*, 20 April 2023, https://rsf.org/en/investigation-mysterious-alexander-malkevich-kremlin-propagandist-ukraine. On his previous career, see Amy Mackinnon, 'Russian Troll or Clumsy Publicity Hound?', *Foreign Policy*, 15 June 2018, https://foreignpolicy.com/2018/06/15/russian-troll-or-clumsy-publicity-hound-putin-russia-troll-factory-russia/.
52. Malkevich Live (@malkevich_live), Telegram post, 29 March 2024, https://t.me/malkevich_live/3527.
53. The Russian Government, 'Mikhail Mishustin vruchil premii Pravitelstva za 2022 god v oblasti sredstv massovoi informatsii', *The Russian Government*, 3 November 2023, http://government.ru/news/47525/.
54. 'Okkupirovav Ukrainskie territorii, Rossiya zakhvatila i vse mestnye universitety', *Bereg*, 20 October 2023, https://bereg.io/feature/2023/10/20/okkupirovav-ukrainskie-territorii-rossiya-zahvatila-i-vse-mestnye-universitety-teper-vlasti-integriruyut-byvshie-ukrainskie-vuzy-i-uchat-studentov-priemam-informatsionnoy-voyny.
55. Reporters Without Borders, 'Mediatopol in South-East Ukraine: Officially a Journalism School, in Reality a Propaganda School in the Service of the Kremlin', *RSF*, 22 September 2023, https://rsf.org/en/mediatopol-south-east-ukraine-officially-journalism-school-reality-propaganda-school-service.
56. Maxim Edwards, 'The Truth over the Dnieper', *London Review of Books* (blog), 1 February 2023, https://www.lrb.co.uk/blog/2023/february/the-truth-over-the-dnieper.
57. YouTube channel: https://www.youtube.com/@MashainMariupol2.
58. YouTube channel: https://www.youtube.com/@walkandtalk_.
59. 'Novoe.Media', 2024, https://novoe.media/.
60. 'Ukrainians Increasingly Rely on Telegram Channels for News and Information during Wartime', *Internews in Ukraine*, 1 November 2023, 67, https://internews.in.ua/news/ukrainians-increasingly-rely-on-telegram-channels-for-news-and-information-during-wartime/.
61. Vasilyeva, 'Vsei semei pereselimsia v odnu komnatu i budem dyshat'.
62. Jeremy Doran, 'Ukrainians Consume More News, Are More Resilient to

Disinformation, and Trust Their Media More During Russia's War in 2022', *Internews*, 28 November 2022, 38, https://internews.org/ukrainians-consume-more-news-are-more-resilient-to-disinformation-and-trust-their-media-more-during-russias-war-in-2022/.

63. Reporters Without Borders, 'Ukraine: RSF Calls on Government to Put an End to Telemarathon', *RSF*, 6 February 2024, https://rsf.org/en/ukraine-rsf-calls-government-put-end-telemarathon.

64. Raiko had only begun painting at the age of 69. Her house was her canvas. She covered the walls with natural murals inspired by the landscapes and animals of southern Ukraine. See Emma Graham-Harrison, '"Masterpiece" House is Latest Victim of Putin's War on Ukrainian Heritage', *The Guardian*, 12 June 2023, https://www.theguardian.com/world/2023/jun/12/masterpiece-house-is-latest-victim-of-putins-war-on-ukrainian-heritage.

65. Bill Whitaker, 'Ukraine Accuses Russia of Looting Museums as Part of Heritage War', *60 Minutes—CBS News*, 12 November 2023, https://www.cbsnews.com/news/ukraine-accuses-russia-museum-looting-church-destruction-60-minutes-transcript/.

66. Konstantin Akinsha, 'Scythian Gold is at the Heart of Russia's Identity War', *The Art Newspaper*, 19 January 2023, https://www.theartnewspaper.com/2023/01/19/scythian-gold-is-at-the-heart-of-russias-identity-war.

67. The Russian Foreign Ministry called it a 'dangerous precedent' and commented that Scythian gold was 'part of the cultural heritage of Crimea, and no decisions of biased courts can annul this indisputable fact': 'Rossiya otvetit na reshenie Niderlandov o peredache zolota skifov Kievu', *RIA Novosti*, https://ria.ru/20230609/zoloto-1877319250.html.

68. Aleksandr Blok, 'Skify', *Sobranie sochinenii Aleksandra Bloka*, Tom 4 (Berlin: Alkonost, 1923), 29.

69. Sakina Nurieva, 'Rogozin protsitiroval stikhotvorenie Bloka, opisivaya rol Rossii v mire', *Gazeta.ru*, 29 November 2023, https://www.gazeta.ru/science/news/2022/03/07/17391481.shtml.

70. Whitaker, 'Ukraine Accuses Russia of Looting Museums'.

71. 'Fihurant rozsliduvannia TsZhR melitopolskyi rekonstruktor Horlachov otrymav pidozru za uchast v "batalioni Sudoplatova"', *Center of Journalistic Investigations*, 21 September 2023, https://investigator.org.ua/ua/news-2/258698/.

72. 'Voennye RF vernuli skifskoe zoloto i drugie relikvii v muzei Melitopolya', *Krasnaya Vesna*, 14 May 2022, https://rossaprimavera.ru/news/90441aa0.

73. 'Zo otvazhnoe vorovstvo—v Melitopole okkupanty nagradili medalyu odioznogo kollaboranta', *RIA-Pivden*, 21 June 2023, https://ria-m.tv/news/322484/za_otvajnoe_vorovstvo_v_melitopole_okkupantyi_nagradili_medalyu_odioznogo_kollaboranta_(foto).html.

74. 'Okkupanty proverili, kakie artefakty eshche ostalis v Maryupolskom kraevedcheskom muzee', *0629.com.ua*, 15 December 2023, https://www.0629.com.ua/ru/news/3705465/okkupanty-proverili-kakie-artefakty-ese-ostalis-v-mariupolskom-kraevedceskom-muzee-foto.

75. Aleksandr Yankovskii and Alena Badyuk, 'Banalnyi grabezh. Chto proskhodit s muzeyami na okkupirovannykh zemlyakh?', *Krym.Realii*, 12 March 2024, https://ru.krymr.com/a/okkupant-rossii-vyvezli-muzeynyye-eksponaty-yug-ukraina/32857143.html.
76. Aleksandr Yankovskii, 'Vyvezennyi Kuindzhi, Aivazovskii i Dubovskii. Rossiyane grabyat muzei yuga Ukrainy', *Krym.Realii*, 4 May 2022, https://ru.krymr.com/a/rossiya-ukraina-voyna-rossiyane-grabyat-muzei-uga-ukrainy/31832614.html.
77. Maria Kutnyakova, 'Pravda pro Mariupolskyi kraieznavchyi muzei. Bloh Marii Kutniakovoi', *0629.com.ua*, 11 April 2023, https://www.0629.com.ua/news/3578241/pravda-pro-mariupolskij-kraeznavcij-muzej-blog-marii-kutnakovoi.
78. 'Okupanty vykraly kartyny Kuindzhi v Mariupoli. Khto vidkryv skhovyshche rossiianam, i shcho vzahali vidbuvalos v muzei', *0629.com.ua*, 29 April 2022, https://www.0629.com.ua/news/3380322/okupanti-vikrali-kartini-kuindzi-v-mariupoli-hto-vidkriv-shovise-rosianam-i-so-vzagali-vidbuvalos-v-muzei-foto-video.
79. 0629.com.ua, 'Okupanty vykraly kartyny Kuindzhi v Mariupoli'.
80. 'Vykradachka kartyn Kuindzhi, eks-dyrektorka mariupolskoho muzeiu provela vystavku "Zvychainyi fashyzm" v Rostovi', *0629.com.ua*, 11 April 2023, https://www.0629.com.ua/news/3578089/vikradacka-kartin-kuindzi-eks-direktorka-mariupolskogo-muzeu-provela-vistavku-zvicajnij-fasizm-v-rostovi-foto.
81. Yankovskii and Badyuk, 'Banalnyi grabezh'.
82. Human Rights Watch, 'Ukraine: Russians Pillage Kherson Cultural Institutions', *Human Rights Watch*, 20 December 2022, https://www.hrw.org/news/2022/12/20/ukraine-russians-pillage-kherson-cultural-institutions.
83. Igor Burdyga, 'Kak Ukraina ishchet propavshie muzeinye kollektsii', *DW*, 18 March 2024, https://www.dw.com/ru/kartiny-prestuplenia-gde-iskat-propavsie-muzejnye-kollekcii-iz-ukrainy/a-68601208.
84. Human Rights Watch, 'Ukraine: Russians Pillage Kherson Cultural Institutions'.
85. Alya Shandra, 'Take a Look at the Unique Paintings Russia Looted from the Kherson Art Museum', *Euromaidan Press*, 27 January 2023, https://euromaidanpress.com/2023/01/27/take-a-look-at-the-unique-paintings-russia-looted-from-ukraines-kherson-art-museum/.
86. Vasilyeva, 'Vsei semei pereselimsia v odnu komnatu i budem dyshat'.
87. James Beardsworth, 'Kherson Museum Art Collection Looted Ahead of Russian Retreat', *The Moscow Times*, 11 November 2022, https://www.themoscowtimes.com/2022/11/10/kherson-museum-art-collection-looted-ahead-of-russian-retreat-a79342.
88. Yelyzaveta Kamenieva, 'Kherson Museum: What Did the Russians Steal, and How Did the Staff Save the Exhibits?', *Svidomi*, 31 January 2023, https://svidomi.in.ua/en/page/kherson-museum-what-did-the-russians-steal-and-how-did-the-staff-save-the-exhibits.
89. Jeffrey Gettleman and Oleksandra Mykolyshyn, 'As Russians Steal Ukraine's

Art, they Attack its Identity, Too', *The New York Times*, 14 January 2023, https://www.nytimes.com/2023/01/14/world/asia/ukraine-art-russia-steal.html.

90. '"Iakby ne kolaboranty, my by vriatuvaly muzei vid rosiian". Interviu z dyrektorkoiu Khersonsoho khudozhnoho muzeiu', *Ukrainska pravda*, 12 November 2022, https://life.pravda.com.ua/culture/2022/11/12/251267/.

91. Dmitrii Shvets, '"It's Sacred: Once it's in a Museum, it's Beyond Return". How War Artifacts and Stolen Kherson Exhibits Make Their Way into Russian Museums', *Mediazona*, 25 January 2024, https://en.zona.media/article/2024/01/25/museums.

92. US Department of State, 'The United States Takes Sweeping Actions on the One Year Anniversary of Russia's War Against Ukraine', 24 February 2023, https://www.state.gov/the-united-states-takes-sweeping-actions-on-the-one-year-anniversary-of-russias-war-against-ukraine/.

93. Mark Santora, 'Why Russia Stole Potemkin's Bones from Ukraine', *The New York Times*, 27 October 2022, https://www.nytimes.com/2022/10/27/world/europe/ukraine-russia-potemkin-bones.html.

94. Sergei Khazov-Cassia and Robert Coalson, 'Russian "History Parks" Present Kremlin-Friendly Take on the Past', *Radio Free Europe/Radio Liberty*, 13 October 2019, https://www.rferl.org/a/russian-orthodox-church-gazprom-history-parks/30214143.html.

95. 'Kiriyenko otkryl istoricheskii park "Rossiya—moya istoriya" v Melitopole', *Izvestiya*, 23 September 2023, https://iz.ru/1578487/2023–09–23/kirienko-otkryl-istoricheskii-park-rossiia-moia-istoriia-v-melitopole; Nikolai Korsakov, 'V Melitopole otkrylsya istoricheskii kompleks', *Gazeta.ru*, 23 September 2023, https://www.gazeta.ru/social/news/2023/09/23/21349441.shtml.

96. Yekaterina Kudasova, 'Istoriya Azova. V parkakh vystavleno pyat multimediinykh shedevrov', *Argumenty i fakty*, 25 May 2023, https://aif.ru/culture/art/istoriya_azova_v_parkah_vystavleno_pyat_multimediynyh_shedevrov.

97. Alena Samokhvalova, '"Russkii Azov": Otpravlyaemsya v multimediinoe puteshestvie vo vremeni', *Argumenty i fakty*, 13 April 2024, https://aif.ru/culture/art/russkiy_azov_otpravlyaemsya_v_multimediynoe_puteshestvie_vo_vremeni.

98. Samokhvalova, 'Russkii Azov'.

99. Kudasova, 'Istoriya Azova'.

100. Samokhvalova, 'Russkii Azov'.

101. Samokhvalova, 'Russkii Azov'.

102. Yulia Yurasova, 'Novye subyekty kino', *Kommersant*, 7 July 2023, https://www.kommersant.ru/doc/6085019.

103. '"Everything from Love to Heroic Death". The Kremlin's New Cultural Policy Puts the War against Ukraine Front and Center in Russian Art', *Meduza*, 24 July 2024, https://meduza.io/en/feature/2024/07/24/everything-from-love-to-heroic-death.

NOTES

104. Svetlana Reiter, Kristina Safonova and Maria Zholobova, '"They're Ready to Forgive You." How the Kremlin's "Penance System" for Artists Works—and the Compromises They Make to Keep Their Jobs', *Meduza*, 21 November 2023, https://meduza.io/en/feature/2023/11/21/they-re-ready-to-forgive-you.
105. Reiter, Safonova and Zholobova, 'They're Ready to Forgive You'.
106. Valerie Hopkins and Georgy Birger, 'Changing His Tune for Mother Russia', *The New York Times*, 9 March 2023, https://www.nytimes.com/2023/03/09/world/europe/shaman-putin-russia-ukraine-war.html.
107. Ivan Stanislavskii, 'Teatr absurda. Kak Mariupolskii dramaticheskii izbavilsya ot glavnogo rezhissera', *LB.ua*, 21 September 2018, https://rus.lb.ua/culture/2018/09/21/408104_teatr_absurda_mariupolskiy.html.
108. Ukrainian media sources, 'Theatre Officials Try to Suppress Opening of Play in Mariupol', *Euromaidan Press*, 16 May 2016, https://euromaidanpress.com/2016/05/16/theatre-officials-try-to-suppress-opening-of-play-in-mariupol/.
109. The term *vatnik*, from the Russian for an old-fashioned quilted jacket, commonly used by poorer Russians, was widely used as a pejorative label for people with pro-Russian views. According to the anthropologist Deborah Jones, a vatnik was 'a sort of dystopian SpongeBob whose body consists of a cheap, scratched, and patched government-issue jacket filled with batting (vata), and who has an alcoholic's red nose, missing teeth, and a shiner over one eye'. Deborah A. Jones, 'The "Fascist" and the "Potato Beetle"', *American Ethnologist* 50, no. 1 (2023): 30–42 (39).
110. Isabel Coles, 'In Shattered Mariupol, Russia Uses a Theater to Legitimize its Occupation', *Wall Street Journal*, 21 June 2023, https://www.wsj.com/articles/in-shattered-mariupol-russia-uses-a-theater-to-legitimize-its-occupation-7af6fb8.
111. Coles, 'In Shattered Mariupol'.
112. Taisiya Bakhareva, '"Skazali, esli ya ne budu sotrudnichat s okkupantami, menya rasstrelyayut": mariupolskogo rezhissera Anatoliya Levchenko 10 mesyatsev derzhali v plenu', *Fakty.ua*, 20 November 2023, https://fakty.ua/ru/429225-quot-skazali-esli-ya-ne-budu-sotrudnichat-s-okkupantami-menya-rasstrelyayut-quot-mariupolskogo-rezhissera-anatoliya-levchenko-10-mesyacev-derzhali-v-plenu; Ivan Stanislavskyi, '"He Called to Set Kremlin on Fire,"—Theater Director Was Accused of Terrorism for a Chewing Gum Wrapper', *Kharkiv Human Rights Protection Group*, 2 November 2023, https://khpg.org//en/1608812999.
113. Coles, 'In Shattered Mariupol'.
114. Bakhareva, 'Skazali, esli ya ne budu sotrudnichat s okkupantami'.
115. Ksenia Bogdanova, 'Aleksandr Beglov: Peterburgskie stroiteli k 2025 g vosstanovyat Dramaticheskii teatr Mariupolya', *Komsomolskaya pravda*, 7 March 2024, https://www.kp.ru/daily/27577.5/4901050/.

116. Semen Shirochin, 'Mariupol Drama Theater: History, Architecture, Future after the Air Strike', *Zaborona*, 22 September 2022, https://zaborona.com/en/mariupol-drama-theater-60-years-of-history-from-construction-to-air-strike/.
117. Shirochin, 'Mariupol Drama Theater'; Andryushchenko Time, Telegram post, 28 August 2022, https://t.me/andriyshTime/2568.
118. Amnesty International, 'Ukraine: Children's Education is One More Casualty of Russian Aggression', *Amnesty International*, 11 December 2023, 10, https://www.amnesty.org/en/documents/eur50/7508/2023/en/.
119. Darya Poperechna, '"Na urotsi moiemu uchnevi z 2-ho klasu povidomyly pro zahybel tata". Iak tse—buty vchytelem pid chas viiny', *Ukrainska pravda*, 1 October 2023, https://life.pravda.com.ua/society/2023/10/1/256834/.
120. Poperechna, 'Na urotsi moiemu'.
121. Yaffa, 'A Ukrainian City'.
122. Sergei Prudnikov, 'Tyazhelo v reshenii: kak khersontsy gotovilis perebratsya na levoberezhe', *Izvestiya*, 10 November 2022, https://iz.ru/1423471/sergei-prudnikov/tiazhelo-v-reshenii-kak-khersontcy-gotovilis-perebratsia-na-levoberezhe.
123. Poperechna, 'Na urotsi moiemu'.
124. Amnesty International, 'Ukraine: Children's Education is One More Casualty', 9.
125. Valeria Pavlenko, 'The Underground School. How Kherson Teachers Taught Children Ukrainian Curriculum During Russian Occupation', *Texty.org.ua*, 1 February 2023, https://texty.org.ua/articles/108862/underground-school-how-kherson-teachers-taught-children-ukrainian-curriculum-during-russian-occupation/.
126. 'Uchitelya sabotiruyut, a uchenikov privlekayut v shkoly za 10 tysyach rublei', *Kholod*, 1, September 2022, https://holod.media/2022/09/01/1-september/.
127. Kholod, 'Uchitelya sabotiruyut'.
128. Kholod, 'Uchitelya sabotiruyut'.
129. Administratsiya Khersonskoi oblasti (@VGA_Kherson), Telegram post, 26 August 2022, https://t.me/VGA_Kherson/3027.
130. 'Kholod, 'Uchitelya sabotiruyut'.
131. Matthew Luxmoore, 'A Ukrainian School Grapples with the Legacy of Russian Occupation', *Wall Street Journal*, 16 December 2022, https://www.wsj.com/articles/a-ukrainian-school-grapples-with-the-legacy-of-russian-occupation-11671188815.
132. Human Rights Watch, 'Education under Occupation: Forced Russification of the School System in Occupied Ukrainian Territories', *Human Rights Watch*, 20 June 2024, https://www.hrw.org/report/2024/06/20/education-under-occupation/forced-russification-school-system-occupied-ukrainian.
133. Anna Murlykina, '"Lessons of Love". How Russian Schools Work in Mariupol,

and What They Teach the Children', *Texty.org.ua*, 2 November 2022, https://texty.org.ua/articles/108139/lessons-love-how-russian-schools-work-mariupol-and-what-they-teach-children/.

134. Kholod, 'Uchitelya sabotiruyut'.
135. Andrei Kots, 'Nichego ne zapreshchayut', *RIA Novosti*, 15 October 2023, https://ria.ru/20231015/yazyk-1902629224.html.
136. Natalya Podobed, 'Roditeli uchenikov shkoly No. 3 Genicheska vozmushcheny, chto pravila russkogo yazyka detyam obyasnyayut na ukrainskom', *Hersonka.ru*, 18 October 2023, https://hersonka.ru/news/167308.
137. 'Po menshei mere 250 uchitelei iz Rossii soglasilis rabotat na okkupirovannykh territoriyakh Ukrainy—SMI', *Censor.net*, 10 August 2022, https://censor.net/ru/news/3359843/uchitelya_iz_rf_o_rabote_na_okkupirovannyh_territoriyah_ukraina_30_let_promyvaet_mozgi_svoim_grajdanam.
138. Irina Babicheva, 'Uroki rossiiskogo. Kak tysyachi ukrainskikh pedagogov proshli perepodgotovku v Rostove', *161.ru*, 19 August 2022, https://161.ru/text/education/2022/08/19/71582156/.
139. Babicheva, 'Uroki rossiiskogo'.
140. Babicheva, 'Uroki rossiiskogo'.
141. Babicheva, 'Uroki rossiiskogo'.
142. Human Rights Watch, 'Education under Occupation'.
143. Murlykina, 'Lessons of Love'.
144. Murlykina, 'Lessons of Love'.
145. Online interviews, May–June 2024.
146. Murlykina, 'Lessons of Love'.
147. Murlykina, 'Lessons of Love'.
148. 'Uchitelya Donbassa sravnili ukrainskie i rossiiskie shkolnye programmy', *MK*, 8 May 2022, https://www.mk.ru/social/2022/05/08/uchitelya-donbassa-sravnili-ukrainskie-i-rossiyskie-shkolnye-programmy.html.
149. Human Rights Watch, 'Education under Occupation'.
150. Babicheva, 'Uroki rossiiskogo'; MK, 'Uchitelya Donbassa sravnili ukrainskie i rossiiskie shkolnye programmy'.
151. 'V shkolakh osvobozhdennykh territorii Ukrainy budut prepodavat ukrainskii yazyk', *RIA Novosti*, 9 July 2022, https://ria.ru/20220709/yazyk-1801458352.html.
152. Maria Fedotova, 'V Khersonskoi oblasti ofitsialnymi yazykami priznany russkii, ukrainskii i krymsko-tatarskii', *Kommersant*, 11 June 2023, https://www.kommersant.ru/doc/6042089.
153. Marina Rassolova, 'Kak teper izuchayut ukrainskii i russkii yazyki v khersonskikh shkolakh—razyasneniya ministra obrazovaniya', *Hersonka.ru*, 25 September 2023, https://hersonka.ru/news/164594.
154. Podobed, 'Roditeli uchenikov shkoly No. 3'.
155. Zhanna Golubitskaya, 'Trudnosti uchitelei novykh territorii napomnili minnoe pole: roditeli ne otpuskayut detei v shkolu', *MK*, 4 October 2023, https://

156. 'Piat shkil Khersonskoi oblasti vidmovylys perekhodyty na ukrainsku movu navchannia u pershykh klasakh', *Center of Journalistic Investigations*, 13 September 2017, https://investigator.org.ua/ua/news-2/201778/.
157. Golubitskaya, 'Trudnosti uchitelei novykh territorii napomnili minnoe pole'.
158. Human Rights Watch, 'Education under Occupation'.
159. Yurii Vasilev, 'Khersonskie shkoly izbavlyayutsya ot Ukrainskikh strakhov', *Vzglyad*, 31 August 2022, https://vz.ru/world/2022/8/31/1175310.html.
160. Yurii Vasilev, 'Khersonskie shkoly'.
161. Kasianov, 'In Search of Lost Time? Decommunization in Ukraine, 2014–2020', 7.
162. Kots, 'Nichego ne zapreshchayut'. The "Heavenly Hundred" (*Nebesna sotnia*) refers to those protestors who died during the Maidan revolution in 2014.
163. Aleksandr Fadeev, *Molodaya gvardiya* (Moscow, 1946).
164. Posylnyi, 'The Soviet Pillar of Belonging'.
165. Murlykina, 'Lessons of Love'.
166. Murlykina, 'Lessons of Love'.
167. Murlykina, 'Lessons of Love'.
168. Amnesty International, 'Ukraine: Children's Education is One More Casualty', 11.
169. 'O geroizme pedagogov, vnedrenii federalnykh standartov i preodolenii mrachnogo naslediya Ukrainy', *Donetskoe Agenstvo Novostei*, 30 October 2023, https://dan-news.ru/interview/o-geroizme-pedagogov-vnedrenii-federalnyh-standartov-i-preodolenii-mrachnogo/.
170. V. P. Medinskii and A. P. Torkunov, *Istoriya Rossii: ot 1945 god—nachala XXI veka* (Moscow, 2023), 403. See also 'V Moskve pokazali novye uchebniki po istorii s operatsiei na Ukraine', *RBK*, 7 August 2023, https://www.rbc.ru/politics/07/08/2023/64d1016a9a794763ffc7ab63.
171. Medinskii and Torkunov, *Istoriya Rossii*, 407–08.
172. Lilia Yapparova, '"Oni mogut nachat protivodeystvovat": Rossiiskie vlasti boyatsya detei, nasilno vyvezennykh iz Ukrainy. Ikh pytayutsya "perevospitat" i postavit pod zhestkii tsifrovoi kontrol', *Meduza*, 1 March 2024, https://meduza.io/feature/2024/03/11/oni-mogut-nachat-protivodeystvovat.
173. Yaffa, 'A Ukrainian City'.
174. 'Tysyachi izdanii s ekstremistskimi materialami izyaty iz bibliotek osvobozhdennykh rayonov', *Donetskoe Agenstvo Novostei*, 25 May 2022, https://dan-news.ru/obschestvo/tysjachi-izdanij-s-ekstremistskimi-materialami-izjaty-iz-bibliotek-osvobozhdennyh/.
175. Felix Corley, 'Occupied Ukraine: After 4 Months, are "Disappeared" Greek Catholic Priests Still Alive?', *Forum 18*, 23 March 2023, https://www.forum18.org/archive.php?article_id=2820.
176. Corley, 'Occupied Ukraine: After 4 Months, are "Disappeared" Greek Catholic Priests Still Alive?'.

177. 'Kak nikogda ranshe chuvstvuyetsya russkii dukh', *Verstka*, 21 November 2023, https://verstka.media/kak-rossiya-prodvigaet-svoyu-molodezhnuyu-politiku-na-okkupirovannyh-territoriyah.
178. Tatiana Tikhonova, '"Yug Molodoi"—bolshe tysyachi aktivistov v Zaporozhskoi oblasti za god', *Komsomolskaya pravda*, 5 August 2023, https://www.zap.kp.ru/daily/27538.5/4804300/.
179. Denis Dmitriev and Andrey Pertsev, 'Russian Lawmakers are Launching a New, Pioneers-Style Children's Movement Run by Vladimir Putin', *Meduza*, 10 June 2022, https://meduza.io/en/cards/russian-lawmakers-are-launching-a-new-pioneers-style-children-s-movement-run-by-vladimir-putin.
180. Verstka, 'Kak nikogda ranshe chuvstvuyetsya russkii dukh'.
181. Verstka, 'Kak nikogda ranshe chuvstvuyetsya russkii dukh'.
182. '"Mashuk" Tsentr znanii dlya translyatorov tsennostei', *RBK*, 22 December 2023, https://rostov.plus.rbc.ru/partners/6585365e7a8aa97a7c85fa11.
183. Donetskoe Agenstvo Novostei, 'O geroizme pedagogov, vnedrenii federalnykh standartov i preodolenii mrachnogo naslediya Ukrainy'.
184. Verstka, 'Kak nikogda ranshe chuvstvuyetsya russkii dukh'.
185. Yapparova, 'Oni mogut nachat protivodeystvovat'.
186. Yapparova, 'Oni mogut nachat protivodeystvovat'. According to its official website, Profilaktika focuses on the threat of suicide, mass shootings in schools, criminal subcultures and cyber-bullying. See the official website at https://www.cism-ms.ru/chasto-zadavaemye-voprosy/. In reality, it also monitors extremism, including opposition political content, anti-war posts or anything related to Ukrainian nationalism.
187. Cited in Yapparova, 'Oni mogut nachat protivodeystvovat'.
188. Yapparova, 'Oni mogut nachat protivodeystvovat'.
189. Yapparova, 'Oni mogut nachat protivodeystvovat'.
190. Yapparova, 'Oni mogut nachat protivodeystvovat'.
191. Valerie Hopkins, 'Their City in Ruins, a Ukrainian University and its Students Persevere', *New York Times*, 21 July 2023, https://www.nytimes.com/2023/07/21/world/europe/mariupol-university-ukraine.html.
192. The Russian Government, 'Marat Khusnullin prinyal uchastiye v otkrytii obrazovatelnykh uchrezhdenii i infrastrukturnykh obyektov v Mariupole', *The Russian Government*, 26 January 2024, http://government.ru/news/49411/.
193. Figures from official website: https://donvuz.ru/vuz/mgu/.
194. Interview, Natalia Falko, Kyiv, May 2024.
195. Interview, Natalia Falko, Kyiv, May 2024.
196. 'Melitopolskii universitet vozglavil Nikolai Toivonen', *TASS*, 6 June 2023, https://tass.ru/obschestvo/17946281.
197. Bereg, 'Okkupirovav Ukrainskie territorii, Rossiya zakhvatila i vse mestnye universitety'.
198. Personal communication, September 2024.
199. Hanna Lopatina, Natalia Tsybuliak, Anastasia Popova, Ihor Bohdanov and Yana Suchikova, 'University Without Walls: Experience of Berdyansk State

Pedagogical University During the War', *Problems and Perspectives in Management* 21, no. 2 (2023): 4–14 (7).
200. Iuliia Mendel, 'Every Ukrainian Knows Both Patriots and Collaborators', *The Washington Post*, 17 November 2022, https://www.washingtonpost.com/opinions/2022/11/17/kherson-liberation-collaborators-patriots/
201. McGlynn, *Russia's War*, 169.
202. 'Feykovyi rektor Khersonskogo gosuniversiteta, kollaborantka Tatyana Tomilina zaochno poluchila podozreniye v posobnichestve gosudarstvu-agressoru', *Centre of Journalistic Investigations*, 4 July 2023, https://investigator.org.ua/news-2/253341/.
203. 'Doklad o realizatsii plana deyatelnosti Ministerstva nauki i vyshego obrazovaniya Rossiiskoi Federatsii v 2022 godu i zadachakh na 2023 god', Russian Ministry of Science and Higher Education (MinNauka), Moscow, 2023, https://minobrnauki.gov.ru/upload/2023/06/%D0%94%D0%BE%D0%BA%D0%BB%D0%B0%D0%B4%20%D0%98%D0%A2%D0%9E%D0%93%20%D0%BD%D0%B0%20%D1%81%D0%B0%D0%B9%D1%82.pdf, 7.
204. MinNauka, 'Doklad o realizatsii plana deyatelnosti Ministerstva'.
205. David Lewis, 'Ideology in Wartime: How Civilisational Geopolitics is Shaping Russian Foreign Policy', Conference Paper, CEEISA-ISA Joint International Conference 2024, Rijeka, 19 June 2024.
206. Bereg, 'Okkupirovav Ukrainskie territorii'.
207. For a two-level framing of how Russian propaganda functions, see Jade McGlynn, 'Russian Propaganda Tactics in Ukraine's Newly Occupied Territories', *Russian Analytical Digest*, no. 313, 21 May 2024.

6. MONEY

1. Lewis, 'Contesting Liberal Peace'.
2. Michael Schwirtz, 'Russian Anger Grows Over Chechnya Subsidies', *The New York Times*, 8 October 2011, https://www.nytimes.com/2011/10/09/world/europe/chechnyas-costs-stir-anger-as-russia-approaches-elections.html.
3. Yuliya G. Zabyelina, 'Buying Peace in Chechnya: Challenges of Post-Conflict Reconstruction in the Public Sector', *Journal of Peacebuilding & Development* 8, no. 3 (2013): 37–49.
4. State Council of the Republic of Crimea, 'O voprosakh upravleniya sobstvennostyu Respubliki Krym ot 30 aprelya 2014', *Resolution*, 30 April 2014, https://docs.cntd.ru/document/413901094.
5. Roman Romanovskii, 'How Putin's Friends "Bought Out" Occupied Crimea', *IStories*, 1 February 2023, https://istories.media/en/stories/2023/02/01/how-putins-friends-bought-out-occupied-crimea/.
6. 'V Krymu pod natsionalizatsiyu popali do 70 obyektov', *RIA Novosti*, 19 February 2023, https://ria.ru/20230219/natsionalizatsiya-1852940782.html.

NOTES

7. 'Predpriyatiya ukrainiskikh oligarkhov v DNR pereshli v sobstvennost Rossii', *RIA Novosti*, 10 February 2023, https://ria.ru/20230210/natsionalizatsiya-1851259493.html.
8. Arutunyan, *Hybrid Warriors*; Konstantin Skorkin, 'All Change: Donbas Republics Get New Russian Business Boss', *Carnegie Endowment for International Peace*, 29 June 2021, https://carnegiemoscow.org/commentary/84859.
9. Anastasiya Boiko, 'Rossiiskii biznes poluchit v upravlenie broshennye v novykh regionakh kompanii', *Vedomosti*, 25 October 2022, https://www.vedomosti.ru/economics/articles/2022/10/26/947345-biznes-poluchit-broshennie-v-novih-regionah-kompanii.
10. Konstantin Skorkin, 'Subyekt rossiiskoi okkupatsii. Kak Kreml pytaetsya upravlyat regionami, yakoby vklyuchenymi v sostav Rossii', *The Insider*, 22 October 2022, https://theins.info/politika/256178.
11. Federal Tax Service of Russia, 'Zavershilsya perenos v YEGRYuL svedenii o kompaniyakh iz reyestrov LNR, DNR, Zaporozhskoi i Khersonskoi oblastei', *Federal Tax Service of Russia*, 5 December 2022, https://www.nalog.gov.ru/rn77/news/activities_fts/12928780/.
12. David Lewis, 'Economic Crime and Illicit Finance in Russia's Occupation Regime in Ukraine', *SOC ACE Research Paper No 20*, University of Birmingham, September 2023.
13. Garner, *Black's Law Dictionary*.
14. Antoine Duval and Eva Kassoti, eds., *The Legality of Economic Activities in Occupied Territories: International, EU Law and Business and Human Rights Perspectives* (New York: Routledge, 2020); Lieblich and Benvenisti, *Occupation in International Law*.
15. Hague Convention (IV) respecting the Laws and Customs of War on Land and its annex: Regulations concerning the Laws and Customs of War on Land, The Hague, 18 October 1907, https://ihl-databases.icrc.org/en/ihl-treaties/hague-conv-iv-1907.
16. ICRC, 'Pillage', *Customary International Humanitarian Law Database*, 2005, Vol. 1, https://ihl-databases.icrc.org/en/customary-ihl/v1/rule52.
17. 'V Melitopole okkupanty razgrabili zavod "Biol"', *RIA-Melitopol*, 4 May 2022, https://ria-m.tv/news/285317/v_melitopole_okkupantyi_razgrabili_zavod_biol.html.
18. Olexsandr Fylyppov and Tim Lister, 'Russians Plunder $5M Farm Vehicles from Ukraine—to Find They've Been Remotely Disabled', *CNN*, 1 May 2022, https://www.cnn.com/2022/05/01/europe/russia-farm-vehicles-ukraine-disabled-melitopol-intl/index.html.
19. Ilya Davlyatchin, 'Lyudi gibli za metall. Kto i kak vyvozit imushchestvo ukrainskikh predpriyatii iz okkupirovannogo Mariupolya', *Poligon*, 22 June 2023, https://www.poligonmedia.net/lyudi-gibli-za-metall/.
20. 'Russia "Looting" Steel Bound for Europe and UK, Says Metinvest Boss', *BBC News*, 21 July 2022, https://www.bbc.com/news/business-62252704.
21. Mamonova, Skibitska and Kobernyk, 'Oleksandr Yakymenko, Head of the SBU'.

22. Zakharov, Lotareva and Gerasimenko, 'Skoro perestroites'.
23. Zakharov, Lotareva and Gerasimenko, 'Skoro perestroites'.
24. Mamonova, Skibitska and Kobernyk, 'Oleksandr Yakymenko, Head of the SBU'.
25. Interviews, Kyiv, May 2024.
26. 'New Front Lines: Organized Criminal Economies in Ukraine in 2022', *Global Initiative against Transnational Organized Crime*, 22 February 2023, https://globalinitiative.net/analysis/organized-criminal-economies-ukraine-2022/.
27. Sofiya Guseva, 'Dve vetki vliyania khotyat razdelit Mariupol—andryushchenko o tom, kak sotrudnichayut okkupanty', *24 Kanal*, 22 August 2022, https://24tv.ua/ru/okkupanty-borjutsja-za-vlast-marupole-andrjushhenko-rasskazal_n2140305.
28. Katerina Serdyuk, '"Privet, 90-ye!": v okkupirovannom Mariupole postoyanno proiskhodyat perestrelki i "banditskiye razborki"', *TSN*, 25 August 2023, https://tsn.ua/ru/ukrayina/privet-90-e-v-okkupirovannom-mariupole-postoyanno-prohodyat-perestrelki-i-banditskie-razborki-2397697.html.
29. 'Shootout between Kadyrovites and Military Police in Occupied Village near Mariupol Leaves Multiple Dead', *Novaya gazeta Europe*, 13 August 2023, https://novayagazeta.eu/articles/2023/08/13/shootout-between-kadyrovites-and-military-police-in-occupied-village-near-mariupol-leaves-multiple-dead-en-news.
30. President of Russia, 'Zasedanie Soveta Bezopasnosti'.
31. President of Russia, 'Zasedanie Soveta Bezopasnosti'.
32. President of Russia, 'Zasedanie Soveta Bezopasnosti'.
33. 'Putin: V byudzhete ezhegodno predusmotreno svyshe trilliona na novye regiony', *Kommersant*, 14 December 2023, https://www.kommersant.ru/doc/6397397.
34. Anna Galcheva and Ivan Tkachev, 'Vlasti raskryli dotatsii iz federalnogo byudzheta dlya novykh regionov', *RBK*, 21 April 2023, https://www.rbc.ru/economics/21/04/2023/6440f0559a7947983b98d930.
35. Olga Ageeva, 'Vlasti zaplanirovali snizit dotatsii byudzhetam novykh regionov v 2024 godu', *Forbes*, 22 January 2024, https://www.forbes.ru/finansy/504636-vlasti-zaplanirovali-snizit-dotacii-budzetam-novyh-regionov-v-2024-godu.
36. Anastasiya Boiko and Sergei Gavriliuk, 'V proyekt byudzheta vklyuchili gosprogrammu vosstanovleniya novykh regionov', *Vedomosti*, 27 September 2023, https://www.vedomosti.ru/economics/articles/2023/09/27/997295-v-proekt-byudzheta-vklyuchili-gosprogrammu-vosstanovleniya-novih-regionov.
37. Anastasiya Larina, 'Moskva potratit 95 mlrd rub. na vosstanovlenie Donetska i Luganska', *Kommersant*, 17 October 2023, https://www.kommersant.ru/doc/6281968.
38. Tenisheva, 'Russian Towns Get Ukrainian "Twins" in PR Drive, Political Deflection Tactic'.
39. Pertsev, 'Vitse-korol Donbassa'.

40. President of Russia, 'Zasedanie Soveta Bezopasnosti'.
41. Mikhail Kolokoltsev, 'Lenoblast profinansirovala vosstanovlenie Yenakievo na 870 mln rublei', *78.ru*, 20 April 2023, https://78.ru/news/2023-04-20/lenoblast-profinansirovala-vosstanovlenie-enakievo-na-870-mln-rublei.
42. 'Yenakiyevskii tramvai. Novaya dlya Rossii, odna iz samykh zhivopisnykh sistem. Zamena PS uzhe nachalas', *Udobno zhit* (blog), Dzen, 18 February 2023, https://dzen.ru/a/Y9Fw7OcvNhsV1iGH.
43. Novosti Kuzmolovo i okrestnostei (@vk.com/kuznews), *47News*, VK post, 29 September 2023, https://vk.com/wall-211175282_10035.
44. 'Deti iz Yenakievo prodolzhayut priyezzhat v letnie lagerya Leningradskoi oblasti', *LenTV24.ru*, 7 August 2023, https://lentv24.ru/deti-iz-enakievo-prodolzayut-priezzat-v-letnie-lagerya-leningradskoi-oblasti.htm.
45. 'Regiony nazvali istochiki finansirovaniya shefskoi pomoshchi Donbassu', *RBK*, 29 June 2022, https://www.rbc.ru/politics/29/06/2022/62b9b0019a7947318feb8b10; Andrey Pertsev, '"Putin i Kiriyenko zastavili rossiiskiye regiony vzyat" "shefstvo" nad gorodami i rayonami Donbassa', *Meduza*, 8 July 2022, https://meduza.io/feature/2022/07/08/putin-i-kirienko-zastavili-rossiyskie-regiony-vzyat-shefstvo-nad-gorodami-i-rayonami-donbassa-meduza-vyyasnila-kak-ustroena-eta-sistema-na-kotoruyu-iz-byudzheta-potratyat-milliardy-rubley.
46. 'Gubernator Peterburga poobeshchal vosstanovit Dramteatr v Mariupole', *Meduza*, 9 June 2022, https://meduza.io/news/2022/06/09/gubernator-peterburga-poobeschal-vosstanovit-dramteatr-v-mariupole.
47. Mack Tubridy, 'How St Petersburg is Put in Charge of Rebuilding Annexed Mariupol', *Russia Post*, 7 November 2022, https://russiapost.info/society/spb_mariupol.
48. 'Fond Peterburga napravil za god 11.8 mlrd rublei na vosstanovlenie Mariupolya', *78.ru*, 25 April 2023, https://78.ru/news/2023-04-25/fond-peterburga-napravil-za-god-118-mlrd-rublei-na-vosstanovlenie-mariupolya.
49. Larina, 'Moskva potratit 95 mlrd rub. na vosstanovlenie Donetska i Luganska'.
50. President of Russia, 'Itogi goda s Vladimirom Putinom', *President of Russia*, 21 December 2023, http://kremlin.ru/events/president/news/72994.
51. Larina, 'Moskva potratit 95 mlrd rub. na vosstanovlenie Donetska i Luganska'.
52. Anastasia Kornya, 'Rossiyane prismotrelis k novym regionam', *Kommersant*, 7 November 2023, https://www.kommersant.ru/doc/6321342.
53. Ekaterina Vinogradova and Ivan Tkachev, 'Mintrud razrabotal osobyi poryadok vyplat pensii dlya novykh regionov', *RBK*, 17 January 2023, https://www.rbc.ru/economics/17/01/2023/63c532ce9a7947d4abda5f6e.
54. Olga Ageeva, 'Sobstvennye dokhody chetyrekh novykh regionov prevysili 40 mlrd rublei', *Forbes*, 10 August 2023, https://www.forbes.ru/finansy/494346-sobstvennye-dohody-cetyreh-novyh-regionov-prevysili-40-mlrd-rublej.
55. '"Novyye vlasti" Zaporozhskoi oblasti zayavili o vvedenii rublya i stremlenii voyti v sostav RF. Ob etom zhe govorili v Khersonskoi oblasti', *Meduza*, 25 May 2022, https://meduza.io/news/2022/05/25/novye-vlasti-zaporozhskoy-oblasti-zay-

avili-o-vvedenii-rublya-i-stremlenii-voyti-v-sostav-rf-ob-etom-zhe-govorili-v-hersonskoy-oblasti.

56. Michael Billig, *Banal Nationalism* (London: Sage, 1995).
57. Ukrainian resistance campaigns often used Photoshopped versions of Russian banknotes with slogans such as 'This is not Russia' or 'Crimea is Ukrainian'. Some were shown in an exhibition about Ukrainian resistance under occupation, 'Nebachena sila' (Unseen Force), in Ukrainian House, Kyiv, 18 May–2 June 2024, https://unseen-force.com/the-unseen-force-exhibition-in-kyiv-ukrainian-house/; see also Katya Aleksander, '"My zdes i my prodolzhaem borotsya"', *Vazhnye istorii*, 27 March 2024, https://istories.media/stories/2024/03/27/mi-zdes-i-mi-prodolzhaem-borotsya/.
58. Maria Yakushchenko, 'Diryavi hroshi, abo iak Saldo pidtrymuvav hryvniu pid chas okupatsii Khersona', *Most*, 24 May 2023, https://most.ks.ua/news/url/dirjavi-groshi-abo-jak-saldo-pidtrimuvav-grivnju-pid-chas-okupatsiji-hersona/.
59. Yakushchenko, 'Diryavi hroshi'; see also Tom Burgis, 'Mr Fifty Percent: The Former Ukraine Mayor Doing Putin's Work in Kherson', *The Guardian*, 19 December 2023, https://www.theguardian.com/world/2023/dec/19/mr-fifty-percent-the-former-ukraine-mayor-doing-putins-work-in-kherson.
60. 'Promsvyazbank Buys SMP for Russia's Second Major Banking Tie-Up in Dec', *Reuters*, 30 December 2022, https://www.reuters.com/markets/deals/russias-promsvyazbank-says-it-has-bought-smp-bank-2022-12-30/.
61. Anastasia Fedorchenko, 'Promsvyazbank nachal rabotu v Khersonskoi i Zaporozhskoi oblastyakh', *Izvestiya*, 30 June 2022, https://iz.ru/1357849/2022-06-30/promsviazbank-nachal-rabotu-v-khersonskoi-i-zaporozhskoi-oblastiakh.
62. Skorkin, 'Subyekt rossiiskoi okkupatsii'.
63. Yulia Kochkina, 'Banki v Donbasse: komu doverit dengi', *Ura News*, 19 April 2023, https://ura.news/articles/1036286620.
64. Olga Sherunkova, 'PSB rasstavlyaet otdeleniya', *Kommersant*, 13 March 2023, https://www.kommersant.ru/doc/5873538.
65. TsMBR (OOO), 'Ofisy i filialy', https://www.cmrbank.ru/offices.
66. Sherunkova, 'PSB rasstavlyaet otdeleniya'.
67. Tatyana Katrichenko, 'Nenuzhnaya privilegiya. Kak Rossiya zastavlyayet poluchat pasporta na okkupirovannykh territoriyakh', *Fokus*, 10 August 2022, https://focus.ua/ukraine/524988-kak-rossiya-zastavlyaet-poluchat-pasporta-na-okkupirovannyh-territoriyah.
68. David H. Petraeus, 'Learning Counterinsurgency: Observations from Soldiering in Iraq', *Military Review* 86, no. 3 (2006): 2–12 (4).
69. Lewis, 'Contesting Liberal Peace'.
70. Yaffa, 'A Ukrainian City'.
71. President of Russia, 'Zasedanie Soveta Bezopasnosti'.
72. Interviews, Kyiv and online, 2023, 2024.
73. Sergei Mingazov, 'Mintrud raskryl srednii razmer pensii v chetyrekh prisoedinen-

nykh regionakh', *Forbes*, 26 July 2023, https://www.forbes.ru/finansy/493533-mintrud-raskryl-srednij-razmer-pensii-v-cetyreh-prisoedinennyh-regionah.

74. 'V Rossii uzhe svyshe milliona zhitelei novykh regionov poluchayut pensii', *RIA Novosti*, 4 December 2023, https://ria.ru/20231204/pensiya-1913613812.html.
75. 'Mery podderzhki sotsialnogo fonda v novykh subyektakh RF', *Sotsfond RF* (Social Fund of Russia), 2022, https://sfr.gov.ru/grazhdanam/newregion/.
76. President of Russia, 'Zasedanie Soveta Bezopasnosti'.
77. Daria Talanova, Sergey Teplyakov and Antonina Asanova, 'How Russia Seizes Ukrainian Businesses on Occupied Territories—Thousands of Companies in Mariupol, Melitopol, and Other Occupied Cities Have Been Re-Registered in Russia', *Novaya gazeta Europe*, 25 March 2023, https://novayagazeta.eu/articles/2023/03/25/how-russia-seizes-ukrainian-businesses-on-occupied-territories-en.
78. Mikita Panasenko, 'Iak rosiiany kradut biznes na okupovanii Zaporizhchyni', *Center of Journalistic Investigations*, 30 November 2022, http://investigator.org.ua/ua/publication/249235/.
79. Katrichenko, 'Nenuzhnaya privilegiya'.
80. Federal Tax Service of Russia, 'Zavershilsya perenos v YEGRYuL svedenii o kompaniyakh iz reyestrov LNR, DNR, Zaporozhskoi i Khersonskoi oblastei'.
81. Talanova, Teplyakov and Asanova, 'How Russia Seizes Ukrainian Businesses'.
82. Zapgov, 'O sozdanii Ministerstva imushchestvennykh i zemelnykh otnoshenii Voyenno-grazhdanskoi administratsii Zaporozhskoi oblasti', Government of Zaporozhe oblast, 22 August 2022, https://zo.gov.ru/docs/show/916.
83. Daria Talanova, Sergey Teplyakov and Antonina Asanova, 'Vso skhvacheno: Rossiya ustroila peredel sobstvennosti na okkupirovannykh territoriyakh. Kak ukrainskiye predpriyatiya perekhodyat v ruki "novykh sobstvennikov"', *Novaya gazeta Evropa*, 24 March 2023, https://novayagazeta.eu/articles/2023/03/24/vse-skhvacheno.
84. Talanova, Teplyakov and Asanova, 'How Russia Seizes Ukrainian Businesses'.
85. The Ministry of Property and Land Relations of Zaporozhe region published frequent lists of 'abandoned property' in 2022–24. See 'Vyyavlennoe beskhozyainoe imushchestvo', https://zo.gov.ru/news/show_group/vyyavlennoe_besxozyajnoe_imushhestvo/all/2024.
86. 'Sotni predpriyatii Zaporozhskoi oblasti pereshli pod vneshnee gosupravlenie', *RIA Novosti*, 27 December 2022, https://ria.ru/20221227/koltsov-1841548120.html.
87. 'Vystupleniye Konstantina Zatulina na forsayt-forume "Kakaya Ukraina nam nuzhna?', YouTube [video], uploaded by Institut stran SNG @user-tn5fy6ue5b, 2 June 2023, https://www.youtube.com/watch?v=q2lCSMrWZ8k.
88. Boiko, 'Rossiiskii biznes poluchit v upravlenie'.
89. Boiko, 'Rossiiskii biznes poluchit v upravlenie'.
90. Yaffa, 'A Ukrainian City'.
91. Aleksandr Volobuev, '"Rosatom" gotovitsya vzyat na sebya upravlenie

92. Zaporozhskoi AES', *Vedomosti*, 4 October 2022, https://www.vedomosti.ru/business/articles/2022/10/04/943871-rosatom-gotovitsya-vzyat.
92. President of Russia, 'Ukaz Prezidenta Rossiiskoi Federatsii ot 05.10.2022 No. 711', *Official Internet-Portal of Legal Information of the President RF*, 5 October 2022, http://publication.pravo.gov.ru/Document/View/0001202210050022.
93. 'ZZhRK prodolzhaet podderzhivat rabotnikov, nesmotrya na zakhvat predpriyatiya rossiyanami', *Korrespondent.net*, 9 November 2022, https://korrespondent.net/business/companies/4533604-zzhrk-prodolzhaet-podderzhyvat-rabotnykov-nesmotria-na-zakhvat-predpryiatyia-rossyianamy.
94. Ivan Lizan, 'Ot Zaporozhskogo k Dneprorudnenskomu: Istoriya grabezha i perezapuska unikalnogo zhelezorudnogo kombinata', *Ukraina.ru*, 29 September 2022, https://ukraina.ru/20220929/1039155802.html.
95. 'Rosiiany vyvoziat rudu z TOT—Tsentr natsionalnoho sprotyvu', *National Resistance Center*, 6 March 2023, https://sprotyv.mod.gov.ua/2023/03/06/rosiyany-vyvozyat-rudu-z-tot/.
96. Talanova, Teplyakov and Asanova, 'How Russia Seizes Ukrainian Businesses'.
97. Talanova, Teplyakov and Asanova, 'How Russia Seizes Ukrainian Businesses'.
98. Talanova, Teplyakov and Asanova, 'How Russia Seizes Ukrainian Businesses'.
99. 'Mariupolskii kombinat im Ilycha peremenuyut v chest drugogo Ilycha', *0629.com.ua*, 14 April 2016, https://www.0629.com.ua/news/1190543/mariupolskij-kombinat-im-ilica-pereimenuut-v-cest-drugogo-ilica-dokument.
100. 'Chechnya's Grozny Establishes "Sister City" Ties With Occupied Mariupol', *The Moscow Times*, 9 August 2023, https://www.themoscowtimes.com/2023/08/09/chechnyas-grozny-establishes-sister-city-ties-with-occupied-mariupol-a82096.
101. Ksenia Churmanova and Andrei Goryanov, 'Zavod v Mariupole i magaziny OVD. Kak biznesmen, blizkii k Ramzanu Kadyrovu, poluchaet inostrannyi biznes vo vremya voiny', *BBC News Russian Service*, 13 February 2023, https://www.bbc.com/russian/features-64599582.
102. Ksenia Churmanova, 'Uz Akhmata v Mariupol. Rukovoditel chechenskogo boitsovskogo kluba poluchil doli v kompaniyakh v okkupirovannoi "DNR"', *BBC News Russian Service*, 22 June 2023, https://www.bbc.com/russian/articles/cv2qxnk5979o.
103. Benoit Faucon and Oksana Pyrozhok, 'Russia Turns Mariupol's Steel Mills From Battle Zone to Spoils of War', *Wall Street Journal*, 21 October 2024, https://www.wsj.com/world/russia/russia-turns-mariupols-steel-mills-from-battle-zone-to-spoils-of-war-d9281aff
104. 'Kombinat imeni Illicha v Mariupole vozobnovil rabotu posle razminirovaniya', *RBK*, 13 December 2023, https://www.rbc.ru/rbcfreenews/657913bd9a79476beedf6713.
105. Talanova, Teplyakov and Asanova, 'How Russia Seizes Ukrainian Businesses'; 'Predprinimatelya Goika, torgovavshego goryuchim dlya okkupantov, v zakh-

vachennom Melitopole, zaochno osudili na pyat let', *Center of Journalistic Investigations*, 20 October 2023, https://investigator.org.ua/news-2/259499/.

106. 'V Melitopole Yevgenii Balitskii s okkupantami RF obvoroval zavod bolee chem na 2 mln Evro', *RIA-Melitopol*, 15 April 2022, https://ria-m.tv/news/283414/v_melitopole_evgeniy_balitskiy_lichno_reshil_otjat_predpriyatie_u_konkurenta_(foto_video).html; 'Yak Balytskyi "vidzhav" dlia piterskykh zavod u Melitopoli', *Center of Journalistic Investigations*, 25 January 2023, http://investigator.org.ua/ua/topics-video/251004/.

107. 'Melitopolskii zavod avtotraktornykh zapchastei prodolzhayet narashchivat obemy proizvodstva', *Lenta novostei Melitopolya*, 13 February 2023, https://melitopol-news.ru/economy/2023/02/13/25016.html.

108. Yevgeniya Koroleva, '"My dumali, chto nado proderzhatsya neskolko nedel": CEO HD-group Boris Shestopalov o tom, kak predpriyatiya perezhili okkupatsiyu', *The Page*, 12 January 2023, https://thepage.ua/business/kak-zavody-hd-group-perezhili-okkupaciyu; Ukraine Crisis, '"We'll Bake Bread as Long as We Can. Even under Bullets"', *Uacrisis.org*, 2 December 2022, https://uacrisis.org/en/pekty-hlib.

109. Data from the Russian State Register of Legal Entities (EGRYUL).

110. 'V Melitopole okkupanty uzhe otzhali myasokombinat', *RIA-Melitopol*, 25 May 2022, https://ria-m.tv/news/287409/v_melitopole_okkupantyi_uje_otjali_myasokombinat.html.

111. Talanova, Teplyakov and Asanova, 'How Russia Seizes Ukrainian Businesses'.

112. Pershii Zaporizki, 'Na okupovanii terytorii Zaporizkoi Oblasti Rosiiany zakhopyly shche try zavodi', *1News*, 10 November 2022, http://1news.zp.ua/na-okkupirovannoj-territorii-zaporozhskoj-oblasti-rossiyane-zahvatili-eshhe-tri-predpriyatiya/.

113. 'Tri predpriyatiya Zaporozhskoi oblasti vzyaty pod vneshnee upravlenie', *TASS*, 26 October 2022, https://tass.ru/ekonomika/16164309.

114. 'John Greaves, ili chto na Zolotoy Nive pokazal progressivnyi berdyanskii zavod?', *GlavPahar.ru*, 30 May 2023, https://glavpahar.ru/news/john-greaves-ili-chto-na-zolotoy-nive-pokazal-progressivnyy-zaporozhskiy-zavod.

115. GlavPahar.ru, 'John Greaves, ili chto na Zolotoy Nive'.

116. 'Nardepa Ponomareva otpravili pod strazhu bez zaloga po delu o gosizmene. chto o nem izvestno?', *Strana.ua*, 24 July 2023, https://ctpaha.media/news/440658-nardepu-ponomarevu-soobshcheno-o-podozrenii-v-hosizmene-za-sotrudnichestvo-s-rf-v-berdjanske.html. See also the investigation by Radio Svoboda: Nataliia Sedletska, Olha Ivlieva, Oleksandr Chornovalov, 'Plivky Ponomarova. Kontakty z FSB, zapusk biznesu ta povernennia u VR–shcho nardep piv roku robyv v okupatsii?', *Radio Svoboda*, 24 July 2023, https://www.radiosvoboda.org/a/skhemy-piv-roku-v-okupatsiyi-nardepa-ponomarova/32516802.html

117. Natalia Skorlygina, 'Na "Azovmash" podgonyat novyi sostav', *Kommersant*, 27 December 2023, https://www.kommersant.ru/doc/6427342.

118. Roman Neyter, Sergiy Zorya and Oleksandr Muliar, 'Agricultural War Damages

119. Anne Quinn and Agnieszka de Sousa, 'Russia Reaped $1 Billion of Wheat in Occupied Ukraine, NASA Says', *Bloomberg*, 3 December 2022, https://www.bloomberg.com/news/articles/2022-12-03/russia-reaped-1-billion-of-wheat-in-occupied-ukraine-nasa-says.
120. Quinn and de Sousa, 'Russia Reaped $1 Billion of Wheat'.
121. Yevhenia Drozdova and Nadja Kelm, 'Vrozhai z okupovanykh terytorii', *Texty.Org.Ua*, 22 November 2023, https://texty.org.ua/projects/111036/vrojai-z-ocupovanyh-teritorii/.
122. 'How Russia Increases Export of Crops Stolen in the South of Ukraine', *Center of Journalistic Investigations*, 10 December 2023, https://investigator.org.ua/en/publication/south-articles/261860/. Other figures are slightly lower. In Kherson region, Saldo claimed to have harvested 1.5 million tonnes by August 2023; http://en.kremlin.ru/events/president/news/72102.
123. Oleksandra Shevchenko, '"Natsionalizovani" ohirky ta pomidory. Yak v okupovanomu Enerhodari zakhopliuiut ahrobiznes', *Radio Svoboda*, 22 April 2022, https://www.radiosvoboda.org/a/novyny-pryazovya-enerhodar-zakhoplennya-ahrobiznesu/31821310.html; 'Ukrav, vyviz, u Moskvu. Yak okupanty namahaiutsia prodaty kradene ukrainske zerno inshym krainam', *Ekonomichna pravda*, 6 May 2022, https://www.epravda.com.ua/publications/2022/05/6/686713/.
124. Tom Burgis and Pjotr Sauer, '"Forged Documents": How Ukrainian Grain May Be Enriching Putin's Circle', *The Guardian*, 11 December 2023, https://www.theguardian.com/world/2023/dec/11/forged-documents-how-ukrainian-grain-may-be-enriching-putins-circle.
125. Alistair MacDonald and Oksana Pyrozhok, 'Russian Oligarch Seizes 400,000 Acres of Ukrainian Farmland, Owners Say', *Wall Street Journal*, 6 December 2022, https://www.wsj.com/articles/russian-oligarch-seizes-400-000-acres-of-ukrainian-farmland-owners-say-11670338956.
126. MacDonald and Pyrozhok, 'Russian Oligarch Seizes 400,000 Acres'.
127. MacDonald and Pyrozhok, 'Russian Oligarch Seizes 400,000 Acres'.
128. MacDonald and Pyrozhok, 'Russian Oligarch Seizes 400,000 Acres'.
129. Anatolii Kostyrev and Alina Savitskaya, 'Agrarii snaryazhayut magaziny', *Kommersant*, 12 April 2023, https://www.kommersant.ru/doc/5927146.
130. Polina Ivanova, Chris Cook and Laura Pitel, 'How Russia Secretly Takes Grain from Occupied Ukraine', *Financial Times*, 30 October 2022, https://www.ft.com/content/89b06fc0-91ad-456f-aa58-71673f43067b.
131. Slavisha Batko Milacic, 'Russia's Role in Preventing World Hunger', *Modern Diplomacy*, 27 May 2023, https://moderndiplomacy.eu/2023/05/27/russias-role-in-preventing-world-hunger/.
132. Oleksandra Hubytska and Nataliya Onysko, 'Ukradene zbizhzhia. Yak i kudy Rosiiany vyvoziat Ukrainske zerno', *NGL.media*, 29 March 2024, https://ngl.media/en/2024/03/29/stolen-grain/.

133. Jonathan Saul, Maha El Dahan and Maya Gebeily, 'Exclusive: Crimea Showers Syria with Wheat, Ukraine Cries Foul', *Reuters*, 19 December 2022, https://www.reuters.com/world/russian-annexed-crimea-showers-syria-with-wheat-ukraine-cries-foul-2022-12-19/.
134. Saul, Dahan and Gebeily, 'Exclusive: Crimea Showers Syria'.
135. 'FAO "ROSKAPSTROI"—logisticheksii tsentr g. Mariupol', YouTube [video], uploaded by @RosKapStroi, 15 May 2023, https://www.youtube.com/watch?v=kUNFnuKiQ6g.
136. Ivanova, Cook and Pitel, 'How Russia Secretly Takes Grain from Occupied Ukraine'.
137. Burgis and Sauer, 'Forged Documents'.
138. Tom Burgis, 'UK Company Set Up in Name of Top Putin Official in Ukraine', *The Guardian*, 27 April 2023, https://www.theguardian.com/world/2023/apr/27/volodymyr-saldo-uk-company-set-up-in-name-of-top-putin-official-in-ukraine.
139. Rachel Hall, '"Hull is Inspirational": Mariupol Academics Look to Yorkshire as They Plan for Rebuilding of City', *The Guardian*, 3 March 2024, https://www.theguardian.com/world/2024/mar/03/hull-is-inspirational-mariupol-academics-look-to-yorkshire-as-they-plan-for-rebuilding-of-city.
140. Mariupol Reborn, 'About Mariupol', *Mariupol Reborn* (2024), https://remariupol.com/en/about-Mariupol.
141. 'Ekskluziv The Village: Plan Mariupolya do 2035 goda, razrabotannyi v Moskve', *The Village*, 12 October 2022, https://www.the-village.ru/all-village/rassledovanie/master-plan-mariupolya. The plan was also published at: https://meduza.io/static/pdf/minstroy-mariupol-ps-29-07-itogovaya.pdf
142. Aleksandr Gamov, 'Russkii Mariupol vosstaet iz ruin: Chto proiskhodit seichas v gorode', *Komsomolskaya pravda*, 11 December 2022, https://www.kp.ru/daily/27482.5/4690881/.
143. 'Russia Scrubs Mariupol's Ukraine Identity, Builds on Death', *AP News*, 22 December 2022, https://apnews.com/article/russia-ukraine-war-erasing-mariupol-499dceae43ed77f2ebfe750ea99b9ad9.
144. Alla Konstantinova, 'Mapping the Ruins. The Reconstruction and Demolition of Occupied Mariupol', *Mediazona*, 31 January 2024, https://en.zona.media/article/2024/01/31/mariupol_housing.
145. President of Russia, 'Zasedanie Soveta Bezopasnosti'.
146. President of Russia, 'Zasedanie Soveta Bezopasnosti'.
147. Polina Smertina, 'Zapitaites, regiony', *Kommersant*, 21 August 2023, https://www.kommersant.ru/doc/6172107.
148. Online interview, June 2024.
149. 'Pochemu nuzhen Mariupolskii zhilishchnyi sertifikat?', YouTube [video], uploaded by @walkandtalk_, 2023, https://www.youtube.com/watch?v=1-cBK7UglsM.
150. Kholod, 'Oni khotyat ves gorod prosto kinut'.

151. Kholod, 'Oni khotyat ves gorod prosto kinut'.
152. Kholod, 'Oni khotyat ves gorod prosto kinut'.
153. YouTube, 'Pochemu nuzhen Mariupolskii zhilishchnyi sertifikat?'
154. Kholod, 'Oni khotyat ves gorod prosto kinut'.
155. Kholod, 'Oni khotyat ves gorod prosto kinut'.
156. Kholod, 'Oni khotyat ves gorod prosto kinut'.
157. 'Marat Khusnullin posetil stroiploshchadku GK "YugStroiInvest" v Mariupole', *YugStroiInvest*, 12 July 2023, https://gk-usi.ru/novosti/marat-husnullin-posetil-strojploshhadku-gk-yugstrojinvest-v-mariupole/.
158. Nurhan Abujidi and Han Verschure, 'Military Occupation as Urbicide by "Construction and Destruction": The Case of Nablus, Palestine', *The Arab World Geographer* 9, no. 2 (2006): 126–54.
159. Martin Coward, *Urbicide: The Politics of Urban Destruction* (Abingdon: Routledge, 2008).
160. Kholod, 'Oni khotyat ves gorod prosto kinut'.
161. Konstantinova, 'Mapping the Ruins'.
162. Vita Chiknaeva, '"Voina ne budet idti vechno"', *Bumaga*, 28 June 2023, https://paperpaper.io/vojna-zhe-ne-budet-idti-vechno-kto-i-za/.
163. Chiknaeva, 'Voina ne budet idti vechno'.
164. Advertisements on the Russian real estate marketplace, Avito, 2023.
165. Advertisements on the Russian real estate marketplace, Avito, 2024. See https://www.avito.ru/mariupol/kvartiry/2-k._kvartira_734_m_45_et._4102860909.
166. Konstantinova, 'Mapping the Ruins'.
167. 'OOO SZ 'RKS-Development'', *Rusprofile*, 2024, https://www.rusprofile.ru/id/1239300005526.
168. 'Marat Khusnullin i ego miniony', *Transparency International*, 23 August 2023, https://web.archive.org/web/20230823104016/https://transparency.org.ru/special/marat-husnullin/.
169. 'Lazurnaya zhizn semi Khusnullina', *Dossier Center*, 24 April 2023, https://dossier.center/husnullin/.
170. Gamov, 'Russkii Mariupol vosstaet iz ruin'.
171. The Russian Government, 'Marat Khusnullin: V Mariupole zaversheny eshche dva doma-dolgostroya', The Russian Government, 22 August 2024, http://government.ru/news/52441/.
172. 'Sergei Shoigu otsenil rabotu voennykh stroitelei v Donbasse', *Voenno-stroitelnaya kompaniya*, 6 March 2023, https://vskmo.ru/2023/03/06/sergej-shojgu-otsenil-rabotu-voennyh-stroitelej-v-donbasse/.
173. 'Mariupolskii benefitsiar', *Dossier Center*, 30 April 2024, https://dossier.center/hus-ivanov/.
174. Maria Zholobova, 'Stroika posle rasstrela', *Vazhnye istorii*, 9 August 2022, https://istories.media/investigations/2022/08/09/stroika-posle-rasstrela/; Oleg Rubnikovich, 'Zamministra rasschitali obvinenie', *Kommersant*, 25 April 2024, https://www.kommersant.ru/doc/6666223.

NOTES

175. 'Zamministra oborony vedet roskoshnuyu zhizn na dengi ot stroitelstva v Mariupole', *FBK*, 21 December 2022, https://acf.international/ru/news/zamministra-oborony-vedet-roskoshnuyu.
176. 'Millioner iz silovikov. Chto izvestno o bogatstvakh i korruptsii zama Shoigu Timura Ivanova, okazavshegosya v SIZO', *Vazhnye istorii*, 24 April 2024, https://istories.media/news/2024/04/24/millioner-iz-silovikov-chto-izvestno-o-bogatstvakh-i-korruptsii-zama-shoigu-timura-ivanova-okazavshegosya-v-sizo/.
177. Vazhnye istorii, 'Millioner iz silovikov'.
178. Dossier Center, 'Mariupolskii benefitsiar'.
179. 'Khusnullin otsenil chislennost naseleniya Mariupolya', *RBK*, 18 July 2023, https://www.rbc.ru/rbcfreenews/64b69faa9a7947a805e3c052.
180. 'Naseleniye Melitopolya seychas bolshe, chem do okkupatsii—Fedorov', *Regionews*, 30 January 2024, https://regionews.ua/rus/news/zaporozhchina/1706620415-naselenie-melitopolya-seychas-bolshe-chem-do-okkupatsii-fedorov.
181. Ben-Nun, 'Neighboring Military Occupation', 383.
182. According to official Russian statistics, some 206,000 people had migrated to Crimea from Russia in 2014–20: 'V Krym za posledniye shest let pereselilis ne meneye 200 tysyach rossiyan—statistika', *Krym.Realii*, 6 January 2021, https://ru.krymr.com/a/news-krym-pereselenie-rossiyan/31036011.html. Figures were disputed. Ukrainian sources suggested in-migration from Russia to Crimea could range from 600,000 to 1 million people, including members of the armed forces and security services. See Yevheniia Horiunova, 'Social Changes in Crimea Occupied by Russia', *Baltic Rim Economies*, 28 April 2022, https://sites.utu.fi/bre/social-changes-in-crimea-occupied-by-russia/; and Alla Hurska, 'Demographic Transformation of Crimea: Forced Migration as Part of Russia's "Hybrid" Strategy', *Eurasia Daily Monitor*, 29 March 2021, https://jamestown.org/program/demographic-transformation-of-crimea-forced-migration-as-part-of-russias-hybrid-strategy/.
183. 'Deputat Zhuravlev predlozhil vydavat uchastnikam CVO "vostochnoukrainskii gektar"', *Kommersant*, 5 November 2023, https://www.kommersant.ru/doc/6321093.
184. 'Kiriyenko rasskazal, kakim budet novyi gorod na Arabatskoi strelke', *RIA Novosti*, 7 January 2023, https://ria.ru/20230107/kirienko-1843401760.html.
185. 'Avdeevky gotovyat k vosstanovleniyu: sdelayut kak v Mariupole', *MK.ru*, 6 April 2024, https://www.mk.ru/politics/2024/04/06/avdeevku-gotovyat-k-vosstanovleniyu-sdelayut-kak-v-mariupole.html.
186. 'Rossiiskie spetsialisty vosstanavlivayut osvobozhdennuyu Avdeyevku iz ruin', [video], Channel 1, 12 October 2024, https://www.1tv.ru/news/2024-10-12/489175-rossiyskie_spetsialisty_vosstanavlivayut_osvobozhdennuyu_avdeevku_iz_ruin?ysclid=m277aepyqf290297404.

187. Kostyrev and Savitskaya, 'Agrarii snaryazhayut magaziny'.
188. Anatolii Vasiliev, 'Avtotrassu na Krym, prokhodyashchuyu po territorii DNR, rasshiryat do chetyrekh polos', *Komsomolskaya pravda*, 18 October 2023, https://www.donetsk.kp.ru/daily/27570/4838976/.
189. Gennady Kravchenko, 'Poluchitsya li u Rossii "vzyat v koltso Azovskoe more"?', *Krym.Realii*, 7 December 2023, https://ru.krymr.com/a/vzat-v-koltso-azovskoye-more-stroitelstvo-dorogi/32719410.html.
190. President of Russia, 'Vstrecha s vrio glavy DNR Denisom Pushalinim', *President of Russia*, 10 April 2023, http://kremlin.ru/events/president/news/70879.
191. The Russian Government, 'Pravitelstvo utverdilo rasporyazheniye o sozdanii predpriyatiya "Zheleznyye dorogi Novorossii"', *The Russian Government*, 2 June 2023, http://government.ru/news/48604/.
192. UK Ministry of Defence (@DefenceHQ), 'Latest Defence Intelligence Update on the Situation in Ukraine' (tweet), X, 15 October 2023, https://x.com/DefenceHQ/status/1713438505353781498.
193. 'Balitskii: Mezhdu Rostovom-Na-Donu i Krymom nachali stroit zheleznuyu dorogu', *RIA Novosti*, 6 November 2023, https://ria.ru/20231106/doroga-1907661796.html.
194. Greg Miller and Mary Ilyushina, 'Russian and Chinese Executives Discuss Russia-Crimea Tunnel Project', *Washington Post*, 25 November 2023, https://www.washingtonpost.com/world/2023/11/24/russia-crimea-tunnel-china/.
195. Leo Chiu, 'Ukraine's Intelligence Cracks Down on Illegal Buses Between Russia, Ukraine', *Kyiv Post*, 1 December 2023, https://www.kyivpost.com/post/24933.
196. Koshiw, 'What Life is This?'.
197. 'Mariupol i Berdyansk vklyuchili v reyestr morskikh portov Rossii', *RIA Novosti*, 31 March 2023, https://ria.ru/20230331/porty-1862276756.html.
198. Rosselkhoznadzor, 'Iz morskogo porta Mariupolya pod kontrolem spetsialistov Upravleniya Rosselkhoznadzora po DNR otpravleno 24 teplokhoda s zernom pshenitsy Rosselkhoznadzor', *Rosselkhoznadzor*, 23 August 2023, https://fsvps.gov.ru/ru/fsvps/news/220894.html.
199. 'Dva doma na prospekte Lenina v Mariupole-na finishe vosstanovleniya', RuTube [video], uploaded by Mariupol 24, 8 August 2023, 00:09:40, https://rutube.ru/video/ade33cd135f1efa0acb9039901f33223/.
200. 'FAU "RosKapStroi" zaimetsya vosstanovleniem infrastruktury Mariupolskogo morskogo porta', *RosKapStroi*, 16 October 2023, https://roskapstroy.ru/news/news_4888.
201. Sergei Starushko, 'Piratskii flot Rossii v Azovskom more', *Center of Journalistic Investigations*, 6 July 2023, https://investigator.org.ua/blogs/256382/.
202. Vladimir Gelman, *The Politics of Bad Governance in Contemporary Russia* (Ann Arbor, MI: University of Michigan Press, 2022).
203. Gelman, *The Politics of Bad Governance*.
204. Bohdan Logvinenko, *Deokupatsiya: Istorii Oporu Ukraintsiv* (Kyiv: Ukrainer, 2023), 228.

7. LIBERATION

1. Logvinenko, *Deokupatsiya*, 260.
2. Online interview, June 2024.
3. Andriy Kuzakov, '"We Realized We Still Had to Fight": Life in Kherson One Year After Liberation', *Radio Free Europe/Radio Liberty*, 11 November 2023, https://www.rferl.org/a/ukraine-kherson-liberation-anniversary-resistance-collaborators-russian-bombardment-/32680777.html.
4. Logvinenko, *Deokupatsiya*, 228.
5. Logvinenko, *Deokupatsiya*, 231.
6. Tom Burgis, 'Life on the Frontline in Kherson: Dodging Shells, Facing Death and Refusing to Leave', *The Guardian*, 7 November 2023, https://www.theguardian.com/world/2023/nov/07/kherson-residents-frontline-bombardment.
7. Yevheniy Safonov, 'The Scene of the Action. A Big Report from Kherson', *Life in War*, 31 May 2024, https://lifeinwar.com/en/publications/the-scene-of-the-action-a-big-report-from-kherson.
8. Burgis, 'Life on the Frontline in Kherson'.
9. 'A Fraught Path Forward for Ukraine's Liberated Territories', *International Crisis Group*, 20 June 2024, https://www.crisisgroup.org/europe-central-asia/eastern-europe/ukraine/271-fraught-path-forward-ukraines-liberated-territories.
10. Smirnova, 'Chto mozhet byt khuzhe?'.
11. Interviews, Kherson residents, May–June 2024.
12. International Crisis Group, 'A Fraught Path Forward', 4.
13. Burgis, 'Life on the Frontline in Kherson'.
14. Safonov, 'The Scene of the Action'.
15. Interviews, Kyiv and online, May–June 2024.
16. Nicole Gonik and Eric Ciaramella, 'War and Peace: Ukraine's Impossible Choices', *Carnegie Endowment for International Peace*, 11 June 2024, https://carnegieendowment.org/research/2024/06/ukraine-public-opinion-russia-war.
17. President of Ukraine, 'We Must Fight for the Full Restoration of International Law in Relation to Crimea and Any Other Land—Address by the President of Ukraine [Volodymyr Zelensky] on the Day of Resistance to the Occupation of the Autonomous Republic of Crimea and Sevastopol', *President of Ukraine*, 26 February 2024, https://www.president.gov.ua/en/news/mayemo-borotisya-za-povne-vidnovlennya-sili-mizhnarodnogo-pr-89313.
18. 'A Fresh Russian Push will Test Ukraine Severely, Says a Senior General', *The Economist*, 2 May 2024, https://www.economist.com/europe/2024/05/02/a-fresh-russian-push-will-test-ukraine-severely-says-a-senior-general.
19. 'What Should Be Done by the Power to Reintegrate the Residents of Crimea Temporarily Occupied Territory?', *ZMINA*, 2023, https://zmina.ua/wp-content/uploads/sites/2/2023/09/crimea_print_eng.pdf.
20. ZMINA, 'What Should Be Done by the Power'.

21. Ukraine Ministry of Reintegration, '7 pravyl zhyttia na TOT, *Ukraine Ministry of Reintegration*, 22 August 2022, https://minre.gov.ua/2022/08/22/7-pravyl-zhyttya-na-tot/.
22. Andriana Velianik, 'What Does Putin's New Decree on Russian Citizenship Mean?', *Svidomi*, 3 May 2023, https://svidomi.in.ua/en/page/what-does-putins-new-decree-on-russian-citizenship-mean.
23. Velianik, 'What Does Putin's New Decree on Russian Citizenship Mean?'.
24. 'Peace in Ukraine (III): The Costs of War in Donbas', *International Crisis Group*, 3 September 2020, https://www.crisisgroup.org/europe-central-asia/eastern-europe/ukraine/261-peace-ukraine-iii-costs-war-donbas.
25. Amnesty International, 'Russia/Ukraine: 10 Years of Occupation of Crimea', *Amnesty International*, 18 March 2024, https://www.amnesty.org/en/documents/eur50/7805/2024/en/.
26. Ukrainian Helsinki Human Rights Union, 'Action Plan for Implementing the Strategy for the Deoccupation and Reintegration of Crimea. What Has Changed?', *Ukrainian Helsinki Human Rights Union*, 3 May 2023, https://www.helsinki.org.ua/en/articles/action-plan-for-implementing-the-strategy-for-the-deoccupation-and-reintegration-of-crimea-what-has-changed/.
27. Velianik, 'What Does Putin's New Decree on Russian Citizenship Mean?'.
28. 'Ukraine Unveils Plan for Recaptured Crimea—but West "Reluctant" to Help', *France 24*, 4 April 2024, https://www.france24.com/en/europe/20230404-ukraine-unveils-plan-for-recaptured-crimea-%E2%80%93-but-west-reluctant-to-help.
29. Mission of the President of Ukraine, 'Strategy for the Cognitive Deoccupation of Crimea', *Mission of the President of Ukraine in the Autonomous Republic of Crimea*, 6 November 2023, https://ppu.gov.ua/en/documents/strategy-for-cognitive-deoccupation-of-crimea/.
30. Mission of the President of Ukraine, 'Strategy for the Cognitive Deoccupation of Crimea.'
31. 'Shoigu obyavil ob osvobozhdenii Svyatogorska', *RIA Novosti*, 7 June 2022, https://ria.ru/20220607/svyatogorsk-1793710910.html.
32. 'Ukraine's National Guard Confirms Recapture of Sviatohirsk', *Ukrinform*, 12 September 2022, https://www.ukrinform.net/rubric-ato/3570073-ukraines-national-guard-confirms-recapture-of-sviatohirsk.html.
33. Thomas Gibbons-Neff, Natalia Yermak and Tyler Hicks, 'A Gray Area of Loyalties Splinters a Liberated Ukrainian Town', *The New York Times*, 8 December 2022, https://www.nytimes.com/2022/12/08/world/europe/ukraine-russia-loyalty-sviatohirsk.html.
34. Emmanuel Grynszpan, 'Guerre en Ukraine: "Que les prorusses fassent leurs valises!"', *Le Monde*, 4 November 2022, https://www.lemonde.fr/international/article/2022/11/04/guerre-en-ukraine-que-les-prorusses-fassent-leurs-valises_6148483_3210.html.
35. Gibbons-Neff, Yermak and Hicks, 'A Gray Area of Loyalties'.
36. Gibbons-Neff, Yermak and Hicks, 'A Gray Area of Loyalties'.

37. Andrew Kramer, 'Battered by Russian Shells, a Monastery Remains Loyal to Moscow', *The New York Times*, 6 June 2022, https://www.nytimes.com/2022/06/06/world/europe/ukraine-monastery-orthodox-church-russia.html.
38. Anna Pshemiskaya, 'Svyatogorskaya lavra v Donbasse. Chto s nei budet posle voiny', *DW*, 6 June 2023, https://www.dw.com/ru/svatogorskaa-lavra-v-donbasse-cto-s-nej-budet-posle-vojny/a-65829635.
39. 'V seti opublikovali video propovedi za kotoruyu sudyat mitropolita Arseniya', *SPZh*, 25 April 2024, https://spzh.live/ru/news/79917-v-seti-opublikovali-video-propovedi-za-kotoruju-sudjat-mitropolita-arsenija.
40. Toal and Dahlman, *Bosnia Remade*.
41. OHCHR, 'Detention of Civilians in the Context of the Armed Attack by the Russian Federation against Ukraine 24 February 2022—23 May 2023', 32.
42. Interviews, Kyiv, 2024.
43. President of Russia, 'Zasedanie Soveta Bezopasnosti'.
44. Miller and Schmidt, 'In Kherson City, Sympathies for Russia Complicate Reintegration into Ukraine'.
45. Igor Burdyga, '"Kazhdyi poluchit svoe"'. Kak i kogo v Ukraine presleduyut za kollaboratsionizm', *openDemocracy*, 15 August 2023, https://www.opendemocracy.net/ru/kogo-v-ukraine-sudyat-za-kollaboratsionizm/.
46. See Criminal Code of Ukraine, Article 111–1, website of the Verkhovna Rada, https://zakon.rada.gov.ua/laws/main/2341-14.
47. OHCHR, 'Detention of Civilians in the Context of the Armed Attack by the Russian Federation against Ukraine 24 February 2022—23 May 2023', 3.
48. Article 111–1 on collaboration outlawed the '[t]ransfer of material resources to illegal armed or paramilitary formations created in the temporarily occupied territory, and/or armed or paramilitary formations of the aggressor state, and/or implementation of economic activities in cooperation with the aggressor state, illegal authorities created in the temporarily occupied territory, including the occupation administration of the aggressor state'. See: Criminal Code of Ukraine, Article 111–1.
49. 'Criminal Liability for Collaborationism: Analysis of Current Legislation, Practice of its Application, and Proposals for Amendments', *ZMINA*, 2022, 7, https://zmina.ua/wp-content/uploads/sites/2/2022/12/zvit_zmina_eng-1.pdf.
50. Onisia Sinyuk, 'Yak karaly za kolaboratsionizm rizni derzhavy ta chomu tsei termin dosi neodnoznachnyi navit v Ukraini', *LB.ua*, 23 August 2023, https://lb.ua/blog/onysiia_syniuk/571430_yak_karali_kolaboratsionizm_rizni.html.
51. ZMINA, 'Criminal Liability for Collaborationism'.
52. 'Uhody u spravakh pro kolaboratsiiu: shcho z nymy ne tak i yak tse vypravyty?', *Helsinki Human Rights Union*, 2 December 2022, https://www.helsinki.org.ua/articles/uhody-u-spravakh-pro-kolaboratsiiu-shcho-z-nymy-ne-tak-i-iak-tse-vypravyty/.
53. Burdyga, 'Kazhdyi poluchit svoe'.

54. OHCHR, 'Detention of Civilians in the Context of the Armed Attack by the Russian Federation against Ukraine 24 February 2022—23 May 2023'.
55. Aleksei Arunyan, '"Sdelali menya vragom naroda, a ya lyudyam dushu otdala". Kak sudyat dvukh obshchestvennits iz Donetskoi oblasti, kotorye vo vremya okkupatsii Limana stali "glavami mikrorayonov"', *Graty*, 11 September 2023, https://graty.me/ru/sdelali-menya-vragom-naroda-a-ya-lyudyam-dushu-otdala-kak-sudyat-dvuh-obshhestvennicz-iz-doneczkoj-oblasti-kotorye-vo-vremya-okkupaczii-limana-stali-glavami-mikrorajonov/.
56. Arunyan, 'Sdelali menya vragom naroda'.
57. Arunyan, 'Sdelali menya vragom naroda'.
58. Arunyan, 'Sdelali menya vragom naroda'. She presumably had in mind the 10,000-rouble payments that the Russians gave to many pensioners and families.
59. Arunyan, 'Plokhaya energetika'.
60. Arunyan, 'Plokhaya energetika'.
61. Arunyan, 'Plokhaya energetika'.
62. Arunyan, 'Plokhaya energetika'.
63. SBU [Security Service of Ukraine] (@SBUkr), Telegram post, 13 June 2023, https://t.me/SBUkr/8637.
64. SBU [Security Service of Ukraine] (@SBUkr), Telegram post, 13 June 2023, https://t.me/SBUkr/8637.
65. Arunyan, 'Plokhaya energetika'.
66. Burdyga, 'Kazhdyi poluchit svoe'.
67. Miller and Schmidt, 'In Kherson City, Sympathies for Russia Complicate Reintegration into Ukraine'.
68. Miller and Schmidt, 'In Kherson City, Sympathies for Russia Complicate Reintegration into Ukraine'.
69. Burdyga, 'Kazhdyi poluchit svoe'.
70. Burdyga, 'Kazhdyi poluchit svoe'. The Telegram channel was @kherson_kolaborant, https://t.me/s/Kherson_kolaborant
71. Detektor Media, 'Mediini Kolaboranty Khersona: Khto, yak i chomu spivpratsiuvav iz vorohom', *MediaSapiens*, 5 August 2023, https://ms.detector.media/media-i-vlada/post/32614/2023–08–05-mediyni-kolaboranty-khersona-khto-yak-i-chomu-spivpratsyuvav-iz-vorogom/.
72. Burdyga, 'Kazhdyi poluchit svoe'.
73. 'Yurii Petukhov, gaulaiter sela Novovoskresenskoye na Khersonshchine, za sotrudnichestvo s okkupantami provedet 12 let za reshetkoi', *Center of Journalistic Investigations*, 8 June 2023, http://investigator.org.ua/news-2/255408/.
74. Burdyga, 'Kazhdyi poluchit svoe'.
75. 'V Mariupole prepodavat v shkolakh budut tolko te uchitelya, kotorye ne predavali Ukrainu,—gorodskoi golova', *0629.com.ua*, 25 August 2023, https://www.0629.com.ua/ru/news/3650090/v-mariupole-prepodavat-v-skolah-budut-tolko-te-ucitela-kotorye-ne-predavali-ukrainu-gorodskoj-golova.
76. Gettleman, 'He Returned a Dazed Soldier to the Russians.'

77. Gettleman, 'He Returned a Dazed Soldier to the Russians.'
78. See his Facebook page, https://www.facebook.com/karamalikov.ilya.
79. 'Kakoi vopros vy by zadali meru Melitopolya segodnya?', *RIA-Melitopol*, 11 June 2022, https://ria-m.tv/news/289202/kakoy_vopros_vyi_byi_zadali_meru_melitopolya_segodnya.html.
80. 'Alexey [Oleksiy] Arestovych, Public Talk, Tel Aviv, 23 May 2023', YouTube [video] @ 44:32, uploaded by @arestovych, 23 May 2023. https://www.youtube.com/watch?t=2670&v=yDsuwDUudlY&feature=youtu.be.
81. 'Prokuror avtonomii: bolshinstvo krymchan—ne predateli, a opredeleniye "kollaboratsionizm" dlya Kryma sleduyet izmenit', *Interfax-Ukraina*, 6 March 2023, http://ru.interfax.com.ua/news/general/895727.html.
82. Elina Beketova, 'Behind the Lines: Crimea's Collaboration Conundrum', *CEPA*, 29 June 2023, https://cepa.org/article/behind-the-lines-crimeas-collaboration-conundrum/.
83. ZMINA, 'What Should Be Done by the Power'.
84. Beketova, 'Behind the Lines'.

CONCLUSION: FUTURES

1. Giorgio Agamben, *State of Exception*, trans. K. Attell (Chicago: University of Chicago Press, 2005), 35.
2. Michaela Pohl, 'Anna Politkovskaya and Ramzan Kadyrov: Exposing the Kadyrov Syndrome', *Problems of Post-Communism* 54, no. 5 (2007): 30–39 (30).
3. Jeffrey Kahn, 'Vladimir Putin and the Rule of Law in Russia', *Georgia Journal of International and Comparative Law* 36, no. 3 (2008): 511–57 (527).
4. Onuch and Hale, *The Zelensky Effect*.
5. Iryna Balachuk, 'Ukrainians Associate "Ordinary Russians" with Enemies, Non-Humans and Zombies—Poll', *Ukrainska pravda*, 8 July 2024, https://www.pravda.com.ua/eng/news/2024/07/18/7466264/.
6. Malyarenko and Kormych, 'New Wild Fields'.
7. Alexander Etkind, *Russia against Modernity* (Cambridge: Polity, 2023)
8. Michael E. Ruane, 'Putin's Attack on Ukraine Echoes Hitler's Takeover of Czechoslovakia', *Washington Post*, https://www.washingtonpost.com/history/2022/02/24/hitler-czechoslovakia-sudeten-putin-ukraine/.
9. 'War a Real Threat and Europe Not Ready, Warns Poland's Tusk', *BBC News*, 29 March 2024, https://www.bbc.co.uk/news/world-europe-68692195.
10. Taras Kuzio, '"Ukraine is Russia": Medvedev Reveals Imperial Ambitions Fueling Invasion', *Atlantic Council*, 4 March 2024, https://www.atlanticcouncil.org/blogs/ukrainealert/ukraine-is-russia-medvedev-reveals-imperial-ambitions-fueling-invasion/.
11. Remarks by NATO Secretary General Jens Stoltenberg at the Munich Security Conference panel discussion, 'In it to Win it: the Future of Ukraine and Transatlantic Security', *NATO*, 17 February 2024, https://www.nato.int/cps/en/natohq/opinions_222630.htm.

12. Jeffrey Mankoff, *Empires of Eurasia: How Imperial Legacies Shape International Security* (New Haven, CT: Yale University Press, 2022).
13. Pepe Escobar, 'Axis of Resistance: From Donbass to Gaza', *The Cradle*, 16 February 2024, https://thecradle.co/articles-id/23408.
14. 'How to End Russia's War on Ukraine', *Chatham House*, 27 June 2023, https://www.chathamhouse.org/2023/06/how-end-russias-war-ukraine.
15. Casey Michel, 'Decolonize Russia', *The Atlantic*, 27 May 2022, https://www.theatlantic.com/ideas/archive/2022/05/russia-putin-colonization-ukraine-chechnya/639428/.
16. M. E. Sarotte, 'A Better Path for Ukraine and NATO: What Kyiv Could Do Now for a Place in the Alliance', *Foreign Affairs*, 8 July 2024, https://www.foreignaffairs.com/ukraine/better-path-ukraine-nato.

INDEX

Abdurashytova, Milana, 178–9
Abkhazia, 24, 87
Abujidi, Nurhan, 248
Afanasevsky, Yury, 169
Afghanistan, 26, 85, 124, 142
Africa, 186, 219
African National Congress (ANC), 93
Agamben, Giorgio, 286
Agriculture and grain exports, 240–3
Agrinol, 239
Agrocomplex, 242
Agrokoin, 241
Agrotek, 222
Agroton, 241, 242
Aivazovsky, Ivan, 192, 193
Akhmetov, Rinat, 51–2, 220, 227, 237
Akinsha, Konstantin, 190
Aksenov, Sergei, 150
Alekseenko, Andrei, 78–9, 100
Aleppo, 73
Algeria, 27
Amnesty International, 72, 73, 208, 266
Anapa, 81
Andryushchenko, Petro, 72, 199

'Animal style', 190
Anti-Corruption Foundation (FBK), 252
Anti-Terrorist Operation (ATO), 130, 190
Antonov Bridge, 53–4, 79, 165
Apachev, Akim, 212
Arabat Spit, 254
Arestovych, Oleksiy, 279–80
Arie, Pavlo, 197
Article 111–1 (Ukrainian Criminal Code), 112, 272–6, 280
Aseyev, Stanislav, 183
Ashirov, Denis, 211
Atlantic Council, 82
Austria, 23
Avdiivka, 83, 254
Avtogidroagregat, 105
Azmol, 239
Azov Brigade, 55, 69, 71, 73, 74–6, 193, 196
'Azov Ring', 255
Azovmash plant, 240
Azovska Khvylia radio station, 184
Azovstal plant, 70, 75, 76, 179, 223, 236–7, 244.

INDEX

Babushka Anna (Granny Anna), 88
Babych, Oleksandr, 134–5, 153
Bakhmut, 8, 35
Balitsky, Yevgeny 61–2, 95–6, 104, 105–6, 110, 133, 160, 182, 183, 186, 191, 242, 256–7
Baltic States, 1, 23, 155, 288
Bandera, Stepan, 42–3, 160, 210
Bardin, Colonel A., 65
Barkhatnova, Alla, 169
Barnaul, 73
'BARS Kaskad', 101
Bas, Olga, 110
Basyuk, Konstantin, 110
Baturin, Oleh, 57
BBC (British Broadcasting Corporation), 63, 85, 92, 161, 177, 223, 237–8
Bedrik, Colonel Viktor, 65
Beglov, Alexander, 199
Belarus, 22, 28, 31, 32, 33
Belgorod, 156
'belligerent occupation', 3, 9
Belovezha Accords, 28
Benvenisti, Eyal, 9
Berdiansk Harvesters, 239
'Berdiansk ZaVtra' (Berdiansk Tomorrow), 185–6
Berdiansk, 29, 54, 65, 73–4, 131, 132, 135, 146, 168, 212, 221, 236, 239, 256
  protests, 62–3
  See also Russia; Ukraine
Berdiansk State Pedagogical University, 214
Beseda, Sergei, 125
Bevz, Tetiana, 44
Bezimenne, 144, 145, 146–7
Billig, Michael, 229
Bilovodsk, 92

Bilyk, Roman, 197
Black civil rights movement, 47
Black Lives Matter (BLM), 47
Black Sea Fleet, 28, 267
Black Sea, 33, 34, 70, 242–3
Blok, Alexander, 190–1
Bloomsbury, 243
Boevoe bratstvo (Fighting Brotherhood) veterans' association, 101
Bogdan Khmelnitsky Melitopol State Pedagogical University, 214
Bohemia, 23
Boiko, Ihor, 208
Bolshevik revolution (1917), 36
Bolsheviks, 36, 237
Borogan, Irina, 125
Bosnia-Herzegovina, 36–7
Boulevard, Komsomol, 179
Boulevard, Meotida, 179
Bouquet Garni, 105
Boychenko, Vadym, 51, 52, 55, 243, 278
Boyko, Oleh, 168
Bratchenko, Tatyana, 193
Brezhnev, Leonid, 43
Britain, 27
Britsin, Pastor (Grace Protestant Church), 133
British Defence Intelligence, 256
Bucha, 129, 262
Budanov, Kyrylo, 125
Bulaev, Nikolai, 111
Bulvar, Morksoy, 179
Bulyuk, Vitaly, 105, 169
'bureaucratic occupation', 5
Butusov, Yuri, 71
Buyskykh, Julia, 16, 17–18
By the Banks of the Caucasus (Aivazovsky), 192

Carlton, Eric, 19

INDEX

Cathedral of Petro Mohyla, 210
Catherine II, 20
Catherine the Great Street, 180
Catherine the Great, 178
Caucasus, 33
Central Asia, 33, 153, 253
Central Election Commission (CEC), 106, 111
Central Museum of Tavrida, 193
Centre for Humanitarian Aid, 89
Centre for International Settlements Bank (CMR Bank), 231
The Centre for the Study and Network Monitoring of the Youth Environment (TsISM), 212–13
Chatham House, 290
Chechen networks 102, 237
Chechen war, 176
Chechnya, 28, 73, 85, 120–1, 123, 124, 142, 219, 286
Chekhov, Anton, 196, 198
Chelyabinsk region, 99, 104
Cherevko, Sergei, 105
Cherkasy region, 104, 126
Chernov, Mstyslav, 71
Chernyi piar (black PR), 88
China, 1, 17, 22, 94, 288–9
Chonhar Bridge, 53
Chonhar filtration point, 146
Chonhar Strait, 52, 53
Chorniy, Andrii, 241
Chornobaivka, 79
Christian Evangelical church, 133
Chui, Father Andri, 132
Chychera, Dmytro, 70–1
Chychera, Liudmyla, 70
Cinema Foundation (*Fond kino*), 196
Ciro Cerullo, Jorit, 179
Civic Chamber, 186

Civil Assistance Committee, 155–6
Clock House, 250–1
CNN, 80
'cognitive occupation', 2
Collaboration, 66, 68, 109, 112, 181, 193, 215, 234, 239, 270–281
Communist Party of the Russian Federation (KPRF), 107, 108
'Confrontation', 191
Congress of Russian Communities (KRO), 33
Council of Europe, 41
Covid pandemic, 8, 66
Coward, Martin, 248
Crimea, 28–9, 33, 150–2, 153–4, 220, 225, 230, 237, 253, 254–7, 266–8, 280
'Crimea Platform', 266
Crimean Bridge, 70, 255, 257, 267
Crimean Tatar prisoners, 150–1
Crimean Tatars, 153–4, 267
Cry of the Nation, The, 198–9
Cyprus, 250
Czechoslovakia, 85, 288

Dadashov, Alash, 237
Dagestan, 120, 203
Dagin, Izrail, 180–1
Danilchenko, Galina (Halyna Danylchenko), 61–2, 66–7, 106, 183–4
Darenskii, Vitaly,
'Database of Traitors', 277
Day of National Unity, 210
'Day of Victory', 151
DDT, 197
Debaltseve, 227
Decolonisation, scholarship on Ukraine, 16–17

367

INDEX

Decolonisation, of Russia, 290
Decommunisation campaign, 44, 49, 179–180
Demidenko, Alexander, 156
Demidov, Anton, 101
Democratic People's Republic of Korea, 86–7
Denisova, Liudmyla, 87, 154
Deoccupation strategies, 264–8
Department for Implementation of the Special Infrastructure Project of the Ministry of Construction, 251–52
Department for Operational Information (DOI), 124–5
Department of Military Counter-Intelligence (DVKR), 125, 151
Deryugin, Igor, 108
Desyatova, Natalya, 194
Detention centres, 120, 129, 137, 150, 151, 172
Dinstein, Yoram, 10
Dmytro Dontsov Street, 181
Dneprorudny Iron Ore Plant, 236
Dnipro River, 3, 36, 53, 56, 79, 164–6, 262, 284
Dnipro, 53, 134, 276
Dniprorudne, 236
DNR Ministry of Internal Affairs, 144
DNR. *See* Donetsk People's Republic (DNR)
Dominican Republic, 67
Don River, 36, 245
Donbas, 3, 29, 36, 37, 38, 40, 44, 49, 77, 93, 99, 127, 130, 261–4, 267, 288
   expropriation, 234–40
   filtration, 141–50
   forced migration, 154–60
   media, 183–9
   money and banks, 229–31
   occupation, economic activity, 225–9
   plunder and expropriation, 222–5
   Russia's cultural revolution, 194–9
   Russian education, 199–210
   Russian education, youth propaganda, 210–13
   Ukrainian children, 160–4
   Ukrainian prisoners, 150–4
Donetsk Oblast, 142
Donetsk People's Republic (DNR), 7–8, 9, 20, 37, 41, 44, 55, 56, 59, 69, 74, 86–8, 99, 106, 284
   annexation, 90–7
   cultural heritage, 189–94
   deoccupation strategies, 264–8
   elections, 106–13
   expropriation, 234–40
   filtration, 141–50
   forced migration, 154–60
   justice and courts, 116–21
   Kiriyenko visits, 88
   laws and standards, 113–16
   media, 183–9
   money and banks, 229–31
   new monuments and streets, 177–83
   occupation, economic activity, 225–9
   plunder and expropriation, 222–5
   prisoners and abuses, 135–41
   security forces, 127–9
   Russian education, 199–210
   Russian education, youth propaganda, 210–13
   transport, 254–8
   Ukrainian children, 160–4
   Ukrainian prisoners, 150–4

INDEX

Ukrainian resistance, 166–72
universities, 213–16
war profiteers, 249–54
Donetsk region, 5, 21, 29, 37, 39, 56, 57, 59, 69, 77, 83, 87
Donetsk Regional Academic Drama Theatre, 197, 198
Donetsk State University, 216
Dontsov, Dmytro, 181–2
Dotsenko, Alina, 194
Dovhoborodova, Viktoria, 261
Dronov, Yaroslav (Shaman), 96, 197
Dubas, Irina, 200
Dubrovsky, Dmytro, 276–7
Dudka, Alexander, 114
Dugin, Alexander, 23–4, 25, 32, 180
Dugina, Darya, 180
Dunlop, John, 24
Durand, Olivia, 35

East Jerusalem, 291
Eastern Front, 150
Edwards, Maxim, 187
8th Combined Arms Army, 127
82 Nakhimova Street, 247
Empire, 16–17, 24, 27–31
'End of Conquest', 26
Enerhodar, 54, 66, 68–9, 115, 140, 236
England, 243
Etkind, Alexander, 287–8
Eurasian Union, 30
Europe, 1, 2, 22, 25, 123, 155, 159, 190–1, 220, 225, 288
European Commission, 161
European Union (EU), 22, 44, 149, 154, 288
Evangelical churches, 132

Facebook, 60–1, 64, 67, 135, 185

Fadeev, Alexander, 207
Faizullin, Irek, 101, 228, 236, 251
Falklands Islands, 26
fascism, 45, 181
Federal Agency for Youth Affairs (Rosmolodezh), 211
Federal Centre for the Development of Programmes for the Socialisation of Teenagers (FTsRPSP), 213
Federal Constitutional Laws, 96, 117
Federal Migration Service, 113
Federal Security Service (FSB), 5–6, 56, 58, 65–6, 70, 85, 103–4, 108, 118, 123, 140, 169
 detentions and killings, 129–35
 filtration, 141–50
 forced migration, 154–60
 media, 183
 plunder and expropriation, 223, 236
 Ukrainian prisoners, 151–2
 Ukrainian resistance, 171
'Federal Teenager Centre'. *See* Federal Centre for the Development of Programmes for the Socialisation of Teenagers (FTsRPSP)
Federation Council, 46, 96, 110, 113, 122, 235
Fedorov, Ivan, 54–5, 61, 168, 253, 279
Filipchuk, Pavel, 66
Filiponenko, Mikhail, 169
Flood, 164–6
Fomin, Alexander, 252
Forsyth, James, 16
Forum 18, 133
Foundation for Humanitarian Projects, 195

INDEX

Foundation for the Protection of National Values, 186
Foundations of Geopolitics, The (Dugin), 23
Fradkov, Mikhail, 230
Fradkov, Petr, 230
Fraenkel, Ernst, 102
France, 27, 251, 252
France, Vichy, 271
Freedom House, 183
Freedom Square, 169
Fursov, Anatoly, 151–2

Galchenkov, Aleksei, 206
Ganchev, Vitaly, 78–9
García Calatayud, Mariano 152
'Gauleiter', 278
Gavrish, Oleg, 112
Gaza, 289, 291
Gekht, Irina, 99
Gelman, Vladimir 258–9
Geneva Academy of International Humanitarian Law and Human Rights, 9
Geneva Convention (IV), 11, 12 115
Geneva Convention, 68, 116–17, 141, 152, 170
Gentile, Michael, 69
Georgia, 24, 155, 156
Germany, 23, 150, 159
Glazyev, Sergei, 30
global liberalism, 22
Global South, 93, 94
Glory to the Heroes (Arie), 197
Golan Heights, 11, 291
Golubev, Vasily, 150
Goncharov, Sergei, 144
Gorbachev, Mikhail, 32
Gorlachev, Yevgeny, 182, 191–2
Grace Protestant Church, 133
Grainholding Ltd, 243

Graty, 274
Great Game, The (talk show), 28
Great Patriotic War, 44–5, 207
'Great Space', 23
Großraum. *See* 'Great Space'
Grozny, 73, 244
GRU (Russian military intelligence), 103, 123, 125
GSB (Security organisation in Kherson), 126, 128, 139, 223, 241
Gurov, Aleksandr, 187

Habsburg, 16
Hague Conventions (1907), 9, 11, 222
Halabuda, 70
Hale, Henry, 39, 41
HarvEast, 241, 242
HD Group, 238
Heleta, Father Bohdan, 132
Henichesk, 53, 54, 80, 81, 180, 206, 254–5
Herasymenko, Dmytro, 275–6
Hitler, Adolf, 181, 210
Hlukhovska, Anastasia, 184
Hola Pristan, 81, 134, 135, 153, 165–6
Holodomor famine, 42, 178, 207, 210
Holubev, Dmytro, 153
Hong Kong, 22
Hotel Paradise, 227
Hrushevsky, Mikhailo, 191
Hull, 243
Human Rights Watch, 72, 74, 136, 155, 193
Hungary, 37, 85

Ibrahimova, Leila, 191
Independent International Commission of Inquiry on Ukraine, 141

INDEX

India, 22, 94
Instagram, 185
Institute for Strategic Studies, 47
Institute for War and Peace Reporting (IWPR), 69
Institute of National Memory, 43
Internally displaced people (IDPs), 263
International Committee of the Red Cross (ICRC), 67, 141, 153
International Criminal Court (ICC), 11, 160–1, 172, 222
International Settlement Bank (Mezhdunarodnyi raschetnyi bank MRB), 231
Investigative Committee (SK), 120, 128, 152, 153
Iran, 289
Iraq, 11, 24, 26, 28, 232, 289
Ireland, 27
Irpin, 262
Isaac Brodsky Art Museum, 195
Ishchenko, Dmytro, 52
Ishchenko, Volodymr, 17
Israel, 11, 253, 291
Isthmus of Perekop, 52
Ivanov, Timur, 251–2
Izborsky Club, 30–2
Izvestiya (newspaper), 134
Izyum, 78,

'John Greaves', 239
Jubilee Concert Hall, 107
A Just Russia—For Truth (SRZP) political party, 107, 108, 161

Kadyrov, Ramzan, 102, 123, 237–8
Kahn, Jeffrey, 286
Kakhovka dam, 53, 158, 164, 189
Kakhovka, 66
   protests, 62
KAMAZ, 240
Kamynina, Viktoria, 209
Kapustnikova, Natalia, 192–3
Karamalikov, Illia, 58, 278–9
Karaul, 164
Karikov, Alexander, 104
Karpenko, Olga, 206
Kasianov, Georgiy, 42, 207
Kastyukevich, Igor, 89, 101, 110, 113, 162
Katerinichev, Colonel Aleksei, 99–100
Kazakhstan, 31, 32
Kazan University, 250
Kelsen, Hans, 25
Kerch Strait, 29, 70
KGB, 123
Khabarovsk Krai, 227
Khablenko, Andrian, 241
'Khan Ukraine', 35
Kharitonov, Andrei, 107
Kharkiv city, region, 3, 34, 36, 40, 45, 56, 60, 78–79, 82–3, 91, 230, 270
   Ukrainian counteroffensive in, 78–79, 263
   occupation authorities, 78
   planned referendum, 91
   detentions and torture, 130
   money and banks, 29
   Russian education, 203
Kharlashkin, Sergei, 99
Khavronin, Dmitry, 252
Kherson Art Museum, 193–4
Kherson city, region, 3, 5, 8, 29, 36, 39, 57–8, 82–3, 261–4, 284–5
   annexation, 90–7
   cultural heritage, 189–94
   detentions, torture, and killings, 129–40

INDEX

economic activity, 225–9
elections, 107–11
expropriation, 234–40
filtration, 141–50
forced migration, 154–60
governance under occupation, 100–1, 104–5
justice and courts, 118–21
liberation, 268–71
local politics, 102–6
media, 183–9
military seizure, 53–54
money and banks, 229–31
protests, 62–4
public opinon, 39–40
occupation, 57–58, 63, 65–68
Russian withdrawal, 79–83
schools, 201–2
security forces, 126–29
sexual violence, 137
Kherson Maritime College, 277
Kherson Military-Civilian Administration (VGA), 90
Kherson People's Republic, 63, 87
Kherson Region. *See* Kherson city
Kherson State University, 168, 187, 214–215
'Kherson-24', 184
Khersonavtokomunservis, 276–7
Khlan, Sergei, 68, 127, 139
Khortytsia, 35
Khorugv, 177
Khotsenko, Vitaly, 98, 99, 103
Khrimli, Father Khristofor, 132
Khromeychuk, Olesya, 16, 249
Khusnullin, Marat, 101, 159, 214, 233, 236, 247, 250–3, 255
Kim, Vitalii, 56
Kim, Yevgeny, 141–2

Kiriyenko, Sergei, 87–9, 99–100, 135, 195, 211, 254
Kirov region, 121
kleptocracy, 19
Klimenko, Yulia, 210
Kobets, Oleksandr, 65–6
Kokhany, 166
Kolosovych, Liudmyla, 198
Kolotilovka-Pokrovka border post, 155, 156
Koltsov, Anton, 98, 235
Koludarova, Olga, 254
Kolykhaev, Ihor, 54, 58, 60–1, 64, 65, 67–8, 104–5, 130, 134, 153
Kommandatura, 65
Kommersant (newspaper), 153
Komunalny district, 274
Konovalets, Yevhen, 182–3
Korchagin, Valid, 237–8
Kormych, Borys, 287
Kornet, Igor, 169
Kostomarov, Alexander, 99
Kotelva, Kateryna, 273
Kovalchuk, Yegor, 104
Kovalchuk, Yuri, 220
Kovalev, Alexei, 135
Kovalov, Oleksandr, 74
Kozak, Dmitry, 86, 88, 90
Kozlov, Sergei, 104
Kramatorsk, 87
Krasnikov, Gennady, 8
Krasnodar Krai, 239
Krasnodar, 78, 81, 103
Krasnopillia, 155
Krasnoyarsk, 249
Kravtsov, Sergei, 205, 208, 212
Kreminna, 56
Kryvoruchko, Serhii, 52, 56
Krivoy-Rog Soviet Republic, 36
Krotevych, Bohdan, 77
Krym-24, 184

INDEX

Krynky, 166
Kryvyi Rih, 40, 79, 279
Kuchma, Leonid, 29, 209
Kuindzhi, Arkhip, 192, 196
Kukulin, Ilya, 89
Kulyk, Volodymyr, 39
Kumok, Mikhail, 183, 223
Kupiansk, 60, 78
Kurgan region, 98, 104
Kursk region, 83, 286
Kushyn, Viktor, 130
Kuwait, 26
Kuznetsov, Vladislav, 98, 104
Kyiv School of Economics, 240
Kyrylivka, 64

Lahuta, Hennadiy, 68
Lazurne, 114
Lenin Square, 179
Lenin streets, 179
Lenin, 36, 179, 180, 192, 193, 237
Leningrad region, 99
Leningrad regional government, 227
LenTV, 227
Leonov, Valery, 250–1
'Leto i arbalety' (Summer and crossbows), 212
Levchenko, Anatoliy, 197–9
Levytsky, Father Ivan, 132
'LGBT movement', 47
Liashevska, Halyna, 57
Liberal Democratic Party (LDPR), 108
Libya, 24
Lieblich, Eliav, 9
Lieven, Dominic, 16
Linnyk, Svitlana, 134–5
Lipandin, Volodymyr, 104, 125
LNR. *See* Lugansk People's Republic (LNR)

Logvinenko, Bohdan, 259
London School of Economics, 17
London, 243
Longobardo, Marco, 9
Lopukhov, Konstantin, 250
Lubinets, Dmytro, 112, 115, 265
Lugansk People's Republic (LNR), 7–8, 9, 20, 37, 41, 44, 56, 59, 61, 78, 86–8, 106, 220–1, 284
  annexation, 90–7
  collaboration, 271–3
  elections, 106–13
  governance, 103–04
  justice and courts, 118–21
  military units, 127–9
  money and banks, 229–31
  occupation, economic activity, 220–1
  plunder and expropriation, 220–1
  Russian education, 199–210
  Russian education, youth propaganda, 210–13
  Ukrainian resistance, 168–70
Luhansk region, 5, 21, 24, 37, 39, 44, 56, 57, 59, 65, 77, 168, 184
Lviv, 273
Lvova-Belova, Maria, 161
Lyman, 127, 143, 259, 261–2, 274–6
Lysychansk, 56, 132, 234

Maidan revolution (2014), 33, 192
Main Intelligence Directorate of Ukraine, 144
Maksimov, Father Kostiantyn, 132
Maksimova, Yulia, 242, 251
Malgin, Andrei, 193

INDEX

Malinova, Olga, 44
Malkevich, Alexander, 186–7
Malofeev, Konstantin, 101
Malyarenko, Tetyana, 287
Mankoff, Jeffrey, 289
Mann, Michael, 5, 284
Marchenko, Dmytro, 56
Margelov, V. F., 129
Marina, Tetyana, 152
Mariupol Local History Museum, 195
Mariupol Museum, 192
'Mariupol Now', 186
Mariupol port, 236
Mariupol State University, 214
Mariupol University, 243
Mariupol, 2–3, 13, 14, 29, 35, 43–5, 51–2, 99, 101,
   courts and justice, 119
   filtration, 141–48
   forced migration, 156–7
   new monuments and streets, 178–83
   plunder and expropriation, 222–5
   public opinion, 43–45
   reconstruction, 243–9
   siege, 69–77
   Russian education, 199–210
   Russian funding, 227–8
   Russian media, 187–8
   transport, 254–8
   Ukrainian resistance, 169–70
   universities, 213–16
   war profiteers, 249–54
Mariupol, battle of, 55, 69–77
Mariupol Drama Theatre, 73, 75, 189, 197–9
Mariupol–Donetsk route, 256
Mariupoltyazhmash, 240
Marshal Zhukov Embankment, 169

Maruniak, Viktor, 138–9
'Masha from Mariupol', YouTube channel, 187
'Mashuk', 212
Massandra winery, 220
Matos, Christine de, 12
Matsehora, Hennadiy, 60
Matvienko, Valentina, 113
McGlynn, Jade, 169–70
Media Detector group, 277
Medinsky, Vladimir, 30
Meduza, 87, 213
Medvedchuk, Viktor, 46
Melitopol, 54, 69, 81, 82
   detentions and killings, 129–35
   elections, 106–13
   history park, 195
   justice and courts, 116–21
   local politics, 102–6
   media, 183–9
   museum, 190–2
   new monuments and streets, 180–2
   occupation and protests, 56–64
   protests, 62
   Russian attack, 54–5
   Russia's security forces, 124–9
   Russian education, 199–210
   Russian education, youth propaganda, 210–13
   transport, 254–8
   Ukrainian children, 160–4
   Ukrainian prisoners, 150–4
   Ukrainian resistance, 166–72
   universities, 213–16
Melitopol Bread Plant, 238
Melitopol Christian Church, 133
Melitopol Meat Factory, 238
Melitopol State Pedagogical University *See* Bogdan Khmelnitsky Melitopol State Pedagogical University

INDEX

Melitopol Tractor Parts Factory, 238
Melitopol tse Ukraina ('Melitopol is Ukraine'), 184
Melitopolski vidomosti (newspaper), 183
Mennonites, 35
Metinvest group, 223, 227, 237
Metropolitan Arsenii, 269–70
Mezhevyi, Yevhen, 162
Middle East, 24, 289
Mikhailov, Gleb, 120
Mikhalkov, Nikita, 48
Military-Civilian Administrations (Voenno-grazhdanskaya administratsiya—VGA), 65–6, 78
Ministry for Reintegration (Ukraine), 265
Ministry of Construction, Housing and Utilities (Russia) 221, 242–4, 250–1, 259
Ministry of Emergency Situations (MChS) (Russia), 80, 99, 166, 232
Michurinsky Prospekt, 85
Ministry of Emergency Situations (Russia), 99–100, 166, 232
'Ministry of Property and Land Relations' (Zaporizhzhia), 234–5
Minsk agreements (2014–15), 31–2
Minsk I, 38
Minsk II, 38
Miranda-Media, 185
Mironov, Sergei, 161
Mishustin, Mikhail, 186–7, 232, 256
MMK Ilyich metallurgical plant, 69, 223, 236, 237
Mnatsakanian, Vaagn, 52

Moldova, 31
Molodaya Gvardiya (Young Guard), 101, 207, 211, 232
Molotov-Ribbentrop Pact, 23
Monaco, 240
Moravia, 23
Morgun, Oleg, 192
Morocco, 11
Moscow Patriarchate, 132, 269
Moscow State Technical University, 47
Moscow Urbanist Conference, 255
Moskvin, Mikhail, 169
'Movement of the First' (Dvizhenie pervykh) group, 211
Mozheliansky, Viktor, 118
MTV+, 183
'Multifunctional Centres' (MFCs), 116
'Multipolarity Forum' 25
Muratov, Aleksei, 142
Muravlev, Petr, 276
Muray, Yury, 238
Mussolini, Benito, 181
Myanmar, 22
Myasnikov, Alexander, 203
Mykolaenko, Volodymyr, 134, 153
Mykolaiv, 2, 55–6, 79, 82, 120

Naddniepryanskaya pravda, 'The Truth over the River Dnipro', 187
Nagorno-Karabakh, 176
Natalia Falko, 214
National Guard (Rosgvardiya), 123, 129, 141, 223
National Guard forces (Ukraine), 51, 268
National Resistance Center of Ukraine (NRC), 167, 170–2

INDEX

NATO (North Atlantic Treaty Organization), 22, 24, 29, 44, 48, 86, 179, 209, 288, 290
Navalny, Alexei, 252
Nazi Germany, 42, 45, 45, 47, 181, 288
Nazism, 8, 45, 47
'Near Abroad', 124
Nemtsov, Boris, 88
Nesterov, Oleg, 108, 141–2
Netblocks, 68
Netherlands, 190
Nevsky housing complex (Mariupol), 251–2
'New Regions', 100, 117
'New Regions' channel, 186
New York Times (newspaper), 68, 162, 269
New Yorker (magazine), 54–5, 147–8
Nibulon Ltd, 241
Nikolske (Nikolskoe), 145, 148
Nizhny Novgorod, 119
NKVD, 142, 180–1, 196
Noman Çelebicihan Volunteer Battalion, 153–4
North Africa, 289
North America, 33
North Caucasus, 181, 203, 253
Northern Cyprus, 253, 290
Nosachov, Pastor, 132–3
Nova Kakhovka, 53, 57, 79, 87, 133, 139, 177, 180, 200
Novaya gazeta Evropa (newspaper), 234
Novikov, Sergei, 197
Novinskyi, Vadym, 52
Novoazovsk, 145
Novoe Media (New Media), 188
Novorossiya, 29, 33–7, 49, 194, 195, 253, 255
Novovoskresenske, 278

'Novyi Melitopol' (New Melitopol), 185–6
Nuclear, Biological and Chemical (NBC), 65

Obilnoe, 238
October Revolution Avenue, 105
October Revolution Street, 179
Odesa, 2, 33, 35, 40, 56, 64, 79, 82, 158, 277, 279
Office of the United Nations High Commissioner for Human Rights (OHCHR), 140–1
Okhlobystin, Ivan, 96
Okko-Light, 238
Oleshky, 165–6, 189
Olimpsitistroy, 251–2
Omsk, 99, 249
1b Chernomorsky Lane, 247
150th Motorized Rifle Division, 70
141st Special Motorized Regiment, 123
131st Separate Reconnaissance Battalion, 182
Onuch, Olga, 39, 41
Onyschuk, Yury, 168
Opposition Bloc, 61, 105
Orange Revolution (2004), 29–30, 33
Order of Labour medal, 187
'Ordinary Fascism', 193
Organisation of Ukrainian Nationalists (OUN), 181
Organisation of Ukrainian Nationalists (OUN-B), 42–3
Organisation for Security and Co-operation in Europe (OSCE), 38, 137
Orthodox Church of Ukraine (OCU), 132

INDEX

Orwellian, 21, 213
Oshchadbank, 230
Osipchuk, Kirill, 120–1
Ostrovsky, Yefim, 89
Ottoman empire, 16, 35
Ovcharenko, Vitaly, 259, 261

Palestine, 93, 247
Palestinian West Bank, 11
Pamfilova, Ella, 106
Panchenko, Iryna, 261
Party of Regions (POR), 61, 67, 104
Pasechnik, Leonid, 95, 103–4, 110, 169, 207
Pawell (vessel), 242
Pawell Shipping Company, 242
Pedin, Igor, 74
Pensions, 231, 266
'People's Republic of Kherson', 67, 87
Peskov, Dmitry, 90, 97
Pétain, Philippe, 271
Petraeus, General David, 232
Petrov, Andrei, 121
Petrovna, Elizaveta, 57
Petukhov, Yury, 278
Physicians for Human Rights, 115
Pilavov, Manolis, 104
Pinker, Steven, 26
'Pirate Fleet', 258
Plokhy, Serhii, 36
Plotnitsky, Igor, 103
Pobeda Foundation, 228
Podkopaev, Nikolai, 119
Podoliak, Yuri, 80–1
Podolyak, Mikhailo, 53, 76
Pohl, Michaela, 286
Pokhitonov, Ivan, 193
Pokrovsk, 87
Poland, 1, 23, 37, 159, 288

Polish Catholic, 36
Ponochovnyi, Ihor, 280
Ponomarenko, Maria, 73
Ponomarev, Leonid, 133
Ponomarev, Oleksandr, 239
Popov Manor House Museum, 189
Postol, Aleksei, 223
Posylnyi, Ivan, 207
Potapenko, Tetiana, 274–5
'Potemkin village', 252–3
Potemkin, Grigory, 20, 34, 178, 194
'pragmatic Eurasianism', 30
'Pravyi Sektor' (Right Sector), 61
Presidential Academy of National Economy and Public Administration (RANEPA), 98
Presidential Administration (Russia), 32, 33, 87, 103, 108, 141, 176, 186, 197, 211
Prigozhin, Yevgeny, 186
'Profilaktika', 213
Profintern Street, 181
Prokhanov, Alexander, 30
Prokopchukov, Anatoly, 133
Prokopenko, Denys, 71
Prokopenko, Marharyta, 161
Promsvyazbank (PSB), 230–1, 273
Prospekt Myru (Mariupol), 178
Protasova, Kateryna, 64
Pushilin, Denis, 38, 87, 95, 97, 99, 110, 237–8, 254, 256, 274
Pushkin, Alexander, 178
Putin, Vladimir, 1, 8, 19, 20–1, 22, 24–6, 49–50, 59, 86, 88, 90, 106, 115, 118, 170, 176, 211, 224, 236, 246, 250, 256
  annexation, 86–7, 90–7
  economy under, 219–20

INDEX

funding occupation, 225–8
ICC arrest warrant, 160–1
on occupation, 8
organised crime, 224
presidential elections, 111–2
Ukrainian resistance, 170
views of Ukraine, 28–49, 180, 181
visit to Mariupol, 250–1
world order, 22–6
Putinism, 175
Putrid Sea, 52
Pyatigorsk, 212

Qatari government, 163
Quisling, Vidkun, 271

Radchuk, Oleksandr, 162
Raiko, Polina, 189
Railways, 256
Railways of Novorossiya, 256
Rainbow (Kuindzhi), 195
Real estate, occupied territories, 248–9
Red Army, 42–3, 182
Red International of Labor Unions, 181
Red Square (Moscow), 96, 210
Red Sunset (Kuindzhi), 195
Religious groups, repression, 131–3
Reporters Without Borders (RSF), 15, 184
Reuters, 86, 242
RIA-Melitopol, 183–4
RKS-Development, 249, 250
Rogov, Oleg, 127–8
Rogov, Vladimir, 47, 98, 168
Rogozin, Dmitry, 33, 110, 191
Roi, Oleg, 47
Rolls-Royce, 252
Romanenko, Oleg, 236

Romanov empire, 30
Rome Statute, 11, 161, 222
Rosatom, 88, 140, 236
Rosenergoatom, 236
Rosgvardiya (National Guard) 123, 129, 141, 223
Roshchyna, Viktoria, 131
RosKapStroi, 242, 250–1, 258
Rosmolodezh (Federal Agency for Youth Affairs), 211
Rostec, 236
Rostelecom, 68
Rostov region, 121, 150, 155, 204, 256
Rostov-on-Don, 128, 193, 203–5, 207, 255, 258
Rotenberg, Arkady, 220
Rouble, 229–30
Rozhin, Boris, 80
Rubizhne (Rubezhnoe), 65
Rukh Oporu, 167–8
Rukh Opory Kapituliatsii (Movement against Capitulation), 41
Russia
  annexation, 90–7
  budget for occupied territories, 225–9
  cultural revolution, 194–9
  currency, 229–30
  detentions and killings, 129–35
  education, youth propaganda, 199–213
  economic occupation, 219–2, 225–9
  elections, 106–13
  empire, 16–17, 24, 27–31
  Eurasianism, 28–32
  expropriation, 234–40
  filtration, 141–50
  forced migration, 154–60

INDEX

humanitarian aid and welfare, 232–4
ideology, role of, 19
justice and courts, 116–21
media, 183–9
money and banks, 229–31
new monuments and streets, 177–83
occupation authorities, 64–9
passports, 113–16
plunder and expropriation, 222–5
politics, 1–2, 88–89, 106–13, 285–6
prisoners and abuses, 135–41
security forces, 124–9
transport, 254–8
universities, 213–16
war profiteers, 249–54
Russian Academy of Sciences, 8
Russian Agricultural Bank, 99
Russian Armed Forces, 85
Russian Central Bank, 229
Russian civil war, 124
Russian Constitutional Court, 10
Russian Criminal Code, 117, 152
Russian Federal Tax Service, 234
Russian Military Intelligence (GRU), 103, 123, 125
Russian Ministry of Construction, Housing and Utilities, 221, 242–4, 250–1, 259
Russian Ministry of Defence, 129, 251, 259
Russian Ministry of Science and Higher Education, 215
Russian Orthodox Church, 31, 132, 195, 269
Russian Red Cross, 157
Russian revolution (1917), 179
Russian Southern Military District, 127, 128
Russian Soviet Federative Socialist Republic (RSFSR), 27, 32
Russian World, 20, 31, 40, 44, 207, 215
'Russian World', satellite television, 184
Russian-Georgian border, 120, 155
Ryzhenko, Konstantin, 67

Sablin, Dmitry, 101–2
Sakharov Prize, 171
Sakwa, Richard, 102
Saldo, Vladimir (Volodymyr), 67, 80, 95, 104–5, 110, 168, 183, 186, 242–3, 254
'Salvation Committee for Peace and Order', 67, 105
Samoilenko, Mykyta, 66
Samoilov, A. N., 35
Samoilovich, Rudolf, 196
Samoylenko, Oleksandr, 58
Saratov, 119
Sat, Artysh, 98
Saulenko, Alexander, 66
Savitsky, Petr, 30
Savluchenko, Dmytro, 168
SBU (Security Service of Ukraine), 52, 58, 68, 104, 126, 130, 141, 257, 269, 270, 279
  collaboration cases, 274–5
  unofficial prisons, 141
Schmitt, Carl, 23–4, 26
Scott, James C., 172
Scythians, 190–1, 193, 195
  gold artefacts, 190–191
'The Scythians' (Blok), 190–1
Sea of Azov, 35, 53, 54, 55, 70, 82, 195, 221, 249, 254, 255–8
Semenchev, Igor, 105

379

INDEX

Senezh (Moscow region), 212
Sereda, Marina, 142
'Serf 2', 196
Sestryvatovsky, Ivan, 53
Sevastopol, 7, 21, 28, 93, 105, 242, 266, 267
Severodonetsk Azot chemical factory, 236
Severodonetsk, 56, 234
Sexual violence, 137–8, 172
Shakhnazarov, Georgy, 32
Shakhnazarov, Karen, 32
Shaman (Yaroslav Dronov), 96
Shchedrovitsky, Georgy, 88–9
Shutov, Andrei, 111
shefstvo system, 99, 227–8
Sheremetyevo airport, 148–9, 257
Shestopalov, Boris 238
Shevchik, Andrii, 66
Shoigu, Sergei, 251, 254, 268
Shostak-Kuchmyak, Anna, 127
Shovkunenko Museum, 193
Shovkunenko, Oleksii, 193
Shyrokyne, 55
Siberia, 16, 73, 153, 249
Simes, Dmitrii, 28
Simferopol, 150, 151, 152, 193, 255
'Single Contractor in the Construction Sphere' (EZSS), 251
Sirovatko, Yury, 119
Siverskyi Donets river, 269
Skadovsk, 81, 105, 135
Skornyakov, Dmitry, 240
Skynet internet provider, 68
Sobyanin, Sergei, 250
Social Fund (Russia), 233
Social Movement of Denis Pushilin of the Donetsk Republic, 274

Sodol, Lieutenant General Yuriy, 77
Sokurenko, Yelyzaveta, 137–8
Soldatov, Andrei, 125–6
Soledar, 236
Solntsev, Yevgeny, 101
Solzhenitsyn, Alexander, 33
Sorge, Richard, 204
South Africa, 94–5
South Ossetia, 24, 87, 220, 231
Southern Buh River, 55
Southern Mining and Metallurgical Complex (YuGMK), 220
Soviet identity, 42–43
Soviet occupation of Eastern Europe, 23, 142, 155
Soviet People's Commissariat for Internal Affairs (NKVD), 142, 180–1, 196
Soviet Red Army, 42
Soviet Union, 18, 27–8, 30, 42–3, 142, 150, 215, 240
Soviet-Polish border, 142
Soyuz, television channel, 184
Spain, 152
Special Infrastructure Project, 227, 251
'Special Military Operation', 8, 45, 210
Special Operations Forces, Ukraine, 167
Spivakovsky, Alexander, 214–15
Sputnik (media), 176
St Catherine's Cathedral, Kherson, 194
St George's Hall, Kremlin, 20
St Petersburg Nakhimov Naval School, 129
St Petersburg TV, 186
St Petersburg, 99, 197, 214, partnership with Mariupol, 99, 199, 227–8

INDEX

Stalin, 180, 182, 196
Star of David, 146
Stara Zburivka, 138
Starobeshovo filtration camp, 147
Starobilsk Cossack Cadet Corps, 129
Starobilsk, 92
State Bank of the LNR, 273
State Bureau of Investigation (SBI) (Ukraine), 77
Supreme Court (Russia), 118
State Duma, 28, 96, 101
State Grain Operator (GZO), 242
State Property Fund of Kherson region, 105
Steglenko, Katerina, 168
Steinmeier formula, 40–1
Stepashin, Sergei, 244
Stoltenberg, Jens, 288
Strategy for De-occupation and Reintegration of the Temporarily Occupied Territory of the Autonomous Republic of Crimea (Qirim), 266
Stremousov, Kirill, 66, 90
Stus, Vasyl, 198
Sudetenland, 1, 23, 288
Sudoplatov Battalion, 129, 182–3
Sudoplatov, Pavel, 182–3, 196
Sumy region, 77, 257
Surkov, Vladislav, 175
Surovikin defensive lines, 81
Surovikin, Sergei, 79
Surzhyk, 38
Suvorov, Alexander, 178
Sviatohirsk Lavra, 189
Sviatohirsk, 268–70
Svitlodarsk, 180
'Svobodnyi Berdiansk' (Free Berdiansk), 184

SWIFT, 230
Synepalov, Ivan, 44
Syria, 72, 124, 176, 219, 232, 242, 289, 290
Syvash, 52

Taganrog, 196, 255–6
Taiwan, 1, 288–9
Tambov region, 164
Tarasov, Oleksandr, 131, 151
Tasheva, Tamila, 267, 280
Tatarstan, Republic of, 100, 250
Tavrida, 212
Tavriya TV, 186
Teatralnoe café (Kherson), 194
Telegram channels, 66, 98, 165, 167, 186–7, 277
Telegram, 14, 59, 79, 145, 148, 185
'temporarily occupied territories' (TOT), 11, 112
Territorial Defence Forces, 54
36th Marine Brigade, 71
Tkach, Valentyna, 274–5
Tkachev, Alexander, 241–2
Toivonen, Nikolai, 214
Tokmak, 81
'Tombasar Mukataasi', 35
Tomilina, Tatyana, 168, 215
Trenin, Dmitry, 27, 33
Trifanova, Svetlana, 119
Trofymenko, Mykola, 243
'Trojan Horse' policy, 38
Trump, Donald, 11
'Truth Hounds', 140
Tsarist imagery, 78
Tsvetkov, Alexander, 118
Tsyhipa, Serhii, 139
Tula region, 250
Turchak, Andrei, 30, 88, 90, 244
Turkey, 220, 242, 253, 289
Tusk, Donald, 288

381

INDEX

Tuzla Island, 29
Tyva, Republic of, 17, 98
25th Transport Brigade, 54
20 Days in Mariupol (documentary), 71, 74

UK Companies House, 243
UK (United Kingdom), 243
Ukraine Is Not Russia (Kuchma), 209
Ukraine
   agriculture and grain exports, 240–3
   annexation of territory, 90–7
   armed resistance to occupation, 166–72
   collaboration laws, 272–3
   counteroffensive, 77–82
   cultural heritage, attacks on, 189–94
   decolonisation debate, 16–17
   decommunisation campaign, 44, 49, 179–180
   deoccupation strategies, 264–8
   filtration, 141–50
   flood, 164–6
   forced migration, 154–60
   identity politics, 38–45
   independence, 28–29
   language laws, 39–41
   local politics in occupied territories, 102–6
   money and banks, 229–31
   military defence, 51–6
   new monuments and streets, 177–83
   occupation and protests, 56–64
   occupation, economic activity, 225–9
   plunder and expropriation, 222–5
   preparations for war, 51–3
   prisoners and Russian abuses, 135–41
   Russian invasion of, 27
   scholarship, 15–16
   Ukrainian children, 160–4
   Ukrainian prisoners in Russia, 150–4
   universities, takeover and re-establishment, 213–16
Ukrainian Criminal Code, 112, 272–3
Ukrainian General Staff, 76
Ukrainian Greek Catholic Church, 132–3
Ukrainian Insurgent Army (UPA), 43, 197, 209
Ukrainian Ministry of Digital Transformation, 167
Ukrainian Orthodox Church (Moscow Patriarchate) (UOCMP), 132
Ukrainian People's Republic, 178, 210
Ukrainian Soviet Socialist Republic, 27
Ukrainian Union of Journalists, 131
'Ukrainianism', 46–48

UN Charter, 10, 25
UN General Assembly, 93
UN Human Rights Council, 141
UN Independent Commission, 137
UN report, 138, 140–1
UN Security Council, 93
UN (United Nations), 10, 25, 93, 94, 137–8, 140–1, 272–3
UNESCO (United Nations Educational, Scientific and Cultural Organization), 189

INDEX

UNHCR (United Nations High Commissioner for Refugees), 157
Unified State Register of Legal Entities (EGRYUL), 234
Union of Left Forces (Ukraine), 66
Union of Right Forces (SPS) (Russia), 88
United Russia (ER) party (Russia), 30, 88, 89, 90 101, 107, 211, 232, 244
Universitetskie smeny (University Exchanges), 212
University of Aberdeen, 16
'urbicide', 247–8
Urzuf, 224
US government, 134, 141, 154, 186, 194
US (United States), 11, 22, 48
'USA Really', 186
Usmanova, Natalia, 72
USSR, 28, 44, 134, 177, 187
Uzhhorod, 198

Valdai conference, 24
Valencia, 152
Varlamova, Inna, 161
Varvarivskyi Bridge, 55
Vasylivka, 64, 214
Venema, Derk, 86
Venezuela, 22
Venice Commission, 41
Vereshchuk, Iryna, 266
Verkhovna Rada Commissioner for Human Rights, 154
Verkhovna Rada, 61, 67, 104, 105, 272
Verschure, Han, 247
Verstka media, 210
Victory Day, 150
Virlych, Yevhenia, 131

VK, social media (Russia), 185
Vladivostok, 156
Vneshtorgservis, 220
Volgograd, 188
Volnovakha, 56, 88, 256
'Volunteers of Victory' network, 211
Vorona, Dmitry, 235
Vrubel, Mikhail, 193
VSK, construction company, 252
VTV+ channel, 183
vyshyvanka (Ukrainian national dress), 274
Vysokopole, 127

Wagner group, 123, 186
'Walk&Talk' channel, 187–8
Wall Street Journal, 198
Wallace, Ben, 1
Ward, Rowena, 12
Warsaw, 257
Washington, 22, 144, 186
Watkin, Kenneth, 9, 170
Wehberg, Hans, 25
West Bank, 253, 291
West Petrol Market, 238
Western Belarus, 142
Western Sahara, 11, 93
'Wild Fields', 34
Word of Life Protestant Church, 133
World Bank, 262
World War II, 1, 8, 12, 21, 45, 170, 197, 243

Yakymenko, Oleksandr, 104, 125
Yale School of Public Health, 144–5
Yanukovych, Viktor, 29, 33, 37, 61, 126
'Yellow Ribbon' movement, 171
Yeltsin, Boris, 28

INDEX

Yenakieve metallurgical factory, 227
Yenakieve, 99, 227
Yesin, Ivan, 196
'Yevorog', 167
Yizhakovska, Maryna, 204–5
Young Guard organisation. *See Molodaya Gvardiya*
'Youthful South' (Yug molodoi), 210
YouTube, 14, 66, 148, 167, 187, 188, 246
Yurchenko, Yevgeny, 220
Yushchenko, Viktor, 43
'Yuzhnyi Platsdarm' (Southern Bridgehead), 59

Za!Radio, 186
Za!TV, 184, 186
Zabahonskiy, Serhii, 198
Zabyelina, Yuliya, 220
Zakharchenko, Alexander, 95
Zakharova, Maria, 8, 177
Zalizetskaya, Svetlana, 183–4
ZaMedia, 186
Zaporizhzhia city, 35, 91
Zaporizhzhia region, 2, 5, 8, 35, 59, 61, 70, 73–4, 91, 94, 95, 99, 261–4
  annexation, 90–96
  checkpoints, 149
  deportations from, 159
  detentions and killings, 129–35
  elections, 106–13
  expropriation, 234–40
  filtration, 141–50
  forced migration, 154–60
  governance under occupation, 98–100, 104–5
  justice and courts, 119–21
  media, 183–9
  money and banks, 229–31
  occupation, economic activity, 225–9
  plunder and expropriation, 222–5
  prisoners and abuses, 135–41
  religious repression, 133
  Russian education, 203–210
  Youth propaganda, 210–13
Zaporizhzhia Iron Ore Plant (ZZRK), 236
Zaporizhzhia Nuclear Power Plant (ZNPP), 54, 140, 236
'Zaporozhe-24', 184
'Zaporozhye NPP Operating Organisation, 236
Zayarina, Oksana, 135–6
Zelensky, Volodymyr, 40–1, 45–6, 51, 62, 68, 81, 166, 182, 264, 287
Zeonbud, 184
Z-FM (Frontline Radio), 186
Zhuravko, Aleksei, 93
Zhuravlev, Aleksei, 253
Zhurzhenko, Tatiana, 44–5
Zhu-Zhu, 74
Zinchuk, Viktoria, 274–5
Zinichev, Yevgeny, 99–100
'Zla Mavka', 171
ZMINA human rights centre, 137
Zveri, 197